FUTURE FOOD

FUTURE FOOD

Politics, philosophy and recipes for the 21st century

Colin Tudge

Harmony Books
New York

Acknowledgments

Editor **Rachel Grenfell**
Assistant Editor **Gillian Abrahams**
Editorial Assistant **Atalanta Grant-Suttie**

Art Editor **Val Hobson**
Assistant Art Editor **Ingrid Mason**

Production **Martin Elliott**
Photographs **Martin Reavley**
Index **Anne Hardy**

Executive Editor **Alexandra Towle**

FUTURE FOOD was edited and designed by
Mitchell Beazley Publishers Limited
87–89 Shaftesbury Avenue, London W1V 7AD

Printed and bound in the United States of America

Library of Congress Cataloging in Publication Data
Tudge, Colin
 Future Food
Includes bibliographical references and index
1. Cookery   1. Title
TX715.T8793   641.5   79–20634
ISBN 0-517-540142 Hardback edition
ISBN 0-517-541300 Paperback edition
1 2 3 4 5 6 7 8 9 10

In this book all metric equivalents are approximate (weight and
volume measures have been rounded up or down for convenience).
Tablespoons and teaspoons are standard measures;
amounts given are for level spoonfuls.

Contents

What kind of future?

The twenty-first century, so close at hand, could be the most pleasurable and the safest time that the world has yet experienced, for all humanity and for our fellow creatures; or (so present events often suggest) it could bring all kinds of disaster.

We can determine which; the difference depends not upon technological miracle or spiritual revelation but upon the simple day-to-day acts of individuals. And the message of this book is that the most significant of those simple acts, the one that cumulatively but inexorably could yet make this precarious world into a good and safe place to live, is cooking. This may sound ridiculous, or at best fanciful, but I hope to demonstrate that it is true; and, more to the point, to show what is entailed in good cookery, if the twenty-first century is to be fit for our children and our children's children.

The absolute importance of good cooking

I am naïve enough to believe, first of all, that the single most important thing that humanity must get right is food production. If we farm inefficiently, or profligately, then land and energy are squandered. The agricultural sprawl drives other creatures into the margin lands; the overreliance on chemistry within the farmlands (often to compensate for fundamentally unsound husbandry) makes that land inhospitable even to those creatures that could otherwise live happily with mankind; and nobody, in the 1980s, needs reminding that energy is at a premium. Yet it is easily possible to produce enough food for all the world's people—even allowing for the inevitable population increase—without using every square foot for food production, without eliminating our fellow creatures, and without racing through the last few million barrels of oil. What we need, in all the countries of the world, are agricultures specifically designed to feed people, which in recent history has been a fairly unusual ambition.

Such agriculture can be termed "rational." I have described the principles in detail, and some of the obvious economic implications, in another book (*The Famine Business*, St. Martins Press, 1977). In this introductory chapter I want merely to sketch in the outline, so as to put all that follows into context, but I will make two observations. First, that rational agriculture, which I believe is necessary, cannot come into being if farming is geared primarily to produce short-term profits, which is largely the case at present. This does not mean rational agriculture cannot be profitable, or cannot be capitalist, but simply that its principal goal must be to feed people, and not to produce as much wealth as is conceivable. Second, we do live in consumer societies, and consumers, collectively, do have power. If you and I and a million other people choose to cook in a "rational" way, to buy only some foods and allow others to molder on the supermarket shelves, and if we also demonstrate that we can, if we choose, produce a great deal of our own food, then sooner or later, and possibly sooner, the apparently overwhelming might of "agribusiness" and governments must come to heel, for if nobody buys what they have to sell they are impotent. The

Farming for feeding people

6

world needs a food revolution; but revolutions that last, as opposed to coups that do not, begin with a change of mind in individuals; and this most important revolution of all must begin humbly, but appropriately, in the kitchen.

Then there is the fact, inescapable and ugly, that the countries that seem to have solved the perennial human problem of hunger—those of Western Europe and North America, and Australia, New Zealand, and perhaps Japan—have walked straight into the equally unsalubrious pit of overnutrition. Heart disease, an impressive catalog of cancers, diabetes, gallstones, and the obesity that in some parts of the world already makes nonsense of the once beautiful human frame, all have strong dietary connections; and if we, the "developed" world, really do represent the prospect for all mankind, then one may wonder if "development" is such a good idea. Yet nutritional theory—not as often presented in the glossy magazines, but as now evolving in the world's more subtle halls of science—is at least convincing, not least because it has the ring of common sense. We know enough, today, not only to produce enough food for all the world's people, but also to produce food that is nutritionally sound, and which does not lead us straight into the diseases of affluence. Such food is already available; and each of us may preempt the necessary revolution in food production, by selecting the right things now. Which brings us to cookery again.

The pit of overnutrition

But then we seem to hit the snag, the final trap; the idea, demonstrated by many a worthy dietitian and many a modern "health food" shop, that food that does not make people fat or cause cancer in mice must be boring. Above all, this book will show the lie of this; that the finest culinary heights achieved by the world's great traditional cuisines can be, and indeed usually are, built upon ingredients that are cheap to produce (cheap in precious land and energy, that is) and are nutritionally unimpeachable. We can create a world like an emperor's garden, yet leave large parts to go their natural way; we can live out our allotted span; and yet, fulfilling both ambitions, we could each of us eat as richly as a medieval prince. It takes a little subtlety, it takes a little knowledge, and it begins and ends with cooking.

Long life in the emperor's garden

So what sort of food should we be producing, and how, and why not carry on as we are?

What is the Problem?
The first difficulty is that the world population is growing and the world is not. The position is far from hopeless: many countries, including those of Europe and the United States and possibly China, have already shown that growth can be contained and that populations may even diminish. But most of the people now on earth are children, and they will have children of their own before the present generation of adults is dead. World population, now around four billion, is likely to double in the next 25 years before it stabilizes. A commensurate twofold increase in food output in one generation will not easily be achieved.

That the world cannot grow bigger is all too obvious. Time was when biologists proclaimed that the sea would solve all our food problems; but it has never supplied more than a small proportion of human food

What kind of future?

Disappointing oceans

and the few brief years of industrial-scale fishing have already taken several of the major fisheries to the brink of oblivion. We must look to the land, yet there are no fresh continents to discover and the remaining virgin land is either in the wrong place (like Siberia or Antarctica) or else, like the Amazon basin, is proving far less fertile than its jungles promised. Production of ersatz foods—of yeast protein, for example—can solve only marginal problems, if only because their large-scale manufacture requires the skill and capital of major industrial countries. Only agriculture can solve the world's food problems; agriculture practiced on the land that is already farmed. More human food per acre of cultivable land is required.

But can we produce more food per acre without expending more energy? And is it not obvious in the 1980s and beyond that lack of energy is the greatest problem of all?

Elusive energy

In truth, the energy problem waxes and wanes, and waxes again, the more you look at it. The difficulty is obvious. The agricultures of the developed world have vastly increased their use of fossil fuels in each of the past five decades. Nitrogen fertilizer is made with fossil fuels, and Britain now uses 30 times as much as at the turn of the century; yet the increase is subject to the law of diminishing returns. Whereas an ancient hunter-gatherer expended only one calorie to provide himself with 10 calories of food, the modern intensive beef farmer, say, expends 100 fossil fuel calories to provide a single food calorie. We seem to save labor but even that may be illusory, for the ancient hunter-gatherers spent only a third of their waking life in search of food, and we spend a third of our income on food, which requires a third of our working life to earn. We run faster and faster, expend more and more energy, just to stay in the same place; and all the time the oil reserves are dwindling.

The figures, however, suggest that agriculture is far from profligate. Britain and the United States, with two of the world's most technological agricultures, spend only two or three per cent of their total energy on farming and less than a third of that goes on producing fertilizer. Reduce the temperature of offices; insulate private houses; make cars with smaller engines; each and any of these things, modestly applied, could save more than the whole of agriculture expends.

Yet there is still a problem, for the agricultures of Britain and the United States are merely part of a food production chain. These agricultures are geared to mass production, which implies mass storage and mass transport; and they serve a processing industry which in the United States transmogrifies 80 percent of all the food the farmer produces before it passes to the consumer. Include transport, packing, and processing (but leave out cooking and the energy spent in shopping trips in private cars) and you find that Britain and the United States expend more than 12 percent of their total energy on food production. If India produced food the American way, and if Indians increased their modest daily intake of 2,000 Calories to 3,000, they would need to use more energy for food production than they use now for all purposes. At the very least, the British and American methods of producing food cannot provide a model for the rest of the world. So we must increase food output: yet, we must do so in ways more conservative of energy.

No model for India

What kind of food?

First question, then: What must we grow? Human protein needs have been grotesquely exaggerated (as the next chapter will explain), but in designing agriculture it is as well to begin with protein because that is the hardest thing to get right.

It would be all too easy to produce too little and so put people in nutritional peril, or too much, and so waste resources. So what is the easiest or most efficient way to produce protein?

The most prolific sources of protein, by a wide margin, are green leaves—a statement that must appear as a misprint to anyone brought up on the nutritional rubrics of the 1950s and 1960s. Yet it is obvious that this should be so, for the protein that finally finishes up in seeds, in meat, or in human flesh was, for the most part, originally manufactured in green leaves, including those of grass. Absolute figures of yield per acre are somewhat fatuous because they vary so immensely from crop to crop, but at least they show order of magnitude; and 1,000 pounds of protein from an acre of cabbage would not be outlandish. *Outlandish cabbage*

But leaf protein is too dilute. Cows can get all the protein they need from grass—far more than they need in fact—but only because their enormous barrellike bodies are filled with an astonishingly large stomach called the rumen, which can hold vast amounts of it. Human beings can make some use of leaf protein, and some green leaves could be a useful source for adults—whose protein needs are more modest than children's—although some of the most proteinaceous leaves contain mild toxins and should not be eaten to excess. Human beings, however, do not seem to have the physical capacity to subsist on leaves.

The potato is the next most productive source; 400 pounds of protein per acre would be reasonable. The protein in potatoes is not too dilute; adult human beings can eat enough to satisfy their protein needs and whole societies, notably the Irish of the early nineteenth century, did subsist almost exclusively upon potatoes. So the potato, rather than the green leaf, can be regarded as the outstanding staple crop. *Outstanding potato*

The cereals, which in practice are the world's leading staples, are the third most abundant protein source. An acre of wheat might yield 250 pounds of protein. Cereals perhaps have the edge over potatoes in that they are easier to store; in general, the two complement each other. Cereals, like potatoes, are adequate sources of protein for adult human beings, and if a country can grow grain (and there are few that cannot) it need have no outstanding food problems. *Cereals and pulses*

The third of the world's great staples are the pulses, the large edible seeds of the Leguminosae: beans, grams, lentils, chickpeas and peas. Yield of protein per acre is of the same order as with cereals but the concentration of protein per seed is generally higher. For this and other reasons—agricultural, nutritional, and gastronomic—the pulses are an admirable foil for the potato and the grains.

These three classes of food—potato, cereal, pulse—should form the basis of every country's agricultural effort and hence of everybody's

What kind of food?

diet. The prime land, the most fertile and the most equable, should be given over to them. Once they are taken care of there is little else to do except provide some micronutrients—vitamins, minerals, and essential fats—and exciting flavors; after all, an exclusive diet of cereals, pulses and potatoes would be tedious. But the staples are the bedrock. They are Food of the First Kind. Food of the First Kind

The foods whose function is merely to abet and enhance the staples are Food of the Second Kind; and the most notable feature of rational agriculture and the gastronomy it allows, is that meat is demoted to this category. I do not suggest we should all be vegetarians; for nutritional as well as gastronomic reasons I would not like to live in or bring up children in a vegan society, and livestock does have clear and important roles in farming. But the Western world's present concentration on livestock is far out of proportion.

Animals produce far less protein than the major plant crops. The most generous farm animal, the dairy cow, yields about 100 pounds of milk protein per acre. The dairy plus beef enterprise, in which the calves are raised alongside their dams, provides about 80 pounds. Broiler chickens give about 70 pounds of protein in return for an acre's worth of feed, laying hens about 60, pigs about 40, and sheep and beef, the jewel in the crown of Western agriculture, about 20 pounds of protein per acre. The developed world, which contains only one-third of the world's people, uses half the world's supply of cereals and feeds 70 percent of its share to livestock—plus, of course, vast amounts of grass. The Third World, with 70 percent of the world's people, feeds only 10 percent of its share of the world's cereals to animals. The Third World could do with more livestock, in the right contexts; but the rich world's prodigality borders on the absurd. There is plenty for animals to do in rational agriculture, however, and the future world can produce, and should eat, meat and other animal products. We should eat less than we eat today, but it will be more flavorsome. Room for animals

Vegetables are also Food of the Second Kind. As with meat, their nutritional role is as abettors; providing micronutrient vitamins and minerals, dietary fiber and, perhaps above all, flavor. It is probably bad for people to eat too much meat, but it is hard to see that anybody, in practice, could eat too many vegetables provided they ate as varied a selection as possible. Vegetables should be supplied fresh, because freezing impairs the flavor that is their *raison d'être*; and even a temperate country can supply a score or more varieties of vegetables all year round if they are appropriately cosseted and subtly intercropped in market gardens.

Fungi, too, can be regarded as Food of the Second Kind. They are minor but at times crucial sources of nourishment, and their ability to transform an ordinary meal into a dish of wonder is unsurpassed. A hundredfold increase in the cultivation of mushrooms and their allies would not be unreasonable.

Food of the Third Kind is a mixed bag; almost everything that breathes is potentially edible, and wild fungi, wild leaves, flowers, shellfish, nuts and berries as well as the vast pharmacopoeia of spices can each provide unique and exciting flavor.

All countries should move toward self-reliance in food; partly for political safety (even the countries that live by trade, as all do to some extent, are in a much stronger bargaining position if they do not have to import essentials), and partly because one important way to save energy would be to stop shifting food around the world. But self-reliance merely means producing one's own basic foods, so that the people do not starve, even in a blockade. It does not mean an end to all trade, and the tropical spices in particular—which require little land, are cheap to transport, and yet are valuable—should be used and made available worldwide, with the profit going to the producer countries. Agricultural self-reliance has usually been associated with "siege economy" and with extreme austerity, as in Britain in World War II; yet if properly conceived, in peacetime, it implies no hardship. Tomorrow's food should be spicy, and where there's spice there's flavor.

Self-reliance is no hardship

The structure of farming must vary from country to country. Most farms would tend to be mixed, because mixtures tend to make best use of the land; yet terrain and climate would inevitably dictate that some areas were predominantly arable, and some pastoral, as is the case at present. Such rational agriculture cannot meet its full potential unless it employs a lot of people; not to take the place of the combine harvesters, in some latter-day Luddite revolution, but to run the inevitably more intricate farms with their often elaborate interplay of crop and crop, and of crop and beast. Yet I make no apology for suggesting that agriculture should employ more people. In a world where unemployment could prove a far more intractable problem than food supply, it would be reasonable to rank the provision of jobs among farming's chief functions; from which it has abdicated.

Jobs for the farmers

In general, overall, the major staples would occupy the most equable and flattest regions; the sheep and cattle would occupy the margin lands; the pigs, ducks and chickens would be kept close to where people live, because leftovers would be their chief source of food; and every group of human habitations would be surrounded by bands of market gardens, pouring vegetables into the town—perhaps, as in modern Peking, in thrice-daily deliveries.

Rational agriculture could be so dramatically productive that it could restructure entire countries; and once farming had concentrated upon the problem of producing human food, it would then be freed for a whole range of other functions. Britain, a middle-sized country with a high population, illustrates the point. It has about 55 million people, and its agriculture (which British farmers claim is "the most efficient in the world") supplies them with about half their food.

Yet one study shows that if Britons were all vegetarian, and the agriculture were adjusted accordingly, Britain could support 150 million people without imports. Livestock does not necessarily reduce total productivity if it is slotted in as described above, so Britain could presumably support at least 150 million, even if people were not vegetarian but had a diet something like that of peasant China. Another estimate suggests that if all Britons cultivated this blessed plot as assiduously as some gardeners do already, then it could support 250 million people. These figures are based on carefully gathered data; but

Could Britain feed the United States?

What kind of food?

even if they are 50 per cent wrong, it is obvious that Britain, which traditionally has been one of the world's most avaricious food importers, could theoretically support its population unaided—twice, or several times over.

So if Britain's agriculture were to become rational, it could also be relaxed. There would be no need to grub up yet more hedgerows in the interests of productivity. The old deciduous woods and copses could be left and extended. The fens and the chalk grasslands, with their astonishingly rich ecosystems, could rest undisturbed. There would be plenty of room for people to live and enjoy themselves in the countryside; no excuse for those fences that now proscribe entry to the most remote hillsides, or for the tedious prairies that offer no way through. Human habitation is not incompatible with wildlife. It is simply a question of design.

Rational agriculture is at least worth thinking about. The diet it would provide would be heavily biased toward the staples, garnished by masses of vegetables and soupçons of meat, and highlighted with spice and whatever else was to hand. The next chapter will show that such a diet would be a considerable nutritional advance on our present one.

Rational, productive and relaxed

What do people need?

So much for efficient food production. But "food," by definition, is what people need to eat. And what is that? The changes in nutritional theory in the past ten years have been dramatic to the point of *volte-face*; but consensus is emerging.

The major areas of change have been with respect to protein and energy; to fat, including cholesterol; to fiber and carbohydrate; and, as a conceptually minor but perhaps supremely important footnote, to salt.

Energy, Protein and Meat

To study protein is almost—and I stress almost—to study all of life, for protein is the material above all others that is the stuff of flesh. The red pigment of blood, hemoglobin, is mostly protein. Hair and nails are hardened protein. The membranes that enclose and traverse all the body's cells, and give form to the entire body structure, are composed largely of protein. The enzymes that control all the more complex reactions within the body are proteins; and these reactions collectively constitute "metabolism." Because of protein's central importance, nutritionists, many dietitians, and large sections of the food industry have sometimes presented protein as an elixir and have suggested that human beings should contrive to eat as much of it as possible. Yet an intake surplus to requirements is simply wasted, and some evidence suggests that that surplus could sometimes be harmful. More to the point, protein is harder to produce in large amounts than, for example, starch, which is the human being's chief source of energy (except in some Western countries where fat and sugar predominate). So the idea that people need a lot of protein has been yoked to the idea that the world could not possibly produce enough. It has been fashionable through much of the past three decades to predict that the human race would succumb to malnourishment. The chief source of that malnourishment, the Jeremiahs thought, would be the "protein gap."

> The stuff of flesh

> Wrong again, Jeremiah

This line of thought was dangerous because it prompted inappropriate action that proved both wasteful and pernicious. Westerners began to eat more meat than was good for them and many Third World countries disrupted their traditional agricultures in favor of more protein-oriented stratagems that they could not sustain. Fortunately for the human race, nutritionists have reduced their recommended protein intakes since World War II by a cool 50 percent.

Thus, in 1948, the National Research Council (NRC) of the United States suggested that toddlers require 3.3 grams of protein per kilogram of body weight; so an average two-year-old weighing around 12 kilograms (26 pounds) would need almost 40 grams of protein per day. A small child (with small jaws and stomach) would find it hard to take in that much protein in a day unless he ate specifically high-protein foods, notably meat. But by 1965, the Food and Agriculture Organization of the United Nations (FAO) was recommending a mere 1.5 grams per kilogram (just over 2 pounds) body weight per day for toddlers

What do people need?

(children weighing 12 kilograms), which is well under half the NRC 1948 recommendation. By 1968 NRC had brought its own equivalent figure down to 2.1 grams per kilogram per day; and in 1969 Britain's Department of Health and Social Security suggested that 1.7 grams per kilogram per day was sufficient. Call it two grams per kilogram per day—24 grams for a 12 kilogram two-year-old—and you will not offend many modern nutritionists. The present FAO/World Health Organization recommendation for adults, who by definition have stopped growing and who require protein only to compensate for wear and tear, is a mere 0.59 grams per kilogram per day. Thus a 70-kilogram (154 pound) man, whom the insurance companies would acknowledge as average, is now thought to need less than 36 grams of protein per day; less, indeed, than two-year-olds were alleged to require in 1948.

Dwindling protein needs

The change in protein theory has perhaps been the most significant single scientific development since World War II. For if people really needed high quantities and proportions of protein as was formerly believed, then they would be obliged to consume milk, meat and cheese, and agriculture would be beholden to concentrate on their production. This in fact has happened, and Britain now uses two-thirds of its prodigious home-grown cereal crop just to feed livestock, while the United States turns four-fifths of its even more prodigious grain output into animal feed. But if human protein needs are modest, as now seems likely, then all of the staples, grains, pulses and potatoes, emerge as adequate protein sources, at least for adults; and even foods such as spinach, mushrooms, turnips and bananas should not be written off as protein sources.

Do not write off the banana

There is a conditional clause: protein quality. Despite their infinite variety, all proteins are constructed from chains and networks of about 20 different kinds of building blocks. These building blocks are the amino acids. The body can happily convert some of these amino acids into other kinds of amino acids so to some extent it does not mind what kind of amino acids it is supplied with, provided it gets enough. But there are about eight amino acids that the body cannot synthesize and these must be supplied ready-made in the diet. These eight are the essential amino acids.

The essential amino acids

The body cannot store surplus protein or surplus amino acids, or at least not in appreciable quantity. So it must have all the kinds it needs available at any one time, and if any one of the essential kinds is missing then work is held up. All the others that may be present are simply wasted. The best food proteins not only contain all the essential amino acids, but also contain them in the right ratio, for if one is under-represented, then some of the rest will not be utilized. Egg protein is of very high quality; it contains all the amino acids people need, in almost perfect proportion. Potato protein is also of surprisingly high quality. But cereal proteins tend to be low in one or other of the essential amino acids, notably lysine, and so their quality is undermined.

Old-style nutritionists made much of these differences in quality, and because cereal protein was flawed it was largely written off—as "second-class protein." Wheat in particular is, however, so rich in protein that the shortfall in quality is probably unimportant in practice;

Supercharged wheat

it is like a car with an overpowered engine that will cover the miles even if the engine is badly made. In addition—one of nature's many serendipities, which almost tempts me to believe in her beneficence—the pulses, including the beans, are rich in lysine and if pulse and cereal are eaten together, then the surplus in the former largely makes good the deficiency in the latter. Pulses and cereals commonly occur together in all the world's great cuisines: beans and tortillas in Mexico; rice or *chapatis* and *dhal* in India; and baked beans on toast in Britain.

Finally, meat protein tends to contain an excess of essential amino acids, so the most efficient way to eat it is in small amounts in conjunction with proteins of lower quality such as those of beans or cereals. The meat is thus used not as a prime source of protein (as it is in some present-day Western diets) but merely as a guarantor of quality. In practical terms, this means demoting meat from its present *prima donna* role in Western cuisine to the role of garnish, as in the cooking of modern China and as in the peasant cooking of all the world through most of history. There is no hardship implied, for Chinese and traditional European cooking scale the gastronomic heights.

Meat as garnish

Modern protein theory seems to fit snugly into the constraints of rational agriculture. If agriculture concentrates on producing maximum food for human consumption then it must concentrate upon the staples—cereals, pulses, and potatoes—and to some extent upon green leaves such as spinach. So be it, since these contain the protein-energy ratio that humans need, let them carry the burden of human nourishment. Rational agriculture relegates livestock to a subsidiary role, and thus reduces their numbers. So be it, since meat is needed only in modest amounts, for its quality rather than for its mass.

The Fat Story

The protein story has largely been worked out in the Third World, and begins with the fact of malnutrition. The fat story belongs mainly to the rich world, and largely concerns the perils of excess.

First, a few definitions. The fats that concern human beings and keep nutritionists awake at night are of two main kinds: the triglycerides and cholesterol. The triglycerides are a large and varied group, with a wide range of qualities and properties. Cholesterol is one single entity, which crops up in an extraordinary variety of contexts.

The triglycerides consist of three fatty acid chains joined to one molecule of glycerol. The glycerol is merely a convenient chaperone for the fatty acids; but the nature of the fatty acids is all-important.

The fatty acid chains can vary in three main ways. They can be long or short; they can be straight or branched; and they can be saturated or unsaturated. Of these three sources of variability it is the last—degree of saturation—that is most germane to a discussion of modern fat theory; so it is worth discussing.

A fatty acid chain consists, for the most part, of a long string of carbon atoms, which are held together by chemical bonds. Each carbon atom carries four chemical bonds, so if each carbon in the chain uses one of its bonds to link to the carbon on its immediate left and one to link with the carbon on its immediate right, then it will have two to spare. But it is

What do people need?

in the nature of chemical bonds to bond. Going spare is not allowed by the laws of the universe. So the spare carbon bonds in the fatty acid chain link up with atoms of hydrogen: one hydrogen atom per bond.

So the "ideal" fatty acid chain—geometrically not nutritionally ideal—consists of a row of carbons, each linked to the carbon on either side, and each flanked by a couple of hydrogens.

Sometimes, and importantly, this ideal structure is not realized. Instead, one or several pairs of carbons along the chain may decide to squander two of their bonds on each other, to form a double bond. If they do this then they have only one bond each to spare for binding to hydrogen. So a fatty acid chain that contains one or several carbon-carbon double bonds will be holding onto fewer hydrogen atoms than one which contains no such double bonds. Putting it another way, the ideal chain, with no carbon-carbon double bonds, contains the maximum possible number of hydrogens, and is said to be saturated (with hydrogen). But a fatty acid chain that is interrupted by one or several carbon-carbon double bonds contains fewer hydrogens than it might, and so is called unsaturated. A fatty acid chain with only one carbon-carbon double bond is monounsaturated; and one with two or more carbon-carbon double bonds is polyunsaturated.

Fats that are saturated, unsaturated and polyunsaturated

The physical properties of fats provide a rough guide to their saturation status. Saturated fats tend to have a high melting point, and so are hard at normal temperatures; suet is the archetypal saturated fat. Unsaturated fats generally have a lower melting point, and so are oily at normal temperatures. But such gross assessment can be highly deceptive. Coconut oil and palm oil are highly saturated, and some plant oils that are naturally unsaturated are deliberately saturated during the refining process to make them more chemically stable. So if you want a fat that is unsaturated you cannot simply plump for oil, but must go for a specific type—sunflower, safflower, corn (maize), or soybean oil.

Deceptive coconuts

Triglyceride fats have two functions. First, they are structural in the sense that some fats are, like protein, the "stuff" of human flesh; indeed the cell membranes consist of layers of fat sandwiched between layers of protein, and the fat is just as important as the protein to the membrane's form and function, and hence to the function of the whole living cell. Some of the fats that are vital to cell function cannot be synthesized in the body. These fats must be supplied in the food and are termed "essential." However, the essential fatty acids are only a small proportion of those that a human being actually consumes, and I take the same attitude to them as to vitamins; that they will inevitably be taken care of if the diet is sufficiently varied, and constrained by consideration of protein-energy ratio, fiber and *gross* fat intake.

Essential fats

The second main function of triglyceride fats is to provide energy—or calories, which are the units of energy. They carry out this function supremely efficiently, for a gram of fat provides nine Calories,* which is twice as much as a gram of carbohydrate (sugar or starch) or a gram of

* *Nutritionists now measure energy in kilojoules; but the Calorie, or kilocalorie (Kcal), is more widely understood. One Calorie equals 1,000 calories.*

protein provides. This is why evolution has favored fat as an energy store; why animals tend to lay down fat before the winter, and plants lace their seeds with oil to nourish the developing embryo.

Cholesterol is an odd molecule. It can be classified as a fat although its structure superficially is quite dissimilar from the triglycerides; for the most part it consists of a characteristic grouping of carbon rings, a grouping described as steroid. Cholesterol is involved in the synthesis of steroid hormones, which include the sex hormones, and it is the root molecule of the bile salts which are important in digestion. It is, therefore, a vital substance; but this does not mean you cannot have too much of it. Oxygen is also vital, but too much can kill you.

Do not breathe oxygen

Indeed, cholesterol is involved in at least two of the major disorders of rich societies—the so-called diseases of affluence—and has therefore been responsible for the intricate, often rancorous, and at times even litigious controversy that has occupied nutritionists for more than a decade. First, cholesterol may crystallize in the gallbladder, in the liver, and so form gallstones, which are common enough in some Western countries to constitute an epidemic. Second, and much more dangerously, they contribute to the fatty lesions—atheromatous plaques, collectively known as atheroma—which begin to build up in Western people's arteries before they are ten years old, and which may block certain vital arteries before they are out of middle age. In particular, atheroma may occlude the coronary arteries, which oxygenate and feed the heart itself. Eventually, a small blood clot blocks the clogged coronary artery, and the result may be a heart attack. This form of heart attack—coronary heart disease—is far more common in men than in women and is now by far the commonest single cause of death in the West. The province of North Karelia in Eastern Finland has the highest rate of coronary heart disease in the world, and I have visited primary schools there in which one-third of the children were fatherless because of heart attacks.

Coronary heart disease, and the orphans of North Karelia

The role of cholesterol in forming the atheroma that underlies coronary heart disease is not straightforward. It is true, or seems to be, that the more cholesterol that people have in their blood, the worse their atheroma; and atheroma, or something very like it, can be produced in laboratory animals by raising their blood cholesterol levels artificially. The atheromatous plaques are complex lesions, containing smooth muscle fibers, connective tissue, and clotted blood; but they also contain crystals of cholesterol. Yet some scientists argue that the cholesterol is involved only passively, or even that its role in atheroma is protective; that you find cholesterol in atheromatous plaques for the same reason that you find policemen at the scene of a crime. This argument does seem perverse, however; for one thing, laboratory animals do not produce cholesterol after they have developed atheroma, they develop atheroma after they have been assaulted with cholesterol. Much evidence now suggests that the role of cholesterol in atheroma is indeed causal, and this is what most people in the field believe.

It is also clear—and this is not a debating point; it is a simple observation—that the more cholesterol people have in their blood, the greater their chance of having a heart attack. This statement is made from

What do people need?

observation of populations, and cannot of course be applied to every individual, if only because blood cholesterol is not the only factor that predisposes a person to heart attack. So you might have a very high blood cholesterol level and yet live to a ripe old age, and I might have a low cholesterol level and yet succumb by the end of this paragraph. But chance is the key word.

High cholesterol need not be dangerous; but why take chances?

In general, plasma cholesterol levels rise with age and if a person's plasma cholesterol never rises above about 120 mg percent, then his chances of coronary heart disease are virtually zero. In some areas—even in Europe, as in southern Italy or peasant Yugoslavia—people's cholesterol levels do indeed remain this low, and heart attacks that are so devastating in many of the countries to the north, are rare.

The healthy peasants of Yugoslavia

The mean cholesterol level among British or American middle-aged men is around 230 mg percent, and this is very much in the "at risk" bracket. In their joint report on *Prevention of Coronary Heart Disease* in 1976, the Royal College of Physicians of London and the British Cardiac Society sought to define a danger level of plasma cholesterol above which an individual and his physician should probably take action. They concluded that there was no clear danger point, but decided that 275 mg percent was a reasonable maximum, above which the chances of heart attack were unacceptably high. Yet 275 is uncomfortably close to the population average. Thus, the blood cholesterol levels of most of the men in Britain and the United States are so high that *all* men are "at risk."

Whether it is worthwhile to lower a raised blood cholesterol level is controversial: but on present evidence it is worthwhile to prevent the rise in blood cholesterol in the first place. So how can this be done?

Diet is the obvious, and for most people the most cogent controllable factor, and of all the dietary factors affecting cholesterol levels the one that apparently has the most consistent and profound effect is fat.

Yet the story is not simple. When coronary heart disease was first shown to be associated with high blood cholesterol, many nutritionists leapt immediately to the obvious conclusion: that people should cut down on dietary cholesterol and, more specifically, should cut out such foods as eggs and variety meats that were extremely rich in cholesterol. Yet only a small proportion of the cholesterol in the human body comes directly from the diet. Most of it is synthesized by the body. So by cutting out dietary cholesterol a person may be damming only a minor tributary, and leaving the flood unstemmed.

Make your own cholesterol

Admittedly, you can raise the blood cholesterol levels of laboratory animals by feeding them enormous amounts of cholesterol; but does this relate to the human condition? For the fact is that people do not eat vast amounts of cholesterol. Eggs are the chief source, and Westerners are not the world's outstandingly conspicuous egg eaters. A superficial glance at the world in general would not indict the egg. The Spanish are very fond of eggs, yet before modern affluence caught up with them they had a very low incidence of heart attack. In short, a specific attack on dietary cholesterol seems unjustified. What seems to correlate far better with the incidence of coronary heart disease is the total level of fat in the diet. The Americans and the British, who have high levels of coronary heart disease, obtain more than 40 percent of their total calories from fat; and fat in this context means triglyceride. The native people of southern Italy, who until a few years ago simply did not have heart attacks, obtained less than 20 percent of their daily energy from fat. The story is consistent worldwide: it seems that high fat diet equals high blood cholesterol equals high risk of heart attack.

The Royal College of Physicians recommended a reduction in fat intake from the present 40 percent, "towards 35 percent of total calories." The McGovern Committee in the United States chose the more ambitious 30 percent as a reasonable target. The target figure is largely arbitrary, but the message—reduce total fat intake—is loud and clear. The cuisine of the Mediterranean and South-East Asia suggest that the "safe," low-fat diet can be far from boring. Ambitious McGovern . . .

There is one final complication—or rather there are several, but only one of direct interest to the cook—which concerns the nutritional differences between saturated and unsaturated fat. Saturated fat, taken in the diet, evidently raises blood cholesterol levels; but polyunsaturated fat apparently lowers blood cholesterol levels. Some doctors are so impressed by this observation that they advise people to consume polyunsaturated fats as if they were a drug, and suggest that people should actually dose themselves with sunflower oil. The Royal College of Physicians adopted a sensible compromise. They pointed out that most Westerners are used to a high-fat diet, and would be reluctant to reduce their fat intake too much; but that it might be a good idea, in addition to reducing fat intake, to replace some of the saturated fat in their diets with polyunsaturates. In other words—broadly speaking—the diet should contain far less animal fat (including butter) but more polyunsaturates, such as corn, safflower and sunflower oil. Olive oil, incidentally, qualifies as a neutral fat. It is mostly monounsaturated, and monounsaturated oil, so the limited evidence suggests, neither lowers nor raises blood cholesterol levels. . . . and sensible compromise

I have more to say about fats later on but in the meantime am content with the generalizations adopted by the Royal College of Physicians: that to reduce total fat intake is a good thing; that a shift in the nature of ingested fat, from saturated, usually hard, fats to polyunsaturates, is a good thing; but the dietary cholesterol is probably not terribly significant because most people just do not eat that much of it. These are the principles adopted throughout this book.

The Stories of Fiber and Sugar

The protein story is one of *volte-face*. The fat story has been refined over the years but in general has pointed inexorably (some feel a little too inexorably) in one direction—toward the recommendation to reduce intake. But the fiber story, which has imposed itself on the medical consciousness only during the past decade, has been a revelation. Revelationary fiber

Ten years ago the expression "dietary fiber," which is now so firmly established in nutrition vocabulary, did not exist, or at least was not defined; it was the British physician Dr Hugh Trowell who provided the definition in 1972. Until then fiber had been referred to misleadingly, dismissively and largely inaccurately as "roughage" or "unavailable

What do people need?

carbohydrate" and had been thought, by most hard-line nutritionists, to be a concept fit only for school matrons anxious to protect their charges from the dire but largely imagined perils of constipation. Now it is clear that fiber is, or can be, a large part of the diet; that it is chemically complex and that it profoundly affects the physiology of the bowel, which in turn profoundly affects the well-being of the whole human animal; and that it is, directly or indirectly, involved or at least implicated in all the diseases of affluence, which affect people in rich countries but not usually people in poor countries. These diseases include somewhat crude mechanical disorders, including constipation, but also diverticular disease, in which the lining of the colon becomes deformed, non-functional, and perhaps painful—but they also include serious metabolic complaints, including diabetes, gallstones and coronary heart disease. Obesity, too, is or certainly can be influenced by the fiber content of the diet. That is a formidable list.

All the "diseases of affluence"

The fat story has been worked out largely in the United States; but the fiber story belongs to Britain. The first person to formulate clearly the idea that fiber might be implicated in the diseases of affluence—or at least, the man whom most fiber protagonists would acknowledge as the pioneer—was Surgeon Commander T. L. Cleave of the Royal Navy. In two books published in the late 1960s he and his co-authors presented some blindingly simple observations and some equally simple but ingenious ideas for which at the time there was little direct evidence but which seem to be growing more convincing by the week as the evidence piles up. Cleave pointed out that one of the principal and most consistent differences between the societies that endure the diseases of affluence and those that do not, was their diet. Negroes or Japanese or Australian aborigines are clearly not genetically immune to gallstones, diabetes and heart disease, for when they move from their villages into the cities, or to the United States, they begin to experience all of those diseases. If genes are not the cause then it must be environment, of which diet is the most direct influential component.

The diet of the rural African differs from the New Yorker's in many aspects. It is smaller, for a start; it contains less of virtually all the major nutrients. It is also *proportionally* less rich in fat and protein. All those aspects—fewer calories, less fat and less protein, both in absolute terms and proportionately—are probably significant. Yet perhaps (and the more you think about it, the more sense it seems to make) it is the fiber content of the diet that unifies these disparate aspects.

What dietary fiber is

Dietary fiber consists of the cell walls of plants. Animals have thin-walled cells, but they also have skeletons, either like hard suits of armor, as in a crab or an insect, or like an internal scaffold, as in vertebrates. If animals did not have skeletons, then their structures would collapse, like an unsupported jellyfish. But plants do not have designated skeletons: they merely confine each cell in a tough integument and it is these integuments—cell walls—that collectively support the plant.

The most well known of all cell wall components is cellulose, one of the few components that really is fibrous. Indeed, cotton and paper consist largely of cellulose. Cellulose consists—as starch does—of long chains of glucose molecules. It differs from starch only in the manner in which the glucose molecules are linked. But the difference in linkage is vital, because starch molecules can be broken down by the enzymes in an animal's (or human's) gut to yield glucose, and glucose in turn is one of the principal sources of energy. But the geometry of cellulose is such that it is not susceptible to the action of animal enzymes. Some animals—such as the cow and sheep—have bacteria in their stomachs that allow them to break down cellulose, and so to use it as a source of energy. But humans have no such bacteria in their stomachs. Cellulose passes through the digestive part of their gut unchanged.

Cellulose is present in all young cell walls, and since all plants have cells and almost all plant cells have walls, cellulose is accordingly the most common compound in nature. But one of the mistakes that nutritionists made in the past was to assume that plant cell walls consisted more or less exclusively of cellulose. Since human beings cannot digest cellulose, and since cellulose in the form of cotton, for example, is obviously inert, they assumed that plant cell walls were also inert and that they could not possibly have more than a rather crude mechanical effect upon the gut. In other words, dietary fiber—alias roughage—might relieve constipation (indeed, demonstrably did relieve constipation); but to posit an effect on heart disease, gallstones or diabetes seems absurd.

More to fiber than cellulose

The traditional method of analyzing the roughage or dietary fiber content of food supported the notion that it could not possibly do anything terribly interesting. It consisted of boiling food in acid, then in alcohol, and finally in alkali, to see what came through. What came through, predictably, was not very much. What came through, in fact, was cellulose. Since the residue of this assault was unimpressive both in quantity and in reactivity, it seemed that roughage must have only minor effects. The thing hardly seemed worth considering.

However the plant cell walls do not consist merely of the relatively uninteresting cellulose. They also contain lignin (wood) and pectic substances, including various kinds of gum and hemicellulose. These pectic substances are liable to predominate in young cell walls, and although they are not broken down by the enzymes of the stomach or the small intestine, they are very reactive indeed. But the laboratory onslaught with acid, alcohol and alkali obliterates the pectic substances which are the most active component of roughage and which exert a profound effect on the large bowel.

Lignin, gums and pectic substances

So, to take just one example, we find that whole wheat flour analyzed by the old boiling acid technique seemed to contain only about two percent roughage, or fiber, which consisted mainly of the physiologically placid cellulose. But modern, more gentle analysis—which approximates the action of the human gut far more closely—shows that whole wheat flour contains about ten percent fiber, and that most of that consists of pectic substances, including hemicelluloses, which are fairly reactive. It now seems that fiber could have important influences, and that its removal from food could be significant. So what difference could ingestion of roughage make? How could it influence obesity, gallstones, diabetes or heart disease?

Modern evidence suggests that the influence of fiber is both negative

What do people need?

and positive; and it may be that the negative effects are in the end more significant. The most important point is that fiber, which by definition is indigestible, makes the food bulky, and yet supplies no energy, protein or fat. And bulk is one important determinant of appetite.

The chief source of energy for most human beings (outside the minority population in the developed world, that is) is carbohydrate, in the form of starch and sugar; and starch and sugar come primarily from plants. If human beings simply eat plants, then they cannot eat starch or sugar without eating plant cell walls, alias fiber. But in modern societies the starch or sugar is extracted from the plant in almost pure form before it is eaten. Modern mills extract white flour from wheat grain and throw away the bran—which is nearly 50 percent fiber. The sugar refiners extract the almost pure sucrose from cane or beet and throw away the fibrous residues of the cane stems or of the massive, hard beet roots. Pure sugar and pure starch—refined carbohydrate—are highly calorific compared to their bulk; and it is possible to eat large amounts of them, and hence to take in enormous loads of energy, without filling yourself up. The feeling of being "full" is not the entire antidote to hunger, but it is at least part of it. Professor John Yudkin, formerly of Queen Elizabeth College, London, has pointed out that the average Briton now eats about five ounces of sugar a day—supplying one-fifth of the daily calories—and surmises that some children may obtain half or even more of their energy from sugar. The conscious eating of sugar in candy is only part of the trouble. People consume sugar without noticing it; in tea and coffee; in soft drinks; even in ostensibly non-sweet foods, including many canned foods, where sugar is used partly as a preservative and partly to improve texture. Sugar eaten in this way—perhaps 1,000 or more Calories a day—hardly even suppresses appetite.

Yet if you eat carbohydrate only in unrefined form—starch in whole grain, or sugar in its parent plant—then you would need to eat relatively enormous quantities in order to obtain 1,000 Calories. Dr Kenneth Heaton of Bristol University, England, has pointed out that if Britons wanted to obtain their daily five ounces of sugar in unrefined form then they would need to eat, for example, almost three pounds of apples, which would be a fairly heroic feat.

The single fact that fiber provides bulk without providing energy (or protein or fat), could well be the key to all the major differences between the healthy diet of, for example, the rural African and the Western diet that seems to be so perilous. The Africans' diet contains a lot of fiber because it consists largely of unrefined roots (cassava) or fruit (plantain) or grains (corn or millet). Such food contains modest but perhaps adequate amounts of protein and very little fat. In order to obtain enough calories to take him through a day, the rural African has to eat an enormous bulk and has neither the time nor the physical capacity to eat excess. Indeed, he is far more likely to settle for a daily 2,000 Calories (with modest protein and low fat) than to aspire to the Westerner's customary 3,000 Calories, rich in protein and awash with fat. It is difficult to see how the rural African could become fat on such a diet, and indeed he does not; and neither can he consume enough fat to damage his arteries. The arteries of the average 40-year-old Westerner

Full without calories

Heroic consumption of apples

Village Africans eat a lot, and stay thin

are invariably atheromatous, and indeed in the kind of condition that would send him scurrying to the emergency plumbing service if it occurred in his water supply. But the arteries of the 40-year-old rural African are as clean as a flute.

The relationship of fiber to diabetes is also eminently conceivable, although it remains speculative. Diabetics are unable to produce appropriate amounts of the hormone insulin, whose task it is to cope with glucose in the blood. Glucose is produced in the gut during digestion of starch or sucrose (table sugar) and streams into the blood immediately after a meal. But if you eat carbohydrate only in its pristine form, in unrefined grains, roots or fruits, then this stream is a mere trickle; the total amount of glucose is small, and it is made available slowly because the digestive enzymes have to battle their way through dietary fiber in order to get to the sugar and starch. If you eat refined sugar or refined flour, then the stream of glucose flowing into the blood after a meal becomes a flood. Dr Cleave suggests that the human body is simply not equipped to cope with such floods, which, after all, are like nothing that could be produced by nature; and that the constant flooding, in people eating the highly refined Western diet, upsets the delicate hormone mechanism that should control blood sugar levels. Speculative or not, this idea makes sense; and the fact remains that rural Africans simply do not have diabetes, although diabetes clinics are springing up like mushrooms in new Western-style towns such as Kampala and Nairobi.

Streams of glucose

In short, the nutritionists' traditional attitude to carbohydrate has been completely reversed. Carbohydrate is the abomination of the dieter. The first thing fat people cut down on is potatoes; and many fashionable high-protein slimming diets are composed almost exclusively of steak and cheese. Yet the diet of the demonstrably svelte, even thin, rural African is very high in carbohydrate. And of course the enemy of the slimmer is not carbohydrate itself, but refined carbohydrate—the white flour which is almost pure starch, and, in particular, the pure sugar that is 100 percent sucrose (and brown sugar is just as bad as white). If you ate carbohydrate only in unrefined form— whole wheat flour, lashings of fruit and vegetables, and all the potatoes you can eat—then it would be difficult to grow fat. You just do not have the physical capacity to eat enough.

Down with refined carbohydrate

There is one important caveat—that high-carbohydrate foods are often laced with fat which undermines their high-bulk, low-calorie status. Thus brown flour in the form of the almost fatless *chapati* is not fattening; but a brown shortcake cookie made with lashings of fat and sugar is highly calorific and potentially very fattening. A boiled potato supplies a mere 80 Calories per 100 grams (about a quarter pound), and you need to eat three and a half kilograms of potatoes per day (more than eight pounds) to supply your daily 3,000 Calories—which I venture to suggest you could not do—and if you live on boiled potatoes (as some people have done) you will lose a lot of weight. But if those same potatoes are sliced thin and deep fried to make what the English call crisps and the Americans call chips, then the energy content increases to a horrendous 533 Calories per 100 grams. Chips are very fattening indeed, as many an overweight child can demonstrate. But the fault lies with the fat; not with the potato.

Thus fiber for the most part does not act in a positive way, like a drug. Its role in diet is like that of the monarch in British democracy, to deny power to other factions rather than to exert power. Yet people do use fiber talismanically; for example, they sprinkle a spoonful of bran on their cornflakes and then eat their eggs and bacon. Their diet is indeed high in fiber—but it is also high in fat and calories. The point is to eat plenty of fiber to the exclusion of other things; and not in the form of boring old bran but as delicious whole wheat bread and *chapatis*, and potatoes and fruit and vegetables.

Yet fiber does have direct, positive effects which are superimposed on its regal role. In particular, fiber absorbs water, and people such as rural Africans who eat a lot of fiber produce large, soft stools, while people on low-fiber diets produce mean, hard stools; and it is the latter who become constipated. In addition, one of Dr Cleave's early surgical collaborators, Mr Neil Painter, suggested that it was the constant effort involved in shifting hard, dry feces through the bowel—an effort involving fierce muscular contractions and generating high internal pressures—that was responsible for diverticular disease. Ten years ago doctors almost invariably told patients with diverticular disease to eat smooth, fiber-free diets, because the fiber was thought to abrade and irritate the already damaged bowel lining. But now, thanks primarily to Mr Painter, their advice is diametrically opposite. Patients with diverticular disease are put on high-fiber diets, and the results are unequivocally better.

Fiber in positive roles

Finally (and this may seem merely an academic nicety, but it could turn out to be supremely important), fiber binds materials other than water, including the bacteria that live in the colon, minerals and bile salts. Evidence on the influence of fiber on colon bacteria and on minerals is at present so sparse and in such a state of flux that it is better left to the specialist journals, but Dr Ken Heaten at Bristol University, and others, have already shown that the effect of fiber on bile salts is certainly measurable and possibly has profound and direct effects upon the genesis of gallstones.

Can fiber prevent gallstones?

Bile is produced in the liver, stored in the gall-bladder, and passed via the bile duct to the small intestine, where it helps to break down fats. The crucial, functional parts of the bile are a group of bile salts which act as detergents—that is, they bind with fat and so make it soluble in water. Quite by chance (I know of no functional explanation) the bile also provides a medium through which the body excretes surplus cholesterol. It dissolves in the bile, and eventually is jettisoned via the small intestine. But sometimes the body loads the bile with more cholesterol than it can hold. In such cases the excess cholesterol crystallizes out. These crystals grow as time wears on and are called gallstones.

The amount of cholesterol that the bile can carry depends on the exact nature of the bile salts that it contains. And the nature of the bile salts in the bile at any one time depends largely on what happens in the colon. For the bile salts that are pushed into the small intestine via the bile duct eventually wind up in the colon, and there they are subjected to bacterial action, which changes their chemical nature. They are then reabsorbed, and incorporated into the next lot of bile. What Dr Heaton and others have shown is that the presence or absence of dietary fiber in the colon influences the action of the bacteria that in turn alters the chemistry of bile salts. If the colon contents include fiber, then different secondary bile salts are formed and a different set of bile salts is resorbed. Hence the bile of people on a high-fiber diet is chemically different from the bile of people on a low-fiber diet. It just so happens that the bile of people on a low-fiber diet is more easily saturated with cholesterol than that of people on a high-fiber diet. In other words, people on a low-fiber diet are more likely to get gallstones, which is what Surgeon Commander Cleave said all along.

Fiber affects bile affects cholesterol

How science came to the aid of imaginative common sense

The message is simple. Eat plenty of fiber, which means eating plenty of carbohydrate—but only in unrefined form: pulses, wholemeal grains, potatoes, vegetables and fruit.

A Note on Salt

The idea that a high intake of salt (sodium chloride) was the root cause of high blood pressure (hypertension) has been around at least since the beginning of the twentieth century, which is when the ingenious inflatable cuff first enabled doctors to measure blood pressure routinely. If it is true that sodium chloride—or, more specifically, sodium—is involved, then salt is very pernicious stuff indeed because hypertension is the outstanding factor in stroke and is one of the three outstanding risk factors in coronary heart disease (the other two being smoking, and high blood cholesterol). Yet the idea never really caught on, partly because people like salt so much once they get hooked on it that they are loath to listen to detractions; and partly because nutritionists had got it into their heads that salt was essential to replace sodium losses during sweating, and positively forced servicemen to swallow it; and partly because the salt story is somewhat complicated and early attempts to present it failed because they were too simplistic. It now seems—and I am referring mainly to the evidence collated by Professor Lot Page of Tufts University School of Medicine, Boston, Massachusetts—that salt is indeed guilty of this serious charge; and (as the Israeli army has shown) that its short-term use to replace alleged losses during sweating is unnecessary.

Salt: pernicious but complicated

The evidence that salt is involved in hypertension is both experimental (based on laboratory studies of rats) and epidemiological (based on observations of human societies living their normal lives). The outstanding figure in the experimental work was the American physiologist, the late Dr Lewis E. Dahl.

Dahl noted what physicians had been noting with alarm for decades, that human beings' blood pressure rises inexorably with age. The rise was so universal it seemed normal, indeed natural, but since the rise was also dangerous, it seemed that this was yet another example of nature's design being less than perfect. Yet human beings are only animals, and the blood pressure of other animals never rises gratuitously with age.

Yet Dahl found he could cause the blood pressure to rise in laboratory rats by various means: by manipulating the blood circulation to the

What do people need?

kidneys, which is involved in blood pressure control; by administering hormones; by inbreeding the rats with the highest blood pressures; or—and in many animals this was the most effective method of all—by putting salt in their diet.

But there were complications. First, the rats' response to the salt was neither consistent nor simple. Indeed, Dr Dahl found that only a proportion of rats increased their blood pressure when given salt, and from these he bred a special salt-sensitive, or S strain. From resistant rats he bred a corresponding R strain.

Second, the nature of the sensitive rats' response to salt was far from simple. Their blood pressure did not rise immediately they were given salt; there was a latent period.

Third, the rats' response was not dose related, or at least not simply so. Blood pressure rose if a certain critical (but variable) amount of salt was given; but it did not necessarily rise more if more salt was given. Increasing blood pressure by giving salt is not like increasing engine speed by pressing the accelerator—a simple continuous reaction to input. It is more like turning on an electric machine by pressing a switch. Once the mechanism is set to work, it runs its own course.

Fourth, the rise in blood pressure was not reversible, or only slightly so. If Dahl gave sensitive rats enough salt, their blood pressure rose after a time to a new high level; and it stayed at the high level, or close to it, even if salt was then withdrawn from the diet. The mechanism set in motion by the initial high salt intake had no effective "off" switch.

Finally, the younger the rats the more sensitive they were to a high-salt diet. Baby rats that began life on a high-salt diet established higher blood pressures than those that began on a high-salt diet late in life.

What evidence is there that human beings do respond to salt in the same way as rats? This is where Professor Page's studies come in: partly his own work, and partly his collation of other people's work. Worldwide research has shown that there are many people whose blood pressure simply does not rise with age. These people are from virtually every racial type—Chinese aborigines, Greenland Eskimos, several Melanesian tribes from New Guinea and the Solomon Islands, Polynesians from isolated islands in Fiji, Cook, Caroline and Tokelau islands, Easter Islanders, Australian aborigines, nomadic tribes in Kenya, Congo pygmies, Bushmen of the Kalahari Desert, Masai from Tanzania, West Malaysians, and South and Central American Indians from Chile, Brazil, and Guatemala. Take any of these people and put them into a city and their blood pressure will rise, so they are not genetically immune from hypertension. Something in their environment allows their blood pressure to stay low and steady throughout life. Or, to put it another way, there is something in the environment created by affluent societies that causes hypertension. The observed rise in blood pressure in members of affluent societies is not innate, after all. It is caused.

So what do the Chinese aborigines, Greenland Eskimos and the rest, have in common? In three words they all have Stone Age cultures, which is not terribly helpful, because Stone Age cultures differ from modern cultures in every conceivable respect, from social values and

Set the mechanism and stand aside

Sensitive babies

What's good about Chinese aborigines?

birth spacing, to dress and language. Yet there are also people in other Stone Age cultures whose blood pressure does increase with age; so what do they have in common with each other, and with modern societies, that they do not have in common with Chinese aborigines?

To cut a long and immensely complex mathematical story short, the factor that Professor Page says "came roaring out of the statistics" was diet; and of all the components of diet, the one that consistently correlated with blood pressure was salt intake. Some of the peoples with low blood pressure were hunters, some were hunter-gatherers, some were fishermen and some were farmers; some were almost vegetarian and some, like the Eskimos and Masai, were well-nigh carnivorous. But all of them consumed less than one gram of sodium per day. The correlation was often subtle, even cryptic. The Polynesian groups had a low salt intake even though they were marine fishermen; but the Lao people of the Solomons boil their food in sea water, and so have a much higher salt intake. Roaring out of the statistics

The loss of sodium during sweating—which is obvious even from the saltiness of sweat—seems primarily to be adaptive. If the body contains too much sodium, it excretes the surplus through the sweat. If it contains no surplus, then it will sweat almost pure water. There is a proviso, that the body takes a few weeks to adapt, and if somebody who is habituated to a high-salt diet goes onto a low-salt diet and then immediately goes on army maneuvers, he is liable to sweat more sodium than he can afford and to run into trouble. But if he first adapts to the low-salt diet, he will conserve his body sodium no matter how much he sweats. People stretched to the limits of their physical endurance, sweating nine liters (almost two gallons) a day lose only two grams of sodium, if they are adapted to a low-salt intake. Indeed, recent studies suggest that the body's basal requirement of sodium (among people not on army maneuvers) is a mere 200 milligrams: one-fifth of a gram. Adapt to a low-salt diet

So the studies of Stone Age societies suggest that one gram of sodium per day may represent the safe upper limit; and other studies suggest that one-fifth of that is the safe lower limit. The sodium intake of Westerners is not known in detail (nutritional science is primitive in many respects), but such studies as there are suggest that the British or American intake is many, many times higher than the safety level. Indeed, data from Johns Hopkins Hospital in Baltimore, Maryland, suggest that the average 16-year-old American takes in about six grams of sodium (14 to 15 grams of sodium chloride) in regular meals alone; and since American adolescents also eat vast amounts of salted peanuts and potato chips, their actual intake may be twice this figure. And of course salt is somewhat addictive; there is a tendency, once you acquire a taste for it, and as the palate loses its sensitivity with age, to pile on more and more of it. How much salt do people eat?

Yet the advice to eat less salt—indeed, to pursue what by Western standards seems almost to be a salt-free diet—seems futile; for people not only like salt, but esteem it almost above all other flavorings. Futile advice?

The mistake, I think, has been to assume that a diet low in salt has to be totally bland; and one of the most famous of the low-salt diets that has been used clinically consisted almost exclusively of rice and fruit. It seems obvious that a diet low in salt should be spiced with other things to compensate. Although the recipes in this book include salt, it should be regarded as optional. They are well laced with spices, lemon juice and yogurt, and it is hard to see how such food can be tasteless.

However, as with sugar and fat, it seems unnecessary to be puritanical. Sugar is fine if used for specific culinary purposes, as a spice, just as bacon fat and beef drippings are acceptable, provided you do not eat enormous amounts of bacon or beef. Similarly, it would be a pity to abandon those dishes, notably pickles and salted meats, where salt is the principal spice. But there is a world of difference between the occasional pickle, eaten as a special culinary event, and the constant intrusion of salt into and onto every item of food from bread and boiled potatoes to porridge and pancakes.

And in conclusion . . .

In conclusion, the details of modern nutritional theory are complex, but the recommendations that emerge are simple enough. The bulk of protein and energy should be supplied by the staples—Food of the First Kind—because these are made bulky and hence filling by their high fiber content, and because they are, for the most part, low in fat. So sound nutrition is based upon pulses, grains, and potatoes cooked as simply as possible.

The role of meat and other animal products in human nutrition is not negligible, but they do not have to be eaten in large amounts. In addition, because of their high saturated-fat content, a high consumption is not recommended. So meat, cheese, and the rest are demoted to the category of Food of the Second Kind, to be used primarily as garnish, for their flavor.

Meat for garnish

Vegetables, too, are Food of the Second Kind, since their role in human nutrition is not vital, at least on a day-to-day basis. They can be regarded primarily as a source of flavor, to make the staples more acceptable. Yet, as with meat, the advice here is not to eat vegetables sparingly. Primarily because of their high bulk—reflecting their high fiber and water content—and their miserly content of fat and other energy sources, vegetables should be eaten *ad lib*. For the Westerner, surrounded as he is by food that is too rich, the more fruit and vegetables he eats, the better.

Salt and sugar should be regarded as spices—Food of the Third Kind—rather than as principal nutrients, which is how they are now regarded. Everything else that is not actually poisonous, from chrysanthemums to cockles, can be pressed into the diet as and when available—not, again, as a prime source of nutrition, but just to create interest: food very much of the third kind.

In general, fat should be eaten sparingly. If you feel that frying really is justified, then use polyunsaturates, such as corn oil or sunflower oil (if you can afford it): and use the succulent saturates, from pork crackling to beef drippings, as delicacies.

Delicate pork crackling

These simple rules will keep you well within the confines of modern nutritional theory and if everyone followed them they might even increase life expectancy. Yet they are not the rubric for a boring diet.

The arts of good eating

What you eat is important: how you eat it is equally so. There are three considerations. The first is that sensuality is one thing and stoking up is another, and the two should not be confused.

The second is that some flavorsome and pleasurable foods are nutritionally potent and perhaps undesirable, while others are perfectly innocuous, and if you are going to acquire tastes for things, as everyone inevitably does, then concentrate upon the latter.

The third principle is always to think about what you are eating, and to surround all intake with ritual.

But what can human beings do in a technological world that surrounds them with high-calorie foods with addictive flavors which they have no innate ability to resist? One answer is to do what slimming buffs are forever recommending—adopt a monotonous diet. Monotony rather than subtlety of nutritional theory is the factor common to the sometimes successful all-fruit, all-cheese, all-salad or sometimes even all-fat slimming diets. But it would be galling to think that civilization had merely led us all to a perpetual round of grapefruit and lettuce. We need a compromise; and that is what traditional cuisines—such as the Japanese—provide.

The traditional Japanese diet is for the most part monotonous. It was designed merely to keep body and soul together and consisted of rice, rice and more rice. It is hard to grow fat on rice both because of its water and fiber content, and because endless bowls of it are so boring. Yet the Japanese are gourmets. The point is that their feasts are of delicacies: tiny slivers of fish, exquisitely marinated and exploding with flavor; endless variations of pickle; little fronds of seaweed that people may risk their necks to gather, but which provide hardly a calorie.

The English high tea is of the same ilk. Calories and basic protein are provided by bread, bread and more bread. Yet there are delicacies on a good English tea table that would bring tears to the eyes, like fine blue cheeses, pastries and little porcelain pots of pink shrimp paste. The whole point of such things is to eat them in tiny amounts.

The antidote to the gloom generated by dietitians—and the way to avoid falling foul of our inappropriate psychological inheritance—is to become a gourmet. Most of the time you should just tick along on whatever food is the regional staple. But when you step outside that simple refueling it should not be to indulge in commercial mayonnaise or sides of ill-considered flesh, but in small amounts of beautiful things lovingly prepared. So long as sensuous foods are eaten reverentially and sparingly, there is little need to bother about their content. It may be inadvisable to eat too much saturated fat, but many of the saturated fats, such as bacon fat and beef drippings, are among cooking's supreme delights. So do not cut the fat off bacon, just eat less bacon, but make sure you enjoy it when you do. And do not give the beef drippings to the sparrows: spread it on good, thick whole wheat bread and do not eat roast beef more than twice a month. Where is the hardship in all this?

What can a person do?

In praise of high tea

Do not cut the fat off bacon

The arts of good eating

Principle two is obvious enough. Some of the most pleasing foods—notably fat and sugar—are highly calorific and perhaps can be harmful in other ways; but many other equally pleasant foods—cumin, onion, garlic, Florence fennel, apples, pears, oranges, peaches—are equally if differently pleasurable, yet have a low or virtually zero calorific content. In many parts of the world people take much of their food as snacks, which theoretically is self-destructive—it is easy to eat too much that way. But if the passing snack is a lovingly pickled fragment of turnip, as it might be in the Middle East, where is the harm? The entire class of vegetables and fruit can virtually be eaten at will provided they are not doused in Thousand Island dressing or heavy cream. Again where is the hardship here?

Loving fragments of turnip

Finally—principle three—thinking about eating, and imposing "form," is vital. "Snacking" in Mediterranean or Eastern style is permissible, partly because many of the tidbits are low in calories and fat, and partly because, despite the informality, the eating is ritualistic. A Western child buys chocolate-covered raisins from a slot machine and nibbles them in passing. A Neapolitan businessman waits by the wayside stall through much cluck-clucking about the state of the Church while the old peasant lady shovels olives into a little cone of paper. The American child comes home from school and takes a tuna fish sandwich and a pint of milk from the refrigerator. The English child, traditionally, had to wait while his mother laid the table and put the kettle on. The ceremonies of the meal serve as psychological cues to begin and finish eating. According to Joyce Nash of the Stanford Heart Disease Prevention Program centered at Palo Alto, California, many American children have never known what it is to feel hungry or to feel sated, and because the concept of the ritualistic "meal" is breaking down, they have no cues either to begin eating or to stop. They simply eat all the time.

So the formalities must return to eating; but the endless meals of Mexico, the pleasant to-ings and fro-ings of Japan, or the prolonged indulgences of France show that this, too, is no hardship.

Prolonged indulgences

Above all, Westerners need a new cuisine. It must be based on the foods that should be eaten and which are liable to be available. It should borrow and adapt all relevant techniques from all the cooks of history, who had often faced and overcome the problems that we now face. The immodest aim of this book is to examine the foods that should in future be available; to review the techniques that have already been applied to them; and to work toward a new cuisine that will demonstrate, I hope, that good living and early death do not inevitably go together.

Wheat, rice, oats and the rest

The grains are half of agriculture, and except for the seed of one glorified dockweed known as buckwheat, and of a relative of Love-lies-bleeding that is called *amaranth*, and *quinoa*, a cousin of the weed Fat Hen, the grains are seeds of the Gramineae, alias grass.

The grasses have done more to determine the kind of creatures human beings have become, and the kind of societies we have developed, than any other outside influence.

The structure and the way of life of grasses is deceptively simple. Often, even characteristically, the stem is short and the growing tip lies close to the ground; the portion that protrudes above the ground to form grass is just leaf, and often what looks like a stem is no more than a leaf base rolled into a tube. Grasses, including cereals, often spread by sending out new shoots (known as tillers) at ground level, but they also reproduce highly effectively by seed. Their sexual activities, manifesting in clouds of wind-borne pollen, are obvious enough to hay-fever sufferers; and the seeds that finally form are distributed in a hundred ways, by wind or water or animals or just by falling to the ground.

Grasses have the simplicity of the artful

Even the seed is a simplified structure; in fact it is fruit and seed combined, as if the whole of the outside of an apple were reduced to a tough integument and fused to the pip; and although farmers are happy to refer to grass seed or cereals as "seeds," the botanists call such a stripped-down, fused fruit-seed structure a caryopsis.

Because the growing tip of grass is close to or even below the ground, it does not "mind" being grazed; all it loses when a deer nibbles off its top are the leaves that it waves in the air, as a cinema sheriff waves his hat to attract the black-hats' fire. Indeed, most grasses "prefer" to be grazed; without this pruning they become overgrown, or rank and moribund. Most plants carry their growing tissue at their apex and if they are nibbled down to ground level they very soon give up the ghost.

Early in the history of terrestrial life a symbiotic relationship was established between the grasses that grew stronger as they were grazed, and the animals that benefited from the earth's generous outpouring of such good food. The grazing animals come from all classes: lizards and tortoises; geese, ducks and swans; rodents and rabbits; elephants, camels, pigs and hippopotamuses; horses; and most significantly, the once endless herds of even-toed hoofed animals—deer, antelope, sheep, goats, cattle and all the intermediate types. Civilization is inconceivable without settled agriculture, and one of agriculture's roots lies in the exploitation of herd animals. Not all herd animals are grass eaters (reindeer, for example, feed largely on lichens), but it was the grassland that gave rise to them, and they that sustained the grassland and provided the basis of pastoral farming.

No grass, no civilization?

The seeds of grasses are nutritious and with their tough, multilayered coats are eminently storable. One theory on the origins of arable

Wheat, rice, oats and the rest

farming, as plausible as any, is that the earliest pastoralists gathered grasses to feed to their beasts, and noted that where seed was shed, new plants grew. One of the many difficulties of cereal breeding is to produce varieties whose seeds adhere to the plant with the right degree of tenacity. If they fall off too readily, they will be lost during harvesting, but if they cling too tightly they are impossible to separate from the straw. If arable farming did indeed rise by the casual dropping of seed from whole harvested grass, this would ensure that cereal breeding started off on the right foot, for the types whose seeds stuck firmly enough to be gathered but not so tightly that they were never released would be perpetuated. But however they were domesticated, it is largely to the big-seeded grasses, the cereals, that we owe agriculture's other and more settled half. The grasses are thus the foundation of both arable and pastoral farming and are 80 percent of agriculture.

Not too loose, not too tight

Seeds are splendid things to eat largely because they evolved, through natural selection, as food repositories; admittedly the food they contain is intended for the embryo plant rather than for us, but it nonetheless includes a quota of protein, carbohydrate, and sometimes of fat, besides minerals and some vitamins, that is more than adequate for such an adaptable creature as the human being.

The cereal seed may be festooned with all kinds of bracts, awns and extraneous wrappings—sometimes loosely termed husks—but the caryopsis itself has three main components. On the outside are the fused layers of the fruit and seed coat; these can be separated during milling, and are then called bran. The bran has a high content of dietary fiber (44 percent by weight in wheat bran) but also (again in wheat bran) an impressive 14 percent by weight of protein, and five percent fat.

Three parts of grain

The bulk of the cereal grain is made up of endosperm; somewhat nondescript tissue whose main function is to act as a food supply. It is the endosperm of wheat that is ground up to make what has become the conventional white flour; it contains only three percent fiber and one percent fat, and is nine to ten percent protein. The rest is carbohydrate, mostly in the form of starch.

Finally, lodged in one corner of the caryopsis is the plant embryo, colloquially called the germ. It tends to be richer in fat, protein and minerals than the endosperm, so its removal in milling slightly diminishes the grain's overall food value; although flour that contains the germ does not store well because the fat becomes rancid.

The food value of all the cereals is roughly similar. With all species, the protein content varies from crop to crop and from variety to variety. The quality of cereal protein is far from perfect—in particular, they tend to lack lysine, one of the important amino acids—but they make up in quantity what they may lack in quality and for most adults at least they are probably adequate sources of protein. In any case they provide humankind with 50 percent of its protein, and some experts suggest that the most effective way to increase protein supplies would be to develop cereals with a higher protein content. The above figures suggest that whole grains, with the bran left on, are the best to eat, partly because the bran is rich in protein and fat and partly because of its high fiber content; and some authorities suggest that cereal fiber is, taken in

Cereals provide half our protein

Paella, a Spanish classic: opulent in appearance but born of austerity and incorporating everything that moves by or under the sea, cooked with spiced rice and pieces of chicken.

*Almost any grain becomes a meal if cooked
according to its lights and garnished with fruit,
vegetable, or slivers of meat.*
Top, *muesli, Dr Bircher-Brenner's invention of
the 1930s, based on oats, wheat and rye.*
Left, *pearl barley with mushrooms and yogurt.*
Right, *wheat thrice cooked with vegetables—a
macrobiotic dish. The wheat is toasted, then
simmered, then fried with vegetables.*

all, the most beneficent of the dietary fibers. In addition, the bran of rice contains vitamin B_1 and rice-eating peoples who eat "polished" rice (without bran) are prone to the vitamin B_1 deficiency disease, beriberi. But the above figures show too that the endosperm, which has a perfectly adequate ratio of protein to carbohydrate and so can satisfy protein needs without providing too many calories, is not to be despised. In short, any country with adequate cereal production need have no major food problems; and for any individual, a high-cereal diet is a good thing.

Grain could solve all major food problems

The no-nonsense, stripped-down quality of grasses has made them supremely versatile. Lichens may upstage them a little in the Arctic Circle and cacti may put up a better show in the harshest deserts but for most regions, from seashore to desert to windswept hillside, there is at least one grass, and usually a dozen or more. In almost every region that is remotely cultivable, there is at least one cereal.

The greatest of the cereals—in area, tonnage, and versatility—is wheat, which almost certainly originated as mountain grass in what was once the fertile crescent of the Middle East. The genetics and interrelationships of the species within the wheat genus *Triticum*, and the overlaps within the varieties of each species—complexities that spring from the natural promiscuousness of grasses and from ten to fifteen thousand years of human manipulation—would take many volumes to describe. Briefly, the cultivated wheats are of four main types. The primitive daddy of them all, favored in the Iron Age and still grown in a few countries, is emmer; and to grow a primitive wheat in places where agricultural conditions are uncertain is far from foolish, as plants that have not been selectively bred are liable to be more adaptable than their modern, thoroughbred counterparts.

Ancestral wheats, bread wheats and wheats for pasta

Rivet, cone, or English wheat—also primitive, or at least now largely superseded—was once the principal wheat of southern England, but now lingers on only in a few countries, and only for animal feed.

The durum wheats are of great commercial importance; they are the ultrahard kinds grown mainly in warm, dry climates, and produce the flour for pasta.

Most important of all are the bread wheats, which vary greatly in hardness. The harder types, which grow particularly well in North America, are favored for bread. The softer kinds typical of Britain are still classified as bread wheats, but are mainly used either for animal feed or for pastry. The crucial difference lies in the content of gluten, the tough wheat protein. Hard wheats contain a high proportion of gluten, and the "strong" flour that is made from them produces tough, elastic dough that will hold gas bubbles like a sponge and so is readily leavened into a light loaf. Soft-wheat flours, which contain less gluten, produce a "weaker" dough that is not so readily puffed up.

Wheat has undergone some impressive metamorphoses at the hands of the breeders, most noticeably in loss of stature. Cereals as a group tend to be big; big plant, big seed. You could have lost a donkey in the wheat fields depicted by Brueghel, and well into the twentieth century some favored varieties were well over four feet tall. But if you fertilize a cereal crop to increase yield then it grows even taller; and if it grows too

Wheat, rice, oats and the rest

tall it tends to fall over, or "lodge." So heavy fertilization of naturally tall varieties is risky. Accordingly, breeders set to work to shorten the straw. Varieties now in favor are only waist high, and new dwarf strains, introduced from Japan via Cambridge and Mexico, will reduce at least some of the next generation of wheats to a little above knee height. Some of the modern semi-dwarf types that could withstand heavy fertilization were involved in the famous (or some would say infamous) "green revolution" of the previous decade; perhaps some of the Third World recipients of these sophisticates would have been better off with old-fashioned, hardy and versatile types—including, perhaps, emmer.

The second of the world's great cereals is rice; the only cereal which needs merely to be husked (which does not mean removing the bran) before cooking. No milling, or even cracking, is necessary.

The archetypal rice grows in tropical or subtropical wetlands; indeed, it spends most of its growing life in water, which is drained when the plant is mature to allow the grain to ripen. But it is also grown to a smaller extent on dry land; and it will grow in Mediterranean climates— in Japan, in southern Europe, and of course in the United States, which has become the world's biggest rice exporter. There are long-grain types, which tend to stay separate when cooked; rounder types that shed their starch and tend to conglomerate, which the English use for rice puddings and the Chinese turn into delightful savory porridges (congees); and sticky glutinous types, which are used by the Chinese in a range of sweet and sweet-savory dishes. *Archetypal rice . . .*

Rice, at least traditionally in the East, is the supremely labor-intensive crop. Each shoot, after a four-week sprouting period in the nursery, is planted by hand in the paddy fields that are the principal feature of Eastern landscape painting. In the United States, rice farmers drop germinated seed into the flooded fields from airplanes. The agriculturist who could induce rice to grow farther north, or develop varieties of wheat or barley that cooked as easily and as delightfully as rice, would deserve the gratitude of the temperate world. *. . . the supremely labor-intensive crop*

Rice is *Oryza sativa*, and comes from Asia. "Wild rice" grows in North America, and more specifically in north Minnesota and around the Great Lakes, and is a quite different species, *Zizania aquatica*. It has little in common with true rice except that it grows in water. *Wild rice: best left wild*

Zizania aquatica is an impressive plant; up to 12 feet tall with two-inch-broad leaves and sweeping seed heads up to two feet long. Gourmets pay enormous prices for its seeds, although non-gourmets are at a loss to understand why. They are expensive because harvesting is difficult. Traditionally, it is done by Indians who go out on the water in flat-bottomed boats; they bend the seed heads over the boat and whack them until the seeds fall off. The seeds that miss the boat sink into the lake or river and provide the following year's crop.

Indians, motivated by the gourmet market and supervised by conservationists and game wardens, some in helicopters and some armed to the teeth, still make a living from wild rice, and they and their quiet boats fit snugly enough into the precarious ecosystems of the wetlands. But where there is a gourmet market there is, at least in theory, the chance of a quick buck; and wild rice is now cultivated, its yield increased tenfold with fertilizer and pesticide, its companion plants and animals banished, its genes rearranged, and the Indian boats replaced by combine harvesters. The semi-domestication of wild species has sometimes produced new and delightful environments as well as exciting food; but sometimes, as perhaps with *Zizania*, the point of the crop is lost in the exploitation.

Corn, or maize as the British call it, alias *Zea mais*, is even more intricate in origin than wheat, having been bred from at least three American wild grasses and been subject to radical genetic revision that has transformed the feeble ears of its ancestors into today's grandiose cobs. Corn can be ten feet high or more, and with its tassels of pollen-bearing male inflorescences on top, and its cobs halfway down, it is one of agriculture's most extravagant creations.

Grandiose cobs

Corn, like wheat and rice, manifests itself in several distinct types. The hard kinds are used for animal feed and for distilling into grain spirit (much of which turns up in blended Scotch whisky). The soft types are milled for flour. Popcorn, as every American knows, blows up when dry-heated. Corn on the cob is now available in astonishing colors, including darkest black. Corn is the staple food in much of South America and in parts of South and East Africa; but it is also favored as animal feed and is spreading northward rapidly. British farmers grow more and more of it, but since they have difficulty in ripening the cobs (corn needs three to five months of reasonable warmth to mature) they are often content merely to chop up the entire plant and ferment it into silage, for cattle feed. After all, the total biomass per acre of this grass is little short of fabulous; provided, that is, that the crows do not ravage it at the seedling stage, and that it escapes the dreaded stalk-rot.

The great merit of the hodgepodge of grasses collectively known as millet, which I take to include the large-grained sorghum, is that they can withstand drought. Sorghum itself, *Sorghum vulgare*, probably originated in Africa, where it still provides meal for porridge and is fermented into beer, while in the United States it is grown mainly for cattle feed and for the syrup that some varieties yield from their stems. Finger millet, *Eleusine coracana*, probably hails from India. It is still grown on a large scale in the dry areas of the south, as well as in Sri Lanka. *Eleusine* has also become a staple food in the dry parts of South and East Africa. Bulrush millet, whose white-seeded types are sometimes called pearl millet, is *Pennisetum typhoideum*. This grain too is probably a native of Africa, and is vital to the people along the southern fringe of the Sahara; but it is also grown in India and Pakistan.

Hodgepodge of millet

This chapter is too short to delve into all the culinary possibilities of millet; but it deserves close study.

Barley has played a powerful role in the Western world's history. The ancient and hardy type, *Hordeum vulgare*, found in carbonized form from the New Stone Age and featured on Greek and Roman coins, has six rows of seeds, while the one now favored in Britain, *Hordeum distichum*, is down to a mere two rows. The best barley is used for malting, to make beer, whiskey and vinegar, and the rest goes to livestock. It is not easy to grow good malting barley; if it is given too

Wheat, rice, oats and the rest

little nitrogen it will not yield heavily; if it is given too much the grain takes up the excess and is no good for malting. But beer, rather than pork, is perhaps the best form in which to store this ancient grain. Barley flour produces admirable cookies, and lends a sweet cakelike edge to wheat-based loaves. It deserves at least a small corner of the kitchen.

Rye, *Secale cereale*, is perhaps too obliging for its own good. It will tolerate cold; it has extensive roots which enable it to tolerate drought; and it can grow in acid soils. Consequently, it has often been grown in soil so sandy and so acid that it does well to survive at all. Rye began its agricultural career inauspiciously, probably as a weed of wheat, but many people appreciate the dark, heavy breads that can be made from its flour (pumpernickel is a superior example), and the East Germans were growing more rye than wheat as recently as 1957. Now it tends to fill odd specialist roles. Its tall stems are still used in some countries for thatching houses and barns; and if the farmer plants it in summer he can graze sheep on the emergent leaves in November and harvest a grain crop the following summer. Obliging rye

The decline in the acreage of oats is a minor tragedy. Oats have roughly the same protein content as wheat but a much higher content of fat (more than eight percent), which is largely polyunsaturated. The Scots in particular have shown how marvelously versatile the oat may be and have pressed the groats, meals and flours into porridges, cakes, breads, puddings and gruel; but oats occur worldwide, and there are recipes from India and Mexico. If rye began its agricultural career as a weed, oats positively thrust themselves upon farmers, and their status remains ambiguous. In Britain, the favored cultivated type is *Avena sativa*; but the related *Avena fatua* (perhaps one of *sativa*'s ancestors) is the notorious wild oat, which has become a metaphor for dissipation and in truth may present the cereal grower with his biggest single problem. Yet in some countries farmers cultivate *fatua* for animal feed. Ambiguous oat

Oats, as is obvious, tolerate a wide range of soils and climate. They do not mind the cold and the wet and they even enjoy mild acidity, which explains their success in Scotland. I wish that the Scots and the Welsh would cling to their heritage more tenaciously, and that the rest of the world would afford the oat a place in the big league of culinary cereals; almost, but not quite, on a par with wheat and rice.

In spite of 15,000 years assiduous cultivation it may be that we have only just begun to realize the cereals' full potential. The wild ancestral emmer wheats that are still to be found in the highlands of the Middle East have qualities that the first agriculturists were content to leave behind but which may yet prove useful. In particular, as Professor Moshe Feldman and Dr Lydia Avivi, of the Weizmann Institute of Israel, have discovered, there are strains of emmer that grow or at least survive in spite of the virtual absence of water. Israel itself is mostly arid, with Sinai occupying the south; and one-third of all the world's cultivated area is semi-arid. Desert wheats would not yield as heavily as a British wheat in East Anglia, or even as highly as an American wheat in Oklahoma. But yield per acre is not what counts, for there is no shortage of space in the desert. Yield per gallon of water is what matters. The cereals' potential is still unrealized

Irrigation might alleviate some of the dry lands' water problems; but the arch-enemy is salt, leached out of the parched earth and left to crystallize at the surface. Salt, as every farmer knows, is toxic to crops.

But is it? Emanuel Epstein and J. D. Norlyn of the University of California (Davis) argue that since many flowering plants will grow in salt-marshes or on dunes, or even in the sea, the toxicity of salt need not be taken as a botanical absolute. A few crop plants, including asparagus and beets, are at least partially salt tolerant, and one crop, the date palm, is highly tolerant. Other crops, including cereals, have salt-tolerant relatives. Could this quality be extended? Are modern crops salt sensitive merely because early farmers did not select their ancestors for salt tolerance?

Barley on the seashore . . .

Epstein and Norlyn germinated seeds of barley from a laboratory strain, appropriately called Composite Cross XXI, which, in contrast to the inbred cultivated varieties, contained a wide variety of barley genes. When the germinated seeds were eight days old, Epstein and Norlyn assaulted them with saline—and then more, and more, at three-day intervals, until the plants were growing in salt water that was 75 percent as concentrated as seawater. Six percent of the original seedlings survived, and matured to produce seed.

This seed was required actually to germinate in saline, equivalent to 85 percent seawater; but those that did so were grown on to maturity in non-saline nutrient. Only one-third of one percent of the plants entered in the original trial came through this second test.

Then came field trials, in sand dunes at the Bodega Marine Laboratory on the Pacific coast. Sand dunes are normally regarded as an agriculturist's nightmare, but for farmers battling with salt they may have an advantage over stable soil, since their constant shifting and extreme porosity militates against the formation of solid salt pans. The best varieties at Bodega yielded the equivalent of more than half a ton per acre after irrigation with pure seawater; equivalent to more than half the average yield in the United States.

. . . gave half the yield of the average American farmland

In short, the quest for saline-tolerant barley has been far more successful than most farmers would have thought reasonable, even after what has been no more than a preliminary foray into the plant's genetic pool. What might be achieved when simple selection has been complemented by crossing, and by a search for more genetic material among ancestral or arcane strains, and by the emergent techniques of genetic engineering? Already the Davis group is working on salt-tolerant wheats; and they have crossed wild, coastal tomatoes from the Galapagos Islands with cultivated varieties, to produce types that will thrive in 40 percent seawater.

Why not a salt-water wheat?

Yet seawater barley is not the ultimate heresy. Seawater contains 11 of the 13 nutrients essential to plants, but the two it lacks are nitrogen and phosphorus which land plants need in greatest quantities. Indeed, when agriculturists and politicians predict a world shortage of fertilizer they mean shortage of nitrogen and phosphorus. Yet some plants have bacteria in their roots which trap or "fix" nitrogen gas from the atmosphere which plants cannot use, and convert it into soluble forms—mainly nitrates—which the plants can utilize. Such plants, which include the Leguminosae (beans, laburnum, and the rest) but

Wheat, rice, oats and the rest

also many wetland plants such as the alder, are virtually self-fertilizing. Why should many varieties of cereals not be bred with such bacteria in their roots?

. . . or a self-fertilizing wheat?

No reason at all, it seems. There are three possible strategies, each being pursued somewhere in the world. The first is simply to develop more vigorous strains of nitrogen-fixing bacteria which will live free in the soil, and which could be injected into agricultural fields whatever crop is to be planted.

The second is to modify free-living, nitrogen-fixing bacteria by breeding, so that they become able to establish symbiotic relationships with the roots of existing cereal crops—in other words, to speed up the evolutionary processes that formerly created such relationships within the legumes.

The third approach is to modify the genetic make up of existing cereals so that they become hospitable to bacteria of the kind that already form symbiotic relationships with other plant species.

Self-fertilizing cereals are not exactly poised to enter the seedsmen's catalogs; but at the University of Rio de Janeiro strains of corn have already been produced which will play host to nitrogen-fixing bacteria that are normally found in the roots of tropical grasses. The grain that behaves like a bean is perfectly feasible.

The fourth and perhaps crucial development in the offing, is to increase dramatically the protein content of cereals. Present-day cereals are probably an adequate source of protein for adults, as is emphasized throughout this book; but they leave little margin for error and small children would be hard-pressed to meet their protein needs exclusively through cereals. But present-day cereals have a modest protein content partly because the first farmers who selected the ancestors of our modern varieties did not specifically select for high protein content. Some of the primitive wheats that Professor Feldman and Dr Avivi found in the Israeli hills had a protein content of between 25 and 31 percent. Fourteen percent is the highest recorded among cultivated types, and 18 percent was the highest previously recorded among wild types. Theoretically, future agriculturists could develop wheat strains with a protein content comparable with that of soybean; and then the specter of the "protein gap," which has haunted nutritionists, scientists and politicians, really could be exorcized once and for all.

. . . or a wheat with as much protein as soybeans?

What of the non-cereal grains? In the United States enthusiasts grow buckwheat, *quinoa*, and *amaranth* and in general the greater the variety of grains there is, the better. The Incas favored *quinoa*, and the Aztecs were fond of the highly nutritious *amaranth*—too fond, for they mixed it with human blood and deified it. Cortez objected, and banned the grain. I have been unable to obtain *quinoa* or *amaranth*, and without wishing to offend can find no outstanding reason for persevering with buckwheat. Many of the buckwheat recipes I have come across seem to be a cheat; lashings of butter, molasses and sweet spice, which would do wonderful things for sawdust. But it is dangerous to comment on things that you have not learned to mold to your purpose, and I would be grateful for evidence that the non-cereal grains do have a part to play in future cuisines.

Going against the grain

Grain recipes

No grain is positively awful even if eaten raw (although some, when dry, would defy all but the strongest teeth), and many become appetizing if they are simply boiled, or toasted in a dry skillet. But it is difficult to define the point where fodder ends and food begins, and at which the workaday bowl of rice becomes a *pilau* fit for a sultan. Enjoyment is influenced by preconception, and macrobiotic buffs indulge in gruels and cereal salads that leave the uninitiated scanning the horizon in an atavistic search for passing wildebeest. Dr Johnson's definition of oats—"a grain which in England is generally given to horses, but in Scotland supports the people"—expresses the ambivalence of cereals.

The outstanding nutritional merit of grains—well balanced in protein and energy, low in fat and high in fiber—is easily squandered because of their insatiable appetite for fat (as is also true of potatoes) and for sugar. With a few deft dabs of butter or molasses, the cook can transform innocent grains not only into things of delight but also into some of the most calorific and atheropathogenic of all foods. In the éclair or shortbread this trap is obvious enough; but even the apparently ascetic oat-cakes, at least as sold commercially, contain more fat than is desirable.

Grain cookery forms a spectrum; soups grade into porridges and porridges grade on the one hand into *pilaus* and on the other hand into puddings and pastries, and the attempt to find themes in this continuum is somewhat subjective. Nonetheless, grain dishes seem to fall into three main categories: those in which the individual grains are kept separate, so that the texture of each seed is emphasized; those in which the seeds are at least partially broken down in water, to form a porridge, gruel or congee; and those in which the grains, either whole or pounded down to meal or flour, are bound together, either by their own starch or abetted by fat, in puddings, cakes, dumplings, noodles, pastry, batters, and bread.

Theme I
The grains kept separate

MUESLI
Muesli was one of the outstanding features of the famous Swiss raw food diet that Dr Bircher-Brenner advocated in the 1930s. He originally conceived it rich in fruit, although more and more cereal has crept into the modern versions. Muesli is well balanced nutritionally if properly conceived, and is certainly high in fiber. Although it is known as a breakfast food it makes a good meal at any time. The ingredients can be varied at will, although oats generally feature. A little honey or orange juice may be added to ring the changes. Make this version the day before you want to eat it.
Serves 6

4 tablespoons rolled oats
2 tablespoons cracked wheat
2 tablespoons cracked rye
2 tablespoons roughly chopped nuts
6 eating apples
2 tablespoons dried mixed fruit
Juice of 1 lemon
1¼ cups milk

Toast the cereals to bring out their nuttiness. Chop the apples finely, but leave the skins on and the cores in. Thoroughly mix all the ingredients together and keep in a cool place overnight.

WHEAT THRICE COOKED WITH VEGETABLES
Macrobiotic *aficionados* make much of wheat. It is not as pleasant as rice when cooked whole—nothing is; rice is one of nature's supreme inventions—but its robust, incorrigibly chewy nuttiness should not be treated with disdain.
Serves 4

¾ lb (360 g) whole wheat berries
A pinch of salt
Black pepper
1 onion or 6 shallots
3 tablespoons oil
2 carrots
2 tablespoons soy sauce
Watercress or parsley

First toast the wheat in a dry iron pan, stirring all the while, for 5 to 10 minutes, until the berries are beginning to brown and their nutty aroma is well in evidence. This is the first cooking.

Simmer the toasted wheat in 5 cups of water with the salt for 1½ or even 2 hours; an hour is recommended even in a pressure cooker. This is the second cooking. When the wheat is tender, drain in a colander. Thus cooked, the berries can be kept for days.

To prepare the finished dish, chop the onion or shallots—shallots are better—and fry in the oil with the thinly sliced carrots until the carrots are tender. Add the cooked wheat berries, and stir-fry for another 5 minutes or so until all is hot and well mixed. Add the seasonings and about half a cup of water containing the soy sauce. Cover, and allow to simmer for another 5 minutes. This is the third cooking.

Turn out onto a hot shallow dish and garnish with watercress or parsley. Serve immediately.

CASSEROLED MILLET WITH NUTS

Millet, like wheat, is customarily toasted in a dry pan to enhance its flavor before it is boiled. Millet also requires a long simmer, although not quite so long as wheat. This recipe is a kind of macrobiotic millet *pilau*.

Serves 4

1 lb ($\frac{1}{2}$ kg) millet
A small amount of corn oil
  (2 tablespoons should be enough)
2 drops sesame oil
1 onion
$\frac{1}{2}$ lb (240 g) root vegetables: carrot,
  turnip, rutabaga, oyster plant, or
  (preferably) a mixture
$\frac{1}{2}$ lb (240 g) cabbage
A pinch of salt
1 cup split almonds, cashews or walnuts

Wash the millet, then toast in a dry pan to drive off moisture, and continue toasting for 1 to 2 minutes to bring out the nuttiness. Then add just enough corn oil to coat the seeds. Add the sesame oil, and continue to sauté for 5 to 10 minutes, until the millet is golden. Add 8 cups of water, bring to a boil and simmer for 30 minutes. Ideally, it should be possible to add exactly the amount of water that the millet will take up as it cooks; but millet, as bought in the store, is so variable that it is impossible to recommend a particular amount. When the grain is tender, simply drain off the surplus.

Cut the onion, root vegetables and cabbage into thin strips while the millet is boiling. Lightly fry the onion and root vegetables in the oil; when they are

tender add the cabbage and the salt. Stir-fry the mixture for another 5 minutes or so. When the millet has been boiling for about 20 minutes, set the oven at 350°F (180°C).

Make the *pilau* by putting alternate layers of boiled drained millet and the stir-fried vegetables into a casserole, with millet at the bottom and the top. Sprinkle with the chopped nuts, and bake in the oven for 5 to 10 minutes or until the top is browned and the nuts pleasantly toasted.

Barley is superficially similar to rice in grain size and texture, and in my restless search for temperate-zone rice substitutes I have often made barley *pilau*. But for me at least, barley has one crushing disadvantage; it is the standard feed of the modern pig and its characteristic flavor, although far from unpleasant, reminds me too pungently of the barnyard. Those for whom this fine little grain has no such connotations might care to try this recipe.

BARLEY PILAU WITH GROUND BEEF

Here, incidentally, is a classic example of meat extension; a small amount of meat being used to flavor a relatively large amount of staple. This theme is examined fully in the chapter on meat.

Serves 4

1$\frac{1}{2}$ cups whole barley
2 onions
2 garlic cloves
2 tablespoons oil
$\frac{1}{2}$ lb (240 g) ground beef (chuck is
  excellent)
1$\frac{1}{2}$ teaspoons ground cumin
$\frac{1}{2}$ teaspoon nutmeg
A pinch of salt
1 egg

Wash the barley and boil in 8 cups of water for 25 minutes, and then drain.

Slice the onions and garlic thinly, and fry in the oil until well softened, then turn up the heat and stir in the meat. When the meat is beginning to brown and exude juices, sprinkle in the spices and salt and stir well. Cook for a few more minutes until the spicy aroma is in full flood.

Mix the almost cooked spicy meat with the boiled, drained barley and the beaten egg, and cook in a covered casserole in the oven at 350°F (180°C) for 20 minutes. The idea of this oven stage is not so much to cook the ingredients (which after all are already cooked) but merely to bring them into a convincing union, and the timing is not critical.

BARLEY WITH MUSHROOMS
Serves 4

1⅓ cups pearl barley
Salt
1 tablespoon fresh or 2 teaspoons dried, mixed herbs
1 large onion
2 tablespoons oil
1 garlic clove
½ **lb (240 g) mushrooms**
1¼ **cups yogurt**
Black pepper
1 tomato

Simmer the barley in 2½ cups of water with the salt and herbs, until it has absorbed all the water and is tender.

Slice the onion finely and fry in the oil until soft; then add the chopped garlic and the sliced mushrooms and stir to heat through and to coat with the juices. Stir in the yogurt, sprinkle generously with black pepper, cover the pan and simmer for 10 minutes.

Put half the barley into a baking dish, spread the mushroom-yogurt mixture over it, and finish with the rest of the barley. Slice the tomato thinly, and lay it over the top. Bake in a 375°F (190°C) oven for 20 to 30 minutes.

RICE: the pilau proper

The next chapter—on bread—belongs to wheat; but a section on the use of whole grains must concentrate upon the incomparable rice, which needs merely to be hulled and boiled to become one of the world's finest foods.

The simplest way to prepare rice is to wash it—not so much to remove dirt as to eliminate the surface starch that tends to stick the grains together—and then soak it in a large amount of water to soften it. Boil the softened rice in a lot of water for about 10 minutes, and then drain in a colander. This elementary "boiled potato" method is adequate for producing the bowls of fluffy white rice that might accompany a Chinese meal.

In India rice is treated with slightly more care: it must be brought to the boil in exactly the amount of water it will take up by the time it is tender, so that no draining is needed and the grains remain separate.

The rice can be fried, after soaking and before boiling, spiced during frying, and regaled as it fries and then boils with any kind of meat, shellfish, vegetable, nut, or egg; the only difficulty, if such it is, is to ensure that the rice and its inclusions are all properly cooked at roughly the same time. This is the basis of the Middle Eastern and Indian *pilau*, the Italian risotto and the Spanish paella.

CHICKEN PILAU

Here, first of all, is a fine but simple *pilau* which illustrates all the principles. The apportionment of chicken—preferably an old but tasty hen—is miserly. This is a rice dish, and the bird is there just for flavor.
Serves 6

2 cups long-grain rice
1 small chicken
1 large onion
3 tablespoons corn oil
6 garlic cloves
Generous inch (2.5 cm) fresh ginger root
2½-**inch (6 cm) cinnamon stick**
6 cloves
½ **teaspoon chili powder**
1 teaspoon ground coriander
1 teaspoon tumeric
½ **teaspoon fennel seed**
½ **teaspoon mustard seed**
4 cardamom pods
A pinch of salt
Chinese parsley

To prepare the rice, wash it in several changes of water and then soak for 30 minutes in exactly 3 cups of water. Drain off this soaking water and reserve. The rice will already have taken up some of the initial 3 cups, and the amount left is what is needed to allow the rice to cook.

The chicken has to be thoroughly cooked, and slight overcooking is acceptable. The easy and decorous way is simply to boil the bird for about 1 hour, and then when it is cool enough to handle, take the flesh off the bones.

Take half the onion, chop it finely, and fry in the oil until translucent. Then add

Wheat, rice, oats and the rest

the finely chopped garlic, the finely chopped ginger, the broken cinnamon stick and the chicken and stir-fry for 5 to 7 minutes until all is well heated and mixed. Then stir in the rest of the spices (break the cardamom pods open before adding) and stir-fry for another 3 to 4 minutes, until the meat is well covered with spice and is aromatizing strongly.

Now add the soaked, drained rice to the meat-spice mixture and continue to stir-fry until the rice first clarifies, then again goes opaque, and then, here and there, begins to turn golden. At this point add the reserved water and the salt, give a good stir, bring back to a boil, then turn the heat well down, put the lid on the pan, and allow to cook through for about 15 minutes.

Turn the *pilau* out onto a hot oval serving dish and garnish with the rest of the onion, raw and thinly sliced, and the Chinese parsley.

RISOTTO

Anything you like may be incorporated in the risotto—mussels, kidneys, fish, chicken—but the point of it is to flavor the rice with fine stock.
Serves 6

4 tablespoons olive oil
1 onion
1 lb ($\frac{1}{2}$ kg) Italian (Aborio) rice
5 cups good strong stock
A pinch of salt
$\frac{1}{2}$ cup grated Parmesan cheese

Heat the oil in a saucepan and fry the thinly sliced onion until it is soft. Add the rice and fry, stirring, for 5 minutes.

Add 1 cup of boiling stock and the salt. Cook until the stock has been absorbed before adding another cupful. Regulate the heat so that the rice bubbles gently all the time. Continue cooking the rice in this way, stirring occasionally with a fork, until it is tender but moist.

Turn off the heat and stir in the cheese. Leave covered for 2 minutes and serve.

PAELLA

Spanish paella is one of those strokes of culinary genius that deserves special mention. It appears opulent, yet it was born of austerity like many great dishes,

and need contain nothing more than an old boiling hen (including some of its giblets) and some seafood. But the saffron, which has become obligatory, is an undoubted luxury.

The prime difference between the paella and the *pilau* is that the Spanish dish is conspicuously oily, with the delectable olive oil acting as spice.
Serves 6

2 cups patna rice
2$\frac{1}{2}$ lb (1$\frac{1}{4}$ kg) mussels
$\frac{1}{2}$ chicken
$\frac{1}{2}$ lb (240 g) white fish fillets—and whatever marine invertebrates you can lay hands on, canned or fresh; whole crayfish or jumbo shrimp are a fine decorative bonus
2 onions
4 garlic cloves
2 green or red sweet peppers
2 chicken livers
12 black olives
$\frac{2}{3}$ cup olive oil
2 cups cooked shrimp
4 tomatoes
Salt
Saffron

For this dish you need a big iron pan—preferably a special paella pan.

Wash the rice and soak it for 30 minutes. Scrub the mussels and then boil them until they open. When they open they are cooked. If they are open before you cook them, they are dead, and should—must—be thrown away.

Cut the chicken into pieces. Cut the fish into bite-sized pieces. Slice the onions, chop the garlic, peppers, and chicken livers, and pit and halve the olives. Now you are ready to start.

Fry the chicken pieces in a little oil until the flesh is tender and the skin is browning or even beginning to burn. Chicken in general needs to be thoroughly cooked and the singed skin is a fine "spice."

Then add the rest of the oil and the sliced onions and cook for 7 to 10 minutes until the onions are beginning to turn golden.

Add the peppers, garlic, chicken livers, olives and white fish pieces, and stir until all is well mixed and you catch the whiff of garlic.

Drain the rice—you can throw away

the water—and stir it into the mixture in the pan until all the oil is absorbed. Add the shrimp, and whatever other shellfish you have, the chopped tomatoes and salt and pour on 4 cups (less if you are using a saucepan instead of a paella pan) of boiling water, made yellow with a large pinch of saffron.

Simmer on low heat for another 15 minutes or so, until the rice is tender and barely moist. Add the mussels 10 minutes before the end.

Serve straight from the dish.

DOLMADES
In many cuisines a kind of *pilau*-risotto mixture is served wrapped in leaves. This is the basis of the Greek-Turkish dolmades and the Japanese *sushi*.
Serves 6

Vine leaves (about 40)
2 onions
$\frac{2}{3}$ cup olive oil
$\frac{1}{2}$ lb (240 g) ground lamb
$\frac{2}{3}$ cup rice
1 tablespoon chopped parsley
A pinch of salt
Pepper
$2\frac{1}{2}$ cups stock or water
Juice of $\frac{1}{2}$ lemon
1 tablespoon tomato paste

If you are using fresh vine leaves, put them in boiling water for 1 minute and then allow to drain. Otherwise, just take them out of the can and drain.

Chop the onions, and fry in half the oil until they are translucent. Add the meat, rice, parsley and salt, sprinkle well with black pepper, and stir-fry for another 5 minutes. Then add the stock or water and lemon juice, and simmer for 15 to 20 minutes, until all the liquid is absorbed.

Spoon a little of the rice mixture onto a vine leaf—enough to make a 2- by $\frac{3}{4}$-inch (5 by 2 cm) sausage, when the leaf is rolled and the ends tucked in.

As each leaf is stuffed, pack it into a large, heavy saucepan, which should be lined at the bottom with spare vine leaves. When the bottom is filled with stuffed vine leaves, put more spare vine leaves on top and then begin another layer of stuffed leaves until the mixture is all used up.

Next, make a simple sauce by mixing the remaining oil with the tomato paste and a little seasoning. Beat in a cup of water. Pour the sauce over the dolmades, put the lid on, and simmer slowly for 1 hour.

Serve hot or cold.

Virtually any kind of leaf can be stuffed in similar fashion. But the pleasure of this dish lies in the sharp flavor and resilient texture of the vine leaves. Large onions (Spanish or Bermuda) are also well worth stuffing—as in the following Middle Eastern dish.

MAHASHA
This dish may be served hot with other stuffed vegetables or cold as a first course.
Serves 4 to 6

6 large sweet onions
3 to 4 tablespoons olive oil

The stuffing
6 tablespoons long-grain rice
1 lb ($\frac{1}{2}$ kg) ground chicken, beef or lamb
1 lemon
3 tomatoes
1 tablespoon finely chopped parsley
1 teaspoon turmeric
1 teaspoon sugar
Salt
Black pepper

Put the unpeeled onions into a large saucepan. Add water and bring to a boil. Cover the pan, reduce the heat to low and simmer for about 20 minutes or until the onions feel tender when prodded with a skewer.

Drain the onions and leave to cool. Then, using a sharp knife, slice off both ends. Make a longitudinal cut through the side of each onion to the center. Remove and discard the outer skin. Then carefully slip off the layers (skins) one by one until they are too small to be stuffed.

To make the stuffing, wash the rice and soak it in cold water for 30 minutes, then drain and put in a bowl. Mix in the meat, the grated rind and juice of the lemon, the chopped tomatoes and all the other ingredients for the stuffing.

Using your hand, lift out a little of the stuffing. Shape it into a sausage without squeezing too hard—the mixture must retain its moisture or the rice will have no liquid to absorb. Put the stuffing into an onion skin and fold the skin over—it folds over quite naturally to form an elipse. When all the stuffing has been used up, reserve any liquid that is left in the bowl.

When all the onion skins have been stuffed, heat the oil in a large sauté pan or deep frying pan. When the oil is hot, put in the stuffed onion skins in one layer; cook over moderate heat for 5 minutes or until they are browned underneath. Then turn them over. Pour over the reserved liquid, cover the pan and cook over low heat for 45 minutes.

Remove the cover after 30 minutes and if there is too much liquid in the pan, cook uncovered for the last 15 minutes.

BIBER DOLMA
Peppers are obvious candidates for stuffing. This version is from Turkey.
Serves 6

$1\frac{1}{4}$ cups long-grain rice
6 green peppers
2 large onions
8 tablespoons olive oil
$\frac{1}{2}$ cup currants
$\frac{1}{4}$ cup pine nuts or pistachio nuts
Freshly ground black pepper
$\frac{1}{2}$ teaspoon sugar
Salt
A handful of parsley

Wash the rice thoroughly, let it soak in water for 1 hour and drain.

Cut around the stem bases of the peppers and lift them out carefully—later they will serve as lids. Scoop out and throw away the seeds and pith. Wash the peppers and leave them upside down to drain.

Slice the onions and fry them in the oil until they begin to turn a golden color. Stir in the rice, currants, pine nuts or pistachios, sprinkle liberally with black pepper, add the sugar and a little salt. Fry the rice, stirring constantly, until it is golden too. Then stir in the finely chopped parsley.

Spoon the rice mixture into the peppers, leaving room for expansion, and cap with the stem bases. Put the peppers upright, side by side in the bottom of a large saucepan. Pour in boiling water to come halfway up their sides. Then bring the water back to a boil, reduce the heat, cover, and simmer for 45 minutes to 1 hour, or until the rice is tender.

Allow the peppers to cool in the pan, and serve cold.

Theme II
Porridge

Any very thick soup is a porridge and so the form of porridge is infinite since, with the aid of a blender, any soup can be made as thick as you like. But the porridges made with grains—rice, millet, cracked wheat, buckwheat, barley, oats—occupy a special place in human history, if only because the grains are the most storable and most universal of foods. To crack them and boil them and to add flavor with whatever is to hand, and to leave the finished dish wet in its pot, is surely to practice the simplest of all cookery. I like the idea of porridge—the one-course, simple meal that discourages gluttony but demands the ceremony of spoon and bowl. The best are the exquisite and infinitely variable Chinese congees, based on rice, and the Scottish oat porridge.

FISH CONGEE
Serves 2 to 3

$\frac{2}{3}$ cup short-grain rice
1 slice fresh ginger root
1 small piece orange peel
1 tablespoon peanut oil
$\frac{1}{2}$ lb (240 g) white fish fillets
1 teaspoon cornstarch
1 teaspoon sherry
A pinch of salt
1 cup toasted almond flakes
2 or 3 scallions

Simmer the rice in $2\frac{1}{2}$ quarts (2 liters) of water, together with the ginger, orange peel and peanut oil, for 3 hours, stirring occasionally. Then remove the orange peel and ginger.

Cut the fish fillets into thin slices. Coat each slice with cornstarch, and add to the simmering rice. Add the sherry and salt and cook for a further 3 to 5 minutes.

Pour the congee into a deep, hot serving bowl and garnish with toasted

almond flakes and scallion "flowers."
Note: To make scallion flowers, cut the
stems into 2-inch (5 cm) lengths, and
then slit the ends like tassels, leaving an
intact "waist," of about $\frac{1}{2}$ inch (1 cm), in
the middle. Drop the split scallion
lengths into a bowl of iced water and
leave for 30 minutes. The tassels should
curl back on themselves like the petals
of a flower.

SCOTS PORRIDGE
Here is a macrobiotic approach, using
whole oats. If you do not have an old-
fashioned cooking range on which the
porridge can safely be left to cook all
night, it is best to use one of the new
electric slow-cooking pots. Serve the
porridge with plenty of dried fruit or
crushed toasted nuts, and/or a
sprinkling of toasted sesame seeds.
Serves 4

1 cup whole oat groats
A large pinch of salt

Wash the whole oats well and discard
any hulls that float. Drain and toast the
oats in a dry skillet over a high flame,
stirring constantly, until the oats are
slightly browned and nutty.
  Bring 5 cups of water to a boil, and
sprinkle in the oats with one hand,
stirring with the other (a feat requiring
wondrous co-ordination) so that the
groats remain separate, and produce no
lumps. Transfer the porridge to the
slow-cooking pot and cook gently all
through the night.

The gourmet Scot, however, uses oats, preferably from Midlothian, that are earmarked
for porridge and already adequately hulled. The
five to one ratio of water to oats would be
maintained, although the cook would think in
terms of a handful of oats and a large pinch of
salt per person (too much for nutritional comfort) in a cupful of water. The water is brought
to the boil, and the oats sprinkled in as above;
but the sprinkling is prolonged over an hour or
so (a handful here and a handful there) so that
the finished porridge contains oats in all stages
of cooking; the first almost disintegrated, the
last almost raw. The salt is added after about
15 minutes, when the first oats are fairly well
cooked. The timing is said to be important. In
principle, this exploitation of the single grain at

all stages of cooking, in the one dish, is good
cookery. It shows a fine appreciation of a
humble ingredient.

Theme III
Grains re-formed

Grains, whether whole, partially comminuted
to groats or meal, or ground to flour, can be
stuck together with their own starch or with fat
to make a range of dishes from primitive
puddings to the finest bread. Wheat deserves
pride of place; with the possible exception of
rice noodles and the light rice-flour-based
pastry used in some of the Chinese stuffed
dumplings, the other grains serve primarily as
alternatives for wheat in its marvelous range of
puddings, pies, pastries, dumplings, cakes and
all kinds of bread.
  Many of the recipes much favored by macrobiotic buffs and featuring such grains as
buckwheat and barley, strike me as nonsense;
there is very little reason for using such materials as long as wheat and potatoes are
available. But each grain fills an ecological niche
and is worth considering.

BUCKWHEAT PANCAKES
The pancakes may be filled with
whatever you like, from sautéed
vegetables to pureed fruits, or nuts.
Serves 4

$\frac{2}{3}$ cup buckwheat flour
2 tablespoons flour
A pinch of baking powder
1 teaspoon sugar
A pinch of salt
1 teaspoon baking soda
Oil
$1\frac{1}{4}$ cups buttermilk

Mix all the dry ingredients in a bowl.
Add 1 tablespoon oil and enough of the
buttermilk to make a batter. Drop large
spoonfuls of the mixture into a hot,
oiled skillet. Turn the pancake over
when it is set and the edges are crisp.

To make buckwheat flour into something positively pleasant seems to me to require more effort
and subsidiary ingredients than the material
merits; molasses, rye flour, wheat flour, sesame
seeds and oil feature in one recipe I have for
buckwheat pancakes. But with molasses and oil

Wheat, rice, oats and the rest

(halfway to toffee) you can hardly fail to make something eatable, whether you use buckwheat flour or floor sweepings. I can see the point of exploiting buckwheat flour if buckwheat is all your climate allows you to grow; but I can see little point in rescuing it from its innate mediocrity if more subtle crops are to hand. There is no reason except nostalgia for commending such intrepid sorties into the primitive.

MILLET CROQUETTES
Makes 6 croquettes

½ cup millet
1 onion
Oil
1 tablespoon chopped fresh herbs
A pinch of salt

Boil the millet in 1½ cups of water until all the water is absorbed and the grains form a solid mass.

Chop the onion and fry in a little oil until it is soft. Toss in the herbs and stir-fry for 30 seconds. Mix the millet with the other ingredients; divide into six balls and flatten into cakes about ¾ inch (2 cm) thick. Brown both sides on a lightly oiled griddle.

CORNMEAL PANCAKES
Serves 6

1 cup cornmeal
2 teaspoons sugar
A pinch of salt
2½ cups milk and water mixed in equal
   quantities
1 egg
½ cup flour
1 teaspoon baking powder
Oil

Toast the cornmeal in a dry skillet for 1 to 2 minutes to bring out the flavor. Put it into a bowl with the sugar and salt. Bring two-thirds of the milk and water to a boil and stir it into the cornmeal. Set aside to cool.

Beat the egg with the remaining milk and water, the flour, the baking powder and 2 tablespoons of oil. Mix this into the cooled cornmeal mixture.

Ladle the batter into a hot, oiled skillet. Turn the pancake after about 3 minutes. Repeat until all the mixture is used up.
Serve immediately.

Wheat is so absurdly versatile that many cooks devote their entire lives to single aspects of its cuisine. Rather than plunge into a necessarily superficial discussion on buns, muffins and the rest, I would like to mention two ridiculously simple "recipes" to show how accommodating wheat can be.

HOMEMADE NOODLES I
This is a macrobiotic recipe using whole wheat flour. Primitive though they are, such noodles are little different from the thin pancakes that the Chinese use in Peking duck; and if they were made with the ultra-hard durum flour, they would be lasagne.
Serves 2

2 cups whole wheat flour
½ cup cornstarch
A pinch of salt
A large pinch of mixed herbs
4 tablespoons corn oil
4 tablespoons cold water

Mix the flour, cornstarch, salt and herbs together. Blend in the oil, then add the water until you have a stiff dough (and I mean stiff). Knead for 10 minutes or until the dough becomes elastic.

Roll the dough out as thinly as possible. Cut it into strips about ½ inch (1 cm) wide and 3 to 4 inches (8 to 10 cm) long and allow it to rest for 10 minutes.

Boil in water or soup for 7 to 8 minutes. Serve immediately.

HOMEMADE NOODLES II
A medieval English recipe for making noodles in which the batter is petrified by trickling into hot fat. They resemble the Chinese crispy noodles. I mention it just to prove Aristotle's contention that there is nothing new under the sun. Nutritionally, the concentration of egg, milk and fat is in the disaster zone.
Serves 2

About 6 tablespoons milk
4 tablespoons 85 percent wheat flour
Salt
2 egg whites
Oil for deep frying

Add enough milk to the flour to make a smooth, runny batter, then add a small pinch of salt.

Beat the egg white in a bowl until frothy and then stir into the batter.

Make sure the oil is hot—almost smoking—and then dribble the noodle batter into it so that it forms a long separate twirl, rather than a mass.

Dorothy Hartley remarks in *Food In England* that the skilled cook allows the batter to dribble down the fingers, giving one noodle twirl per finger.

Such noodles as these would be an admirable accompaniment to fish and huge piles of mixed Chinese-style vegetables, to compensate for the noodles' horrific calorie content.

While Western cookery writers emphasize the desirability of fluffy rice with each grain as separate from its neighbor as skittles in a box, the Chinese, who have been cooking rice for about 8,000 years, happily contrive to stick the grains together to produce a vast range of sweet and savory puddings.

CHINESE RICE PUDDING WITH PORK AND SHRIMP

In this recipe, the boil-in-a-bag treatment is identical with the Scottish mealy pudding, except that the cereal is steamed rather than boiled. Serve the rice with stir-fried mixed vegetables.

To make ginger sherry bring $1\frac{1}{4}$ cups of medium sherry to a boil with about a 1-inch (2.5 cm) piece of fresh ginger root, finely sliced. Remove the pan from the heat and allow to cool. Strain the sherry into an empty bottle and use whenever the Chinese idiom is appropriate.
Serves 2

$\frac{1}{2}$ **cup round-grain rice**
Salt
1 scallion
1 tablespoon pork drippings
$\frac{1}{2}$ **cup finely sliced lean pork**
A large pinch of sugar
1 cup cooked shrimp
$\frac{1}{2}$ **teaspoon ginger sherry**

Soak the rice overnight. Drain the rice, add a pinch of salt and tie loosely in a cheesecloth bag, so that as it swells during cooking it is constrained and pressed together. Steam for 30 minutes, then take out the bag and sprinkle it with cold water. Return the bag to the steamer for a further 30 minutes.

Meanwhile, chop the scallion and fry gently for 1 minute in the pork drippings. Add the pork (fine slices are preferable to dice), the sugar, shrimp, a pinch of salt and the ginger sherry, and stir-fry for another minute. The pork really does cook almost instantly.

Untie the cheesecloth bag and flop the rice on to a heated dish. Break it up a little with a fork and add the shrimp and pork. It is ready now for serving.

Oats have been poking their prickly heads into man's agricultural efforts for at least 10,000 years, and oat recipes of greater or lesser subtlety appear in Mexican, Indian and Middle Eastern cuisines, as well as in the famed oat cookery of Scotland and Wales. The crushed oats—groats—are made into porridge; the coarse meal is made into broths; the medium oatmeal goes into bannocks and oatcakes, and is mixed with other flours; and fine oatmeal is used for thickening soups, for all manner of biscuits and pastries, and for flouring herrings to form a crisp batter as the fish shed their juices.

SCOTCH OATCAKES

The Scots, Welsh and northern English each have their own version of oatcake, with the local differences depending partly on the kinds of fuel available, and hence on the method of cooking that is possible. The Scottish kind, traditionally baked in a cool oven or on a griddle, are appropriate to the modern stove.

Oatcakes need a little fat to bind them, but avoid excess. Dorothy Hartley suggests that Scottish soldiers probably made them with greasy water from the boiled meat.

Such oatcakes can be served in the traditional manner, with bacon or with sweet things—raspberry jam or honey.
Makes 12 oatcakes

$1\frac{1}{3}$ **cups medium oatmeal**
A large pinch of salt
$\frac{1}{2}$ **tablespoon bacon drippings**
Fine oatmeal

Mix the medium oatmeal with the salt. Melt the drippings by stirring into some boiling water, and knead it into the oatmeal. Add boiling water a little at a time, stirring the while, until you have a soft dough.

Dust the board and rolling pin with

Wheat, rice, oats and the rest

fine oatmeal, and roll out the dough as thin as possible. Then cut into 4-inch (10 cm) squares (or whatever shape you like) and cook on a lightly greased baking tray in a 300°F (160°C) oven or on a griddle until the edges curl up and almost begin to crisp.

INDIAN OATCAKES
In this Indian version, yogurt takes the place of the Scottish soldiers' greasy water. These oatcakes are an excellent foil for curries and pickles and (a pleasing example of the cereal-pulse theme) for dhal.
Serves 2

1 green chili
1 onion
1 garlic clove
1⅓ cups rolled oats
A pinch of salt
1¼ cups yogurt
Oil for frying

Chop the chili, onion and garlic, and mix with all the other ingredients to make a batter. Pour the batter a tablespoon at a time onto a hot, lightly oiled griddle, and brown on both sides. Serve immediately.

ENGLISH MEDIEVAL OATMEAL DUMPLING
Serves 4

1⅓ cups medium oatmeal
Meat broth

Here is "meat extension" at its simplest; a way of bulking a meat stew. Simply wet the oatmeal with some of the broth, and then tie loosely in a cheesecloth bag. Allow the dumpling to bob alongside the meat for an hour so that it picks up all the stew's flavors as it swells.

GOLD BELLY
This simple idea—oatmeal swelling in a confined space—manifested itself in Scotland as the sweet Gold Belly, and in Scotland and Ireland as the savory White or Mealy Pudding. The temptation is to pile in the fat, which was more appropriate to the austerities of pre-World War I Britain than to the

affluent present. Serve as a dessert or with bacon as a main course. If you have any Gold Belly left over, bind it with an egg and use it to stuff a chicken—the sweet-savory combination works beautifully.
Serves 4

½ cup suet
1 lb (½ kg) "old-fashioned" oatmeal
2 tablespoons butter
⅓ cup raisins
1 tablespoon chopped mixed candied peel
1⅓ cup sliced, pitted prunes
1 tablespoon brown sugar

Grate the suet finely and rub thoroughly into the oatmeal with the butter. Mix in all the other ingredients. Tie the mixture loosely in floured cheesecloth, and simmer, covered, for at least 1½ hours in water. This dish should be served steaming hot.

WHITE PUDDINGS
Serve the puddings sliced with bacon, or with apple sauce.
Serves 4

1 lb (½ kg) "old-fashioned" oatmeal
½ cup suet
1 small onion
1 teaspoon mixed dried herbs
¼ teaspoon white pepper
A pinch of salt
Sausage skins or **a piece of cheesecloth**

First dry the oatmeal: spread it on a tray and leave for 10 minutes or more in a low oven, 300°F (160°C).
  Grate the suet and chop the onion, and add them to the oatmeal with the herbs, pepper and salt. Mix thoroughly.
  Stuff the mixture into sausage skins or tie it loosely in the cheesecloth and boil in water for at least 1½ hours.

RAISIN BREAD
Makes 1 large loaf

3 cups whole wheat flour
⅔ cup oatmeal
1 heaping teaspoon baking powder
A pinch of salt
2 tablespoons brown sugar
⅔ cup raisins
1¼ cups yogurt

Three classic ways to stuff a vegetable:
left, *mahasha, from the Middle East, in which
onions are filled with rice, herbs, spice and
touches of meat;* **top,** *biber dolma, a vegetarian
version from Turkey, with nuts, currants and
rice in sweet peppers; and* **in the foreground,**
*vine leaves stuffed with rice and finely ground
lamb, in Greek-Turkish dolmades.*

A miscellany of grain, region and idiom: **back, left to right,** *Scotch oatcakes; Chinese rice pudding with shrimp and pork; gold belly—a classic sweet pudding, again from Scotland.* **In the foreground,** *noodles made from 100 percent wheat flour, and buckwheat pancakes.*

A repertoire of breads.
Whole wheat, **top left** *; a rye loaf,*
made mainly with wheat, **top right** *;*
chapatis, **left** *; an unleavened wheat*
loaf, **center** *; barley bread,* **bottom right.**

Mix all the dry ingredients in a bowl. Add the yogurt and stir to make a soft dough. Knead the dough on a floured board until it is smooth. Shape it and put it into a lightly greased, large bread pan. Bake in a 400°F (200°C) oven for 40 to 45 minutes or until the bread is well risen and golden brown on top.

CORNMEAL BREAD
Makes 1 small loaf

$\frac{3}{4}$ cup cornmeal
1 cup whole wheat flour
2 teaspoons baking powder
2 heaping teaspoons sugar
A pinch of salt
1 egg
1$\frac{1}{4}$ cups buttermilk

Mix all the dry ingredients in a bowl. Beat the egg into the buttermilk and mix it into the flour mixture. Beat well to mix to a smooth batter. Pour the batter into a small, lightly greased bread pan and bake at 400°F (200°C) for 30 to 35 minutes or until the bread is well risen, firm to the touch and nicely browned.

CORNMEAL MUFFINS
Makes 15 muffins

1 generous cup cornmeal
$\frac{1}{2}$ cup flour
2 teaspoons baking powder
2 teaspoons sugar
1 tablespoon grated hard cheese
1 cup buttermilk
2 tablespoons corn oil

Put all the dry ingredients into a bowl. Combine the buttermilk and oil and mix them into the flour mixture. Beat well to make a smooth batter.
 Spoon the batter into greased muffin pans, filling them two-thirds full. Bake at 425°F (220°C) for 15 minutes or until the muffins are well risen and nicely browned. Cool on a rack.

CORN BREAD
Makes 1 small loaf

1$\frac{1}{2}$ cups cooked corn kernels
1 egg
1 tablespoon butter

2 teaspoons sugar
A pinch of salt
1 heaping teaspoon baking powder

Put all the ingredients in a blender to make a smooth purée. Pour the mixture into a small greased bread pan and bake at 375°F (190°C) for 1 hour.
 Cool on a rack.

SINGIN' HINNIES
Serves 6

3 cups all-purpose flour
$\frac{1}{3}$ cup rice flour
A pinch of salt
2 teaspoons baking powder
2 tablespoons lard
$\frac{2}{3}$ cup currants
$\frac{2}{3}$ cup milk or buttermilk

Mix the flour, rice flour, salt and baking powder in a bowl. Mix in the lard and then mix in the currants. Add the milk or buttermilk and mix to a soft dough.
 Roll the dough out $\frac{1}{4}$ inch (0.5 cm) thick. Cut into circles about 3 inches (8 cm) in diameter and prick all over.
 Make your griddle fairly hot and cook the cakes on both sides until they are nicely browned. Serve hot and split.

As shown throughout this book, the cereal-pulse combination serendipitously recurs throughout world cuisine. Here are two examples, from opposite sides of the globe, in which cereal and pulse are fused in the same dish.

Theme IV
Grain and pulse

RYE AND LENTIL PILAU
Serves 4

2 cups brown lentils
$\frac{1}{2}$ cup cracked rye
2 onions
2 to 3 tablespoons corn oil
1 teaspoon caraway seeds
A pinch of salt
Pepper to taste

The garnish
Tomato
Onion
Cucumber
Hard-boiled egg

Wheat, rice, oats and the rest

Wash the lentils and soak them for at
least 2 hours. Simmer in 5 cups of water
for 30 minutes or until tender (but *al
dente*), and drain.

Wash the rye thoroughly, then toast in
a dry skillet for a few minutes to bring
out the nuttiness. Put the rye in a
saucepan with 5 cups of water, simmer
for 45 minutes, and drain.

Slice the onions and stir-fry in a little
oil until tender. Then mix them into the
lentils and rye, together with the
caraway seeds and seasonings, and
moisten, if necessary, with a little water.

Put the mixture into a covered
casserole and cook in a 350°F (180°C)
oven for 20 to 30 minutes, both to heat
and to allow the spices to permeate.

To serve, turn out onto a heated dish
and garnish with slices of tomato, onion,
cucumber and hard-boiled egg.

RICE WITH LENTILS

This traditional Indian dish, or
something very like it, is echoed, albeit
distantly, in the kedgeree of Scotland,
which incorporates haddock; and this
mild rice-lentil mixture is indeed a
pleasant foil for fish, including the
admirable and oily broiled mackerel.
Serves 6

$1\frac{1}{3}$ **cups lentils**
$1\frac{1}{4}$ **cups long-grain rice**
2 onions
1-inch (2.5 cm) piece fresh ginger root
2 tablespoons butter
$\frac{1}{2}$ **teaspoon turmeric**
Salt

Wash the lentils and rice and soak them
in water for 30 minutes. Drain and put
them in a saucepan. Cover with water—
the water should not extend more than $\frac{1}{4}$
inch (0.5 cm) above the ingredients. Add
a pinch of salt and bring to a boil. Cover
the pan, reduce the heat to very low and
cook for 20 minutes.

Meanwhile, slice the onions and ginger
finely, and fry in the butter until soft.
Stir in the turmeric, cook for a few
seconds, then tip the contents of the pan
into the cooked rice and lentils. Toss it
all well together with a fork and serve.

A repertoire of breads

The Old Testament tells of migrations and wars and dialogues with God, but at the root of the wars and migrations and of half the stories and metaphors was bread: the growing of grain, the grinding, the baking, the rituals of eating.

Through most of history bread was made from whole grain, or nearly whole grain, and so included all the protein, fiber, minerals and vitamins that whole grain contains. It was often awful; made from poor-quality, moldy, or badly selected grains, which were badly milled, badly mixed and unevenly cooked. It was also often deliberately adulterated by millers and all shades of middlemen. But when the bread was good it was very, very good and people ate a lot of it, not simply because they liked it but because they were poor and it was at least affordable, although it did not become cheap until the last few decades. The people who had access to good bread did not starve, but they did not get fat either. They were exempt from a whole range of deficiency diseases, and did not suffer from coronary heart disease or any of our other modern epidemics of affluence. Indeed, the greatest single nutritional disaster of the past 100 years in Western countries has been the decline of bread; in its nutritional quality and in particular in its fiber content; in its texture, from robust to vapid; in its flavor; and in the amount that people eat. With modern wheats and technology it is possible to make good bread every time. With the benefit of modern nutritional theory, we can see that to restore good bread to its central position in the diet is the best thing we could do. And if you really like food you must like bread.

The decline of bread—the greatest nutritional disaster

I hope the decline in bread is a temporary aberration, brought about partly by overemphasis on mass production and technical shortcuts, and partly by the old-style nutritionists' exaggeration of the role of animal protein and their disregard of dietary fiber. More intriguing is the reason for bread's initial ascendancy. It has been such a familiar part of life for so long that some languages do not differentiate "bread" from "food." Yet it is a supreme artifice, whose production—growing, milling and cooking—has not only been at the nub of world politics and religions since at least the beginning of agriculture but has been one of the main spurs in the advance of technology. How can a thing so artificial have become so "natural"?

Bread, defined loosely, is a reasonably homogeneous blob of pre-dominantly carbohydrate material, stuck together with water—or, more accurately, through the action of water on starch or mucilage. It can be made from the flour or meal of any kind of cereal, beans or other seeds, and many roots, tubers, bananas and seaweeds. It differs from gruel in being stiffer and more resilient and hence more portable. Through the addition of fat it develops into puddings and pastries; through the addition of fat and egg it becomes cake and pancakes; and if extremely "strong" (durum) flour is used, with a minimum amount of water, the result is pasta in all its many forms.

Bread from seeds, bread from potatoes, bread from seaweed

Of all kinds of bread, by far the most interesting are those made from

A repertoire of breads

grain. Potato breads, banana breads and cassava breads have never been much more than local contrivances built around local ingredients. But bread based on the grass seeds known as cereals, sometimes but not necessarily augmented with other seeds, is almost universal and may well have developed independently among hundreds of different societies throughout the world.

Such universality alone suggests there is something natural about bread, and indeed there is. The plant seed is the obvious food for the omnivore; a structure designed by nature as a food supply, and hence both nutritious and storable. But the seed is also hard (for its own protection) and dry (to guard against decay), so although it is nutritionally unimpeachable, it is not the easiest thing to eat. Indeed, the fossil skulls of those ancestral men or men-apes who ate seeds have teeth that are worn flat, although few such primitive people would have been more than 25 years old when they died. An early task for the first farmers and their predecessors would have been to render this supremely desirable food palatable.

What had to be done? The grain had to be crushed, of course, to take some of the burden from the teeth. If you do that crudely you get meal, and meal always includes some finely powdered endosperm, alias flour. This is one of nature's many serendipities, for nobody surely could have predicted that the mere crushing and grinding of hard brown seeds would produce those small, soft, white and supremely useful flecks.

The meal must then be moistened, for only a termite could enjoy such arid material. If you moisten it, you produce gruel. But if you leave damp gruel around it quickly goes sour and it tastes awful. Yet another universal artifact—fire—will both arrest decay and improve flavor.

If you boil the meal in a pot, you produce a kind of porridge; but if you use less water to produce a dough rather than a gruel, and put it on a hot stone or in a nest of hot stones, you have broiled or oven-baked bread; desperately simple, but it is cooking of a kind that still has a place in the finest cuisine.

Porridge in the sun

In short, bread is a contrivance; the archetypal proof, if proof were needed, that man is a technological animal. Yet its origin, the most convenient rendering of the most nutritiously convenient food, is at least as explicable as the production of flint axes.

The decision to crush grain with artifacts instead of with the teeth was, technologically, the most significant that human beings have ever taken. The rendering of grain into meal and flour has been, for the past 6,000 years, the pre-eminent technical preoccupation of civilized societies. For grain is not only unbelievably tough, but must also be pounded down in enormous quantities.

The first artifacts for breaking down the tough seeds were stones, which were pounded, rubbed and ground together. Favored stones would have become molded to each other and thus, so some archaeologists suggest, may have given rise to the mortar and pestle.

The mortar and pestle works upon one batch at a time: fill, pound, reserve; fill, pound, reserve. The quern, through which the passage of grain is continuous, was an enormous conceptual advance, just as the conveyor belt is a mechanical advance over the work bench. The first querns were saddle querns: the top stone was lifted and allowed to slide down the one beneath, shearing, rather than simply crushing, the grain between. These devices were often worked by slaves and were the "mills" of the Old Testament, Homer and Ancient Egypt. It was to such an appalling machine that Samson was put when imprisoned by the Philistines.

The rotary quern came next. It may be hard to turn a poorly lubricated stone—lubricated, that is, only by the grain beneath—but rotary milling did not involve the perpetual lifting required by the saddle quern. Rotary querns were in general use in Britain and presumably through all the civilized world, by 100 to 50 BC. The first in Britain were no more than 16 to 20 inches across and six to eight inches deep. Presumably they were intended to serve only one household, and were turned by hand. Animal power was introduced as the advantage of bigger stones became apparent—or, equally to the point, as the technology for producing bigger stones was developed.

Then, evidently in Greece and Asia Minor, came the third and perhaps most significant conceptual leap in the development of milling: the introduction of water power, and of the waterwheels that have been so much a feature of world landscape for 1,000 years and are still in operation, even in the United States of America. The transition from ox to water power may seem simple enough. But an ox moves horizontally, like the quern he rotates. The waterwheel spins vertically. The angle of rotation must be turned through 90 degrees by great whirring cogs of wood and iron. The capstan quern is a modest refinement of Old Testament ingenuity; the water mill is a machine. By Domesday, AD 1086, Britain had 6,000 water mills south of the Severn and Trent, serving 3,000 communities. Here, at this astonishingly early date, with the Middle Ages scarcely begun, was the mechanical foundation of industrial revolution.

The millers' second exploitation of natural power was evident in Britain by the twelfth century. The windmill arrived. Was the idea imported from Sistan, in Persia, where mills (albeit with horizontal vanes) were recorded in the tenth century? Or, as Elizabeth David posits in her excellent *English Bread and Yeast Cookery* (1977), did the idea arise in England and Holland as "an independent invention of the Gothic North"? If the origins are unclear it is certain that windmills fired the medieval imagination, and they were widespread in Britain by the fourteenth century. With their arms spread against the sky on the high point of the land, they are dramatic machines; yet more dramatic even than they seem, for the power transmitted to the great emery querns was proportional to the cube of the windspeed. A tenfold variation in gust would theoretically have been translated to the stones a thousandfold. The whole structure—the wooden husk of the building, the spinning querns, the swirling motes of bran—must have been a tinderbox, and one primed by the most excitable of elements. Those jolly red-faced millers of the nursery tales must have watched their machines as anxiously as ocean yachtsmen watch their sails.

All rotary querns, whether turned by hand, animal, water or wind, work like a centrifuge. The corn is fed in through a hole in the center of

The pestle and the saddle quern

The rotary quern is born

The water mill arrives

But where did the windmill come from?

A repertoire of breads

the top stone and, as the querns rotate, the corn is squeezed between the stones and pushed ever outward until it falls, in various states of comminution, off the edge. Smooth running and a consistent degree of milling depend upon the geometry of the grinding faces, and, especially with large querns, this geometry becomes critical. Hence the top stone was not smooth but "dressed" with a pattern of centrifugal grooves which had constantly to be recut. The pattern of these grooves was continually modified and improved from before Roman times to the nineteenth century, when stone milling was superseded.

For in the nineteenth century came the technology that is still with us; an inevitable development, in retrospect, based not on counter-rotating stone faces but on whirling cylinders. The corn was simply channeled in on one side and then sheared by the rollers with fine mechanical precision to produce a flour of any required grade at the flick of a handle. This was—is—roller milling.

The stone gives way to the cylinder

So we come to one of many controversies surrounding the modern milling and bread industry. Is the old-fashioned, stone-ground flour, as sold in healthfood stores, really superior to the modern, roller-milled flour? Is it more wholesome? The answer is that stone-ground flour generally is more wholesome, but this is not inevitable. In brief, stone milling is more gentle than roller milling, and so produces a flour containing more of the original grain; but roller milling is versatile and can produce almost any flour the miller chooses.

Is stone-ground flour more "wholesome"?

Grain of all kinds has three separate components: the germ, which is the embryo of the new cereal plant, and includes the primordial leaf and root shoots; the endosperm, which is the starchy, fairly amorphous structure, equivalent to the yolk of an egg, which contains the embryo's food store; and the seed coat fused with the hard wall of the fruit, and sometimes with the odd bract or awn as well, which constitute the husk. Stone grinding, for all the subtlety of the "dressing" and the miller's craftsmanship, is an intrinsically crude process. It crushes, shears and scissors the whole grain and minces all three components together, reducing the endosperm to white powder, the embryo to yellow flecks, and the husk to brown, or more usually fawn, flecks of bran. The whole flour—100 percent—can then be sieved or bolted to remove the coarser bits, which inevitably lightens the color since a high proportion of bran is thereby removed. But a high proportion of the wheat germ remains. The wheat germ is rich both in proteins and in oils, and, inevitably, in flavor. Hence the flour containing wheat germ is indeed more nutritious and more flavorsome than flour that does not; and what else does "wholesome" mean? However, flour which contains wheat germ also tends to go rancid, because of the oil in the wheat germ. Stone-ground flour had to be produced in manageable quantities for almost immediate consumption, and this is partly why Britain had so many windmills—at least ten in London in the early seventeenth century.

In roller milling the wheat berry is sheared open by break rollers to release the endosperm within; this, as a granular semolina, is then readily separated from both bran and embryo, and can be pulverized at will into flour. The bran can be put back and so can the wheat germ, to produce various kinds of wholewheat flour. But the bulk of the roller mill's product is pure ground endosperm; only 70 percent of the original grain remains, and the flour is therefore known as 70 percent extract. Its whiteness must have pleased the consumers who first set eyes upon it at the end of the nineteenth century, for people had been trying for thousands of years to make flour white, and still whiter. Its lack of oil and its consequent storage qualities certainly pleased the millers. We know now, however, that white is not necessarily all right, and that brownness does not mean coarseness. We have discovered that flour can be stored, covered and in a cool place, so that rancidity is less of a problem; and the modern mills can produce flour of up to a 95 percent extract if the millers choose. So for the present, stone-ground flour does emerge more wholesome, but only by default. I for one am not against modern, precise, easy technologies—including roller milling—which enable us to do anything we want, and have no nostalgia for ancient crafts unless they offer something of value that we have lost. I wish only that we used our improved technologies for our real benefit and not simply to make life easier for producers.

White bread was a feast for the eyes

Who cares for ancient crafts?

All you need to do to make bread is to mix flour with water and cook. The *chapatis* of India are made this way, and yet deserve ubiquity. They do not require butter (what good bread does?) and are as superb as moppers-up of eggs and bacon or jam or honey as of curry. The equally straightforward barley bread, too, has an "honest" quality that is easy to find addictive. The cook of the future should play with flour: blends, degrees of coarseness, addition of spices, herbs, fruits and stuffings. It is at this primitive, unleavened level, of doughs baked, cooked on a griddle, broiled and fried, that the experiments and the rewards are quickest and the failures most expendable.

Although I have tried to show in this book that all flours and meals deserve serious treatment (and the sliding toehold of oats in Western cooking is a minor tragedy), I will not try to disguise, in a chapter on bread, the overwhelming superiority of wheat. For wheat contains in abundance a protein—gluten—that is present in other grains in miserly amounts if it is present at all, and which lends to wheat dough an elastic resilience that makes it one of the supreme architectural materials, as versatile as modeling clay. Because of gluten, wheat dough may be leavened: puffed up with tiny bubbles of carbon dioxide produced by yeast that has been put to feed upon the dough, and able to hold those bubbles within its miraculously close, elastic fabric. Leavening, by use of yeast, is only a refinement; no more, it seems, than the addition of fat or spice. But it is the kind of refinement that raises simple, workmanlike and reliable bread into a quite new level of grace.

Leavening depends upon fermentation, which is the controlled (or partly controlled) decay of edible material by fungi, bacteria or yeast. As a culinary technique, fermentation may even predate agriculture. Dogs ferment the bones they bury and so disgustingly unearth, and the ancient Icelanders buried Atlantic sharks on the seashore, for a prolonged bacterial and saline pickling.

Fermenting bread . . . and bones and sharks

Yeast is the supreme fermenting agent. It exists everywhere, in air-dust and on every surface, in thousands of varieties, waiting for an organic substrate on which to settle and there practice the single

A repertoire of breads

supreme skill that has made it the organism to be prized above all others: the conversion of sugar to alcohol and carbon dioxide. Without that there would be no beer, no cider, no wine, no spirits, no leavened bread —a situation too dreadful to contemplate.

Because yeast is a living material (although it plays possum skillfully enough in the dried form in which it is often sold), it must be handled as delicately as befits all life. This is why the technique of leavened bread-making is so exacting; it also, unfortunately, explains why technique has so often been frozen into high ceremony and hence so often seemed inaccessible. A hundred and fifty years ago, when cottage ovens were small and the heat from their expensive fuels was uncertain, cooks could be forgiven for leaving bread-making to the baker. Now that bakers' bread is so often so appalling, and domestic ovens work with such easy precision, it really is a pity that so many competent cooks shy from this central task.

It is easy enough to explain the origins of bread itself: it evolved through nothing more than dogged application to obvious problems. Leavening at first sight seems to be a wild and quite unprecedented conceptual leap. Yet this is not so: if dough is left lying around in the right conditions it will ferment naturally with wild yeasts, and we can imagine that barley breads especially might have been left to ferment, simply to improve the flavor, through alcohol production.

The logical path to leavened bread

Natural fermentation would certainly explain the first excursions into wine- and beer-making; since grapes are covered with a bloom of wild yeast, their fermentation is almost inevitable. Brewing and baking have been closely linked activities since Ancient Egypt; partly, presumably, because they both involved the large-scale use of grain, and partly because they both required large-scale and prolonged heating, and why use two furnaces when one will do? But the rapidly reproducing yeast in the fermenting beer—the barm—would equally well have fermented the bread dough if added to it, and with the two processes operating side by side this discovery again seems inevitable. Until Louis Pasteur launched microbiology as a science in the nineteenth century, such barm was also the chief source of bread yeast, although sometimes, as in the sourdough technique, a piece of dough from one baking was kept back as a starter for the next. Much of the nineteenth-century literature on bread-making is concerned with the husbandry of yeast. But yeast is now a standard product with perfectly predictable behavior; and, as explained in the recipes, it requires nothing more subtle than a little warm, sugared water and a warm place in which to sit to stir up its metabolism, and a little time to work.

Bread-making is worthwhile, perhaps the most worthwhile thing to do, even if you only cook *chapatis*; but even the most complex breads that once required the skills of a lifetime are now within everyone's compass. Bread should again be served with every meal, and predominate in most, nutritionally if not gastronomically; and it would be good to see tables laid, as I have sometimes seen them in Germany, with breads of every variety, some spiced, some of mixed grains, some dense, some light. If people were connoisseurs of bread as they often strive to be of wine, their nutritional problems could all but disappear.

On every table, a variety of breads

56

Many of the grain concoctions surveyed in the last chapter could be regarded as bread; as could the potato, lentil and spinach cakes of later chapters. This chapter is mainly about wheat, which tastes good and contains a high proportion of the rubbery protein known as gluten, and so can be molded into a tough dough which—as a form—is as distinct from and as important as all the other forms of all other grains put together. Wheat bread alone is infinitely variable; there are at least a dozen distinct routes to variety, and each route offers infinite byways. You can vary the strain of wheat: the very hard, ultrahigh-gluten (durum) wheats are used to make pasta; the high-gluten hard wheats, mainly from North America, which are ground into strong flour, produce elastic dough that can be puffed up (by leavening) to form light loaves; and the lower-gluten soft wheats of Europe make a weaker dough that cannot be so stretched and so produce heavier loaves.

Wheat of all kinds can be milled to different degrees; simply cracked, or ground through a complete spectrum of meals to flour. The flour can be left intact—100 percent—so that it contains bran, embryo (germ) and all, or extracted to various extents. Seventy percent extraction means that 30 percent—the bran and germ—is taken out, and only the white, starchy endosperm is left (in commercial circles it may then be bleached and generally added to).

The bread can be made with or without fat, which may be hard or oily; a little fat or oil—one ounce (30 g) of fat or one to two tablespoons of oil to each pound ($\frac{1}{2}$ kg) of flour—increases the elasticity of the dough and encourages the bread to rise, although if you put in a lot of fat the boundaries are blurred between bread and cake. Eggs and milk push the dough toward batter (although many entities that most people would call bread contain either or both); and batter becomes popovers or pancakes.

The bread may be leavened or unleavened; and if leavened may be puffed up by the carbon dioxide bubbles breathed out by yeast, or by the same gas produced from chemical baking powder. But unleavened bread may also be puffed up by sealing the outside and then heating, to swell the moisture within into expanding steam.

The bread may be cooked on a griddle or baked (moist or dry) or fried (deep or shallow) or by some combination of means. The wheat may be mixed with other flours that directly affect its texture and flavor—barley, rye, oatmeal, potato, rice, corn, millet, pulse, buckwheat; or

with molasses, which adds weight, color and flavor; or spices in combinations that often blur the margins of sweet and savory. The bread may be spiked or doused with extraneous materials: grains etched into its surface; fruit, onions and seeds held in the dough like ants in amber; and tomatoes and soft things eased into its surface as it cooks, as in the Neapolitan pizza.

When you have finally produced the bread, by whatever little sheep-track you chose among the maze of possibilities, you face yet another infinity of stuffings and spreads and toastings. A man who is tired of bread, to misquote Dr Johnson, is tired of food.

But here is a basic repertoire.

Theme I
Breads at their simplest

CHAPATIS
The astonishingly simple *chapati* is a marvelous form of bread. In India it is eaten with everything. I like them with eggs and bacon and tomatoes; their almost complete fatlessness is a fine counterbalance and their texture complements both the crisp bacon and the mushy tomatoes.
Makes about 24 chapatis

1 lb ($\frac{1}{2}$ kg) whole wheat flour
A pinch of salt
1$\frac{1}{2}$ tablespoons oil

Put the flour and salt into a bowl, make a well in the center and pour in the oil and 1 cup of water. Mix to a soft dough, adding more water if necessary. Then fold and knead the dough for 10 minutes until it is smooth and pliable.

Divide the dough into walnut-sized knobs. Flatten the knobs and roll them out evenly on a well-floured board and with a floured rolling-pin into discs as thin and round as possible. Or, if you want to enter into the spirit of village India, slap the dough from hand to hand, palms flat, until it forms the required shape. There is something about dough that brings out the manual in people: Indians slap their *chapatis*, English bakers turn and twist their uncooked loaves with cabalistic flicks of the wrist, and Italian chefs twirl their pizza dough above their heads, and not only for the benefit of the tourists.

A repertoire of breads

Heat an iron frying pan (or a frying pan with a non-stick lining) thoroughly. Put in a *chapati* and cook it, moving it around in the pan with your fingers, until its edges turn up. Turn it over, and continue cooking until the *chapati* puffs up—which it sometimes does in disappointing little hillocks and sometimes in a great opulent dome.

Serve hot.

POTATO DOSAS

South Indians eat *dosas* for breakfast and Americans eat pancakes. Potato *dosas* are a fine alternative; easier to make than the *dosa* and theoretically easier on the arteries than the traditional eggy pancake. Eat them either with lemon and sugar or with broiled tomatoes.

This recipe shows that cold cooked potatoes, like cold cooked beans and old bits of cheese, are good to have around the kitchen.

Makes six 6-inch (15 cm) dosas

1 cup cold mashed potatoes
1 cup whole wheat flour
2 tablespoons oil
Salt
Pepper
Herbs

Mix the potatoes into the flour with your fingertips, as if you were working fat into flour for pastry. In a minute or two you will have a smooth and pleasant dough. Work in the oil, seasoning and any herb or herbs that you fancy.

Press the dough as flat as possible on a well-floured board (you will have to repair the edges as you go) and then roll out as thinly as possible; an eighth of an inch (0.25 cm) or less is desirable. Cut into circles (I use a 6-inch/15 cm saucepan lid) and cook in a dry skillet. Press down and flip over at intervals until both sides are crisped and speckled dark brown. Serve hot.

SIMPLE BREAD TASSAJARA STYLE

Chapati-making uses heat efficiently, but if you have the oven on anyway you might like to try the comparable form recommended by Edward Espe Brown of the Tassajara Zen Buddhist Monastery in Monterey County, California. This bread makes what scoutmasters would call a hearty sandwich. Split it through the middle, put in a small thin omelet or slivers of meat and whatever raw vegetables are around—shredded cabbage, cucumber, tomato, celery and onion—add a touch of oil and a sprinkling of cayenne pepper and you have a robust version of the kebab in pita.

Makes 4 loaves

1 lb ($\frac{1}{2}$ kg) whole wheat flour
A pinch of salt
1$\frac{1}{4}$ cups water
1 tablespoon oil

Make the dough as for *chapatis*, then divide it into 4 pieces and roll each piece into a flat oval cake $\frac{1}{2}$ inch (1 cm) thick, about 6 inches (15 cm) long and 4 inches (10 cm) wide.

Bake the bread on oiled trays in a 350°F (180°C) oven for 25 to 30 minutes.

Serve warm or cold.

BARLEY BREAD

Many ancient breads were made from mixed grain flours, largely because the crops themselves were mixed. Farmers sometimes planted different grains together so that whatever disaster struck, drought or blight or tempest, one of the grains with luck would survive; and rogue crops, notably oats, crept in willy-nilly. Now that grains are grown "pure," we can mix them for fun as in the following recipe.

Makes 4 loaves

2 tablespoons corn oil
2 cups barley flour
About 4 tablespoons millet meal,
  sunflower seeds or sesame seeds
4 cups whole wheat flour
A pinch of salt

Heat half the oil in a heavy pan. Add the barley flour and the millet or seeds and cook, stirring, until they are warm and aromatic. Put the mixture into a bowl with the whole wheat flour, the salt and the rest of the oil. Pour in 3$\frac{3}{4}$ cups of boiling water, stirring all the while with a wooden spoon. When you have a thick dough, knead with your hands (cooling them in cold water whenever necessary) until the mixture is soft, springy and homogeneous.

Shape the dough into flat loaves about 1 inch (2.5 cm) thick and bake on oiled cookie sheets at 350°F (180 C) for about 40 minutes.

Cool on a rack.

The point is made: good bread can be ludicrously simple. If you use mainly wheat flour, if you do not make the dough too wet, if you mix it thoroughly, and if you make sure it is cooked through, then anything goes. It is just a question of doodling intelligently. Indeed, I am, between paragraphs, preparing a brand new bread that may well be a contribution to the literature: one part couscous, fried in a little corn oil until beginning to brown, two parts whole wheat flour, a sprinkling of caraway seeds and a touch of cinnamon; a stiff dough shaped to a disc a half-inch (1 cm) thick, and then cooked in an iron pan over a low flame for ten minutes each side. When the bread is cool, slice through the middle and fill with sliced vegetables, meat or cheese.

PARATHAS

The correct attitude to fat in (or on) bread is the same as for potatoes. A bread shot through with fat—like the delectable *paratha*—is nutritionally suspect, like the comparably delectable Swiss potato dish called Rösti; but a bread that is just fried so that the fat merely sticks to the surface, like the *puri*, is acceptable, as is the comparable French fried potato. I include recipes for *parathas* and *puris* just to follow the fat theme through, but I do not think that *parathas* should be eaten except in the context of an otherwise ascetic, Indian vegetarian diet.

Makes 8 parathas

1 lb (½ kg) whole wheat flour
A pinch of salt
1 cup butter or *ghee* (a kind of clarified butter)

Put the flour and salt into a bowl and blend in 1 tablespoon of the butter. Add 1 cup of water and mix to a soft dough, adding more water, if necessary. Then fold and knead the dough for 10 minutes until it is smooth and pliable.

To make the *parathas*, divide the dough into 8 pieces and shape into balls.

Flatten one ball and roll it out on a floured surface into a circle approximately 7 inches (18 cm) in diameter. Melt the butter and brush the top of the circle lightly; fold the circle in half and brush again with butter. Fold again to make a triangle. Roll out into a circle again and repeat the process. If you do this 4 times you will have 16 microtomically thin strata of butter and dough.

Lightly butter and heat a griddle or iron frying pan. Put one of the *parathas* in the pan and when the top is a mottled light brown turn it over and spread a little butter over the top. Cook for 2 minutes, turn it again and spread with a little more butter. Cook for 1 minute more. Remove the *paratha* and keep it hot while you make the others.

Serve hot.

PURIS

The Indian gourmet, with cavalier disregard for life and his blood vessels, piles in with the *ghee* and salt. This recipe is more restrained.

Makes 12 puris

2 cups whole wheat flour
A pinch of salt
1 tablespoon butter or *ghee*
Oil for deep frying

Put the flour and salt into a bowl, add the fat and blend it in. Make a well in the center and pour in ½ cup of water, a little at a time, mixing well after each addition until you have a firm dough.

Knead the dough for about 10 minutes or until it is smooth and pliable.

To make the *puris*, lightly grease your hands with oil or melted butter and pinch off a piece of the dough about the size of a Ping-Pong ball. Flatten the ball and roll it out on a lightly oiled surface into a circle approximately 4 inches (10 cm) in diameter.

Heat oil in a deep-frying pan until it is very hot (about 350°F/175°C). Put in one *puri* at a time; it will puff up irregularly, but keep pressing it down into the oil with a spatula. After 1 minute turn it over, press it down and when it is quite golden brown and puffed up it is ready. Remove the *puri*, drain thoroughly and serve warm.

A repertoire of breads

Leavened breads

The difference between leavened and un-leavened bread is not absolute, as I used to think before I started experimenting with unleavened bread; a plain flour and water dough can be remarkably springy, especially if puffed internally with steam. But leavening with yeast opens a whole new vista nonetheless.

If ever leavened bread-making seems complicated it is because it combines two technologies: the subtle technology of yeast, which is akin to husbandry, imposed on the simple manipulation of wheat. But once you have a feel for the biological needs of yeast the reasons behind the rituals become obvious.

Yeast is not exactly a fungus but it is a fungus-like thing; a single-celled organism that reproduces by budding and splitting, and in the course of respiration performs one simple bio-chemical trick that has influenced human culture almost as profoundly as photosynthesis has influenced human biology. It transforms starch, one of nature's commonest compounds, first into sugar and then into carbon dioxide gas and alcohol. Without this humble ubiquitous plant-let there would be no big crusty loaves; and no wine, no cider, no Guinness and no brandy. It hardly bears thinking about.

You can buy yeast in a fresh puttylike mass or in a possumlike state of desiccation. The first requirement if it is to be used to leaven bread is to rouse it from dormancy. Like all living things, yeast is killed by excessive heat and made sluggish by cold; and it needs moisture and it needs food just to activate its metabolism. So you first mix it into a little tepid water with a pinch of sugar.

When the yeast froths and puffs up it is introduced to the flour. Its task is to break down some of the wheat starch to carbon dioxide and alcohol; the former to be trapped in little bubbles to lighten the dough, the latter destined to escape in baking with the intoxicating whiff of new bread. The flour should be blood-warm when the yeast goes in (pre-warmed perhaps in a gentle oven if the kitchen is cold) or it will work too slowly.

The yeast must be brought into close contact with the flour grains, or it cannot work upon them. So the fresh-made dough is kneaded, to spread the yeast evenly throughout. Then the yeast is allowed to work; or, to use the jargon, the dough is left to prove. This takes time—a couple of hours or more—but it is not your time. Bread needs no baby-sitters and if you leave the dough for a few hours more for your own convenience, it matters little.

At the end of this first proving the dough should have blown up like a balloon. But to make sure that the finished loaf is as evenly textured as possible, you first give the swollen dough a punch and then knead again. Then you allow a second proving, which this time results in an unequivocally even-textured spongy mass, the tiny gas bubbles held in the tough gluten fabric of the wheat. Only wheat dough will rise so pleasingly. Doughs made from low-gluten cereals have no elastic matrix to hold the gas and it just drifts off.

When you cook the dough the yeast is killed and the dough hardens, thus trapping the bubbles irrevocably.

So that is the principle; and here are the fundamental examples.

PITA
Pita is one of the flat breads from the Middle East that looks unleavened but which is made with yeast. Flat breads are useful; the pita splits open through the middle to form a bag, for beans, *hummus*, *falafel* or kebabs, and olives and vegetables.
Makes 8 pitas

One $\frac{1}{2}$-oz (15 g) cake fresh yeast or one $\frac{1}{4}$-oz (8 g) package dried yeast
Sugar
1 lb ($\frac{1}{2}$ kg) bread flour
A pinch of salt
Olive oil

Mash the yeast with a pinch of sugar and $\frac{1}{2}$ cup of lukewarm water and set aside in a warm place until it begins to froth. Warm the flour and salt in a large bowl. Pour in the yeast, $\frac{3}{4}$ cup of lukewarm water and 1 tablespoon of olive oil and mix to a dough. If the dough feels sticky, knead in a little more flour.

Knead the dough until it is smooth and elastic; cookbooks always recommend 10 minutes or more, but I find 5 minutes or even less perfectly adequate. Cover and leave in a warm place for at least 2 hours, by which time it should have doubled in bulk.

Punch down the dough and knead it again. Divide the dough into 8 pieces. Roll into balls, a little larger than golf balls, place on a floured plate, cover and set aside in a warm place for about 20 minutes to prove. Flatten the dough balls with a floured rolling-pin into $\frac{1}{4}$-inch (0.5 cm) thick oval shapes.

Preheat the oven to 475°F (240°C). Oil some baking sheets and put them in the oven to get hot. Put the pitas on the sheets and bake for 5 to 8 minutes. They will puff up but should hardly brown at all. Cool the pitas on a dish towel—they will flatten but retain a pocket inside, which is revealed when they are cut in half or split.

ENGLISH WHOLE WHEAT LOAF
To call this archetypal bread an English loaf is pure chauvinism, especially as it is made with hard North American wheat. But the English have always favored family-sized loaves, sliced away through rambling high teas.
Makes 1 large loaf

One $\frac{1}{2}$-oz (15 g) cake fresh yeast or one $\frac{1}{4}$-oz (8 g) package dried yeast
Sugar
5 cups whole wheat bread flour
A pinch of salt

Mash the yeast with a pinch of sugar and 2 tablespoons of lukewarm water and leave in a warm place for 10 minutes until it begins to froth.

Warm the flour and salt, make a well in the middle and pour in the yeast. Trickle in $1\frac{1}{4}$ cups or more of water, stirring the while with a fork or your hand until you have a pliable dough; then knead for 5 to 10 minutes. Cover the dough with a damp cloth and leave in a warm place for 2 hours or until it has doubled in bulk.

Punch down the dough and knead it again for 3 to 4 minutes. Shape the dough and put it onto an oiled baking tray or into an oiled bread pan. Cover and set aside in a warm place to prove for 30 minutes or until the dough has risen to the top of the pan.

Bake at 350°F (180°C) for 40 to 45 minutes or until it is done.

To test the bread, turn it upside down and rap it with your knuckles; if it sounds hollow, it is done. Cool the loaf on a rack and store it wrapped in a linen cloth.

BARLEY OR RYE BREAD
Whether or not the barley loaves that Jesus broke after the Sermon on the Mount were or were not mixed-grain loaves, the truth is that most so-called barley or rye loaves are made mainly with wheat, because only wheat can be relied upon to rise. I say "relied upon" rather than "will" because an eminent British scientist who bakes for relaxation told me that he makes 100 percent barley loaves that do rise. I believe all that this particular professor tells me, but such bread has never risen in my house. Barley or rye bread is made exactly like the whole wheat loaf but with up to half the wheat flour replaced by barley or rye flour.

Theme III
Flavoring the bread

WELSH FRUIT LOAF
You can flavor bread with herbs or spices that permeate the dough or with fruit held in suspension or with seeds such as sesame or caraway. The spectrum of possibility is infinite, but here is a Welsh classic, the famous bara brith, that makes the point. This is the kind of bread that British people used to cook on special occasions and has scores of local variations.
Makes 1 large loaf

One $\frac{1}{2}$-oz (15 g) cake fresh yeast or one $\frac{1}{4}$-oz (8 g) package dried yeast
3 tablespoons brown sugar
1 cup milk
$\frac{1}{4}$ cup butter
1 lb ($\frac{1}{2}$ kg) 85 percent wheat flour
$\frac{2}{3}$ cup currants
$\frac{2}{3}$ cup seedless raisins
$\frac{1}{3}$ cup mixed candied peel
$\frac{1}{2}$ to 1 teaspoon mixed spices: cinnamon, cloves, nutmeg, ginger

Mash the yeast with a pinch of the sugar. Warm the milk and stir half of it into the yeast. Set it aside in a warm place for about 10 minutes to froth.

Melt the butter and the sugar in the remaining milk. Warm the flour, make a well in the middle and pour in the yeast and the milk mixture. Mix to a light dough and leave, warm and

A repertoire of breads

covered, to rise for about 2 hours or until the dough has doubled in bulk.

Punch down the dough and knead it well, then mix in all the fruit and the spice. Shape the dough into a loaf and put into a large, warm, buttered bread pan. Let it prove in a warm place for 1 to 2 hours or until the dough has risen to the top of the pan.

Bake the bread in a 425°F (220°C) oven for about 30 minutes. Cover the bread with foil if it shows signs of burning. Leave in the pan for 10 minutes before turning the bread out to cool on a rack.

Theme IV
Bread in concert

Bread eaten alone tends to be a shade ascetic. Its proper role is as a foil and platform for less restrained flavors: a mopper-up of sauces, or a vehicle, as in the sandwich, pizza, or *masala dosa*. But we modern Westerners have lost our sense of balance. The ordinary people of many countries would never dream of eating any meal without bread. In rural France, Greece, India, the Middle East or southern Italy—all the countries with a low incidence of coronary heart disease, in fact—bread often dominates a meal nutritionally even when it appears simply to be an accompaniment. The Englishman in an Indian restaurant orders a *chapati* as an afterthought; yet in much of rural India there would be no meal without the *chapati*.

To reestablish good bread at the center of cooking and the center of diet would be by far the greatest single advance that the Western countries could make—nutritionally, gastronomically and agriculturally. A pox on restaurants that serve no bread, or only burnished rolls in little baskets with nothing inside but air and intended only for decoration and as vehicles for butter. Even rich Neapolitans never used to put butter on the dinner table to accompany the copious bread. They could afford it, but they were not accustomed to it and did not particularly want it. But now, I am told, the middle-class Neapolitans are learning that butter is smart. A sad day for their cooking and their arteries.

The sandwich, too, should be seen as a device for flavoring bread; but the bread has simply become the means whereby the hands are kept off the goods. The paradox is—again—that the old-fashioned, working man's sandwich, a slice of bacon and a touch of mustard between two doorsteps, is far more delicate, nutritionally, than the vicar's tea-party equivalent—egg mayonnaise between soft, wafer-thin, fiberless white bread and butter. Triple-decker sandwiches are grotesque inventions. I remember them in California; layers of cream cheese and cold bacon between strata of vapid bread. Most of the calories came from fat (in the cheese, bacon and butter) and a few from the refined carbohydrate (in the bread starch). The cheese and bacon—whose only justification was to supply flavor—supplied none; this came courtesy of a gherkin, pinned to the sandwich surface by a little wooden stake, like a Transylvanian vampire. In a proper bacon sandwich the bacon does provide the flavor. There is little need to bother about its fat, because most of the calories are provided by the unrefined carbohydrate of the thick bread; and the delicious, delicate bacon drippings, rather than tedious butter, moistens the sandwich. Mediterranean peasants do not die of heart disease, and if they are not impossibly poor they eat very well indeed. Eat like a peasant. When it comes to bread, that is.

PIZZA

There are breads in which the filling is not applied as in the sandwich, *masala dosa* and pita, but cooks on top of the bread and merges with it. Pizza is the best-known example, which generally has Italianate toppings of tomato, cheese and olives. But there are versions from all around the Mediterranean. Here is one from the Middle East.
Makes 1 large pizza

One $\frac{1}{2}$-oz (15 g) cake fresh yeast or one $\frac{1}{4}$-oz (8 g) package dried yeast
2 teaspoons sugar
1 cup warm milk and water, mixed
2 cups 85 percent wheat flour
A pinch of salt
3 tablespoons olive oil

The Topping
1 egg
1 small onion
2 large tomatoes
1$\frac{1}{2}$ tablespoons toasted mixed aromatic seeds: cumin, fennel, poppy and sesame
2 tablespoons chopped mixed nuts
Black pepper
A pinch of salt

Mash the yeast with the sugar and half the milk and water and set aside in a warm place for 10 minutes to revive.

Warm the flour and salt, make a well in the middle and pour in the yeast mixture and the olive oil. Trickle in the rest of the milk and water, stirring all the while, until you have a soft dough. Knead for 5 to 10 minutes. Cover the dough and put aside in a warm place to rise for 1 to 2 hours.

Meanwhile, make the topping: beat the egg, chop the onion finely and the tomatoes coarsely and mix with all the remaining ingredients.

Punch down the risen dough and knead again for a few minutes. Roll the dough out into a ½-inch (1 cm) thick circle. Put the circle onto an oiled baking sheet and spread the topping over the bread. Leave to prove for about 15 minutes.

Bake in the oven at a modest 350°F (180°C) for about 30 minutes.

Theme V
Old bread

Old bread, like cold potato, is a great asset in the kitchen. Here it is employed in two classics.

SUMMER PUDDING
Serves 6

½ cup sugar
2 lb (1 kg) soft fruit, berries or rhubarb; but especially raspberries
About 8 slices stale bread

Dissolve the sugar in ⅔ cup of water over low heat, then pile in the fruit and stir and simmer until hot and beginning to disintegrate, which with raspberries takes about 6 minutes.

Cut the crusts off the bread. Line a mixing bowl with the bread, making sure there are no gaps. Pour in half the fruit, add a layer of bread, then pour on the rest of the fruit and finish with a final layer of bread. Cover with a plate, put a heavy weight on top, and leave in a cool place, or in the refrigerator, overnight, or longer. Unmold the pudding and serve.

Summer Pudding is a traditional bread pudding without which no English summer is complete.

In the autumn and winter a similar and equally interesting pudding can be made using coarsely pureed apple, and dried fruit that has been soaked in rum for several hours or overnight. Line the bowl with bread and sprinkle it with a syrup made with rum. Fill with the apple puree and plenty of dried fruit. Put a layer of bread on top, sprinkle with more rum syrup and finish as for Summer Pudding. Other fruit such as pears and rhubarb can also be used in this way.

FREE KIRK PUDDING
A bread pudding that does need cooking.
Serves 4

8 tablespoons flour
8 tablespoons breadcrumbs
4 tablespoons butter
1 large cooking apple
6 tablespoons mixed dried fruit
2 teaspoons mixed spices: cinnamon, nutmeg, ginger, clove
4 tablespoons sugar
1 teaspoon baking soda
About 1 cup milk

Mix the flour and breadcrumbs and work in the butter. Do not bother to peel or core the apple, but chop it into roughly ½-inch (1 cm) cubes. Then mix all the fruit, spice and sugar in with the flour and crumbs.

Dissolve the baking soda in a little of the milk and stir into the fruit mixture thoroughly. Then mix in enough milk to make a soft dough.

Put the mixture into a heat-proof mixing bowl. Cover the bowl with a piece of foil, leaving a pleat (for expansion) in the center, and tie it down securely with string. Steam for at least 2 hours. If you do not have a steamer put the bowl into a saucepan of boiling water—the water should come halfway up the sides of the bowl. Cover the pan, reduce the heat and simmer away, adding more water if necessary.

Where would we be without potatoes?

If a latter-day Columbus were to rediscover South America, and if his successors were to bring potatoes afresh to Europe, the tubers would surely be hailed as a wonder food. They contain protein of astonishingly high quality (low only in the essential amino acid methionine, but otherwise approaching the quality of egg) and five pounds would supply an adult's daily protein needs.

Also, as the modern analyst would quickly discover, five pounds of potatoes a day would not make people fat; indeed, since a quarter pound of boiled old potato supplies only about 80 Calories, he might be disappointed by its energy content. The poor Irish of the early nineteenth century, who lived virtually exclusively on potatoes, had to eat a heroic eight pounds a day each to meet their daily energy needs.

Potatoes for dieters . . .

Potatoes also contain a fair spectrum of minerals (they are positively rich in potassium) and are a fine source of vitamin C. Indeed, a freshly dug potato contains about 30 milligrams of vitamin C per 100 grams (approximately a quarter pound) although this falls to eight milligrams per 100 grams by springtime if a potato is stored through the winter and although Americans, on average, now consume a mere quarter pound of potato a day, it is still a significant source of the vitamin.

. . . and for vitamin C

Oranges may contain twice to ten times as much vitamin C as potatoes, weight for weight, but they are more expensive, less versatile, and eaten in smaller quantities. The most significant foods are not necessarily the richest.

So what would the nutritionist, confronted with this wonderful food for the first time, tell the public? That potatoes, at least when either boiled or baked, could be eaten whenever desired; for if people ate generous but not ridiculous amounts they would meet their protein requirements, and their vitamin C and several mineral requirements many times over, but if they did so they would be obliged to eat so much fiber and water that they would be hard pressed to meet daily energy requirements. In short, the nutritionist might point out that in addition to its broad-spectrum nutritional benefits, the potato was almost the ideal food on which to lose weight.

So why has the humble spud been so notoriously abused—considered "heavy" by the old-style dietitians, shunned by the dieter (usually a fat person who clearly does not know what foods are non-fattening) and often written off as being nothing but—in the phrase beloved by old-style nutritionists—empty calories?

Ignorance is at the heart of the trouble. The old-style nutritionists believed that human beings needed vast amounts of protein, and even assumed that only animal products should be considered as protein sources. Yet if potatoes had not contained protein, the Inca civilization could hardly have begun and the poor Irish and western Scots of the last

How else would the Incas have conquered the Andes?

Potatoes make some of the finest stuffings and "meat extenders." Top, Cornish pasties; in the middle, samosas—same idea, different idiom; and, in the foreground, English potato patties, flavored with parsley.

Top, *potatoes cooked whole with beans. If the potatoes are sliced thinly the combination is a fine substitute for rice.* **Center,** *a simple potato salad, flavored with bacon.* **In the foreground,** *a classic potato soup from Switzerland.*

century would never have survived even until the blight years of the 1840s; and since people have at times lived almost exclusively on potatoes, it is obvious even at a common-sense level that they are a fairly complete food. But the power of accepted if unexplored truth is such, even in science, that the protein content of potatoes has been largely disregarded until the past few years.

Coupled with ignorance has been subjective judgment. Potatoes are starchy, are they not? And pastry is starchy, is it not? So the two are equivalent, both being classified as "heavy"? Yet the dumplings that may bob alongside the potatoes in a stew and are superficially so similar contain, by virtue of their fat content and their relative dryness, five or six times as many calories (weight for weight) as the potato. Subjective assessment is a dangerous guide in nutrition.

Behind the lack of knowledge and the superficial judgment, however, lies a prejudice that at least has some rational basis. The history of the potato is not one of unqualified beneficence.

Although the potato is now a fine, safe food (even the recent suggestion that blighted potatoes might be implicated in *spina bifida* has now been disproved) it has not always been so. Potatoes are the underground stem tubers (not roots) of *Solanum tuberosum*. *Solanum* belongs to the family Solanaceae, which also includes, among others, the deadly nightshade; and, as will be seen again in connection with the Leguminosae, a tendency to do nasty things runs in botanical families. Potato berries are poisonous; potatoes that have been exposed to light and turned green are poisonous; and the wild, misshapen, deep-eyed tubers that the Incas first dug out on their native Andes (and which in the end helped them to inhabit the Andes) were often poisonous too. The Incas deified the potato because they recognized their debt to it; but they knew too (as all religious peoples have known since the beginning of time) that gods are fickle.

Poison runs in families

When the potato was first introduced to Europe—by the Spaniards, probably, and not by Drake or Raleigh as the English like to think—it was regarded with the suspicion that greeted all American exotics, including tobacco and the tomato (two more members of the Solanaceae). Although its food value was soon recognized, albeit without the benefit of scientific analysis, it tended to be used largely as a cheap food for poor people—and indeed, as Redcliffe Salaman comments in his classic work *The History and Social Influence of the Potato* (1949), it came to be used as an agent of exploitation. What better way for a landowner or manufacturer to keep a hold over his work force and to cut down his own costs, than to supply them with a sustaining fodder that could be grown virtually without trouble and at minimal cost? The potato did not only sustain the Irish and western Scots in the early nineteenth century, it also provided the means by which they could be kept in abject and uncomplaining poverty.

William Cobbett perceived the political insidiousness of the potato, and it was this, and not irrational prejudice, that prompted his famous tirades against it. The potatoes that he saw growing in gardens in Hexham in the north of England prompted the following sober passage in *Rural Rides* (1830), which illustrates his rather subtle attitude: "As

The subtlety of William Cobbett

Where would we be without potatoes?

garden stuff and used in that way [the potato] is very good. . . . It is the using of it as a substitute for bread and for meat that I have deprecated it, and when the Irish poet, Dr Drennan [1754–1820] called it 'the lazy root' and 'the root of misery', he gave it its true character."

The "root of misery"?

I do not of course deprecate the potato as a substitute for bread or meat (rather the opposite), but then I do not envisage people in the twenty-first century being fed on it like cattle, as they sometimes were in centuries past.

The potato has also suffered from its too frequent and too easy association with fat. Because potatoes are floury and moist and contain only one-tenth of one per cent of fat, they can soak up fat almost as readily as muffins. The modest amount of butter that people commonly put into mashed potatoes increases its calorie content by 50 percent, while the French fry, which loses non-calorific weight in the form of water and picks up fat instead, is about three times as calorific as boiled potato. Potato chips are both dry and fatty, and are seven times as calorific on a weight-for-weight basis as boiled potatoes. Indeed, the potato chip, with 533 Calories per quarter pound, is almost as high in calories as any tolerable food can be; only fat that is almost pure, which most people would certainly not find tolerable, is significantly more calorific.

French fries, however, are far from indefensible. They contain 250 to 290 Calories per quarter pound, which is less than dry toast—297 Calories per quarter pound—and considerably less than crackers, which are both dry and (even without butter) are rich in fat. Thus unbuttered soda crackers contain 440 Calories per quarter pound (at least 50 percent more than French fries) and even starch-reduced crispbread, with 388 Calories per quarter pound, far outstrips the much-maligned French fry. I have sometimes suggested to colleagues who sit down to their ascetic dieter's lunch of crackers and Cheddar cheese (406 Calories per quarter pound) that they would be better off with a nice warming plate of French fries, but they think I am being silly, so I have given up. Yet the analyses have been carefully done, and the figures are in *The Composition of Foods* (A. A. Paul and D. A. T. Southgate, 1978). If you work from first principles, the true facts are obvious; potatoes are fibrous and watery, while crackers, made from refined flour, are dry, and are "shortened" with fat. Of course crackers are calorific; and of course the potato is nothing like as calorific (weight for weight) until it too has been dried and shot through with fat as in the potato chip.

The eminently defensible French fries

Fat should never be used gratuitously (always stop to consider whether the dish would be as good—different, but as good—without fat) and dishes in which potatoes are used virtually as blotting paper for fat, as in Swiss Rösti, probably should be avoided. But dishes in which the fat merely sticks to the outside of a piece of vegetable or potato (for example, French fries, or roast potatoes) are, in context, quite acceptable. Big pieces of potato hold less fat than small pieces, since they have a smaller surface area relative to their volume. Roast potatoes contain only 157 Calories per quarter pound, which is twice as many as boiled potatoes but far fewer than French fries. Big French fries, as made in Greece and in old-fashioned truckers cafés, are preferable to the delicate little "crisp golden fries" of the modern hamburger joint. In cooking, delicacy comes in strange guises.

In short, the potato's role in obesity—if indeed it has played such a role—is rather subtle. The potato itself clearly is not fattening; you would have to be a masochist to get fat on boiled potatoes. Even the French fry, commonest manifestation of the "fatted" potato, is not outrageously calorific.

The point about potatoes is, I think, that they enable people to eat more of everything. People cannot tolerate powerful, unrelieved flavor: fatty meat on its own, or greasy gravy on its own, are monotonous and overbearing. But the potato dilutes, absorbs and rarefies; it can make almost anything acceptable and if you build a meal around potatoes you can eat a great deal. Greed, therefore, is to blame. Attach no blame to the potato.

As a crop, potatoes are wonderful. Yield admittedly is fickle, but that is because they are so responsive to growing conditions. The obverse is that if you treat them well they will yield as much food per acre as any crop. Given plenty of moisture and heavy feeding, and provided that the farmer earths them up to give the tubers room to develop and keeps a careful watch for the dreaded *Phytophthora infestans*, alias blight, maincrop potatoes can yield 10 to 25 tons an acre, containing 300 pounds of protein.

In a Canadian study, only soybeans (with 400 pounds per acre) out-yielded potato on the protein stakes, while other beans (160 pounds of protein per acre) and spring wheat (130 pounds) lagged far behind; and of these crops, the potato is by far the easiest to grow. (Green leaves, such as cabbages, would yield far more protein per acre than even soybeans, but leaf protein is so diluted by water and fiber that it is of less direct use to human beings.)

I hope that people will again become connoisseurs of potatoes, for the tendency today is to breed them primarily for yield and for resistance to disease, and for the high sugar content required by the manufacturers of potato chips.

The old varieties that were each suited to different dishes are being allowed to die out. They are harder to grow, of course; lower yielding, often less hardy and more prone to disease than the modern types. But we should demonstrate that they are worth the effort by being prepared to pay for them. The breeders could, in future, achieve far more variety than they ever have in the past, because all the present varieties were bred from the South American stocks that were originally brought to Europe in the sixteenth century—and then taken back to North America. But scientists at the Scottish Plant Breeding Station in Edinburgh, and elsewhere, are now gathering indigenous wild and primitive cultivated types from South America, to broaden the breeding stock and produce a whole new series of potatoes with a whole new range of interesting flavors.

I trust that people in the twenty-first century will at last realize what a splendid thing the humble potato really is, and will urge the breeders to do their job well.

Where would we be without potatoes?

The cook's first question—why cook at all?—is only too readily answered when applied to the potato, the raw flesh of which is one of nature's least appetizing contrivances. But the transformation wrought by cooking is wondrous, and pursues three paths. Mere heat, applied by boiling or steaming or oven baking, makes the flesh soft and floury. Direct radiant heat or hot dry metal breaks down the flesh to produce a brown, sweet, chemically complex patina. Hot fat crisps the outside.

Potatoes may be served as whole, discrete things, which is how they appear in the traditional meat-and-potato meal. They can be broken down a little, so their surface starches take up the surrounding juices, and leak out to thicken them. They may be pounded a little more to produce a puree (mash) or broken up completely to thicken soups, like flour; or indeed turned into flour, which is sometimes used in bread. At all grades of comminution the potato will pick up and hold surrounding flavors: of mint, thyme, young carrot, or (although the potato came late to India) the whole astonishing array of Indian spices.

The potato, once mashed, is as pliant as modeling-clay; it can be mixed with anything and everything and molded to whatever shape you please. To examine the potato's cuisine is to explore all cooking.

Theme 1
The road to dissolution

The potato begins as a solid orb and can be successively sliced or mashed through all degrees of comminution to a fine puree, being spiced or not as you choose. The easiest form is the boiled potato. I would not presume to write about boiled potatoes if I had not so often seen them ruined. The skins, unless too warty, are best left on. They are waterproof, so there is no need to plunge potatoes into boiling water as is sometimes suggested—they sit in wet earth throughout the summer without going soggy and a few minutes in slowly warming water will do them no harm. Salt in the cooking water will not flavor them (and in any case should be avoided) but it will raise the boiling point of water; since potatoes cook at slightly below the normal boiling temperature of water this is no great advantage.

Potatoes boil well when about the size of a large hen's egg; if the pieces are not roughly equal sized, they will not all cook at the same

pace. If they are substantially bigger than a hen's egg, cut them, or bake them in the oven.

In short, put the egg-sized bits into a saucepan of cold water, bring them to a boil and allow to simmer for about 20 minutes. When a fork penetrates the potatoes easily, they are done.

Boiled potatoes look distinguished if they are sliced fairly thinly and then sprawled edge-on like collapsing dominoes down the middle of a long, thick, hot, earthenware serving dish, with roast onions or two colors of cabbage or root vegetables playing aisles to their nave on either side; and the whole decorated with watercress.

POTATO SALAD
Serve as an accompaniment for fish or with other salads.
Serves 4

$1\frac{1}{2}$ lb ($\frac{3}{4}$ kg) potatoes
4 slices bacon
12 scallions
1 teaspoon dill seeds

The Dressing
2 tablespoons wine vinegar
2 teaspoons prepared Dijon mustard
$\frac{1}{2}$ teaspoon sugar
A large pinch of salt
Pepper
6 tablespoons olive oil

Peel and cube the potatoes. Boil them for 15 to 20 minutes or until they are tender.
Meanwhile, broil the bacon until it is crisp; chop the green and white parts of the scallions; and prepare the dressing by mixing the vinegar with the mustard, sugar, salt, and a generous sprinkling of pepper. Beat in the oil until you have a homogenized mixture.
Drain the potatoes and put them in a large bowl. While they are still hot, mix in the crumbled or chopped bacon, the scallions and the dill seeds. Pour the dressing over and toss to mix well.

SPICY POTATOES IN INDIAN STYLE
The Indian approach to boiled (and in this instance baked) potatoes is a little more subtle. Note the marriage of potato and dairy produce—yogurt, in this recipe—which recurs throughout world cooking.
Cows like grass, and grass needs a wet climate; so do potatoes.

Serves 4

2 lb (1 kg) potatoes
1 teaspoon ground coriander
½ teaspoon ground cumin
A large pinch of salt
A pinch of ground cinnamon
⅔ cup yogurt
3 broken bay leaves
½ teaspoon chili powder
1½ tablespoons corn oil
½ teaspoon brown sugar
2 tablespoons chopped Chinese parsley

The idea is to impregnate the potato surface with the spices; so peel them and boil them for 10 minutes until half-cooked, then prick the surface with a fork until the potatoes are spongy.

Mix the coriander, cumin, salt and cinnamon with the yogurt, and stir in the potatoes.

In a casserole dish, fry the bay leaves and chili powder in the oil for 2 minutes. Add the sugar and when it begins to darken stir in the potatoes and yogurt mixture.

Cover the casserole, and put it in a moderate oven, 350°F (180°C), for 15 to 25 minutes. Garnish with chopped Chinese parsley.

ALU RAITA

Once the potato is broken up a little to expose yet more surface, it becomes even more receptive to spices. Here is another Indian approach—a kind of salad, served as a side dish.
Serves 4

1 lb (½ kg) potatoes
½ lb (240 g) tomatoes
Black pepper
A pinch of salt
½ teaspoon cumin seeds
2 cups yogurt
1 tablespoon chopped Chinese parsley

Boil the potatoes and slice when cool, then mix with the sliced tomatoes.

Mix a generous sprinkling of black pepper, the salt and the cumin seeds with the yogurt, and pour over the potato-tomato mixture. Decorate with the chopped Chinese parsley.

Potatoes for mashing can be peeled or unpeeled; if left unpeeled, the brown flecks of skin in the finished mash add color and "spice." To make mashed potatoes, boil them until tender, then drain and pound with a fork or masher. Today, people seem usually to add butter (the potato-dairy link again), but this is unnecessary, although a dash of milk improves the texture. Black pepper is mandatory.

A well-made dish of mashed potatoes is a meal. Mashed potato is also one of the most versatile cooking materials that can be used as a bed for any kind of garnish (just as Chinese cooks use beds of rice) or as a pie crust. But first, a look at the second main route into the potato.

Theme II
Potatoes and fat

Potatoes can absorb as much fat as you care to load them with. The muffin is hardly more accommodating. The fat need not be overwhelming if it is used simply to coat the surface (and perhaps hold a few spices), especially if the potatoes are cut in large bits, so that the ratio of surface area to volume is low. I present a few very fatty dishes here—just to pursue the theme of comminution to its logical conclusion. But the nutrition-conscious cook should try only the first three of the following five recipes.

FRENCH FRIES

I am insulting you with this simple recipe just to make a few generalizations.

Although potatoes will not absorb water unless deliberately macerated, they will absorb hot fat—unless the fat is so hot that it first vaporizes the water on the outside of the potato, to create positive steam pressure which repels the invasive fat; and then, almost immediately, seals the outside into an impermeable coat.

French fries are food for kings and, as explained in the text, far from unacceptable nutritionally. They contain fewer calories per unit weight than dry toast (and far fewer than dry crackers) and if they are cooked in polyunsaturated corn oil (sunflower oil seems a little extravagant in this context) there seems no good reason why they should damage the arteries. Their chief drawback is their tastiness. They encourage greed.

Where would we be without potatoes?

Serves 4

1½ lb (¾ kg) potatoes
Frying oil or drippings

Peel the potatoes and cut the pieces big and fat, to reduce surface area relative to volume. Wrap these in a cloth as you prepare them, to stop them going brown and to dry them—because the more damp they are when you put them in the fat, the more they will cool it, and the more they will froth and splash.

Have the fat hot—350° to 400°F (175° to 200°C) is recommended; but a feel for the rightness of things is a good substitute for a thermometer, and the fat is hot enough when a single piece of potato tossed into it immediately sizzles and rises to the surface. Do not put in too many at a time, or you will cool the fat and the potatoes will be soggy or cause the whole pan to froth over.

When the potatoes are almost done, take them out of the fat and let them sit in the air in their basket while the fat, over high heat, becomes really hot; then plunge the fries in again for a final browning. Give the potatoes a good shake before serving.

ROAST POTATOES

The point of roasting potatoes (as opposed to baking) is to encourage them to absorb the fat (drippings) and the fresh juices from the roasting meat. So just boil the potatoes for 3 to 5 minutes to soften their surface. Then put them in a roasting pan, in just enough hot dripping and meat juices to baste them, and put them at the top of the oven, above the meat, for about 1 hour.

The "flat roast" (a term coined by my daughter; I can find none better) is a hybrid between the French fry and the roast potato, and is versatile and delicious. I have served flat roasts with cold poultry (the remains of Christmas turkey and all the stuffings) or beef, with pot roasts, with Hen of the Wake and with Roast Lamb and beans and they are not out of place with curries. As with French fries the idea is to repel fat, so the potatoes—peeled, sliced into ⅛-inch (0.25 cm) thick rounds, and blotted dry—are put into hot fat; but the right amount of fat, as with roasts,

is just enough to baste them.

Preheat the oven—containing a roasting pan with ¼-inch (0.5 cm) or so of drippings—at 425°F (220°C) for about 20 minutes. Then pile the sliced potatoes into the hot fat, tossing them about to give them a thin covering. Put them near the top of the oven for about 1 hour, and baste at least twice. Oil, instead of fat, can be used for cooking flat roasts. Sesame, caraway and other aromatic seeds and perhaps German red cabbage can transform what is essentially an English roast beef idiom into a fine, strong, vegetarian dish.

If you break up the potatoes a little more, and then fry them, you enter a theme that runs right through world cooking. The following are too fatty for comfort, but I cannot bring myself to ignore them.

FRIED POTATOES

An ancient English technique, making use of cold cooked potato—which, incidentally, is one of those left-overs that no kitchen should be without.
Serves 4

2 cups mashed potatoes
Drippings
Pepper
A pinch of salt

Melt the drippings in a frying pan until it is smoking hot, then press in the well-peppered and lightly salted potato. As the bottom colors, stir the mixture around until the whole thing is browned all over and shot through with brown bits and pieces.

Rösti is the national potato dish of German-speaking Switzerland. The dish is virtually the same as the English one above, except that the potatoes are first boiled in their skins and when they are completely cold they are peeled and shredded on a special grater, or cut in julienne strips. They are then fried in butter and flattened into a cake. After a minute or two the cake is turned over. When the potatoes are nicely golden the pan is covered, and the flat potato cake cooked for another 15 to 20 minutes until the bottom is brown and crusty. The rösti is served crusty side up. Cheese, bacon, and onions are sometimes cooked in with the potato. A non-stick pan is useful for this dish.

Theme III
Potatoes in concert

Potatoes mix well with every other kind of vegetable. They may simply be cooked alongside—new potatoes boiled with baby carrots and a sprig or two of wild thyme are a supreme delicacy—or merged with other ingredients through all degrees of admixture to the point of amalgamation. Potato and onion, potato and root vegetables, potato and bean, all offer endless scope; but here, first, is the honored theme of potato and greens, that may manifest in the idiom of any of the great cuisines.

BUBBLE AND SQUEAK
"It was bubble-and-squeak, between two plates, and its fragrance filled the narrow cell. The penetrating smell of cabbage reached the nose of Toad as he lay prostrate in his misery on the floor, and gave him the idea for a moment that life was not such a blank and desperate thing as he had imagined. . . . Toad, between his sobs, sniffed and reflected, and gradually began to think new and inspiring thoughts: of chivalry, and poetry, and deeds still to be done. . . ." I offer this quotation from Kenneth Grahame's *The Wind in the Willows* to reiterate the point that regard for food is largely in the expectation. Come to Bubble and Squeak naïvely or, like Toad, with memories of rambling aristocratic breakfasts and it becomes a thing of delight.

Disbelieve whomsoever tells you to mash the potatoes; no matter if they are already mashed, but the correct condition is the point of disintegration, small bits held together by their own mushiness. Use of butter is gratuitous; this is an ideal vehicle for bacon fat.

Serve Bubble and Squeak with broiled tomatoes or zucchini.
Serves 4

4 cups cooked cabbage
2 cups cooked potato
Pepper
A pinch of salt
Bacon drippings

Shred the cabbage and mix it in well with the disintegrating potato. Pepper generously as you go and add the salt. Put enough bacon drippings in the pan to cover the bottom when melted—you can always add more, but the intention is to use the minimum—and heat. Press the potato-cabbage mixture into the fat, to make a flat cake. Do not stir. You want the bottom browned and the rest merely hot. Serve brown side up.

POTATOES AND GREEN BEANS
This is an Italian-Swiss version, from the Valle-Maggia.
Serves 4

1 lb ($\frac{1}{2}$ kg) potatoes, peeled
1 lb ($\frac{1}{2}$ kg) green beans
1 sprig thyme
Pepper
A pinch of salt
2 tablespoons butter

Boil the potatoes and beans together, with the thyme. Then mash with pepper, salt and butter. The Swiss, of course, use lots of butter; but although this dish calls for it, use it with discretion.

POTATOES AND BEANS
I am always on the look-out for temperate substitutes for the sub-tropical rice, because the basic form of the peasant South-East Asian meal—a bed of rice with a few sprinklings of whatever's going on top—is almost the archetypal simple meal; aesthetically, nutritionally, and economically acceptable. Potatoes mixed with beans are texturally comparable to rice or pasta and nutritionally superior to either. Anything can be used as garnish; but crisp slivers of pork belly or bacon and lots of green or Chinese cabbage, sprinkled with soy sauce and plenty of pepper, is a fine combination.
Serves 4

1 lb ($\frac{1}{2}$ kg) potatoes
1$\frac{1}{3}$ cups navy beans or black-eyed peas, boiled (see page 85)
Pepper
A pinch of salt

Boil the potatoes with their skins on. Drain, slice thinly, or leave whole, and mix in with the boiled beans. Season with plenty of pepper and the salt.

Where would we be without potatoes?

SPICY LENTILS WITH POTATOES

Unleavened bread is a fine accompaniment and the dish is perfectly at home with other curries and rice. I would serve it with flat roast potatoes and thus establish a neat counterpoint between the two forms of potato; sprinkle the whole lot with watercress for decoration and toss on a few raisins.

Serves 4

½ lb (240 g) lentils (brown are good in this robust context)
½ lb (240 g) potatoes
1 carrot
Juice of 1 lemon
2 green chilies
2 teaspoons mustard seeds
½ teaspoon fennel seeds
1 teaspoon ground cumin
2 teaspoons ground coriander
1 cup grated coconut
2 teaspoons corn oil

If you are using brown lentils, first soak them for 3 hours. Drain and set them boiling in 1 quart (9 dl) of water. After 20 minutes add the chopped potatoes and the scrubbed, chopped carrot. You want them all to reach their moist and tender peak at the same time. When they are tender (after another 20 minutes or so) add the lemon juice.

Chop and fry the chilies with the mustard seeds, fennel seeds, cumin, coriander and coconut for a few minutes in the oil. The spice mixture should not taste "raw" but should still be pleasantly aromatic. Stir the spice mixture into the lentil mixture.

Serve immediately.

The sharpness of onion of course complements the potato; and the combination of potato and the more substantial leek has served many a poor family as a substitute for meat. Which shows once more that when it comes to eating, poverty has many advantages.

PAN HAGGERTY

Serves 2

1¼ lb (¾ kg) potatoes
1 large onion
2 tablespoons bacon or beef drippings or 1½ tablespoons oil
1 cup grated hard cheese
Salt and pepper

Scrub the potatoes and slice them paper thin. Slice the onion finely.

Heat the drippings or oil in a large frying pan. When it is hot remove the pan from the heat and put the potatoes, onions and cheese in layers, with a good sprinkling of pepper and the salt. End with a layer of potatoes. Put the pan back on the heat, cover and cook over low heat.

When the vegetables are cooked increase the heat for the bottom to brown. Then put under the broiler to brown the top.

The sad thing is that many a modern mother would feel she was selling her children short if she served Pan Haggerty for supper; yet in all the main respects this dish is nutritionally unimpeachable. Potato, eked out by cheese, provides adequate protein and energy; potato, and to a small extent onion, provide fiber; the fat content is low and the vitamin-mineral content of the potato-cheese mixture is impressive. Yet those same modern mothers would happily prize an ersatz hamburger (containing the talismanic soybean) from the deep-freeze or open a package of frankfurters; unaware, perhaps, that 80 percent of the energy in the all-American frankfurter is supplied by saturated fat. The trouble with Pan Haggerty is, quite simply, that it is too cheap; and so long as dishes are cheap, the food industrialists can find no lever for profit, and where there is no profit there is no propaganda. A book should be written in praise of Pan Haggerty, and if I have nothing to do next winter, I will write it.

Which brings us neatly to the fourth method of mixing potatoes with other vegetables—simply mashing the potato together with compatible vegetables. An old Welsh dish, Punch Nep, exploits the felicitous affinity for turnip.

PUNCH NEP

This dish is as smooth and white as alabaster, and although simple it is astonishingly good. But it is the principle that counts: one despised root and one disprized tuber, fused into a thing of beauty.

Serves 4 to 6

2 lb (1 kg) potatoes
2 lb (1 kg) white turnips
A large pinch of nutmeg
A pinch of salt
⅔ cup milk

Peel the potatoes and turnips and boil them together until soft. Drain them well and mash together with the nutmeg, salt and milk.

Theme IV
Soups, stews and curries

The potato's fiber—that is, its cell walls—tends to keep it intact; its starch, leaking from the cells, fuses the potato flesh with its surroundings. There are no finer qualifications for an ingredient of soups, stews and casseroles. Here, first, a simple recipe from Switzerland, where people esteem potatoes and like soup. The potato-dairy-onion theme continues yet again.

SWISS POTATO SOUP
Serves 4

1¼ lb (¾ kg) potatoes
2 onions
2 tablespoons butter
5 cups stock
A pinch of salt
Pepper
A handful of chopped parsley

Peel the potatoes and cut them into tiny cubes; slice the onions thinly. Cook the onions and potatoes in the butter in a heavy saucepan over low heat. Cover tightly but stir frequently, until the potatoes are half-done, which will take about 10 minutes.

Then add the stock and salt, pepper well, and simmer until the potatoes are tender. Serve sprinkled with parsley.

With only minor variations—less liquor, the potato cut a little larger, and fried until browned, and the addition of spices—a simple potato soup becomes a superficially complex (but technically just as simple) curry. Yet again, a fine potato dish from India.

VEGETABLE CURRY
Serves 4

2 lb (1 kg) potatoes
1 turnip, about ½ lb (240 g)
2 zucchini
2 onions
4 tablespoons corn oil
1 to 2 green chilies
2 garlic cloves
1½-inch (3.5 cm) piece fresh ginger root
½ teaspoon black pepper
1 teaspoon turmeric
2 teaspoons ground coriander
1 teaspoon ground cumin
2 tomatoes
A pinch of salt

Chop the potatoes and turnip into ½-inch (1 cm) cubes, and cover to prevent browning. Slice the zucchini. Chop the onions and fry them in the oil until soft. Then add the finely chopped chilies, garlic and ginger and, after 1 minute, stir in all the spices.

When the spices are well fried, stir in the potatoes, turnip and zucchini and fry until browned. Then stir in the tomatoes, cut into quarters, and the salt and add 1¼ cups of water. Allow to simmer for 10 to 15 minutes, until all the vegetables are tender.

PORK BOULANGÈRE
Potatoes, usually sliced but sometimes diced, associate with all kinds of meat and fish in all kinds of soups and casseroles, from hotpot (a casserole topped with potato) to the egregious Potato Pie of Lancashire (page 116). Here is a simple but distinguished potato and meat hotpot to illustrate the genre. Serve this dish with plenty of spicy red cabbage.
Serves 4

3 lb (1½ kg) potatoes
2 large onions
4 pork chops
1 tablespoon flour
2 tablespoons oil
A pinch of salt
Pepper
1 teaspoon dried sage
2 cups milk and water mixed

Peel the potatoes and cut into ½-inch (1 cm) thick slices; this is the standard hotpot style potato, big enough to have body, but small enough to absorb plenty of flavor. Peel and slice the onions. Then coat the chops in flour and fry in the oil until browned on both sides.

Put half the sliced potatoes in a wide ovenproof dish, followed by half the sliced onions, add the salt and pepper liberally. Put the chops in next, sprinkle

73

with the dried sage, then add more seasoning and another layer of onions. Finish with a top layer of potatoes. Pour in the milk and water mixture and cover with a tight lid, or with foil.

Cook in a hot oven, 400°F (200°C), for 1¼ hours; but remove the cover for the last 15 minutes to brown the potatoes.

Serve immediately.

Theme V _____
Potatoes as pie crust

In Pork Boulangère, as in all hotpots, the potato slices melt and cake at the surface to form a texturally interesting crust, with the browning adding spice. But mashed potato makes outstanding pie crust, and stretches sparse fillings to great lengths. Shepherd's Pie is the archetype; but if for ground cooked meat you substitute flaked cooked fish, or (in vegetarian vein) mushrooms and a touch of *miso*, you can hardly go wrong.

SHEPHERD'S PIE
I would (often do) serve Shepherd's Pie with French fries or flat roasts: there is musical wit in using the same ingredient twice in the same meal in vastly different contexts, and you just cannot eat too many potatoes.

Here is the basic Shepherd's Pie; all the ingredients (except the tomatoes, which are included to freshen the flavor) are cooked before the final baking, the function of which is merely to consummate the marriage—a technique that takes the panic out of cooking.
Serves 4

2 lb (1 kg) potatoes
A pinch of salt
Pepper
2 cups cooked roast lamb or beef (or however much you have left over)
2 large onions
Beef drippings (the minimum needed to prevent burning)
4 tomatoes

Boil the potatoes (no need to peel, in such a bucolic dish) and mash with the salt and plenty of pepper.

Grind the meat and chop the onions, and fry in a little of the fat until the onions are soft. Season with plenty of freshly ground pepper.

Spread the meat and onion mixture in a fairly shallow oven dish; slice the tomatoes and lay them on top of the meat and onions. Spread the mashed potatoes over all, and flatten with a fork—leaving a furrowed pattern: this is not merely decorative, for the ridges will brown and add flavor and texture.

Put the dish near the top of a hot oven, 400°F (200°C), until the pie is thoroughly hot and the potato is browned.

Serve immediately.

Theme VI _____
Potatoes incarcerated

So much for potatoes on the outside of things: they also serve as the innards of a vast spectrum of pies and pasties (turnovers). Here are three classics, which differ only in idiom.

VEGETARIAN CORNISH PASTY
It occurred to me one day that if you left the meat out of a Cornish pasty you would still have a splendid dish. And so it proved. This pasty is delicious hot and magnificent cold. It is made from nothing much and is not at all ascetic.
Makes 4 pasties

½ lb (240 g) potatoes
½ lb (240 g) turnips
½ lb (240 g) carrots
½ lb (240 g) parsnips
1 garlic clove
2 onions
Oil for frying
A pinch of salt
Pepper
1¼ cups grated Cheddar cheese
A large pinch of thyme
½ cup margarine
2 cups whole wheat flour

Scrub or peel the potatoes, turnips, carrots and parsnips. Cut them into egg-sized chunks, and boil for 15 to 20 minutes until all are soft. Then drain.

Meanwhile, crush the garlic clove and peel and slice the onions and fry them in minimal oil until soft. Add to the other vegetables. Add the salt, a generous sprinkling of pepper, half the

74

cheese and the thyme and mash and stir with a fork until all is integrated; but do not reduce to a puree. Then put to one side to cool.

Blend the fat into the flour and then mix in the remainder of the grated cheese. Mix to a dough with water and divide the mixture into 4 pieces. Shape each piece into a ball and roll out into a circle about 6 inches (15 cm) in diameter. Put 2 good tablespoons of the vegetable mixture across the middle of each circle, leaving 1 inch (2.5 cm) uncovered at each end. Dampen around the edges of the circle and then bring the two sides together, pinching the pastry well together so that it forms a ridge across the top. Bend the ridge one way, and then the other at 1 inch (2.5 cm) intervals, for strength as well as decoration (like the edges of a scallop). Bake in a 400°F (200°C) oven for 30 minutes. Do not let them get too brown.

In India the same dish, with a bit of spicing here and there, has become a classic. It is traditionally eaten in South India for breakfast.

MASALA DOSA

A *dosa* differs from a Cornish pasty in that the *dosa* is made separately, and then stuffed; not cooked with the stuffing. Begin making the *dosas* the day before you intend to serve them.
Serves 4

$\frac{3}{4}$ cup long-grain rice
$\frac{2}{3}$ cup *urad* lentils (split black beans)
Baking soda
2 tablespoons rice flour or fine white
   wheat flour
A pinch of salt
1 green chili
Butter

The Filling
1 lb ($\frac{1}{2}$ kg) boiled potatoes
1 tablespoon grated coconut
2 green chilies
1-inch (2.5 cm) piece fresh ginger root,
   peeled and chopped
1 onion
1 tablespoon sunflower oil
1 teaspoon mustard seeds
$\frac{1}{2}$ teaspoon turmeric
$\frac{1}{2}$ teaspoon ground cumin
A pinch of salt

To make the *dosa* batter, clean and wash the rice and lentils. Soak them separately in cold water for at least 3 hours or preferably 8 hours.

Drain the rice and puree it in a blender with about 4 tablespoons of water; the puree should have a consistency of a thick batter. Drain the lentils and puree them in the same way, adding more water, if necessary. Mix the two purees in a bowl, cover tightly and leave in a warm place for 12 hours to ferment slightly.

To prepare the filling, peel the potatoes and mash roughly. Puree the coconut, chilies and ginger in a blender with a little water. Chop the onion and fry it in the oil until soft. Add the mustard seeds, turmeric, cumin and salt and stir-fry for 2 to 3 minutes. Add the potato and the coconut mixture and fry for another 5 minutes. Keep hot.

When you are ready to serve the *dosas*, beat the fermented rice and lentil puree well. Beat in a large pinch of baking soda, the rice flour, salt and the very finely chopped chili. The batter should have a pouring consistency, so mix in a little water if necessary.

Heat a heavy frying pan and grease it with a little butter. Pour in a little batter, tilting the pan to spread it evenly. Fry for 2 minutes and when blisters appear on top smear with a little butter and turn the *dosa* over. Cook for a further 2 minutes, by which time the *dosa* should be lightly browned. Cover and keep warm while you make the other *dosas*.

Put a little of the potato stuffing on each *dosa*, fold the *dosa* over and serve.

SAMOSA

Another classic, and an important form, is the *samosa*.

The *samosa* is of course comparable to the fritter and *pakora*, which is discussed in the chapter on vegetables; it is a highly satisfactory way of keeping well-matched, well-spiced ingredients together in bite-sized packages, and a grand way to use up small amounts of left-over potato and vegetables.
Samosas are traditionally eaten with a fresh coconut or Chinese parsley chutney. To make a fresh chutney, soak

Where would we be without potatoes?

two heaping tablespoons of desiccated coconut in half a cup of yogurt for two hours; then blend with the juice of one lemon, one to two chili peppers, the leaves from a bunch of Chinese parsley, salt and sugar to taste. When the chutney is smooth, chill it.
Makes about 18 to 20 small pasties

2 tablespoons butter
2 cups flour
Oil for deep frying

The Filling
$\frac{1}{2}$ lb (240 g) potatoes
2 to 3 tablespoons oil
$\frac{1}{2}$ teaspoon mustard seeds
1 onion
$\frac{1}{2}$-inch (1 cm) piece fresh ginger root
2 green chilies
$\frac{1}{4}$ teaspoon turmeric
$\frac{1}{4}$ teaspoon ground cumin
1 teaspoon ground coriander
A pinch of salt
Juice of $\frac{1}{2}$ lemon
1 teaspoon finely chopped fresh
   Chinese parsley

To make the pastry, blend the butter into the flour and add enough water to make a smooth dough. Knead well, cover with a damp cloth and set aside.

Next make the filling. Boil the potatoes; when they are nearly but not quite tender, drain, peel and cut them into small cubes.

Heat the oil in a large frying pan, add the mustard seeds and when they begin to crackle and pop, put in the finely chopped onion, the grated ginger and the finely chopped chilies. Fry, stirring, until the onions are soft. Add the turmeric, cumin and coriander and fry for a minute before putting in the potatoes and salt. Stir in the lemon juice and the parsley and set aside to cool.

Knead the dough again. Pinch off a piece of the dough the size of a large marble—about 1 inch (2.5 cm) in diameter—and roll it out as thinly as possible into a circle. Cut the circle in half and shape each half into a cone. Fill the cone with the potato mixture—it will take about a rounded teaspoonful. Dampen the edges of the pastry and pinch to seal.

Deep fry the cones until they are crisp and golden. Drain and serve hot.

Theme VII
Koftas and cakes

Once potatoes are mashed, they can be mixed with just about anything—cheese, fish, ground meat, spices, other vegetables—and then pressed into a cake, perhaps with a little egg for binding, and then deep or shallow fried. Such patties not only can be but are in every great cuisine. Here are three illustrations, working from West to East; but there are a thousand others in between.

ENGLISH POTATO AND PARSLEY PATTIES
The main point of this dish is to dispose of ancient potatoes; but it is not without piquancy.
Serves 4

1 lb ($\frac{1}{2}$ kg) potatoes
1 tablespoon bacon drippings
A big handful of parsley
A pinch of salt
Pepper
Flour
Oil

Boil the potatoes. Peel and mash them with the drippings and the finely chopped parsley. Add the salt and pepper. The parsley should turn the whole mass bright green. Form the mixture into small spheres, flatten into patties and fry in a little oil.

BEMUELOS
This version, based on a Middle Eastern Jewish recipe, is slightly more complex.
Serves 4

2 lb (1 kg) potatoes
1 egg
$1\frac{1}{4}$ cups grated old Cheddar
A pinch of nutmeg
A good handful of chopped parsley
A pinch of cayenne pepper
1 chili pepper
Pepper
A pinch of salt
Flour
Matzo meal
Oil for deep-frying

Boil, peel and mash the potatoes, and pound in the beaten egg, grated cheese, nutmeg, chopped parsley, cayenne, chopped chili, pepper and salt. Add a little flour or meal to thicken if the mixture seems too moist.

Shape into small spheres, coat thickly in meal, and deep fry.

The point is now made, but in India, as always, the cooks are able to go one better. The *kofta* is a fine form.

ALU KOFTA
Such *koftas* go well with cold meat, crisp sticks of celery and with salad.
Makes about 30 koftas

1 lb ($\frac{1}{2}$ kg) potatoes
1 green chili, finely chopped
1 small onion, finely chopped
1 teaspoon grated fresh ginger root
A pinch of salt
Juice of $\frac{1}{2}$ lemon
All-purpose flour or *besan* (chickpea) flour
Oil for deep frying

Boil and mash the potatoes, mixing in the rest of the ingredients (except the flour and oil) as you go. Divide the mixture into about 30 little balls; roll in flour and deep fry in hot oil.

Theme VIII
Potatoes and fruit

I was faintly surprised when I first came across potatoes hobnobbing with fruit. Yet they do so in many cuisines and contexts. Here, first of all, is an outstanding pie which comes from Wales (also made in Ireland).

CELTIC POTATO APPLE CAKE
Serves 4

1 lb ($\frac{1}{2}$ kg) potatoes
2 tablespoons butter
1 teaspoon sugar
A pinch of ground ginger
A pinch of salt
1 cup flour
2 medium-sized apples

Boil the potatoes and mash them with the butter, sugar, ginger and salt, stirring in the flour to make the mixture

drier. Divide the mixture into two slightly unequal lumps, and roll each into a circle just over $\frac{1}{2}$ inch (1 cm) thick. Put the smaller circle on a baking sheet, arrange slices of apple on it (do not peel and core; it is a waste of time and of good seeds) and put the bigger circle on top as a lid. Press all around to seal. Cover with foil and bake in a medium oven, 375°F (190°C) for 20 minutes, then uncover and bake for a further 15 minutes or until the potatoes brown and the apples finally soften.

And here is a surprising variation from the rural areas of Switzerland, where home-dried fruits are a way of life.

SCHNITZ UND ERDAPFEL (Dried Fruit and Potato Casserole)
Such an association of apples and potatoes and onion should immediately conjure up thoughts of pork and this is indeed a common accompaniment.
Serves 4 to 6

2$\frac{1}{2}$ cups dried apples or pears
1$\frac{1}{2}$ lb ($\frac{3}{4}$ kg) potatoes
1 large onion
2 tablespoons butter
A pinch of salt
2 tablespoons honey

Soak the dried fruit in water for 2 hours. Chop the potatoes and onion coarsely.

Fry the onion in butter until transparent, and then add the potatoes, salt, fruit and honey, and give a good stir. Add just enough water to cover, then bring to a boil. Put on the lid, turn down the heat and allow to simmer for 20 to 30 minutes or until all is tender.

The Germans, of course, have been mixing fruit with potatoes for a long time. They make potato pancakes and serve them with apple or cranberry sauce. Other fruit purees would be equally delicious with the pancakes. Coarsely mashed potatoes layered with apricots and then baked goes well with boiled ham or roast pork.

Beans by many other names

Pulses have good qualities and bad qualities; but their bad qualities are largely, although not entirely, in the imagination and their beneficence is so overwhelming that they must take their place at the heart of human nutrition and gastronomy, as they have in many cultures for the past 10,000 years.

They must do so, however, in their pristine form, as peas and beans and lentils and chickpeas and grams; not as the appalling ersatz "textured vegetable protein," or TVP, that has suddenly become the basis of a boom industry. Their texture needs no improvement and their versatility is infinite, without the intercession of high technology.

The bad things first. Pulses are the large and meaty seeds of plants of the worldwide and highly successful Leguminosae group; but the Leguminosae share with the Solanaceae, provider of the potato and tomato, a proclivity for playing nasty tricks. Thus one of the potato's relatives in *Atropa belladonna*, the deadly nightshade; and one of the Leguminosae is the laburnum, whose seeds can have extremely unpleasant effects, as can those of some of the lupins. The potato itself can be poisonous; many of the primitive, wild forms certainly are and even the modern cultivars become toxic if they are exposed to light and allowed to become green. Similarly, some of the pulses that people eat have at times done them harm, and in a variety of ways. A severe form of anemia, which occurs in Mediterranean countries and is known as favism, is thought to be caused by eating too many broad beans; the big-seeded jack bean has poisoned people; and paralyzing lathyrism can result from overconsumption of the grass pea, *Lathyrus sativus*— although people do not normally eat this pulse except in times of famine. Much less serious (although they irritate some people) are the oligosaccharides (complex sugars) that are contained in many pulses and which escape digestion by the enzymes produced in the gut. The bacteria in the large bowel ferment the unchanged oligosaccharides to produce socially embarrassing barrage balloon volumes of carbonaceous gas of the kind that was once used to fire street lamps.

The pulses have undesirable relatives

Snobbery surrounds the pulses; they have been despised largely because they have been one of the standbys of poor people. The word pulse comes from the Latin *puls*, meaning pudding. Yet some of the reservations were justified in the past, before there were plant breeders and toxicologists to develop safe varieties. The Greeks recognized their debt to the broad bean, *Vicia faba*, and offered bean feasts to Apollo; but, in words that I regret must remain anonymous, "Beans be damned by Pythagoras, for it is said, that by oft use thereof the wits are dulled and cause many dreams, for dead men's souls be therein."

Yet the agricultural, nutritional and gastronomic advantages of pulses are profound, and the old suspicions should be encouraged to die. As crops, pulses have three advantages. First, they are not grasses, and they therefore do not share the diseases of grasses and cereals. The

Three profound advantages

leafy leguminous plants—alfalfa, sainfoin and the clovers and vetches—have therefore often been grown in the wetter areas to complement grass. The legumes grown for their seeds—the pulses—similarly may alternate with the grasses that are grown for their seeds—the grains. Indeed, grains and pulses are a grand little knockabout team; they grow together, or side by side, and they can with advantage be eaten together.

Second, the legumes, which are not unique but are at least outstanding among plants, fertilize themselves. They have bacteria—*Rhizobium*—living symbiotically in little nodules in their roots; and these bacteria fix atmospheric nitrogen, which means they capture the somewhat uninteresting gas that makes up four-fifths of the atmosphere and form it into soluble nitrates and nitrites, which are the chief plant food. In practice, Western farmers put additional fertilizer onto pulse crops; but legumes can grow in astonishingly unfertile soil and leave it more fertile than they found it.

Third, the legumes are almost as versatile as the grasses. Some, such as the peanut, or groundnut, and in particular the Bambarra peanut of West Africa (named after a district in Mali), can grow in virtual desert; and others, like the tepary bean of Central America and Arizona, produce a crop after the most miserly shower.

Other pulses, such as the scarlet runner, like wet conditions. Some kinds, the pigeon pea for example, one of the most valued crops in India, are tropical; others, like soybeans, are unhappy in a climate that is less than Mediterranean. But a few types, notably the broad bean, are among the hardiest crops known to agriculture.

Nutritionally, the pulses are perhaps the most desirable of all simple foods. Raw navy beans provide about 250 Calories for every quarter pound—which makes them about three times as calorific as potatoes; although by the time they have swollen in cooking, the calorie value per unit weight is roughly equal to that of the potato. But the navy bean also contains 25 percent fiber, so it would be hard to get fat on a diet of navy beans; and it provides 20 percent protein, which is easily in excess of human needs. Furthermore, the protein of navy beans—indeed of all beans—is rich in lysine, which is the essential amino acid most likely to be deficient in grain protein. Hence grain protein and pulse protein together meet human requirements more exactly than either alone; and it is at least a happy accident that the grain-with-pulse theme is so prominent and so popular in all the world's cuisines, as *dhal* with rice in India, kidney beans and tortillas in Mexico, beans on toast in England, or rice and soybeans in China.

Only two obstructions (besides prejudice) stand between the cook and the pulse. The first is that pulses are dried seeds and although some, such as lentils, can be cooked without further preparation, the bigger beans need soaking, which means that the cook needs to think ahead.

Two disadvantages besides prejudice

The second impediment is the nomenclature. Pulses have a host of names not only because there are many different kinds but because different people name them for different purposes. The botanists give them names that reflect their ancestry; the plant breeders name their new creations like racehorses; the farmers' names describe the places where they grow and the things for which they can be used; and the

Beans by many other names

market gardeners tend to give them names that reflect their form. Cooks are interested mainly in shape and size, and retailers, these days, faced with a mass of pulses imported from the ends of the earth, sometimes pluck names out of the air. The beans now growing in my garden could be called *Phaseolus vulgaris*, The Prince, kidney beans, dwarf beans or green beans, depending on whether they were being sold, grown, eaten or bequeathed to the botany school.

Aliases galore

This proliferation would not be quite so bad if the names were consistent; but only the scientists' Latinesque inventions and, to a lesser extent, the breeders' names enjoy formal and universal recognition. Thus when an American farmer talks of horse beans he generally means *Canavalia gladiata*, which is also called the sword bean, and sometimes the jack bean; although jack bean usually refers to the related *Canavalia ensiformis*. But the British horse bean is *Vicia faba*, alias the tic bean or field bean, which is related to the broad bean. Again, the pigeon pea, *Cajanus*, is not related to the English green pea, *Pisum*, the asparagus pea, *Lotus*, the chickpea, *Cicer*, or the cow-pea, *Vigna*; and its small round seeds are much favored in India, where it is called red gram. But green gram is *Phaseolus aureus*, which is a kind of kidney bean, and is sometimes called the mung bean. *Phaseolus mungo* ought to be called the mung bean, but usually is not. It is called black gram.

Familiarity dispels confusion

The only sure antidote to such confusion is familiarity, through which a bean tastes as pleasant by any other name; but here is a potted guide to the main types.

The pulses that most people call beans come from three main botanical groups: *Glycine*, the soybean; *Phaseolus*, the kidney bean, and *Vicia* (formerly called *Faba*), of which the chief is the broad bean.

Glycine, the soybean, is one of nature's most astonishing creations. It is native to Asia, and has been cultivated for thousands of years in China; but it has spread all over the world (there are more than 1,000 varieties) and it is now the second biggest export crop of the United States. The Chinese and Japanese cook it fresh, or dry it, or turn it into bean curd, or ferment it to make soy sauce and *miso* (soybean paste). They make flour from it and a kind of milk, and use it as one of several sources of bean sprouts. The ancient Chinese could not have known that soybeans' protein content—up to 40 percent—was as high as that of meat; but it kept them alive nonetheless.

The overrated soybean

The soybean is not a bad bean, but its merits have been greatly exaggerated, mainly by agribusinessmen who have been growing it for decades for its oil, and now are using the alleged and hypothetical protein gap as a pretext for selling it as human food. In truth there is no specific protein gap, so there is no reason for growing one specific high-protein food. There is no good reason either for any country which does not traditionally grow soybeans, or which has too cool a climate to do so, to import it. The ersatz meat industry, based on soybeans, is one of this century's more intriguing confidence tricks and is discussed at the end of this chapter. Because it is oily, the soybean is excellent when cooked by dry heat in an iron pan or roasted, as are oily peanuts (groundnuts), sunflower seeds, sesame seeds, almonds and oats. Roasted soybeans make a good crunchy side dish and, like other oily seeds, can add textural

Top, *navy beans make a fine autumnal bed for roast lamb and mixed vegetables in this robust dish from Provence.* **Bottom,** *a little farther south and east chickpeas are pounded to make a paste, hummus, often flavored with tahina paste made from ground sesame; thus do simple seeds provide one of the world's great delicacies.*

Poor people from most countries have often all but lived on beans, and produced some of the world's great dishes in the process.
Top, *pease pudding, outstanding companion for boiled meats.* **Left,** *black bean soup.* **Right,** *a modified version of classic Boston baked beans, made with apples and pork.*

interest when floated on a thick soup. But the soybean's oiliness makes it one of the most difficult beans to cook, and since Westerners do not actually need the vast amount of protein it contains, I feel Western cooks would be far better advised to use the established and versatile kidney beans and lentils.

The archetypal beans of the West belong to the *Phaseolus* series: the kidney beans. The outstanding species is *Phaseolus vulgaris*, native to South America, which includes the range of climbing dwarf varieties that are grown for their pods—that is, as green beans; and the range (often the same varieties) whose pods are allowed to ripen and whose seeds are then eaten as white, brown, black or multicolored haricots. One variety, the navy bean, was made famous by H. J. Heinz of Pittsburgh as the baked bean.

A bonanza of beans

The other big-seeded *Phaseolus* of note, also native to South America, are *Phaseolus coccineus*, the scarlet runner, grown mainly for its pods, and *Phaseolus lunatus*, the butter bean, or Lima bean, whose large white seeds are the biggest of all the *Phaseolus*. *Phaseolus coccineus* was first cultivated in Britain in the eighteenth century as a decorative creeper. With its scarlet or white flowers (or red and white or pink in some modern cultivars) and slim green pods up to two feet long, it is certainly handsome. In a future, more crowded world, crops that please the eye will be especially desirable.

Vicia faba comes in several forms. The ones eaten by humans are the broad beans, which helped to sustain the civilizations of Greece and Rome (even though the patricians regarded them with suspicion), and they still seem to be grown in every odd corner of southern Italy. They dry well, but their grey-brown leathery skins take some softening. Broad beans are extremely hardy—they are often sown in autumn, and withstand the winter—and their humbler varieties, tic and field beans, are good animal feed.

The grams are a mixed bag of small beanlike pulses much favored in India for making *dhal* and also for sprouting. Red gram, alias the pigeon pea, or *Cajanus cajan*, is a perennial shrub (many of the Leguminosae are shrubs or trees) native to Africa. It has become the second most popular pulse in India (after chickpeas) and it is canned in the West Indies. Black gram is another *Phaseolus*, namely *Phaseolus mungo*, and it probably originated in India, where it is sometimes called *urad*. Green gram is *Phaseolus aureus*, often called by its Indian name of mung and commonly used for sprouts, which are an outstanding emergency source of vitamin C.

The chickpea, *Cicer arietinum*, is probably another native of Africa, but it has become the chief pulse of India where, just to add to the confusion, it is also called Bengal gram. The Indians cook it with spices, but the Arabs have created the particular form *hummus*, which is renowned all through the Middle East and deserves universal acceptance. It is an inspired amalgam of softened chickpeas, lemon juice, garlic, olive oil and, sometimes, the subtle and delectable *tahina* paste made from sesame seeds.

Then there are the ubiquitous and versatile lentils, the green, brownish, reddish, or mottled seeds of the vetchlike *Lens culinaris*, one

Beans by many other names

of the world's oldest leguminous crops. They probably originated in the Near East and Mediterranean, and were certainly known to the Greeks and Ancient Egyptians. They still grow where they always grew, although they can be grown as far north as the British Isles. Roman Catholics traditionally ate lentils during Lent and it would be nice to think that the two words have a common origin. But lentil evidently derives from *lens* meaning lens, and Lent comes from *lenten* meaning spring. Yet the original meaning of *lenten* was lengthen; and since lenses, which are lentil-shaped, also make things look longer, there is probably a devious connection after all.

How long is a lentil?

And so to the highly variable group that the English call peas, which are all varieties of the single species *Pisum sativum*. One hardy group of peas—sometimes called *arvense*—are eaten dried, and are often sold as split peas. But peas are also eaten fresh, and in several forms: the marrowfats have large, wrinkled seeds, the round-seeded types are hardier, the petit pois of France are especially tender and small seeded, and the snow peas, or mangetout, are grown for their pods. Peas have been largely taken over by the frozen food industry and this is a minor tragedy, for the fresh garden pea is a thing of wonder, and as it ages, through the summer, it gradually slips into mealier guises that are all different and delectable. I refuse to eat frozen peas on principle; the thought of what has been lost is too sad.

Then there is that odd group of pulses that fruit and even flower underground: the peanut, groundnut, or monkey nut. *Archis hypogaea*, originally from South America but now grown widely in Asia, Africa and the United States, is the best known. With its 30 percent protein content and 40 to 50 percent oil content, it vies nutritionally with the soybean. Cooks treat it as a nut, rather than a pulse; but there can be few more inappropriate ways to serve such a high-calorie, high-fat food than as a predinner cocktail nibble. The peanut can be a versatile and imposing ingredient, as the cuisine of South-East Asia abundantly demonstrates; but the salted peanut, eaten between meals, must be one of the most pernicious foods on the Western scene.

Pulses under the ground

Several legumes that have been drifting in and out of cultivation in odd pockets of the world for hundreds and probably thousands of years are now recognized as crops of enormous potential. One example is the Bambarra peanut of Africa, *Voandzeia subterranea*. It has a high-protein content like *Arachis*, but contains much less oil. Its ability to grow in dry conditions is a potential boon, since a good third of the tropics is semiarid.

The winged bean from tropical Asia, *Psophocarpus tetragonolobus*, has proteinaceous seeds, pods that are said to taste like mushrooms, leaves that are said to taste like spinach, stems like asparagus, and edible tuberous roots; you can also eat the flowers. The National Academy of Sciences, Washington DC, has emphasized that the winged bean and the tepary bean, *Phaseolus acutifolius*, which can withstand extraordinary degrees of drought and which some United States and Mexican Indians still cultivate in unirrigated desert, have marvelous potential both as food for local people in hot countries and perhaps as cash-earning export crops.

Pulses are now enjoying a revival; even supermarkets stock whole herbariums of them. But the new and encouraging vogue is being marred by cynical, or at least muddle-headed, commercial opportunism. I mean, of course, the sale of textured vegetable protein, TVP, which is pulse dressed up as meat; an inferior product sold at an inflated price to people who have no need of it. Since TVPs are now big business, but for no other reason, they deserve a brief discussion.

A Note on TVPs

Textured vegetable protein, which is bean—usually soybean—protein spun into fibers like nylon and then bundled to resemble muscle, has been on sale in unobtrusive packages in vegetarian food stores for some decades. But in the 1950s and 1960s, a combination of bumper harvests and agricultural technology transformed pastoral farming into intensive factory farming; and so long as meat could be produced as if from a conveyor belt, there was no conceivable call for ersatz, except, of course, from vegetarians, who, in the old unsophisticated days, seemed to favor imitations of meat (for example, the ubiquitous nut cutlet, and even, in a final flight of fancy, nutmeat pâté carefully sculpted into the shape of turkeys for Christmas) even though they rejected meat itself.

Bean fibers that resemble muscle

By the 1970s, and especially after the disastrous year of 1973, when crops failed in four continents at once, it became clear that meat production could not be expanded indefinitely. But the idea that people needed to eat vast amounts of protein had become well established; indeed, the world's food shortage was widely considered to be, specifically, a protein gap. Protein in those far off days was equated with meat; and if meat was in short supply, what were people to do?

In addition, meat sales had boomed in the 1950s and 1960s, not least because meat had become relatively cheap and people do like it. Nutritionists, farmers and government departments, however, managed to conclude not simply that people buy what they like when there is a lot of it about, but that human beings like meat above all other kinds of food. Some nutritionists argued, in romantic vein, that human beings had inherited the blood lust of their hypothetically predatory ancestors and would eat meat, meat and more meat as long as they could afford it. Although this idea is little more than pleasant fantasy, it caught on; it fitted the economic mood of the time, and scientific hypotheses are heavily influenced by economic mood. Thus to the idea that people needed meat was added the idea that they would demand meat if ever it was in short supply; and just in case anyone should feel that they would happily eat baked beans on toast instead, nutritionists clamored to assure them that animal protein was the only proper thing and that to serve their families with lesser foods was irresponsible.

Our predatory ancestors

And so by the beginning of the 1970s the time was ripe to take TVPs—ersatz meat—out of the health food stores and launch them on to the mass market. The minor irritation known as consumer resistance was easily overcome. The aesthetes (including many food writers) who said ersatz was nasty were told they were irresponsible; for the technologists had come up with a world-saver, and the complaints of gourmets were merely effete. The housewives' objections to this newfangled stuff

Beans by many other names

were dismissed as old-fashioned prejudice. Textured vegetable pro- "One of the great food developments"? teins, said Georgetown University's Professor Aaron M. Altschul when Rank Hovis McDougall launched their ersatz *Protena* in Britain in 1974, were "one of the great food developments of all time."

The idea was irresistible to the dietitians, who aspire to be scientists and can influence what people eat. Ersatz was introduced into American school meals in 1971 and by 1973 it was being consumed by the thousand ton. Today, more and more schoolchildren's meals include textured vegetable protein.

Yet the whole idea was never more than nonsense. It simply is not true that people need vast amounts of protein. If you put protein-rich, soybean-based TVP into a pie to extend the meat (to use the technologists' term), then you merely provide the consumer with a surplus of protein; and since humans cannot store protein, they simply burn off the surplus as fuel. Nutritionally, it would be just as effective to extend the meat with potato, to make, for instance, a Cornish pasty; or to extend it with cereal, as in haggis or bacon sandwiches, or with unprocessed pulses, as in the recipes in this chapter. TVPs are also economic nonsense, for although they are cheaper than meat they are nothing like as cheap as potato, bread, Freaks of marketing or unprocessed pulse; if ever they are, it is only through a freak of marketing.

People survived before the post-war boom in meat consumption; indeed, if they did not die from war or infection, they were healthier than we are today. Cooks extended meat in a thousand delectable ways, according to principles that I endeavor to describe in this book. It is astonishing that anyone could ever have believed that the grisly, ersatz-flavored TVP was ever necessary; and even more astonishing that people not only believe it, but sanction its use in their children's food and buy it for their own consumption.

Or rather it would be astonishing but for two considerations. First, that many people in Britain and the United States have already forgotten the old cooking skills, and prefer the convenience that processed food seems to offer. They also seem to have no knowledge, or only a folk memory, of the traditional ways of eating, for if they had they would see the nonsense of ersatz.

Second, the ersatz boom shows the power of big business, and of the propaganda it can disseminate. Soybeans, the basis of the ersatz industry, have been grown in the United States for decades, not for their protein but for their oil. The protein was almost an embarrassment. It could be sold off for animal feed, but since fishmeal was until recently ridiculously cheap there was not much profit in that. Henry Ford was Line your car with TVP among the industrialists who realized the potential for texturized soybean protein, but he wanted it for car upholstery, not for ersatz meat. The events of the late 1960s and early 1970s—the continuing protein gap myth, the end of the bumper harvests and of the meat boom, the energy crises, and the growth in food processing generally—provided an almost miraculous opportunity not only to flood the food market with an otherwise embarrassing surplus but also to persuade governments and public alike that this was a responsible thing to do.

So far they have got away with it; but I hope not indefinitely.

Theme I

Texture one way, flavor another

Pulses are mealy things, which usually have a skin; if you cook them just enough to make them tender without stirring them too much the seeds remain whole and discrete and provide a range of textures from the big mealy butter beans or more chewy broad beans down to the small, almost crunchy brown lentils. But if you cook them a little more, or break them up with a spoon, you can produce an additional range of textures from the slightly disintegrating *fagioli all'uccelletto* of Italy, through *dhals* and *hummus* to purees and thick soups. And if you stick pulses together, with or without pounding them first, you can produce a range of cakes and fritters and puddings and *falafels*.

Because pulses are essentially bland, as well as mealy, they are ideal vehicles for spices, herbs and sauces, and because they grow worldwide in one form or another, they have been integrated into almost every great cuisine. Thus pulses provide the means by which to create idiom; with just small shifts of spicing the same dish of beans can be pushed into an Italian, Mexican, French, English, Middle Eastern or Indian mode. Pulses are to the cook what clay is to the sculptor. They are infinitely obliging; you can mold them as you will.

Beans need soaking before cooking. Soak them overnight in plenty of water and discard any that float. A quicker way is to bring the beans slowly to a boil, then turn off the heat and let them swell in the hot water for an hour. Drain the beans, cover them with fresh water and simmer until tender. To test, remove a few beans and blow on them; if the skins burst they are done.

The following recipes are organized to move down through the range of textures, drifting into different idioms along the way.

SPICY BEANS

This is modified from a recipe for Mexican beans. The simplified but effective spicing makes the dish presentable in a vast range of contexts; I have, for example, served it with well-cooked shoulder of lamb, pot roasts of beef and as part of a vegetarian meal. Note the use of flour, only as a thickener, but showing yet again the affinity of pulse and grain.

Serves 4

1 lb (½ kg) red kidney beans
1 large onion
4 fat garlic cloves
2 teaspoons flour
1 teaspoon ground cumin
1 teaspoon chili powder
1 tablespoon corn oil
1 drop Tabasco sauce
A pinch of salt
Freshly ground black pepper

Soak and drain the beans. Cover them with fresh water and simmer with the finely chopped onion and garlic until the beans are tender but still intact, which takes about 1 hour. Then drain again.

Mix the flour, cumin, chili powder, oil and Tabasco to a smooth paste and stir into the beans. Cover with water, add the salt, sprinkle generously with black pepper and cook, covered, for a further 45 minutes until the sauce is thick.

FAGIOLI ALL'UCCELLETTO

Similar in conception to the recipe for Spicy Beans but in a different idiom.
Serves 4

1 lb (½ kg) navy beans, soaked
½ lb (240 g) beefsteak or plum tomatoes, fresh or canned
¾ cup olive oil
3 to 4 bay leaves
Generous sprigs fresh rosemary and sage
A pinch of salt

Drain the beans and simmer in fresh water until tender but not mushy—40 minutes should be long enough. Drain again and add the tomatoes (chopped if fresh), olive oil, bay leaves, other herbs and salt. Simmer, covered, very slowly for about 1 hour until the sauce is very thick and the beans are on the point of disintegration. Remove the bay leaves and the herb stems and serve.

DHAL

In India the pulse porridges known as *dhal* are a ubiquitous accompaniment of rice dishes and breads. Scooped up in a *chapati*, they provide an outstanding example of the nutritionally unimpeachable grain plus pulse theme.

Beans by many other names

Dhals are made from grams, lentils or chickpeas and can be spiced at will. Here is a straightforward version intended for mung beans, although other grams or lentils will serve as well.
Serves 4

1 lb ($\frac{1}{2}$ kg) mung beans
2 onions
2 fat garlic cloves
1-inch (2.5 cm) piece fresh ginger root
4 tablespoons corn oil
$\frac{1}{2}$ teaspoon turmeric
$\frac{1}{2}$ teaspoon ground cumin
1 teaspoon ground coriander
A pinch of salt
A handful of Chinese parsley, chopped

Soak the mung beans for at least 1 hour. Drain, cover with fresh water, add the salt and simmer for about 45 minutes. While the mung are cooking chop the onions, garlic and ginger and fry in the oil. Add the turmeric when the onion is well softened, and the more delicate ground cumin and coriander when the onion is almost melted. Cook for a further 3 minutes, stirring all the while.

Turn the oniony-spicy mixture into the *dhal*, just as the mung beans are approaching tenderness. Serve garnished with the Chinese parsley.

SAG DHAL

By way of diversion on this journey from the whole bean to the puree, I must mention *sag dhal*, the magical combination of pulse and spinach. In fact a separate recipe is unnecessary, although a touch of fenugreek cooked alongside the turmeric and onion is a pleasant addition.

After you have added the final spices in the recipe for *dhal*, simply stuff the saucepan with finely chopped spinach—1 pound ($\frac{1}{2}$ kg) goes a long way. This will wilt in the heat and after a few minutes can be stirred into the *dhal*. You could, if you like, at this point stir in a small carton of yogurt. The dish is now worthy of any guest; it is low in fat, has adequate protein, high fiber and a sharp, coherent flavor.

At the very simplest, the mealier pulses (yellow or red lentils, white or green peas or lima beans) may simply be boiled to the point of mushiness,

then drained and peppered and pounded or sieved; and the resulting puree is an admirable foil for sausage or pork; contrasting in texture, taking up fat, and offering no competition in flavor.

In England, traditionally, old broad beans were boiled, pushed through a sieve and served on toast, on which, in this context, it is even reasonable to risk a little butter; and scrambled egg is another recognized accompaniment. Broad beans were also boiled in mutton broth, then pounded to a puree and served on coarse oatcakes; a robust and nourishing variation of the grain-pulse theme, exactly comparable to *dhal* with *chapati*.

HUMMUS WITH TAHINA

Hummus is a Semitic invention, a puree of chickpeas often flavored with the paste of sesame seeds known as *tahina*, which is available from most delicatessens. *Hummus* is traditionally served with pita, but it can be accompanied by almost any unleavened bread. It is often used as a first course and the quantities served are small.
Serves 4

$\frac{2}{3}$ cup chickpeas
Juice of 2 lemons
2 fat garlic cloves
A pinch of salt
2 to 3 tablespoons *tahina*
1 tablespoon olive oil

The Garnish
Virgin olive oil
Cayenne pepper
Chopped parsley

Chickpeas can be tough; soaking overnight is not too long and simmering for 2 hours is minimal. Drain them when they are cooked, but save the liquor. Put 4 tablespoons of the liquor into a blender with the lemon juice, garlic and salt and, as the blades are whirling, alternately feed in the cooked chickpeas and the *tahina*. If it clogs, add more liquor and the olive oil. The result should be a smooth, creamy purée.

Serve the *hummus* in bowls with a whorl of virgin olive oil, a dusting of cayenne and a sprinkling of parsley.

What excites me about *hummus* is not simply that it is a pleasant and easy starter but that it is a form of unlimited potential; a pulse porridge which is nourishing and flavorsome on its own account but can absorb almost any flavor (or additional nourishment) you care to impose on it. Oat porridge, as favored by the Scots, was traditionally left to bubble all night; porridges of the tougher pulses could similarly be left, to be served for breakfast on toast or oatcakes. The Arabs seized on sesame paste because it was there; but the infinite range of *misos* are an obvious substitute; and any bean could theoretically stand in for chickpeas.

So we arrive at lima bean *hummus* flavored with *miso* and served on oatcakes for breakfast; an Arab form using American and Japanese ingredients and served in the manner of Scotland; pulse, cereal and fungus combined. Outlandish but logical; and it works.

BLACK BEAN SOUP

From the southern states of America. You must start making the soup the day before you intend serving it.
Serves 6 to 8

1 lb (½ kg) black beans
1 ham bone or chicken carcass
2 bay leaves
10 peppercorns
2 onions
2 garlic cloves
1 celery stalk
1 leek
Salt
Pepper
4 tablespoons dry sherry
1 hard-boiled egg, optional
1 lemon, optional

Soak the beans in cold water overnight. The next day drain the beans and put them into a large saucepan with 2½ quarts (2 liters) of water, the ham bone or chicken carcass, bay leaves, peppercorns, chopped onions, garlic, celery and leek. Bring to a boil, removing any scum as it rises. Reduce the heat, cover the pan and simmer for 3 hours, skimming occasionally.

Remove the bone or carcass and the bay leaves. Blend or sieve the soup and let it get quite cold in a bowl. When cold remove the grease from the top and return the soup to a clean pan. If the soup is too thick stir in a little more water. Add plenty of black pepper, and a little salt, if necessary (this depends on whether you have used a ham bone or

chicken carcass for the stock).

Bring the soup to a boil. Pour the soup into bowls, add a tablespoon of sherry to each bowl and garnish with thin slices of hard-boiled egg and lemon, if you wish.

Theme II
The pulse cake

So much for pureeing; but once a pulse has been broken up it can be stuck together again to form a pudding or cake.

Such pulse cakes appear in virtually every great cuisine. They can be held together simply by the starch of their own mealiness, or sometimes by a dash of grain or *besan* (chickpea) flour. Their texture can be varied from the porridgy to the crunchy, both by varying the kind of pulse used and by slight variations in the cooking. In pease pudding, for example, the pulse is boiled almost to the point of mushiness; but the beans used in *falafels* are not boiled at all—they are merely soaked to soften them, pounded to a paste, shaped into patties and then fried. They can be spiced or herbed in any way you please (or not at all) and thus can express any idiom, from English peasant to grand Indian. Pulse cakes can be eaten with bread as a light lunch or with curries and vegetables for an Indian or Indonesian banquet. They can merely be boiled, or finished by dry frying, shallow frying, or deep frying; and when they are fried they can be spiced again.

In short, the pulse pudding or cake is one of the great forms in cooking. Here are a few simple and classic examples to give a hint of the range. Once the principle is grasped, the recipes write themselves.

PEASE PUDDING

This dish is designed to accompany boiled meat; it is primitive and easy to make but fine cooking.
Serves 4

Scant 2 cups dried peas or fresh, mature peas with a mealy texture
A pinch of salt
A few sprigs of mint or thyme

If the peas are dried they should be soaked for at least 3 hours or all day if that is more convenient.

Tie the soaked peas or fresh peas loosely in cheesecloth together with the salt and herb sprigs (mint or thyme are not mandatory, but they go well with old peas). Put the peas in with the meat to boil alongside. At least 30 minutes' simmering is desirable but timing hardly matters; this is a dish for the long, slow simmer. The peas swell (taking up the broth of the meat) until they are constrained and finally pressed together by the cloth. You finish up with a tight, round pudding that you untie and pull apart with forks.

RED LENTIL CAKES
Such cakes as these are unendingly versatile. I boiled some lentils one Sunday afternoon and made some cakes to serve with Sunday dinner and we had the rest with jam for breakfast the following morning.

Lentil cakes can be laced with virtually any spice or herb or carrot shreds, or they can be left unflavored and allowed simply to take up whatever sauce you care to bathe them in, from spiced yogurt to mutton broth. Or you can put some flavors into the cakes and others into the sauce and so strike a counterpoint between the two.
Serves 4

2 cups red lentils
A pinch of salt

Wash the lentils and put them in a saucepan with the salt and plenty of water and simmer for 15 to 20 minutes or until the lentils are on the brink of mushiness but still *al dente*.

Drain the lentils in a sieve and let them dry and cool a little. Take handfuls of the lentils and mold them into cakes about $\frac{3}{4}$ inch (2 cm) thick. They are not strong but hold together well enough. Dry fry the cakes in a non-stick pan.

LENTIL CAKES INDIAN STYLE
These cakes are a worthy accompaniment to any curry, or, served with *chapatis*, make a frugal but pleasant lunch.
Serves 4

$\frac{2}{3}$ cup *urad* lentils
$\frac{1}{2}$-inch (1 cm) piece fresh ginger root, sliced
1 garlic clove

$\frac{1}{2}$ teaspoon cayenne pepper
$\frac{1}{2}$ teaspoon ground coriander
A pinch of salt
2 teaspoons chopped Chinese parsley
Oil for deep frying

The Yogurt Mixture
2 cups yogurt
A pinch of cayenne pepper
A pinch of salt

Wash the lentils thoroughly and soak them in cold water overnight. Drain the lentils and put them in a blender with the ginger, garlic, cayenne pepper, ground coriander, salt and Chinese parsley. Add water a little at a time and blend until the mixture is reduced to a smooth puree.

Heat the oil and drop in tablespoonfuls of the lentil puree. Do not overcrowd the pan. Fry the lentil cakes for 2 minutes or until they are puffed up and golden brown. Drain on paper towels.

Whip the yogurt in a bowl. Mix in the cayenne pepper and salt. Put in the lentil cakes and turn them to mix well. Serve immediately.

FALAFEL
Falafel is traditionally served in envelopes of pita with *tahina* (sesame seed paste) dip. Dried broad beans of the kind used in the Middle East are available from Greek or Italian delicatessens.
Serves 4

1 generous cup dried white broad beans
1 large onion
2 garlic cloves
1 cup Chinese parsley
1 scant teaspoon ground cumin
1 scant teaspoon ground coriander
Black pepper
Cayenne pepper
A pinch of salt
$\frac{1}{2}$ teaspoon baking powder

Soak the beans in water overnight or for 3 hours in water in which they have been brought to a boil.

Slice the onion and garlic, chop the Chinese parsley, and puree them together with the soaked beans in a blender. Add the spices, salt and baking powder as you go to ensure their even distribution.

Put the whole mixture aside for an hour in the refrigerator. Then form it into little cakes and either deep fry them or shallow fry them in oil until their outsides are puffed up and they become crisp and brown.

Theme III
Pulses as meat extenders

The food technologists invented the term "meat extenders" to describe textured vegetable protein, or TVP. Since the beginning of time cooks have been extending meat according to exactly the same principle and with far more pleasing results, using potatoes, bread, pulses and fungi. Pulses are supreme meat extenders, with their *al dente* contrasting texture, their bland flavor and (soybean and peanuts aside) their fatlessness; and of course whenever they appear on the same dish as meat, or even in the same meal (as *hummus* might precede a meat dish, or a sweet lentil cake might follow one) they are acting as meat extenders. But there are a few classic dishes of great distinction in which the specific conception is to match meat and pulse. Note, incidentally, that meat is used far more sparingly in the classic dishes than in the modern TVP casserole. There is no need to disguise the pristine pulse; the meat is used merely as a garnish.

LENTILS WITH LIVER AND YOGURT
Here is an engaging invention from a friend of mine who likes lentils and has a feel for them.
Serves 2

1 onion
1 carrot
$\frac{2}{3}$ cup red lentils
$\frac{2}{3}$ cup brown rice
1 bay leaf
A pinch of salt
Black pepper
$\frac{1}{4}$ lb (120 g) liver
Oil
A pinch of dried mint
$\frac{1}{2}$ teaspoon ground mustard seed
2 tablespoons yogurt
Watercress sprigs

Slice the onion and carrot thinly and put them into a saucepan with the lentils, rice, bay leaf, the salt and a sprinkling of pepper. Pour in 2 cups of water and bring to a boil. Cover the pan and simmer for 45 minutes. Keep your eye on it and top up with more water if the mixture becomes too dry; there should be just a hint of moisture by the time the rice and lentils are tender without the need to drain.

Slice the liver thinly and cook it in a frying pan in a very little oil—the idea is to make it exude and then lightly cook in its own juices—together with the mint. Take the pan off the heat. Stir the mustard into the yogurt; then turn the mixture into the slightly cooled liver.

Make a nest of the lentils and rice and put the liver mixture in the middle. Decorate with watercress and serve.

ROAST LAMB AND BEANS
The changing nature of pulses as the season progresses is part of their appeal; lamb is served with fresh green peas or beans in summer and perhaps as boiled mutton and pease pudding as the peas grow mealier and, in winter, on a bed of dried beans. Here is my version of a Provençal recipe which is not so much a dish as an ecosystem; easy, opulent, cheap and courtesy of the bean.
Serves 4 to 6

1 shoulder of lamb
2 teaspoons ground cumin
4 to 5 garlic cloves
6 medium onions
$1\frac{1}{4}$ lb ($\frac{3}{4}$ kg) potatoes
2 large carrots
1 parsnip
1 medium turnip
A pinch of salt
Black pepper
1 lb ($\frac{1}{2}$ kg) beans, big white, navy, lima or red kidney, soaked
2 tablespoons yogurt (optional)
Watercress or parsley

Rub the cumin well into the skin of the lamb. Make little nicks in the surface and tuck in the garlic cloves—halved to make them go further. Put the meat into a roasting pan and place in a 375°F (190°C) oven. If the shoulder is a fair size—3 pounds ($1\frac{1}{2}$ kg) plus—then 2 hours is not too long. Baste the roast frequently in its own exuding juices. Put the whole peeled onions into the

Beans by many other names

roasting pan about 30 minutes before the meat is ready. Baste the onions, too; they should be caramelized and soft but not mushy.

Scrub the potatoes, carrots and parsnip and peel the turnip. Cut the vegetables into chunks and put them into a casserole with the salt and a good sprinkling of pepper and about $\frac{1}{2}$ inch (1 cm) of water. Put the casserole in the oven underneath the meat for $1\frac{1}{2}$ hours. Baste the vegetables in the pan juices now and again to avoid too much browning.

Drain the beans and boil them in plenty of water for about 40 minutes or until tender but *al dente*. Remove the pan from the heat and drain.

To serve, spread the beans in a thick layer on a large platter. Drain (reserve the liquid) and arrange the vegetable chunks on top. Slice the meat and arrange it and the onions on top of the vegetables.

Put the roasting pan on top of the stove, pour in the reserved liquid from the vegetables and bring to the simmer. Add the yogurt, if you are using it, and stir to form a rich, sharp gravy.

Pour over enough gravy to just moisten the dish and garnish with sprigs of watercress or parsley.

The affinity of pulse with pig manifests itself in a hundred contexts: the flavor of pork and bacon, and the saltiness and fattiness, are admirably balanced by the pulse's mealiness. Pease pudding, a traditional dish which was often boiled alongside a bacon hock, provides a fine example of the marriage. Here is another classic example, in quite a different vein, to make the point.

BAKED BEANS WITH APPLE

In this derivative of the famous Boston baked beans the ratio of protein to energy is near enough perfect (the sweet, calorific molasses and calorific crackling are balanced by the protein of the beans and pork; the beans and apple provide fiber) and the bitter-sweet combination of mustard, molasses and tomato is typically North American.

The inclusion of apple is something I tried one day partly because apples were on hand but also because apples go so well with pork; and it worked.

Traditionally, baked beans are cooked for up to nine hours but I find the shorter cooking time adequate.
Serves 6

1 lb ($\frac{1}{2}$ kg) red kidney beans
1 apple
1 onion
3 fat garlic cloves
$\frac{3}{4}$-inch (2 cm) piece fresh ginger root
Oil
2 large beefsteak tomatoes or 1 cup canned tomatoes, drained
$\frac{1}{4}$ to $\frac{1}{2}$ lb (120 to 240 g) pork belly, with crackling
1 tablespoon molasses
2 teaspoons ground mustard seed (freshly ground, if possible)
A pinch of salt
Black pepper

Soak the beans for at least 3 hours. Drain and transfer to a deep casserole. Chop the apple (leave the skin and seeds) and gently sweat and fry it with the sliced onion, chopped garlic and ginger root in very little oil in a frying pan until all is mushy. Then throw in the finely chopped tomatoes.

Cut the skin off the pork and put it on one side. Remove any bones and cut the flesh into small slivers about $1\frac{1}{2}$ by $\frac{1}{2}$ inch (3.5 by 1 cm). Add these pork bits to the beans, then add the contents of the frying pan plus the molasses, mustard, salt and a good sprinkling of black pepper. Pour in enough boiling water to cover and stir. Put the lid on the casserole and put it on the middle shelf of a 400°F (200°C) oven.

After about 1 hour the beans should be cooked and the gravy nicely blended. Move the casserole to the bottom of the oven. Put the pork skin on the rack near the top of the oven and stand a roasting pan on the rack beneath to catch the drips. After 30 minutes the skin should be nicely crackled.

Break the crackling into small bits, scatter over the top of the beans and serve immediately.

Beasts of the field

The eating of animals and the keeping of them are the most dramatic things that human beings do in the cause of self-nourishment. Meat eating can have profound effects on human well-being, sometimes saving life but perhaps, at the other end of the scale, being largely responsible for the "diseases of affluence" that now account for most human deaths in the "developed" world.

The hunting and raising of beasts has determined, in large part, the course not only of cultural development but also of human evolution: we are the kind of beasts we are, with deft fingers and agile brains, partly because our ancestors pitted their wits against their fellow beasts, and we occupy almost every terrestrial niche on earth (including those where plants will not grow) partly because they succeeded. Yet the fact that we kill to eat, and the fact that we may subjugate every detail of a beast's biology to make that killing easier and more fruitful, is a kind of indictment. If human beings can exist only by inflicting pain and by slaughter, are they themselves entitled to survival? Have they the right to impose their will so totally on their fellow creatures?

This last question is important not simply as an ethical debating point but also for practical reasons. Human beings are eminently capable of what George Orwell called double-think; they may dote on their own children, yet ignore or even oversee the deaths of others. But societies that indulge in such selectiveness (and there are few in history that have not) seem to me not only to be morally flawed but also to be politically precarious. For simple reasons of personal survival it seems dangerous to overlook violence in our own society, whether the violence is inflicted on other human beings or on animals. Certainly it has often been argued that animals do not suffer; but the same has been said at times about the Blacks, the Irish, the working classes, Poles, or, in recent history, the people of Vietnam. The argument has never been more than an excuse and it is just possible that societies that depend on such excuses contain the seeds of their own destruction.

Some people adopt a position of extreme moral rigor. They argue, with the Buddhists and some Hindus, that all life is one and that it is an offence against life—nature, God—to take other lives. There are monks who sweep the ground ahead of them for fear of treading upon ants, and perfectly respectable middle-class Englishmen who advocate the elimination of the human race to make room for our fellow creatures. Such extremism is easily dismissed as lunatic (albeit attractive, at least in the case of the earnest monks). But the vegans take a position only a little down the scale and cannot be so easily dismissed: they argue that human beings can survive without slaughter, so why should they not? Further along the scale, the lacto-ovo vegetarians contrive to take only what the beasts do not need, yet remain among the healthiest people in the world.

Double-think

Monks who sweep the ground

91

Beasts of the field

If human beings really can thrive without incommoding their fellow creatures, how can they justify the suffering implicit in husbandry and slaughter? I find the vegan-vegetarian argument powerful; yet I do not think it is right.

The inescapable facts are that human beings exist and that no species, human or otherwise, can exist without interfering with the lives of other creatures. This interference may, in some instances, be beneficial, but it also inevitably involves competition to the point of death. Simply refusing directly to kill does not alter the fact: in order to plow, you must destroy the natural woodland that once would have harbored a thousand species. If you want to harvest and finally to eat what you have grown, then you must keep the birds and mice at bay while the crop is in the fields, and the rats and weevils after harvest; and even if you do not directly kill these beasts, you do affect their reproduction—the lives of their actual or potential offspring—by denying them their food supply. To some extent the extremists are right; the only way to avoid destroying some of your fellow creatures is to commit suicide, provided you also arrange burial in some hygienic spot.

Competing unto death

Lacto-ovo vegetarians, for all that they express sincere interest in animal welfare (and, indeed, have influenced many reforms in the treatment of animals), have achieved a logically untenable position. You cannot obtain milk from cows unless you allow the cow to produce calves; and since pregnancy in cows lasts nine months, and lactation peaks about four months after parturition and then falls off for the next six months or so, dairy farmers have found they get the best return by having their cows impregnated once a year.

But a cow may live for at least 20 years, in the course of which she could produce about 18 calves (although it is probably stretching things to get a cow pregnant after 14 years of age). If you do not slaughter her or her calves, then by the time she is in her final lactation you would have to support a herd of 20 cattle; and that is assuming that all her offspring were prevented from reproducing (which is itself a cruel frustration of nature). If the offspring were allowed to reproduce then their numbers would be astronomical by the time the sacred old cow staggered through her final lactations. If dairy farming were practiced without slaughter—of the superfluous offspring and finally of the cow herself—then we would need to fill the United States and Europe with cattle, just to keep Britons in milk. Although it is superficially agreeable, dairy farming is as steeped in blood as the fields of Culloden. Yet there is no conceivable alternative if we want to drink milk: and once the calves or old cows are dead it seems to me perverse not to eat them; perhaps even sinful simply to bury them, and to sanction such waste.

When vegetarianism is perverse

Again, in the care of animals—whether the welfare of individual beasts or the conservation of species—there are sins of omission as well as of commission. In the past 40,000 to 100,000 years, the human species has profoundly influenced most of the major habitats in all six continents. Among the large mammals in particular, the remaining fauna is a thin relic from the Pleistocene era, when there were camels, giraffes and elephants in the United States and rhinoceroses and lions in Europe. The animals that are left are precariously placed and have no chance whatever of surviving the next few hundred years unless they are not simply "protected" (from poachers or road builders) but actively managed. Indeed, one way to kill off a species—any species—is to put a fence around what you consider to be its territory, put a notice up saying "wildlife reserve," and then clear off. Precisely because the area is circumscribed, its ecology will inevitably change; and among the more obvious and immediate changes will be that some species overbreed, or that the nonbreeding adults fail to die and so compete with the young and with lactating mothers. The great packs of lions that have sometimes roamed in African parks like wolves, slaughtering everything that moves, and the overfecund, neurotic elephants, digging and tearing the trees, are examples. Presumably such fluctuations in numbers have always occurred, but temporary instabilities can be accommodated when beasts have a whole continent at their disposal. In the sometimes vast but inevitably circumscribed area of the national park, irregularities in the breeding cycles of major species can lead to permanent detriment; to loss of species or the creation of deserts. If human beings actively care about the fate of animals within sanctuaries then they must at times help adjust their population structure: to fulfil the task that was once fulfilled by a thousand outside influences. "Adjusting population structure" includes killing redundant beasts.

> Don't fence them in

The cautionary note sounded by some vegetarians and religions should be heeded: animals should be regarded as sentient beings, with rights. But the simple idea that all animal life is sacred is an insufficient guide to action because it does not take account of the facts: the fact that human beings exist, and that their existence inevitably interferes with the lives of other beasts; and that the continued existence of other beasts largely depends upon active human intervention in their affairs. Presumably most people want human beings to survive, and I am not alone in thinking that the well-being of other creatures is also important. So what attitude can we take to animals, that will take account both of our needs and of theirs?

> "Thou shalt not kill"?

The idea that does seem to me to meet the case is that of guardianship. Human beings are influential, whether they like it or not. They are stuck with enormous power, whether they like it or not: the power to destroy their own species, in a dozen different ways, and to destroy most of the large mammals in passing; and the power (provided they exert considerable subtlety) to ensure their own and their fellow creatures' long-term survival. The conditional clause that traditionally underlies such seigneurial power is that of *noblesse oblige*; and to adopt the superficially benign Hindu philosophy—which regards cows as sacred but makes no provision for their upkeep—is, I think, irresponsible. We must at least take responsibility for killing some beasts at some time and there seems to be no defensible reason for not eating them afterward.

> No power without responsibility

Such argument might justify culling as an agent of wildlife conservation; but does it justify husbandry, the officious production of beasts for no other purpose than to produce food?

> Culling is acceptable, but what of husbandry?

There are two answers to this. The first is that in the real world the difference between wildlife management and husbandry is only one of degree. We may reject some forms of husbandry on the specific grounds

Beasts of the field

of cruelty; but to reject the idea of husbandry altogether is to fall into the same kind of logical trap that, I believe, has so obviously ensnared the lacto-vegetarians. Is it better to keep sheep on the Welsh hills or to let the hills become barren, giving way first to scrub and finally, in a few centuries, to forest? To press for the extinction of the present flocks seems to me perverse; but to allow those flocks to go feral, as some vegetarians advocate, would be to subject them to an appalling fate, as the experience of Soay sheep on the St Kilda islands demonstrates. Those sheep were left behind by Neolithic farmers. As erstwhile domestic animals, they have lost the ability to adjust their reproductive rate to the conditions. So they breed and breed and breed, until a bad winter causes most of them to starve; and then they build up their numbers again until the next disaster. We are already far too involved in the destiny of animals to reject the idea of husbandry.

The second justification for farming beasts is that human beings are responsible also for their own survival. Other chapters have stressed that a vegan diet is possible and that a low meat diet is probably desirable. But vegans stay healthy only if they are dedicated: if they pay obsessive attention to the protein content of this and the vitamin content of that and, in particular, if they can guarantee an adequate source of vitamin B_{12}. Animal products should not be given a prima donna role in cooking, and should not be regarded as the prime source of protein; but eaten in moderation they are an admirable backstop, providing a range of vitamins, minerals and fats, and ensuring that protein intake never falls to dangerously low levels. At the present state of nutritional knowledge and sophistication it would be irresponsible to advocate veganism as a world nutritional policy, even if people would accept it.

In short, to back away from the idea that animals must be killed is merely effete; and husbandry is justified on conservational grounds as well as for human well-being.

But can the future world afford livestock? Everyone must by now know the economic arguments against keeping livestock; they even appear elsewhere in this book. You can provide many times more protein and food energy per acre or per unit of fuel energy by growing staples for human food, than by growing staples or grass for animal food. In a world in which people are already hungry and resources are already sometimes dangerously extended, it seems grotesque to use most of the finest acres of the most fertile continents for a system of food production in which 90 percent of the protein produced is squandered. Britain provides only half the food its people consume; yet if those people were vegetarian, and British agriculture adjusted accordingly, it could feed four or five times the present population. Since husbandry also involves the restriction and slaughter of animals, there seems to be no possible excuse for it.

Can the world afford livestock?

Yet it is impossible to devise a system of vegetarian agriculture that is 100 percent efficient—in which it would not be possible, with advantage, to accommodate some beasts. If an all-vegetarian Britain could feed 200 million people, then one with a well-chosen and modest assortment of livestock could feed, say, 210 million. And unless there were some beasts, then much of the vegetation would go to unnecessary

Vegetarian agriculture is inefficient

94

waste. What is wrong with present-day agriculture is not the beasts but the numbers that are kept and the ways of keeping them.

Animals have three principal roles in agriculture, and offer several bonuses. Their first role is to utilize the land—which in some countries is the greater part—that cannot be cultivated or which, if disturbed, would turn into desert or swamp: land that is too high to produce regular crops, too steep to take a tractor, too salty, too low to be drained, or in which the soil is too thin. Evolution has provided a hundred different species for such environments and the alternative to husbanding those beasts for food is simply to let the land deteriorate. In many cases—and this is one of livestock's bonuses—unruly land is improved both aesthetically and as a wildlife habitat if controlled numbers of livestock are given their rein: a classic example is the chalk grassland of much of Britain, which supports an astonishingly varied flora, and its accompanying fauna, left over from the grassland of the Ice Age. Now that the ice has retreated, the ancient grass would revert first to scrub then to forest if grazing sheep did not keep it short and destroy the seedling trees. Iceland itself, still an Ice Age country, now has an economy largely based on sheep, which not only graze in the hills during the long days of the short summers but also on the seaweed along the shores. There is no vegetarian alternative to such husbandry.

Maintaining ancient grass

The second role of livestock is as scavengers. Every cropping system produces some waste or at some time leaves patches of land idle; and human beings, who have high aesthetic aspirations, prefer to throw away deformed or wormy things, however theoretically nourishing they may be. In addition, Britons are said to throw away 25 percent of their food—after it has reached the kitchen; and since my family has started keeping chickens, and saving food refuse separately for them, I find that statistic quite believable. Americans may throw away less than this, but only because they eat more processed food; the waste takes place before the food arrives in the kitchen. Yet all this waste food—crops of late turnips, windfall apples, and the mountains and mountains of food refuse—is potentially nourishing; and beasts such as chickens and pigs, which are now fed on custom-grown barley, are very happy to eat it. Indeed, pigs and domestic poultry are omnivorous, like humans, and you cannot raise them on food which could not theoretically nourish a human being; but since human beings throw away at least one-third of all they grow, there is plenty of room for scavengers.

Room for scavengers

The third essential property of livestock is the one that causes most disquiet: that they can eat their way through vast amounts of staples. Yields of crops depend on weather, and thus are unpredictable; so countries that aspire to self-reliance are advised to grow more than they need. Even though they may keep some grain in store, as Joseph advised the Ancient Egyptians to do, they should strive to produce, say, 10 or 20 percent more than they need just in case the frosts come late or the rain fails to fall. Yet in most years, most well-organized countries do achieve their agricultural targets; so in most years the self-reliant country would produce a grain, pulse and potato surplus, and in some years would produce an enormous surplus; all this, simply for insurance. But what should be done with surplus? That is the perennial problem of

Beasts of the field

agriculture; but it is certainly less wasteful to feed it to livestock than to burn it. Thus, livestock serves as a reserve, flexible population, able to smooth the inevitable fluctuations in production.

Beasts as reserve population

The fault in present Western agriculture is not simply that it produces too many beasts but that it has so completely reversed the emphasis of livestock production. Animals are not required simply to soak up the surplus grain produced by agricultures designed to feed people; they have become the *raison d'être* of agriculture and the chief recipients of grain. The grain-consuming role should be secondary to the first two roles, those of marginal grazer and scavenger. Thus it is advisable to have grain or grain-based compound feed in reserve when raising pigs or poultry on household scraps or municipal swill, because swill tends to be unpredictable both in amount and in quality; it is advisable, too, to use grain to feed hill sheep in winter, because if the farmer does not support them then he will not have enough sheep to make full use of the summer grass. Hence, judicious use of feed grain can be thrifty, because it can help the farmer to use livestock to exploit other food sources. But the law in Western countries tends to discourage household chicken-keeping and the use of swill for pigs, partly for health reasons that are only to a small extent justified, and partly because it is administratively much simpler to raise birds and beasts entirely on manufactured, grain-based feed, and to throw alternative feeds on the scrap heap. Thus the argument is not simply that we should keep fewer beasts, and certainly not that we should keep no beasts at all, but that beasts should be used only to abet the cause of rational agriculture—in which role they would increase the number of people that a given agriculture could feed. At present the biological assets of livestock are largely ignored, and the beasts are used not to increase the overall biological efficiency of agriculture but primarily to increase the amount of money flowing into farming, and hence to increase profits. Used in this way, livestock compete with human beings for resources.

Discouraging swill

Of course, if Western agriculture did use beasts only in these rational roles then they would produce far fewer than they do now, perhaps only a half, perhaps only a third; it is worth pointing out, however, that China in the 1960s had as many hogs as the United States, even though grain was in desperately short supply for many years and could not be diverted for pigs. Yet there are sound nutritional reasons for thinking that a meat intake reduced by a half or two-thirds would do the average Westerner a lot of good. Such a decrease need not reduce his present 12 percent protein intake, which could be maintained simply by eating more (unrefined) grain and pulse and less (refined) sugar; a shift that would be well worthwhile for reasons that have nothing to do with protein.

Plenty of pigs in China

But the prime reason for thinking that a reversion to livestock's traditional and rational roles would be no bad thing is that the main function of meat is, after all, to provide flavor; and beasts that have been raised on varied diets and at a relaxed pace tend to be far more flavorsome than those bred specifically for rapid growth and raced from conception to slaughter. Indeed, the modern broiler chickens are almost devoid of flavor, except for the little they may pick up from the burnt

Flavoring chicken with chicken flavor

Top, *this pâté, although here obscured by bacon, is made largely with spinach: its moist fibrousness soaks up the meat juices.*
Left, *brawn, usually made from head meat, is held together by gelatin.*
Right, *under the bacon is another pâté—pork with sugar and spices.*

Cockie-leekie contains a lot of meat—chicken
and brisket or pork—but it should be made
primarily from old beasts. To make it with
custom-grown broilers or young beef would be
aesthetically unsound.

skin or fat. They have become mere vehicles of increasingly bizarre sauces and there is a healthy trade in bouillon cubes designed to impart an albeit crude suggestion of poultry flavor. If meat cannot be produced with flavor, then there is no point in producing it at all. Small delicious roasts and poultry are far, far preferable to great watery hunks of tasteless flesh.

In addition, intensive production in factory farms sacrifices two more of animals' incidental assets: that they fertilize the fields and that they have intrinsic aesthetic merit. Intensive livestock units are usually cleaned out with high-pressure hoses: the dung is thus reduced to a slurry, far too wet and cold to decay rapidly. In such form it cannot easily be used as a fertilizer; instead, it is a pollutant. Free-range animals are a pleasure to look at; and, as with downland sheep, help to maintain fine landscape. The intensive piggery or factory farm appears even uglier if you gaze upon the languishing beasts inside than if you just look at its blank outside walls.

So twenty-first-century rational farmers will find room for plenty of beasts, although fewer than we have now. But what manner of beasts?

Livestock fall into two broad categories. The exploiters of marginal land are the specialist herbivores, who do not simply digest the food they eat but also ferment it with the aid of bacteria living in their gut. Above all (thanks to these bacteria's enzymes), they are able to utilize cellulose, nature's commonest organic compound, as a source of energy, which human beings cannot do. Food that for the human being is merely fibrous—good for the metabolism, but not nourishing—is a feast for the specialist herbivore. The chief of those fibrous foods, one of the few plants that actually benefits from constant grazing, is grass.

Feast for specialist herbivores

The specialist herbivores are of two kinds: the ruminants, and the rest. The ruminants are all vaguely related to one another; "the rest" belong to half a dozen different mammalian orders. Ruminants and nonruminants may be equally "successful" herbivores, but the ruminants, through some quirk of evolution, have contrived to shift the fermenting bacteria from the hind part of the gut into the front part of the gut, into a huge stomach called the rumen.

Food is not only dumped in the rumen as the animal grazes but, later, at leisure, can be shuttled back to the mouth for a further contemplative chew: the act of "rumination." This method of dealing with massive quantities of low-grade, high-fiber fodder has given the ruminants alone as great a dominance and variety as all the rest of the specialist mammalian herbivores put together. Rumination is one of nature's subtlest and finest inventions—and also one of its most unlikely, for it is highly eccentric to allow bacteria to take over the front part of the gut.

A further contemplative chew

The ruminants include the cattle, antelopes, sheep, goats, musk-oxen, deer, camels, llamas and giraffes; all of which (with the possible exception of the giraffe) should play a major part in the food supply and landscape of the twenty-first century. Of course, they have played a large part in human affairs ever since there have been human beings; presumably humans have always hunted ruminants (just as modern baboons or chimpanzees will catch the occasional antelope), and the reindeer was probably the first food animal to be domesticated. But in the

Beasts of the field

more ordered yet adventurous world of the twenty-first century, these beasts' traditional roles could be greatly extended.

Of all ruminants, indeed of all animals, cattle have probably had the greatest influence on human life. The different species have each been domesticated separately, and sometimes several times over. From the aurochs, *Bos primigenius*, in Europe, have been developed the half-hundred breeds from Dexter to Chianina that have become synonymous with "cattle" in Europe and most of the Americas. The buffalo, in Africa, is not easy to tame but has been known to pull the occasional cart. The yak, water buffalo and zebu (*Bos indicus*) have largely determined the course of cultural development in Asia. Even when left undomesticated, cattle have helped to shape human history: it was the bison, or "buffalo," of North America, millions and millions of tons of prime beef "on the hoof," that first enabled the Indians to live on the plains and then helped the white man to subjugate the entire continent.

Influential cattle

Cattle have all the assets of a domestic animal, especially for primitive people; and we, for the most part, have simply inherited the beasts that were domesticated by primitive people. They are strong and can be highly aggressive, yet they can be tamed. They are thrifty, versatile, and can get by on low-grade fodder. At different times for different people they have supplied transport, clothes, shoes, weapons, tools, ornaments, meat, milk, fertilizer, lighting and fuel; the water buffalo in India still plays a crucial part in most of those contexts in many of that country's half-million villages. But the obvious merits of cattle have caused people and governments almost to become fixated upon them; to regard them not simply as obliging beasts that can be slotted into a dozen different niches but as symbols of affluence and success and as the only domestic animals worth taking seriously.

This mentality is obvious among unsophisticated people, such as the Masai, who count their wealth in head of cattle, and live upon the beasts' blood, milk and urine; but it is there, too, in North America and Europe, where beef and milk production are the biggest single industries and steak has become the almost universal symbol of well-being. The Masai cattle fixation has often led to overgrazing, the elimination of other species and the creation of wilderness. The American-European cattle fixation has led to stupendous waste of resources and, through butter and other fats, laid the foundations of the "diseases of affluence." Cattle have much to contribute to twenty-first-century life, but if the mythology that so exaggerates their importance is not stripped away they could pervert the entire course of world agriculture and cuisine. Cattle production, like all animal husbandry, should be regarded as a means of filling in the cracks in a staple-oriented agriculture designed to feed people, and as a perquisite; and all that follows in this book should be seen in that context.

Creation of wilderness

Cattle are, first and foremost, grazers; and grass can be grown to advantage in many contexts. It is the obvious and sometimes the only worthwhile crop in some of the wetter counties of Britain and Ireland, where grain will often fail to ripen; and it should perhaps be grown more extensively in the drier states of the United States, which, if devoted to profitable grain, are still liable to crumble into dustbowls. Grass may be

Where grain will not ripen

permanent, in which case, if left alone, it tends to become interlaced with a marvelously varied flora and fauna; or it can be sown as a temporary pasture, for one to three years, in rotation with other crops. Cattle are not the best grazers in all contexts, and it is a pity that they have often been forced into areas where other beasts would do better; many antelope and other beasts are more tolerant of dry conditions, for example, and moose, red deer and reindeer may thrive on grazing that is too poor for cattle. But every agriculturist would think hard, and rightly, before rejecting cattle in favor of some other species.

The versatility of cattle is, of course, a bonus, but it has raised some knotty logistic problems. Beef animals should obviously be muscular; red meat, after all, is muscle. Since wild cattle tend to be heavy around the shoulders (mainly for offensive purposes) while the most succulent steaks come from the rump, beef breeders have spent much of the past thousand years shifting the beast's bulk from front to back, resulting in oblong beasts, usually on legs as short and solid as a chesterfield, and epitomized by the Hereford, the Beef Shorthorn and the Aberdeen Angus. Some say that the original shape was not all to the bad, and there are gourmets of the hardier kind who speak highly of buffalo hump. I cannot comment on this specific, but accept that beef becomes juicier as you move from nose to tail.

Gourmets of the hardier kind

But dairy cows, in theory, should be thin; they can eat only a limited amount, after all, and the more of their feed they convert into muscle the less they can divert into lactation. The classic dairy cow is gracile, like the Ayrshire or the doe-like Jersey. She is portrayed by European painters from Cruyff to Daumier as a kind of hearth-rug draped loosely over a trestle of indeterminate bones.

This tidy separation of breeds would be all very well if the separation of milk and meat production was equally straightforward. But a cow cannot produce milk unless she has calves; and if, as with the Jersey, the calf is as incorrigibly fleshless as the mother, what can be done with it? A half or a third of the female calves may be kept back as herd replacements, but the rest of the females and all the males have no conceivable function, for they will not grow big enough or fast enough to justify the cost of trying to turn them into beeves. Nowadays attempts are made to produce a worthwhile calf by crossing the tiny Channel Island cows with huge Charolais bulls; but this is a somewhat dicey compromise.

Incorrigibly fleshless Jersey

The same kind of argument applies to the pure beef breeds. If a cow is not kept for milk, then all she does in return for an entire year's feeding is produce one calf, which then has to be fed, probably for two or more years, before it is saleable. Suckler herds probably have a future—in the American prairie, for example, or the Scottish hills—but they are intrinsically inefficient.

So North American and European farmers in particular have moved toward the dual-purpose animal that will give plenty of milk and produce a big-boned calf capable of rapid growth; and the ideal, so it seems, is the black and white (or occasionally red and white) Friesian, alias Holstein. This, then, is the ultimate cattle breed for the commercial farm in temperate climates; and it seems that we can look

Old-fashioned Friesians

Beasts of the field

forward, in the twenty-first century, to fields populated entirely by black and white cattle. As is so often the case, the search for a commercial compromise seems to have produced boring uniformity.

But the game is not yet over; there is no last word in agriculture. Holstein calves do grow well, and the calf of a Holstein cow and a Hereford sire is undoubtedly one of the best beef animals ever bred, for feeding on grass. But the quicker a meat animal grows, then, theoretically, the more economical it is, because it costs money just to keep beasts hanging around whether they are growing or not. Big breeds grow quicker than small ones and the biggest breeds of all are those originally developed for cattle's most primitive agricultural function— that of transport. Europe has retained some of its ancient draught oxen—the Charolais and Simmental of France; the South Devon of England; and the extraordinary Chianina of Italy, which may stand six feet high at the shoulder—and they are all now being bred into cattle herds all over the world.

Meanwhile, the wonderfully milky Holstein is proving to be a little too milky; or, at least, the European Economic Community (EEC) has a chronic dairy surplus which it would have trouble shifting even if the epidemiologists were not now showing that milk is a highly equivocal commodity. Already some British dairy farmers maintain that they barely break even by selling milk; their only clear profit is in the sale of the old cows' carcasses. So there is also a trend toward large, fleshy cows, though not necessarily with an outstanding milk yield.

What can we do with all that milk?

In short, the cattle herds of the next century, besides being far smaller than the present herds, could be a lot more varied; all frightfully well bred, big, yielding well, producing good, big calves, and healthy (which livestock has rarely been), but with plenty of scope for individuality in the bits that show—the coat, the horns and the physiognomy. That at least is the optimistic view; the statement of what should happen.

Finally, as with all livestock, we should pay attention to aesthetics; the whimsically marked Belted Galloway (a black beast with a broad white band) and the somewhat mournful Highland cattle would be worth keeping for their looks (although the "Belty" also produces outstanding beef). One of the potential advantages of living in a crowded world is that we cannot afford to use land *merely* for productive purposes.

Cattle have been the stars of twentieth-century agriculture and will, and should, decline; sheep have been the perennial also-rans, but are already in the ascendancy. They suffer economically (as cattle do) from a low reproductive rate; the average ewe produces only one lamb per year and lambs have a strong tendency to die. Wool is a perquisite, but has nothing like the value of the cow's surplus milk. Lamb is not so sought-after as beef, and has rarely commanded so high a price. Sheep are subject to a bewildering catalog of infections, parasites and nutritional disorders, and the wonder is that anyone keeps them at all. But they do have advantages and they could be far more productive than they are. By the middle of the twenty-first century they could outstrip cattle as a source of meat.

The ascendant sheep

Because the sheep is intrinsically unproductive (contrast the ewe's one offspring a year with the sow's 20), farmers have rarely found it possible to spend much money on their housing, or feed, or general husbandry; and because sheep are versatile and hardy—withstanding winter on the British hills at one end of the scale and subtropical desert conditions at the other—it has been possible to push them into niches where no beast should venture. Thus sheep have hung on through most of the world's agricultures largely because they are cheap: the archetypal low-input, low-output enterprise.

This is all very well so long as land is cheap: which in Europe at least, in the next century, it will not be. The level of husbandry must be stepped up; but can a sheep step up its output accordingly? Can we do a productivity deal with sheep? Can a sheep really be more like a pig?

Why can't a sheep be more like a pig?

Several lines of research in Britain suggest that the sheep could change more profoundly in the next few decades than any other form of livestock. The chief problem is to increase the amount of lamb produced per ewe per year, which can theoretically be done in three ways: inducing small ewes (which are cheap to feed) to produce big, fast-growing lambs; persuading ewes to produce litters of lambs; and inducing them to produce more than one litter per year.

The first of these options—producing big lambs from small ewes—is traditional practice: ewes of hill breeds, such as the petite Welsh, are commonly crossed with big, butch, lowland rams such as the Suffolk or Border Leicester to produce medium-sized, fast-growing lambs.

The second possibility—producing more lambs per litter—offers plenty of scope but raises enormous logistic problems. Prolificacy is no great problem; existing breeds such as the Finnish Landrace or the Greek Chios commonly produce three, four, or even five lambs at a time. But where you have a litter you have runts, and small inviable creatures are simply a waste. Again, the Finn is a skinny beast whose offspring are not particularly desirable; and small lambs that grow slowly are far less useful than bigger lambs that grow quickly. But how can a ewe feed four lambs at a time if they are all to grow quickly?

Prolificacy no problem

Such difficulties might again be solved by mixing genes from different breeds. The Suffolk and Dorset Horn are not overly fecund but they do have a good body shape. The Friesian is milky (and, indeed, might be a better bet for the family smallholding than a house cow). A Welsh-Dorset-Finn-Friesian mother producing three or four Suffolk-style lambs would be at least four times as productive as the average ewe now to be seen in British fields.

Sheep have only a five-month pregnancy; if their lambs could be weaned early, then they could theoretically produce two litters a year. One difficulty is that they are still primitive beasts, responsive to the regulatory signals of nature; and they come into season only during the shortening days of autumn, so as to give birth the following spring. Yet some breeds are less responsive than others to environmental influences, and the Dorset Horn, for example, will sometimes breed out of season. Two litters every year may be a little excessive, but scientists at the Rowett Research Institute at Aberdeen have induced Dorset-Finn crossbred ewes to produce three litters in two years.

Two lamb litters a year

I would hate to see the sheep reduced to the termite-like reproductive machine that the modern sow is being bred to aspire to, and believe that

Beasts of the field

in a crowded world, where livestock are used merely as fillers-in, this would be as inappropriate as it is inhumane. But a ewe that produced three or four strong lambs in the spring, and perhaps another couple in early autumn, now and again, would be more than acceptable.

Yet in confining the discussion to conventional breeds, albeit including the exotic Finns, Friesians and Chios, we may have been too conservative. Zoologists like to think that when they decide that a particular group of animals constitutes a "species," it is henceforth incapable (by definition) of cross-breeding with any other species—at least to produce fertile offspring. Thus the horse and donkey are different species, and although they can be crossed the resulting mules or hinnies are sterile. Conventional domestic cattle have been crossed with North American buffalo to produce the catallo, or with yaks to produce a yakow; and here the offspring may be fertile, but are not reliably so. However, some of the animal populations the zoologists have confidently decided are quite distinct can breed perfectly well together if given the chance, to produce fully fertile offspring. The world's catalog of sheep, and a few of the goats, are in this category.

Catalloes, yakows, and mules

Every environment that a species may come to inhabit imposes its own constraints and allows its own freedoms, and farmers can cash in on the different kinds of adaptation to different environments. Thus beasts from extreme latitudes tend to be highly seasonal in their breeding (it would be disastrous for a herbivore in an arctic climate to give birth in winter), but their offspring tend to grow extremely rapidly during the brief summer—or they would not be big enough to withstand winter. Mountain species tend to be large and chunky, which increases their weather resistance. Animals from regions where the climate is constant tend to have long breeding seasons, or no recognizable seasonality.

If breeders want to produce big sheep, why not look beyond the 200 pound domestic sheep to the 300 pound Marco Polo sheep of Asia? Such beasts, standing over three feet high at the shoulder, might cope with the Scottish Highlands as competently as deer. If nonseasonal breeding is desirable, why not breed from the European mouflon, which has been known to breed from January to November? If the small ewe that produces a large lamb is worthwhile, why not look again at the once-domesticated Soay, which produces the biggest lambs (for its body size) of any sheep?

What price the Marco Polo?

Of course, one of the great merits of sheep is that they are not like cattle: they are only middle-sized, cheap, and fit into all kinds of agricultural niches that could not accommodate cattle. But a sheep as big as a pony with lambs like wolfhounds is an intriguing possibility.

Neither cattle nor sheep (Marco Polos aside) thrive in the worst of the Scottish hills or the subarctic conditions in the north of Scandinavia or North America; only beasts with a high metabolic rate can resist the weather, but the food supply—coarse grass, heather, gorse and lichen— is hardly fitted to supply the necessary energy. Yet deer survive: reindeer in Scandinavia and Russia and caribou in North America; moose, the largest deer, across the whole of the top of the world from Finland to Alaska; and wapiti in the Rocky Mountains and red deer in Europe. Deer have at times been a major source of meat; the Lapps have

More meat from deer?

built their entire culture around the reindeer and European country houses and monasteries (and Cambridge colleges) had their deer parks. Hunting is more usual than farming but it tends to be wasteful, not least because meat from a beast that has been shot and then pounded down the mountain on a mule is something of an acquired taste. Is it possible to take advantage of the deer's ability to exploit impossible land in more ordered fashion, without becoming a full-time Lapp?

Research at the Rowett Institute on Scottish red deer suggests the answer is a cautious yes. About 200,000 red deer live on five million acres of Scotland, usually in conditions that cattle and sheep find very taxing. Deer eat a lot and push their food through rapidly, digesting it far less assiduously than a sheep would; but this is an adaptation to a poor, heather-based diet, which does not repay more than cursory digestion. Deer calves are born in June, and if they are not half-grown by December they will not survive the winter. Accordingly, they double their weight in the first 20 days of life, a feat which takes a calf 47 days, a foal 60 days and the sluggardly human 120 days. In captivity at the Rowett—and deer tame easily, although they are never less than frisky—deer calves have reached 200 pounds within one year (the weight of a full-grown Suffolk ram), to give a carcass that has ten percent more lean meat than fat lamb. A beast that can return such performances under hill conditions is surely heaven sent.

But deer pay heavily for their apparent success. In winter, when there is virtually no food and the search for it simply wastes energy, deer lose their appetite. Because they have very little body fat to act as a food reserve, they burn body protein—muscle—instead. But protein provides only half as many calories, weight for weight, as fat. Consequently hill deer may lose 30 to 40 percent of their body weight.

The calves' rapid growth depends upon a heavy supply of rich milk; and whereas the lactating ewe or suckler cow must increase her feed intake by a mere 30 to 40 percent, the hind must double her intake if she is to feed her burgeoning calf. Because of this enormous physiological burden, and the subsequent drain of winter, hill deer are able to give birth only in alternate years. Even so, 10 to 25 percent of the calves die in their first year. In short, under hill conditions, and for all their astonishing potential, deer are unproductive; a herd produces only about 11 pounds of meat per head per year.

Surviving not thriving

Obviously the deer could be far more productive if they were cosseted: Rowett has shown what they can achieve under optimum conditions (and that is without the benefit of the selective breeding that has produced modern sheep and cattle), and the red deer even of the lowland parks are half as big again as the hard-pressed "monarchs of the glen." But if they are cosseted, where should the line be drawn? If they are to be given the same level of husbandry that cattle expect—winter feed and housing, veterinary care, supplementary feed for the dams— why not keep cattle instead? Can a regular meat trade be maintained unless the animals are killed, bled and inspected in an abattoir? But how can they be brought to the abattoir if they are not ranched, and to some extent tamed? Yet deer survive in the Scottish Highlands partly because they can cover huge distances, and so shelter from the worst weather

Beasts of the field

and seek out the most succulent tips of heather. Can they really be controlled over such vast areas, at least at a justifiable price?

There are compromises: for example, it may prove worthwhile simply to feed the lactating hinds, or to capture at least some of the calves at the end of autumn to be raised on farms. But whether or not Scottish deer graduate into an appreciable meat source, there can be no doubt that the search for compromises between husbandry and wild life management is a crucial issue; assuming, that is, that we want to continue to eat meat, but also want to coexist with other animals.

Husbandry and wildlife management: the crucial compromise

Fortunately the Scots are not alone in taking their half-wild beasts seriously. The moose is the supreme exploiter of northern forests and American and Russian and north European scientists are all exploring its domestication. Its appearance is deceptive; its hindquarters are as massive as those of an ox, and its legs, designed for wading and swimming as much as for running, are—in contrast to those of cattle—well muscled almost to the hooves. The Russians have also pioneered the exploitation of the saiga, a beast about the size of a roe deer, which is usually classed as an antelope but which (like the panda) eludes easy classification. The saiga has an odd labyrinthine nose like the trunk of an ancestral elephant which may serve to warm the dry, freezing air before it reaches the lungs. In any case it was almost extinct 50 years ago; yet it is ideally suited to the steppe, and now that it is managed, the saiga again roams in great herds.

The Russians are also involved with the world's biggest antelope, the eland; there has been a herd at Askaniya-Nova in the southern Ukraine since the turn of the century. The eland is related to the oryxes and is not too far removed from the addax, all of which have an ability to withstand drought that in some instances surpasses that of the camel. Camels do, after all, need to drink now and again, but the addax can get by without surface water. Eland are ranched to a limited extent in their native Africa, and they will grow as big and sleek as a Hereford bull under conditions that will parch cattle to the bone. Only prejudice, it seems—the belief that cattle are supreme and eland are mere "game"—prevents their much wider exploitation. The Ancient Egyptians domesticated the addax (and hyena, gazelle and the ibex), and the Israelis, who have the Negev Desert to fill, are now taking the addax seriously.

The llamas from South America, like the deer, are ruminants that shove food through at a great rate and are able to thrive on poor fodder; but, as the Peruvians have shown, they are more tractable than deer. The alpaca is a llama which the Peruvians developed for its wool; the vicuña is a gracile related from that produces wool that is equalled only by cashmere. At least one scientist at the Rowett has suggested that the llama group could be the ideal Highland beasts, for an animal that can survive the Andes can survive anything. With the Pyrenees, Alps, Himalayas and Rockies also available, it does seem odd that llamas have been left to the South Americans.

Llamas for Scotland

Similarly, the water buffalo, thanks largely to research in the United States and also in Australia, is proving that it is not simply the "poor man's tractor" of South-East Asia that it is so often made out to be. Some modern, well-bred and well-fed water buffalo in Florida are now yielding what some consider to be the finest beef to be had anywhere. Their milk is splendid and becomes, when fermented, the incomparable Mozzarella, and their personality (again in defiance of much of the published literature) is almost too agreeable. (They do not like outsiders, however.) Boys and buffaloes in South-East Asia become friends; and in a predator-prey relationship that is not an advantage.

The mixed bag of nonruminant herbivores offers yet more opportunities. Horses are "good doers" on erratic grazing, and share with deer the ability to run away from trouble. The French keep them for food on the Massif Central, and Icelanders are happy to eat their mountain ponies. Scotland and vast areas of the United States could usefully accommodate meat horses.

The capybara, which is about the size of a sheep and is the world's largest rodent, is a semiaquatic herbivore from South America. The manatees and dugongs, the so-called sea-cows, are ugly beasts; but they have pectoral breasts and, floating upright in the water, may have given rise to the mermaid myth. Whether they did or did not, they are extremely efficient browsers of the weed that tends to choke tropical waterways. A single carcass of a hippopotamus, mightiest of the world's semiaquatic herbivores, is equivalent to those of 60 sheep. The world has a lot of water, and capybaras, sea cows and hippos could help human beings to make good use of it.

And what about the capybara, the sea cow and the hippopotamus?

The final step in the husbandry of unconventional species is not simply to put one or other type into a ranch but to "farm" the entire "natural" ecosystem. Even on a Western farm, where the sward has been simplified to one or a few species of grass, it is easy to see how different classes of livestock may complement each other: calves having the first bite when the grass is young and tender; cows wrenching at it as it "gets away" from the calves; and sheep nibbling the aftermath. When the vegetation is natural and therefore varied, as on the African plains, efficient grazing is possible only through such divisions of effort: the 30 or so African antelope alone—leaving aside the cattle and non-ruminants, such as zebra—all tend to have slightly different grazing habits, so that between them they check all the different plant species and maintain a balance. This balance is vital; much of Africa is both dry and infertile and the alternative to the rich but precarious flora and fauna is not farm but desert. One estimate shows that if the nine most abundant hoofed animals of the Serengeti National Park—a group that includes elephant and giraffe, buffalo and kob, warthog and bushpig—were culled by ten percent each year, they would yield an annual 13,000 tons of carcass. This would amount to only ten pounds live-weight per acre, which is a mere one percent of the output of the most intensively managed British grassland. But it is a great deal more than would be produced if the Serengeti were given over to domestic cattle.

Intricate Serengeti

So much for the exploitation of marginal land, and the fusion of husbandry and wildlife management. But there is another vast category of domestic meat animals: those that live with humans as commensals, or scavengers. They include dogs, pigs, guinea pigs, ducks, geese, chickens, turkeys; and whatever their anatomy might say (the dog, structurally, is a carnivore and the guinea pig is a plant eater) they are

Pigs, ducks and guinea pigs

Beasts of the field

omnivores. They need a diet as rich as a human's, but they don't need it so delicately presented. Apart from dogs (which I mentioned only as a historical aside) all these beasts should feature prominently in twenty-first-century food supply.

To the Iron Age farmer, and still to some semiagricultural hunter-gatherer peoples today, the pig was the universal doer and filler in. It ate what was going, from agricultural surplus to human excrement, and by its nosing and rooting may have done as useful a job of cultivation as the ancient plows. By the 1950s in Europe and America (and in most of the Far East today) pig-keeping had been tidied up, but the ancient foraging-scavenging role was still discernible. Recognizably different breeds were being used for different jobs—the middle-sized Middle White and Berkshire being raised in Britain for pork, and Essex and Wessex, Large Black and Long White Lopeared being also allowed to grow on to become "baconers"—and a few were specialists. The Gloucester Old Spot, for instance, was the archetypal "orchard pig," which liked windfall apples, did not grow too fat, and made good pork and bacon. Swill, whey, crop residues and—particularly for the pregnant sows—grass, were the traditional pigs' diet.

But the pig is at the opposite end of the biological spectrum from the sheep. Sows may produce up to 20 offspring in a litter (although ten is more usual) after a pregnancy of a mere three-and-a-half to four months. With such an output, and such an eager market for pork, bacon, sausages and pies (including the market for beef sausages, which often contain pig fat), there was no need for the caution that held back the sheep farmers. There was nothing to do but invest in housing, breeding, feed and veterinary protection so as to exploit the last iota of the pig's extraordinary potential and then to increase it a little more.

As a result, within 20 years, the pig has become the complete factory animal. The old breeds have largely gone, to be replaced by hybrids from combinations only of the biggest and fastest-growing strains: Large White from Britain; Swedish Landrace; Hampshire from Britain via the United States; and Pietrain from Belgium. The precision of the breeding is matched by that of the nutrition. The standard pig feed today is compounded from whatever grain, soybeans or other protein sources are cheapest, into mixtures whose protein, mineral, fiber and calorie content is prescribed to the nearest fraction of a percent.

Animals in general waste energy by moving about and maintaining body temperature; pigs are therefore confined and raised entirely indoors, in a warm atmosphere. The sows, through the greater part of their pregnancy, are kept in "sow stalls," in which they cannot turn around. They are separated from their young as they suckle by an iron crossbar, and sometimes are chained by the neck to the floor—although this confinement is not purely gratuitous because sows have a strong tendency to lie on their babies. The weaned pigs go into weaner pools, enough per pen to ensure they cannot move too much; and they are sometimes kept in dim light to reduce "vice."

Sows were traditionally allowed to suckle their young for eight weeks; but if this is reduced to five or six, they are just able to produce two litters a year. Weaning at birth is now envisaged, with the piglets being raised on artificial milk in cages, like battery hens; and the sows, spared the enormous physiological burden of lactation, could perhaps manage three pregnancies per year. There is always a disease risk, of course, which increases with confinement; so pig units are sometimes started off by piglets born by Caesarean section, and then maintained "germ free."

The old-style sow might have produced fewer than ten pigs a year. Most in Britain still produce only about 15, and 20 is still considered a good target. But 30 to 32 pigs a year is now considered feasible.

The price of this technical progress has been high. Pig husbandry has rarely been particularly jolly: the sty was not a nice place and pigs tend to be aggressive, so their life has always been one of hassle. They do not like cold and the old-style penning on freezing mud could hardly have pleased them; and piglet mortality, caused partly by the sow's clumsiness and partly by competition between the young pigs, ran at 20 to 30 percent. But pigs are intelligent animals, they love digging and rooting, and their near total confinement from birth to death on concrete floors seems to me to be well beyond the moral pale.

In addition, the fundamental virtue of pigs—that they are **Scavengers** scavengers—has been sacrificed; for who would consider feeding swill **sacrificed** to a Hampshire–Large White–Landrace cross? Flavor, too, the *raison d'être* of all meat, has not been given first priority. Apple, sage, onion and garlic are said to have become the traditional sauces of pork because these were among the foods of the ancient, free-ranging beasts, and would already have aromatized their flesh. Such fineness of feeling hardly seems appropriate to the dull white flesh that nowadays masquerades, cellophane-wrapped and frozen rigid, as pork.

Technologists have suffered some rude shocks during the 1970s; the **Technical hubris** belief that seemed to prevail in the 1960s, that things would inevitably go on getting bigger and faster and more efficient, has given way to the idea that technology must above all be appropriate; that it must fit in with society's conventions or meet its aspirations. In many parts of the Third World (and the developed world) prestige hospitals, or plans for them, are giving way to less spectacular, even workaday clinics that just happen to bring more medical care to more people. High-rise apartment blocks, the pinnacles of achievement in domestic architecture, are pushed over for the reason that was clear enough before they were built, that no one wants to live in them. It is no longer silly to suggest that technology not only can outstrip its purpose, but often demonstrably does so; and that it can be abandoned or reversed. It is old fashioned to keep pigs in backyards. It is rare, nowadays, to keep them in towns or villages, although that used to be common enough. But that is where pigs should be and their breeding should be adjusted accordingly. And that, I trust, is where they will again be in the twenty-first century.

The same kind of argument applies to chickens, which potentially are **Chickens in every** far more versatile than pigs because they are smaller and could be kept **backyard** in every backyard, and give a pay-off every day in the form of eggs. Like the pigs, they have been too potentially productive for their own good, and enjoyed, if enjoyed is the word, too keen a market. The modern broiler is now raced to slaughter at six to eight weeks (again raised in the dark to reduce its activity), while the modern layer (perhaps

Beasts of the field

with her beak clipped off to prevent the "vice" of feather pecking) is stuffed into a cage (with up to four others) in which she lays up to 300 eggs a year and is then killed. Assuming, that is, that she has lived so long and that her claws can be disentangled from the wire of the cage.

Do not believe farmers, if you do, who say that chicken never really did taste like chicken; that the old free-range bird is the same as the modern broiler. I keep hens, and kill them after about two years, and although they are tough and better suited to making curry than for roasting, they are things of wonder. If chickens were kept as they should be kept, there would be plenty of eggs (the Spanish, for example, were traditionally poor but were not short of eggs), but the only chicken flesh to be eaten would be that of the old hens and the superfluous males from the breeding flocks. But if chicken again became a rare and fairly expensive delicacy, it would be worth waiting for.

Ducks, and perhaps geese, could emerge as major meat animals of the twenty-first century. They are excellent both as scavengers and as grazers; they grow fast; and some breeds of duck (the Campbells, for example) lay up to 300 eggs a year. And ducks and geese, like sheep, can be bred with wild species which have many extra desirable qualities.

Major duck

Thus the usual domestic goose, the Embden or Toulouse, is probably derived from the greylag, *Anser anser*. The greylag is a middle-of-the-road species from temperate climates, in no particular hurry to go anywhere: it breeds seasonally, incubates its eggs for 33 to 35 days and grows fairly relaxedly through the summer. But the genus *Anser* and the related *Branta* include about 33 species or subspecies, all of which produce fertile hybrids when crossed with the domestic goose, and between them possessing the qualities suitable for almost all kinds of environment. *Anser caerulescens*, the Greater Snow Goose, must raise its young rapidly or they die: it incubates for only 23 to 24 days. So too does *Branta ruficollis*, the red-breasted goose—and in the first weeks of life its young grow twice as quickly as the Embden. Such high-latitude species have a short breeding season, but *Branta sandvicensis*, the Hawaiian goose or Nene, may lay eggs in winter and is the only wholly terrestrial goose: able to copulate on land and probably less inclined to fat than the aquatic greylag.

Super-goose

The domestic ducks, Aylesbury and Campbell, are almost certainly derived from the temperate mallard. They might similarly borrow the ability to breed all year round from tropical species, and the short incubation and rapid growth of Arctic species, and be a little less prone to fat if crossed with the terrestrial Laysan Teal.

Ducks and geese are fairly easy to manage, and pleasant to have around. There is no conceivable agricultural scene, no matter how hard pressed, that could not accommodate huge numbers of them. The Chinese have long regarded ducks as standard fare, and I for one look forward to seeing a lot more of them.

The guinea pig is worth a passing mention. I do not envisage Europeans or North Americans allowing guinea pigs to scratch around their kitchens as they do in Ecuador, gently fattening on scraps until seized for the pot, any more than I think it likely (or desirable) that we should reintroduce the Fat Dormouse, once beloved of the more effete

Guinea pigs or rabbits.

Romans. Future conditions are not likely to demand that we should be so bizarre. But the fact remains that the people of Ecuador, high in the mountains and desperately poor, can not only find room for guinea pigs but also rely on them as a sole source of meat, and yet stay healthy. This suggests that this little beast is another South American native which, like the llama and perhaps the capybara, has much to offer appropriate groups of people the world over. China and Russia are already interested in rabbits as meat animals, and could perhaps complement them with the slightly more omnivorous guinea pig.

Finally, creatures such as guinea fowl, pigeons and bees strike their own compromise between husbandry and management. All they demand of their owner is a safe place to live; they happily forage for their own food, a fact reflected in some of the cannier architecture of Scotland. The house gables are stepped for pigeons to perch and the attic walls are pierced for them to enter.

Bees, pigeons and guinea fowl

In short, there is no conceivable need for vegetarianism, but there are powerful agronomic and humanitarian reasons to take the heat out of animal husbandry, and sound nutritional and gastronomic reasons to change the role of meat in cooking.

We can expect livestock to become rarer, although this comparative scarcity would have compensations. First, it would no longer be so necessary to worry about saturated fat intake, since the sources of saturation would be fewer, and instead of cutting the fat off the beef we could again begin to savor the delights of beef drippings. Second, because livestock would be raised less intensively—growing more slowly on a more varied diet—and because quality rather than sheer bulk would be at a premium, we can hope that twenty-first-century meat would have the flavors that old men remember and which the technologists try to persuade them never existed.

We can also expect a change in the species hierarchy, with the present leading trio of beef, chicken and pork being challenged or perhaps surpassed by lamb (mutton), various game (especially deer) and duck. The cooking skills appropriate to each—in particular, the handling of relatively fatless game meats—will come to the fore.

The present tendency to equate "meat" with muscle and to disregard the rest has always been gastronomically regrettable and nutritionally undesirable, and when livestock is rarer will be untenable. The cooking of red meat is only one-quarter of meat cuisine: the use of connective tissue, as jellies and thickeners and as crackling skin; the use of bones and nerves; the use of variety meats, each as different from each other and from red meat as mushrooms are from beans; and the subtle use of fat are each the subject of ancient cuisines that should be revived. Carnivorous animals never confine themselves to red meat; indeed, captive lions and falcons quickly languish if they are not given bones and variety meats.

Offal for the lions

Finally, when meat is rare, it cannot simply be used as steaks or roasts, to be vaguely decorated with bits of vegetable. I trust that when people do have roasts they will treat them with suitable ceremony; but the future role of meat, as through most of history, should be as the garnish or the source of permeating stock, its flavor extended and highlighted as befits a rare, delicious food.

Beasts of the field

I see meat as a scarce and precious thing, but scarcity has many advantages. The object of gastronomy is nothing but sensuality and the easy access of beef, pork and pallid poultry in the past decade has caused many of the marvelous subtleties of flavor and texture that are contained within the whole beast to be all but lost; sauces, also, have been degraded to the glutinous excesses of *haute cuisine*, as if chefs were intent on dispersing the rich world's dairy surpluses all by themselves.

It is the excessive production of meat that has pushed agriculture so far off course and raised the problem of dwindling resources; and it is the excessive eating of meat and other animal products, with richer and richer accompaniments, that is largely responsible for the Westerner's fatty arteries and the early death of so many Western men.

If you do not eat much meat or variety meats then you do not need to worry about the fats in it; and all the old indulgences, from suety pie crusts to beef drippings and lush bacon sandwiches, again become acceptable. The recipes that now bring little squeals of mock-ascetic horror to the lips of hostesses were born of austerity; and the people who devised them for the most part were not fat, and did not die of overnutrition.

So I ask you to read much of what follows in the context not of three meaty meals a day with popcorn in-between but of meat taken as a feast; the way that hunting people take it and, indeed, the way that the specialist predators take it.

From the infinite and intriguing catalog of meat cookery, six definite themes emerge that seem to me to be particularly significant for the twenty-first-century cook.

Theme I
Simple and good

The future cook, when meat is scarce, must of course make use of unfashionable cuts and unusual species; but even future beasts will have legs and loins and haunches and one outstanding requirement is to revive the ancient reverence for the roast.

The modern cook puts meat into the oven to "roast," but what actually takes place may be a combination of roasting, baking, braising and deep frying. If meat is hung before an open fire, cooked mainly by fierce, dry, radiant heat, then it is roasted. If it is put in a closed oven, heated largely by the convection of warm, moist air, then it is baked. If it is wrapped in foil (which is useful for dry meats such as venison, but has few other justifications), then it is essentially braised. If it is allowed to sit in its own rising fat in a roasting pan in the oven, then the bottom half is fried; and this, for a cut such as leg of pork, can be disastrous, for when pig skin is fried it turns to leather.

Baked meats should always sit on racks above the roasting pan, the function of which is merely to catch the drips.

The nature of cooking is determined largely by the available fuels; slow, cool-burning peat, for example, gave rise to cuisines of slow simmering; fierce, fast, open wood fires first gave rise to the cuisines of roasts and kebabs. The falling off of cheap fossil fuels in the twenty-first century, and the electricity produced by burning them, will probably drive more and more people to both solar heating and to renewable fuels—of which the chief is wood. I make no excuse therefore for including recipes that require prolonged slow cooking—probably in well-insulated slow ovens that get at least some of their warmth from the hot-water supply that acts as a reservoir of solar heat. Neither is it irrelevant to discuss roasting, for although tomorrow's wood stoves will be astonishingly efficient closed affairs, they should be openable and incorporate a spit.

The three prime techniques in spit roasting large joints of meat are basting, dredging and frothing.

In basting, the fat that drips into the roasting pan beneath the meat is constantly ladled back over it.

In dredging, the meat is dusted with complementary spices or handfuls of herbs, which are carried by the running fat into all the crevices; and with flour, to form a crust and seal in the flavor.

In frothing, the cooked meat is dredged with flour, and then hot water is poured over it, or steam played onto it, until the surface is "cooked transparent"; and then the roast goes back before the fire for a final crisping. If the meat is mutton, then a few sprigs of mint should have been boiled in the frothing water. Venison is traditionally frothed in red wine, rabbit is doused in beer, and hare bathed in red-currant juice.

Roasting is profligate, of course; the meat does not retain its moisture and bulk as it does when foil wrapped and baked. But roasting can produce exquisite, forgotten flavors; and as every future cook should know, it is flavor, not volume, that counts with meat.

Theme II
Pâté, brawn and döner kebab

When meat is scarce you realize how much the cook wastes in time of plenty: the older beasts, the unusual beasts and well over half even of those beasts that are fashionable. One way to use scraps—or rather, a whole spectrum of ways—is simply to press and cook them together, mixing lean and fat, game and pork, flesh and fowl. The ingredients may be bound together with gelatin or egg; or pounded as fine as cream; or simply held together with a giant skewer. Into this category of pressed mixed meats fall pâtés, terrines, brawns and döner kebab, variously spiced and herbed to produce a range of dishes that is infinite; yet the principle is the same throughout and a few examples will illustrate it.

Pâtés can be expensive, but their strength of flavor is compensation; an ounce of pâté is worth five ounces of bland meat, and it is in the spirit of twenty-first-century cooking to use meat as sparingly and flavorsomely as possible with quantities of bread and salad. But pâtés can also be ridiculously economical. One of the best I ever tasted was made from the carcass of a Boxing Day goose. The remains of a cooked duck, with or without a few ham trimmings, will serve as well.

I have given specific quantities in the following recipes but the amounts may be varied according to availability. The principle is of close compression and moderate, even cooking.

A SIMPLE GOOSE PÂTÉ
Serves 2

2 cups meat and 1 cup skin taken from a goose carcass
Ham trimmings and fat, if available
1 large onion
2 garlic cloves
1 egg
3 tablespoons dry sherry
A generous sprinkling of black pepper
A large pinch of salt

Break as much meat as possible off the ravaged carcass; meat should outweigh fatty skin about two to one. Reserve any large pieces of goose meat and grind the rest with the ham trimmings, onion and garlic. Mix in the beaten egg, sherry, pepper and salt, to make a moist sticky mass. Mix in the reserved meat.

Line a small terrine with ham fat, if available, or grease with fat from the bird. Put the pâté mixture in the terrine, seal with foil and stand it in a baking dish half filled with water. Cook at 375°F (190°C) for 1 hour. Cool, then cover with a weighted plate and let it stand in the refrigerator for 1 day before serving.

The following recipes all incorporate pork, which is the principal meat of pâtés and brawns. Any cheap cut can be used, but if you are giving a party for about 50 people (and I mean 50) you could do far worse than buy a pig's head, to be used as the basis for an almost endless range of mixed meat dishes, to which spices or herbs can be added at will. The brains, tongue and ears should be cooked separately, and the rest scrubbed and crammed into a saucepan with enough water to cover. Simmer for six hours, then lift out the meat and bones. The stock should set into a useful gelatin (the ten cups I started with formed a soft gelatin when reduced to seven cups, and became hard when reduced to five cups) and the rest forms an enormous pile of miscellanea. The bones are easily picked out, and the skin is easily sliced off. Much of the meat is of excellent quality, and almost all the remaining fat and gelatin is eminently usable.

Anyway, here is a cheap pork pâté for which I use cooked head meat, although any cut (or mixture of odds and ends) with a roughly fifty-fifty ratio of meat to fat would do. Sugar is used here as a principal spice. Very medieval.

PORK PÂTÉ
A variation on this recipe can be made by layering the pork mixture with an equal quantity of roughly chopped cooked tongue.
Serves 4

1 lb ($\frac{1}{2}$ kg) cooked pork, roughly equal parts fat and lean
1 garlic clove
2 teaspoons flour
2 teaspoons brown sugar
1 teaspoon ground nutmeg
1 teaspoon ground cinnamon
1 teaspoon ground ginger
1 teaspoon white pepper
6 whole cloves
A generous sprinkling of salt
1 tablespoon medium sherry
1 egg
A few strips of fatback

Beasts of the field

Grind the meat and the garlic. Mix in all the other ingredients except the fatback, and grind again. Pack the meat into a well-greased terrine, cover with the strips of fatback, and seal with foil. Place in a baking pan, pour in enough boiling water to come halfway up the side of the terrine, and bake at 375°F (190°C) for 1 hour. When the pâté is cool, cover with a plate and put a weight on top to squeeze out the air.

Serve the next day.

One of the virtues of pâté is that you can incorporate whatever is at hand. One day I found I had a leftover rabbit liver, and made the following pâté.

RABBIT LIVER PÂTÉ
Serves 2

2 dried Chinese mushrooms (*shiitake*)
1 rabbit or chicken liver
½ lb (240 g) pork (equal amounts of
  lean and fat meat)
1 onion
2 garlic cloves
1 tablespoon sherry
1 teaspoon flour
A large pinch of salt
1 small egg
A few strips of fatback

Begin by soaking the mushrooms in hot water for 30 minutes. Grind the liver, pork, onion and garlic twice, then mix in the sherry, flour, salt and beaten egg. Drain the mushrooms, discard the stems, chop the caps and stir into the meat mixture.

Line a small dish with half the fatback strips, press in the pâté, put the rest of the fat on the top and seal with foil. Stand the dish in a baking pan, pour in enough boiling water to come halfway up the sides, and bake at 375°F (190°C) for 1 hour.

PÂTÉ WITH SPINACH AND HERBS
This impressive but simple variant makes much of spinach.
Serves 4 to 6

2 cups cooked fatty pork
1 large onion
2 garlic cloves
1 lb (½ kg) spinach

¾ cup liver
Oil or bacon drippings
¾ cup cooked tongue
1 egg, beaten
1 tablespoon dried rosemary
1 tablespoon dried marjoram
1 tablespoon dried tarragon
1 large bunch fresh parsley
½ teaspoon salt
1 teaspoon cayenne pepper
Slices of fatback

Grind the pork, onion and garlic, Cook the spinach in a saucepan until it is soft, then chop it finely.

Sauté the liver gently in oil or bacon drippings, then chop coarsely. Chop the tongue coarsely, as well. Mix all the ingredients, except the fatback, together thoroughly.

Line a terrine with half the fatback slices. Stuff the pâté mixture in and cover with more fatback slices. Cover the terrine with foil, then stand it in a baking dish. Pour in enough boiling water to come halfway up the sides of the terrine and bake in the oven at 375°F (190°C) for 1 hour.

Let the pâté cool, then cover with a weighted plate and let stand for 1 day before serving.

Brawn is a kind of head cheese held together with meat gelatin, which is poured on as hot stock and allowed to set. There are many ways of making firm jelly, but even more ways of making thick sticky soup that does not set.

The best method is to use a pig's foot. Simmer it for two hours in five cups of water, remove the foot, break it up with a fork (it will fall apart easily), then return it to the stock and simmer for at least another two hours.

Take out the meat and bones (the meat is fine fare) and reduce whatever fluid is left by boiling it furiously to two and a half cups, which will set solid when cold.

PORK AND RABBIT BRAWN WITH HARD CIDER
In this recipe the stock is heavily flavored with hard cider—again the pork and apple theme. Rabbit tends to be lean and dry: its marriage with fatty pork is felicitous. This dish is bland but I like it that way. Brawn is traditionally made from head meat, but for small quantities any cut will do.

All parts of the beast will be eaten in the 21st century; at times in history, all parts have featured in outstanding dishes. **Top,** *tripe with apple and onions, and* **bottom,** *tripe in a hot-sour soup.*

Two ancient ideas for the 21st century: meat as a garnish, rather than as the chief source of protein; and meat sweetened, its protein diluted with sugar or honey.
Top, *honeyed pork with cabbage (in which the cabbage should dominate)*, and **bottom**, *Mexican beef stew, with honey and black-currant jam.*

Serves 6 to 8

4 large onions
4 large garlic cloves
1 small pig's foot
1½ lb (¾ kg) rabbit pieces
½ lb (240 g) pork (equal quantities of lean meat and fat)
A bouquet garni, made with thyme, parsley, savory, marjoram, bay and lovage, if available
2½ cups hard cider
12 peppercorns
2 teaspoons mace
A sprinkling of salt
A sprinkling of black pepper

Peel the onions and cut them in half. Do the same with the garlic. Scrub the pig's foot, and then put all the ingredients—except for the mace, salt and pepper—into a saucepan. Add 6 to 8 cups of water, bring to a boil and simmer, covered, for 1 hour.

Take out and discard the bouquet garni and take out the rabbit and pork. Remove as much meat as possible from the rabbit pieces and return the bones to the pan.

Continue to simmer the stock for another hour, then remove the pig's foot and break it up. Return it to the pan and continue to simmer for another 2 hours. Strain the stock and reduce it to 2½ cups. Cool the stock and remove any grease from the top.

Cut the best pieces of rabbit meat into bite-sized pieces, and grind the rest, together with the pork. Mix the rabbit pieces with the ground meat, mace, salt and pepper. Press the mixture loosely into a dish or bread pan. Melt the stock and pour in enough to cover the meat. When this is set, pour the rest of the stock over the top to form a layer. Refrigerate and when thoroughly cold and set, turn the brawn out of the dish and cut in slices.

PORK BRAWN
Serves 12

1 pig's head with tongue, cut in half
2 pig's feet, halved
2 onions, halved
2 carrots, halved
2 leeks, halved lengthwise
Bouquet garni

8 black peppercorns
4 cloves
6 allspice berries
A pinch of salt
Black pepper

Wash the pig's head and feet thoroughly and put into a large saucepan with all the remaining ingredients except the salt and pepper. Cover with plenty of water, bring to a boil and remove the scum as it rises. Then cover the pan and simmer for 2 hours or until the meat comes off the bone easily.

Detach the meat from the bone, skin the ear and tongue and chop all the meat coarsely. Put the bones back into the pot and boil, uncovered, until there are about 4 cups of liquor left. Strain the liquor into a clean pan, skim off the fat then put in the meat, a very little salt and a generous sprinkling of black pepper and simmer for 15 minutes.

Pour the meat and stock into a mold which has been rinsed out in cold water, and set aside to cool.

When cool cover the mold and refrigerate until set. Unmold the brawn and serve sliced.

DÖNER KEBAB
The dry countries of the Middle East have, of necessity, learned to value the meat of sheep and goat and, indeed, of camel. The meat is often tough, usually lean and with a strong tendency to go off. The meat is better for being cut up and marinated before cooking, and the limited fat carefully distributed to compensate for its lack within the muscle. The scorching and smoking of the open fire provides a patina of flavor.
Serves 6 to 8

1 leg of lamb or goat
½ shoulder of fat lamb
2 onions
4 garlic cloves
2 bay leaves
½ cup oil
1 teaspoon ground coriander
1 teaspoon ground cumin
4 cloves
½ teaspoon cinnamon
¼ teaspoon ground mace
A large pinch of salt
½ teaspoon black pepper

Beasts of the field

Cut the meat into $\frac{1}{2}$-inch (1 cm) thick slices about 4 to 5 inches (10 to 13 cm) across, rejecting the gristly bits.

Chop and pound (or blend) the onions and garlic, chop or crumble the bay leaves and mix with the oil, spices, salt and pepper to make the marinade. Put the meat in the marinade and leave for 2 hours and preferably for 24 hours.

Spear the slices of meat on a revolving barbecue spit, alternating fat pieces with lean and pressing well down to form a pleasant lump. Put the spit in position and start cooking. The outside should be ready to eat within 45 minutes. Slice downwards to serve.

Theme III
Bits and pieces

Any beast is divisible into half a hundred conceptually different entities; and every bit, in the hands of some cooks, at some point in history, in some part of the world has been not simply at the periphery but at the center of great cooking. (I am not sure I would include the bits of lung in garlic butter that are now masquerading as *escargots* in many restaurants, although they do show what a little enterprise can achieve.) Ears, though, are full of promise.

PIG'S EAR SOUP
A strong, clear soup made with pig's ears, which when cooked become translucent.

Begin cooking the soup the day before you intend to serve it.
Serves 6 to 8

2 pig's ears
1 large onion stuck with 6 cloves
Bouquet garni
1 tablespoon vinegar
1 egg shell
1 egg white
A pinch of salt
$\frac{1}{2}$ teaspoon white pepper
$\frac{1}{2}$ teaspoon ground mace
Juice of $\frac{1}{2}$ lemon
6 tablespoons medium sherry

Put the pig's ears, onion, herbs, vinegar and $2\frac{1}{2}$ quarts (2 liters) of water, into a saucepan and simmer, covered, for at least 4 hours. Then set aside to cool.

When the stock is quite cold, skim off the fat and take out the ears. Skin the ears and slice the now softened cartilage into thin strips.

Strain the stock and discard the onion and bouquet garni. Break up the egg shell and beat the egg white until it is frothy.

Put the stock, egg shell and egg white into a large saucepan and, beating continually, bring to a boil. Stop beating as soon as the mixture boils. Without disturbing the crust that will have formed on the top, allow the mixture to rise in the pan and then move it off the heat.

Scald and wring out a piece of cheesecloth and line a strainer with it. Put the strainer over a bowl and tip the crust gently into it, then pour the stock slowly through. The stock should now be clear and sparkling.

Pour the stock into a saucepan and bring to a boil. Throw in the strips of ear, the salt, pepper, mace, lemon juice and sherry and serve in a hot tureen.

ROAST HEART
Here is a recipe, using beef heart as a substitute for goose, which was once made by poor English people at Christmas. The meat is as dark as game and as tender as the finest beef.

The aim of the preliminary cooking is to circumvent the heart's tendency to toughness.
Serves 6 to 8

1 beef heart, about $5\frac{1}{2}$ lb ($2\frac{1}{2}$ kg)
2 large onions
2 tablespoons vinegar
Peppercorns
2 teaspoons chopped sage
A pinch of salt
Black pepper
1 cup fresh breadcrumbs
Flour
2 slices bacon

Wash the heart thoroughly, removing all arteries, veins and blood, but leave a little of the fat. Put the heart in a large pan with the whole onions, vinegar and peppercorns. Cover with water and simmer for 3 to 4 hours. Remove the pan from the heat and allow the heart to go cold in its broth.

Lift out the heart and onions, reserve the broth. Skim off any fat from the top of the broth and keep it. Chop the onions and mix them with the fat, the sage, the salt, a good sprinkling of pepper and the breadcrumbs. Moisten the mixture with a little of the broth— about ½ cup. Pack the stuffing into the heart and sew it up.

Dredge the heart with flour and tie the bacon slices over the top. Roast in a moderate oven, 350°F (180°C), for 1 hour, basting occasionally. Finally, lift out the heart and using the fat in the roasting pan make gravy with a little flour, some of the reserved broth and a little seasoning. Serve immediately.

SPINACH SOUP WITH LIVER

Liver is high in cholesterol but it is also highly flavorsome and a little can be made to go a long way. It easily becomes leathery; gentle heat and solvents to tease out its moisture are the antidote.

This sharp, substantial soup is an admirable starter; rich, but high in fiber and low in fat.

Serves 2 to 4

6 oz (180 g) liver
3 garlic cloves
2 tablespoons corn oil
1¼ cups yogurt
1 lb (½ kg) spinach
A pinch of salt

Gently fry the thinly sliced liver and the sliced garlic in the oil in a large saucepan, stirring all the while. When the meat looks cooked (a pale mauve color) pour on the yogurt and then add the finely chopped spinach and salt. Give it a good stir until the spinach starts to collapse into the general liquid. Put the lid on the pan and leave over very low heat for about 15 minutes. Serve immediately.

There is an awful lot of intestine in an animal and especially in a ruminant; and although long, slow cooking and generous spicing are necessary to avoid the flavor of old wash cloths, the result can be worth waiting for.

The English traditionally eat tripe with onions. The French eat tripe in many forms, but in one classic recipe it is cooked in hard cider and enriched with pig's feet. The following recipe

borrows from both ideas, and reduces the ratio of meat (tripe) to vegetable.

TRIPE WITH APPLE AND ONION

Serve with boiled potatoes or slice the potatoes (as many as you think suitable) and lay them on top of the tripe mixture in the pan about 30 minutes before serving. Bring back to a boil, then reduce the heat and simmer for 20 minutes. In this case, do not bother with the final reduction of the stock.

Serves 4

1 pig's foot
1½ lb (¾ kg) apples
3 large onions
8 garlic cloves
2-inch (5 cm) piece fresh ginger root
6 tablespoons oil
1½ lb (¾ kg) tripe
¼ teaspoon cayenne pepper
Salt
2½ cups hard cider

First make the stock. Simmer the pig's foot for 2 hours in 8 cups of water, then remove and break it apart with a fork. Return the pig's foot to the pan and simmer for another 2 hours. Remove the pig's foot and reserve the choicest pieces of meat. Strain and measure the stock. If you have more than about 5 cups put it back into the pan and boil it down.

Meanwhile, chop the apples, but do not bother to peel or core them. Peel and slice the onions, garlic and ginger and fry with the apples in the oil until the whole mixture becomes mushy.

Slice the tripe finely and stir it into the apple and onion mixture. Add the meat from the pig's foot, cut into bite-sized pieces. Continue to stir-fry gently for another 5 minutes.

Sprinkle on the cayenne pepper and a little salt, then pour on the cider and the stock. Bring to a boil, cover, and simmer for 2 hours.

A few minutes before the end of the cooking time, uncover the pan and bring to a galloping boil to reduce the stock, which in the finished dish should just cover the meat.

Tripe is well suited to the Chinese "hot-sour" treatment; the vinegar helps to soften it.

Beasts of the field

HOT-SOUR TRIPE SOUP
Serves 4

½ lb (240 g) tripe
2 red chili peppers
4 dried Chinese mushrooms
6 cups chicken stock
1 cup cider vinegar
1 teaspoon cornstarch
1 egg
4 scallions
Pepper
A pinch of salt

Slice the tripe and chilies finely. Soak the mushrooms in hot water for 30 minutes. Drain the mushrooms, discard the stems and slice the caps.

Simmer the tripe, chilies and mushrooms for 2 hours in the stock and vinegar. A few minutes from serving time put the cornstarch into a cup, add a little of the stock and stir well to make a thick paste. Gradually add more stock until you have a thin white fluid. Stir the cornstarch mixture into the soup and cook for a few seconds.

Take the soup off the heat, and trickle the beaten egg in, stirring all the while, to produce the thin golden threads of an egg drop. Return the pan to the heat, add the chopped scallions, pepper and the salt, bring back to a simmer and serve immediately.

Theme IV
Extending the meat

The inventors of textured vegetable protein speak of "meat extenders": large amounts of ersatz served with small amounts of meat to give the impression of a lot of meat. But cooks have been using the staples—grains, beans and potatoes—as extenders for thousands of years, and since the staples contain adequate protein, while meat contains an excess of protein, the resulting mixture of staple and meat will contain quite enough for human needs. Because the body cannot store surplus protein, enough is as good as a feast, and meat–plus–potato or meat–plus–pastry are, in context, nutritionally equivalent to meat–plus–ersatz. And a good deal nicer.

Although meat extension is an infinite art, we can distinguish four main principles that are echoed in all the world's cuisines: pastry or potato crusts are added, to seal in and partake of the flavor, or dumplings or puddings are cooked alongside the meat; the meat may be stuffed, with the stuffing taking up the meat's juices and moistening it from the inside; the meat is used as a garnish, on cereal or soup, or made into a sauce; or, finally, the meat is chopped into tiny pieces and mixed in with the staple—it is difficult to decide where a *pilau* ends and a sausage begins.

POTATO PIE
To illustrate the first principle we may take the finest pie in the history of the world, which is Potato Pie from Lancashire. The extension of meat is frenetic—by potatoes inside, and a thick crust on top—and the resulting flavor and texture are astonishing; in this, as in all great dishes, the whole far surpasses the sum of the ingredients. The dish is not, despite appearances, particularly fattening—that is, it does not have a particularly high energy content relative to its bulk. The suet crust is highly calorific, of course (although not more so than other pastry), but the meat is lean and the bulk of the dish is potato—which, without added fat, is not highly calorific.
Serves 6

1 lb (½ kg) lean stewing steak, cut into
  small pieces
2 lamb's kidneys or ¼ lb (120 g) beef
  kidney, cut into pieces
4 lb (2 kg) potatoes, cut into ¾-inch (2
  cm) cubes
1 lb (½ kg) onions, sliced
Black pepper
A pinch of salt

The Crust
1½ cups shredded suet
3 cups flour
2 teaspoons baking powder

You need what Lancashire people call a "potato pie dish"; thick, deep and earthenware, shaped like a flowerpot, and sometimes sold as a "turtle pot." An earthenware casserole with high sides will serve.

Put the meat, potatoes and onion, well peppered, all together into the pot. Add the salt and cover with about 5 cups of water. Put a thick plate over the top (potato pie dishes have no lids) and cook in a moderate oven, 350°F (180°C), for about 3 hours.

To make the crust, blend the suet into the flour and baking powder. Add enough water to make a good firm dough. Roll out the crust $\frac{3}{4}$ inch (2 cm) thick and just big enough to cover the top of the dish.

Remove the pie from the oven, cover with the crust and return to bake for a further 45 to 60 minutes.

The potato pie is little different in principle—and not at all different in ingredients—from a beef stew with suet dumplings. But "dumplings" of a sort can be made to do a dumpling's job—take up the flavorsome juices and provide bulk—without using fat at all; which is very much in the twenty-first-century spirit. One traditional method must date at least from the Middle Ages, when bags or bowls of food were suspended in the perpetually bubbling water of the cauldron.

BOILED BEEF WITH CARROTS AND OATMEAL PUDDING

This English recipe makes use of oats with beef, but dried peas (with pork) and lentils are used in the same way. You may add chopped onion, chives, parsley or any flavorings to the pudding.
Serves 6 to 8

$\frac{1}{2}$ **lb (240 g) carrots**
$\frac{1}{2}$ **lb (240 g) parsnips**
$\frac{1}{2}$ **lb (240 g) turnips**
1 short stalk celery
3 large onions
2 lb (1 kg) boneless round steak in a piece
1 lb ($\frac{1}{2}$ kg) "old-fashioned" oatmeal
A pinch of salt
Pepper

Slice the vegetables and put them in a large saucepan. Pour in enough water to cover the meat when it is put in, and bring to a boil. Tie the meat securely into a round and put it into the water as soon as it boils; then allow merely to simmer. After 20 minutes remove any scum, add the salt and a liberal sprinkling of pepper.

To make the pudding, moisten the oatmeal with some of the broth from the pan and add pepper. Tie it loosely in greased cheesecloth and drop it into

the saucepan alongside the beef.

After 80 minutes the meat should be pleasantly tender and the oatmeal should have swelled into a tight, round pudding, which is exposed by pulling the cloth apart, not by cutting it.

HEN OF THE WAKE (HINDLE WAKES)

This Lancashire recipe, as old as the Pennines, shows how stuffing with humble fruit and cereal may transform an unpromising bird into a thing of rare excitement. The recipe is not difficult and the result is well worth the effort. Note, incidentally, the correct use of sugar; not as a significant source of calories, but as a subtle spice.
Serves 6 to 8

1 large stewing chicken
2$\frac{1}{4}$ lb (1 kg) prunes
3 cups dried breadcrumbs
$\frac{3}{4}$ cup coarsely chopped suet
Mixed herbs
A pinch of salt
Pepper
1$\frac{1}{4}$ cups wine vinegar
2 tablespoons brown sugar
2 tablespoons cornstarch
Finely grated peel of 2 lemons
Juice of 1 lemon

First make the stuffing: soak the prunes overnight then take out the pits. Crack the pits and extract the kernels. Reserve a few prunes for the garnish and chop the rest and the kernels.

Mix the chopped prunes, kernels, breadcrumbs, suet, herbs, salt and pepper and moisten with a cupful of the vinegar. Stuff the mixture tightly into the chicken and sew up both ends.

Put the chicken into a large saucepan, cover with water, add the remaining vinegar and half the sugar and bring to a boil slowly. Cover the pan and simmer gently until the chicken is tender—traditionally, old hens were used for this dish and 3 hours of simmering, or more, was not too long. The modern broiler should take less than an hour. Remove the pan from the heat and set aside to allow the chicken to cool in its broth.

To make the sauce, mix the cornstarch with $\frac{2}{3}$ cup of water. Add the lemon juice to another $\frac{1}{2}$ cup of water and bring it to a boil in a saucepan. Stir this hot lemony water into the cornstarch and water mixture. Return the mixture to the saucepan and bring to a boil, stirring all the time, until the sauce thickens, and then boil for 2 minutes. Remove the pan from the heat and allow the sauce to cool slightly, then stir in the remaining sugar and half the lemon rind.

Take the chicken from its broth and drain. Give it one coat of sauce, and when that cools, coat it again with the rest of the sauce. Decorate the chicken with the remaining grated lemon rind and the reserved prunes.

Turn the stuffed chicken inside out and you have a *pilau*; well, not quite, but the following outstanding *biryani* (which is a form of *pilau*) contains virtually the same balance of cereal, fruit, nuts and meat as Hen of the Wake. The species are different (rice for wheat bread-crumbs, pistachios for prune kernels) but the parallels are more striking than the discrepancies: acid is used in both recipes to break down the meat, vinegar in the English dish and yogurt in the Indian one. But the main difference is in idiom; the Nordic cook traditionally prefers to present meat as meat wherever possible, while the Asiatic cook is content merely to elaborate the basic bowl of cereal. It is the ancient dichotomy between the hunter-pastoralist and the arablist.

CHICKEN BIRYANI

This is an elaborate but exciting dish involving a number of separate components that are brought together at the end. I will describe the preparation of each separately.
Serves 8

3 lb ($1\frac{1}{2}$ kg) chicken
$2\frac{1}{2}$ cups milk
2 teaspoons ground mace
4 cups long-grain rice
1 bay leaf, broken into 4 pieces
Salt
$1\frac{1}{4}$ cups yogurt
1 teaspoon ground cinnamon
$\frac{1}{2}$ teaspoon ground nutmeg
$\frac{1}{2}$ teaspoon chili powder
2 large onions
7 garlic cloves
2-inch (5 cm) piece fresh ginger root
$\frac{1}{2}$ cup oil

15 blanched almonds
5 tablespoons tomato paste
2 tablespoons ground coriander
1 tablespoon raisins
$\frac{1}{2}$ tablespoon chopped pistachio nuts
3 tablespoons chopped Chinese parsley

Scorch the chicken over a naked flame before you begin; the crispy skin can be the best part of the chicken. Then cut the bird into pieces. Put the chicken in a saucepan with the milk and mace and simmer for about 30 minutes—that is, until almost done. When the meat is cool enough to handle, separate it from the bones in neat, bite-sized pieces. Measure the liquid in the pan and add enough water to make it up to $5\frac{1}{2}$ cups.

To prepare the rice, wash it thoroughly and then allow it to soak with the bay leaf in the milk and water mixture for 1 hour. Add a large pinch of salt and boil for 2 to 3 minutes or until the rice is three-quarters done, drain if necessary.

To make the sauce, put the yogurt, cinnamon, nutmeg, chili powder and salt in a bowl. Mix well and set aside. Chop one of the onions, the garlic and ginger and fry in the oil until the onion is soft, then add the almonds and tomato paste. When the paste is just beginning to cook, pour in half the yogurt mixture. When the oil begins to separate, stir in the rest of the yogurt. When the oil separates again, put in the ground coriander.

Finally, broil the raisins by throwing them into a hot, dry frying pan, stirring them until they swell up.

To assemble the *biryani*, slice the remaining onion thinly, and put the slices in the bottom of a large casserole (they will be on top when the dish is turned out). Spread a third of the sauce over the onions and a third of the rice over the sauce. Then make a layer of half the chicken pieces, cover with another layer of sauce and a scattering of pistachio nuts and raisins. Put in a second layer of rice, then the rest of the chicken, nuts, raisins and sauce and a final layer of rice. Cover the casserole and cook in a moderate oven, 350°F (180°C), for 30 minutes.

Turn the *biryani* out onto a heated platter, scatter the chopped Chinese parsley on top and serve immediately.

COCKIE-LEEKIE

The chicken is cooked whole, but by the end of the cooking time it will be almost falling apart and can easily be divided into portions in the pot. Give each person a piece of the chicken, a piece of the brisket or pork butt, a few prunes and leeks and several spoonfuls of the stock. Alternatively, reserve the stock and serve it as soup.

Serves 8 to 10

2 lb (1 kg) brisket or smoked boneless
    pork shoulder butt (if it is very salty,
    soak it for about 6 hours before using)
1 large chicken
A large spiral of lemon peel
A handful of pearl barley
2 medium-sized carrots
$2\frac{1}{2}$ lb ($1\frac{1}{4}$ kg) leeks
Pepper
18 to 20 prunes
A handful of fine oatmeal
3 tablespoons chopped parsley
Salt

Cut the brisket or pork butt into pieces and put them into a large saucepan with the chicken, the lemon peel and the pearl barley. Roughly chop the carrots and half the leeks and add them with plenty of pepper to the pan. Add enough water to cover the chicken by about 2 inches (5 cm) and bring to a boil. Cover the pan and simmer for 1 to $1\frac{1}{2}$ hours.

  Meanwhile, soak the prunes in warm water for 30 minutes. Drain and add to the saucepan.

  After a further 15 minutes add the remaining leeks, chopped into fairly large pieces, and sprinkle on the oatmeal, stirring well to prevent it from forming lumps. After a further 10 minutes stir in the parsley, taste and adjust the seasoning (add salt, if necessary) and simmer for at least 5 minutes more before serving.

GOULASH

Goulash is at its best with beef shank, which makes a fine strong gravy because it is full of connective tissue. The dish has been paraded around the world with everyone adding their own refinements, but the original conception, as with Lancastrian potato pie, is both ridiculously simple and beyond

improvement. The key to its success is the prodigious quantity of onion, and the long, slow cooking. The recipe's apportionment of meat seems mean by modern standards but richness of flavor compensates for lack of bulk. I leave out salt on principle but even traditionalists do not find it necessary in this dish. A two-pound (1 kg) can of tomatoes may be substituted for the fresh tomatoes and the tomato paste. Serve with boiled potatoes or rice.

Serves 8

3 to $3\frac{1}{2}$ lb ($1\frac{1}{2}$ to 2 kg) onions
4 tablespoons oil
$2\frac{1}{2}$ lb ($1\frac{1}{4}$ kg) boneless beef shank
2 tablespoons flour
2 teaspoons hot paprika
2 lb (1 kg) beefsteak tomatoes
2 tablespoons tomato paste
3 tablespoons mild paprika

Slice 1 lb ($\frac{1}{2}$ kg) of the onions. Sauté them in half the oil until they are well colored. Use a perforated spoon to scoop them out and put them into a large, deep, warmed casserole (it must be flameproof as well as ovenproof).

  Cut the meat into fairly big chunks. Roll the chunks in the flour, and sauté in the rest of the oil, tossing them around until they are beginning to brown and produce gravy. Add the hot paprika and toss the meat some more, then transfer to the casserole together with all residues in the pan.

  Chop the rest of the onions coarsely and add to the casserole. Cut the tomatoes up coarsely and pile them into the casserole with the tomato paste. Add the mild paprika. Just cover the whole lot with boiling water, and stir until thoroughly mixed.

  Make sure the goulash is simmering well before putting it in a 325°F (170°C) oven. Cook for at least 6 hours. After 8 hours it is wonderful. Ten hours is just a little too much.

MEXICAN BEEF STEW

In its proportions of meat and accompaniments, this stew resembles goulash, but the idiom is again quite different. The recipe sounds bizarre but the result is superb. Serve with rice or plenty of plain boiled potatoes.

Beasts of the field

Serves 4

1½ lb (¾ kg) chuck steak
2 lb (1 kg) small onions
4 garlic cloves
1 tablespoon dry mustard
1 tablespoon flour
2 tablespoons corn oil
2 lb (1 kg) can of tomatoes
1 tablespoon honey
1 tablespoon black-currant jam
A small pinch of salt
Black pepper to taste

Cut the meat roughly into 1-inch (2.5 cm) cubes. Peel the onions, but leave them whole. Crush the garlic cloves, and mix the mustard to a smooth paste with a little water.

Toss the meat in the flour and fry in the oil until it is browned on all sides. Put the meat into a large, heavy casserole with all the other ingredients. Add 1¼ cups of water, stir well and bring to a boil. Put the casserole in a 325°F (170°C) oven for 2½ hours.

Finally, it is worthwhile to use leafy vegetables—notably spinach and cabbage—as if they were a staple, and then to garnish them with a small amount of highly flavored meat; reversing the balance achieved in steak houses, where wisps of lettuce are used to garnish steaks like the frills around a circus elephant. Of course, leafy vegetables do not have the food value of staples; but Westerners are not short of calories or protein and they are short of the fiber that leafy vegetables provide.

HONEYED PORK WITH CABBAGE
This dish is delicious, easy to make and meets all the nutritional and agronomic requirements of healthy people in a crowded world.
Serves 4

¾ lb (360 g) belly of pork (about five
   ½-inch/1 cm thick slices)
2 small onions
2 garlic cloves
2 lb (1 kg) cabbage
2 tablespoons corn oil
1 tablespoon honey
2 teaspoons mustard (preferably freshly
   ground mustard seeds)
¼ teaspoon ground ginger
½ teaspoon black pepper
A pinch of salt

Remove the skin from the meat and place the skin on the middle rack of a 350°F (180°C) oven. Put a pan underneath to catch the drips. After 30 to 40 minutes, when the skin has become pleasantly crackled, remove and chop or break into small pieces.

Cut the rest of the pork into 1½- by ½-inch (4 by 1 cm) pieces. Peel and slice the onions and garlic. Cut the cabbage in quarters, remove the core and slice the cabbage into ¼-inch (0.5 cm) strips.

Fry the pork pieces in the oil in a large saucepan or wok until they begin to brown and shed fat. After 5 minutes add the onion and garlic and continue frying, stirring, until the onion is soft.

Add the honey, mustard, ginger, pepper and salt to taste, stirring well to mix. After a minute or so of stirring—just enough to ensure that each piece of pork is well coated with the sauce—put the cabbage on top of the frying mixture and mix it in, then put the lid on and allow the cabbage to cook in its own steam. After about 10 minutes add the crunchy crackling and serve.

COUSCOUS
This is a dish that could equally well be included in the chapter on grains, so well balanced is the meat with the grain. The grain (and the dish) is called couscous; it is a kind of semolina or ground wheat.

The couscous grains and the *harissa* sauce (a strong, fiery sauce made from hot peppers) can be bought from the larger supermarkets, healthfood stores and some delicatessens.

There are many different recipes for couscous, each reflecting the national tastes of the three North African countries of Morocco, Tunisia and Algeria. This recipe is my version of the Moroccan dish. Instead of mutton you can use chicken or both meats together and there is also a couscous with fish. The vegetables, too, can be varied and the point is to use whatever is at hand.

If you do not like spicy food, leave out the chili powder and serve the dish without the *harissa* sauce.

It is better—and easier—to make couscous in a *couscousier*, the traditional pan used in North Africa and available here in specialist kitchen shops. The *couscousier* is made in two parts (rather like a large double steamer). The lower pan cooks the meat and vegetable stew; the top pan has a perforated bottom and steams the couscous grains at the same time.

Traditionally, the *couscousier* was made of glazed earthenware or copper, but today aluminum pots are more usual.

Serves 6

$\frac{2}{3}$ cup chickpeas
$\frac{1}{2}$ teaspoon baking soda
1 lb ($\frac{1}{2}$ kg) couscous grains
1$\frac{1}{2}$ lb ($\frac{3}{4}$ kg) lean mutton or lamb
2 carrots
2 onions
6 tablespoons olive oil
2 bay leaves
2 tomatoes
4 garlic cloves
A large pinch of ground saffron
1 teaspoon chili powder
1 teaspoon ground ginger
2 teaspoons ground coriander
1 bunch celery
2 zucchini
2 leeks, white part only
2 sweet peppers
2 eggplants
$\frac{1}{3}$ cup raisins
Harissa sauce

Soak the chickpeas overnight. Drain them and put them in a saucepan with the baking soda and cover with water. Bring to a boil then simmer gently for 1$\frac{1}{2}$ hours or until the chickpeas are almost tender.

Meanwhile, spread the couscous grains out on a baking sheet. Sprinkle them with water and work the grains lightly between your fingers so that they separate and become moistened and slightly swollen. Leave the couscous to rest for 15 minutes and repeat the process 3 times more.

Drain the cooked chickpeas and put them in the bottom half of the *couscousier*. Cut the lamb into cubes, slice the carrots thickly, quarter the onions, add them all to the chickpeas, cover with water and simmer for 30 minutes.

Put the couscous grains in the upper part of the *couscousier* and place it over the bottom half. Make sure that the liquid in the bottom pan does not come into contact with the couscous grains because this will make them lumpy. Steam, uncovered, for 30 minutes.

Lift off the top part of the pan and empty the couscous into a bowl. Sprinkle the couscous with water and stir to get rid of any lumps. Return the couscous grains to the pan and stir in 2 tablespoons of the oil.

Add the bay leaves, chopped tomatoes, the crushed garlic, saffron, chili powder, ginger, coriander and the remaining oil to the lamb and chickpea stew.

Fit the top pan back into position and cook for 15 minutes. Chop the remaining vegetables coarsely and add them and the raisins to the stew. Continue cooking for a further 15 to 20 minutes or until the vegetables and meat are tender.

To serve, pile the couscous (which should be tender but with each grain separate) onto a heated serving dish. Make a large well in the center and spoon the vegetable and meat stew into it. Serve the *harissa* sauce separately in a small bowl.

Theme V
Comminutions

The most economical way to use meat and a method of infinite adaptability is to grind whatever there is (from sheep's lung to cold roast beef) and mix it with something farinaceous—potato, bean, cereal, or all three; add more fat (if necessary), bind with egg and flavor liberally with onion and herbs. The resulting mixture is coated with batter and fried; or put in a bowl or encased in a cloth, or wrapped in vine or cabbage leaves, or a sheep's paunch or a sausage skin, and steamed, boiled, fried or grilled according to fat content and shape. I once made a perfectly acceptable Sunday supper by grinding the remains of a cold roast duck with a touch of garlic and chestnuts that I had gathered in the park. The mixture was heated dry in a cast-iron pan and served on baked potato halves. It would also have been good eaten with the fingers, shovelled up on leaves of Chinese cabbage, a technique I discovered in one of London's better Chinese restaurants which caters for Western tastes but not without feeling. The

Beasts of the field

prime example of the comminution form, or as Burns more elegantly put it, the chieftain of the pudding race, is the haggis.

There must be as many haggis recipes as there are good Scottish cooks, but what they have in common is that they begin with animal odds and ends that by most people's standards are uneatable, and through the addition of oatmeal (the prince of cereals) and robust spices and aromatics, transform them into a thing of wondrous beauty.

HAGGIS

Haggis is a dish that the dieter would regard with horror; yet the haggis itself contains little fat except for the oils in the oatmeal, the small amount of suet and the minute amount adhering to the heart; certainly not more fat than would be contained in an equal weight of tolerably juicy "lean" meat.

Traditionally, haggis is cooked in a sheep's stomach, but if you prefer use greased cheesecloth. Again, traditionally, haggis is served alone, or rather with whisky; but mashed potatoes and neeps (turnips) have become an acceptable accompaniment. If you do not add butter to them their calorific content will be modest.
Serves 2

1 lamb's heart
$\frac{1}{4}$ lb (120 g) liver
1 lamb's kidney (if you like kidneys)
A piece of lung (if available)
1 large onion
$\frac{1}{2}$ cup suet
$\frac{1}{2}$ nutmeg
Black pepper
A pinch of salt
$3\frac{1}{3}$ cups medium oatmeal
A handful of dried currants
A well-greased piece of cheesecloth

Chop the meat and onion finely, grate the suet and nutmeg and grind the pepper. Mix all the ingredients together. Line a bowl with the cheesecloth, pack in all the ingredients and tie the ends of the cloth tightly over the top to make a round pudding. Sew up the ends or fasten with wooden skewers, which are the traditional tools for fastening haggis.

Put the haggis into a large saucepan, cover with water and boil for $1\frac{1}{2}$ hours.

Meat and fruit

Fruit is the perfect foil for meat for several reasons, and although many traditional fruit sauces are creeping back we would do well to recapture some of the medieval abandon. The acid of fruit tenderizes, and (subjectively at least) "takes off" the fattiness; the sweetness of fruit acts as a spice; and the fiber of fruit is a useful antidote to all that concentrated flesh.

Our ancestors did not confine themselves to the addition of fruity sauces; they were content to use apple, for example, the way we might use onion today.

PORK, APPLE AND POTATO PIE

In this recipe it is not simply the association of meat and fruit that is desirable, it is the ratio that counts.
Serves 4

1 lb ($\frac{1}{2}$ kg) pork (you can use belly, hock or meat from the head)
$1\frac{1}{4}$ lb (600 g) apples
1 large onion
2 teaspoons sugar
Pepper
A pinch of salt
Dried sage (optional)
A little stock or water
$1\frac{1}{2}$ lb ($\frac{3}{4}$ kg) potatoes

Cut the meat up very small, chop the apples roughly (leave the skins on and the cores in) and slice the onion as thinly as possible.

Cover the bottom of a deep casserole with some of the pork; add a layer of apple, then a light dusting of sugar, a few onion slices, pepper, salt and a sprinkling of sage, if you are using it. Continue the layers until the dish is full. Press down firmly and add a very little stock or water—the apples will provide the bulk of the juice. Put the lid on and place the casserole in a medium oven, 350°F (180°C), and allow to cook for 45 to 60 minutes after the dish has come to a simmer.

While the casserole is simmering away, boil and mash the potatoes. Remove the dish from the oven, spread the mashed potatoes over the top and put the dish back in the oven until the top is pleasantly browned.

Vegetables ad libitum

Vegetables, creators of texture and fountainhead of flavor, should be at the center of all great cooking. Raw vegetables, the French crudités, should be a universal side dish, to be eaten like bread at every main meal. In the traditional "meat and two veg," the "veg" should dominate; the meat should serve only as a garnish and to provide gravy. You might reasonably strive to eat as many vegetables as you can; if this seems boring you are doing it wrong.

The great enemy of the vegetable is the freezer: despicable not for reasons of romanticism or puritanism but on grounds of simple logic. It wastes time, energy and money; it reduces variety, and it sadly undermines the flavor that is one of the vegetable's greatest assets. Freezers thus achieve the precise opposite of their makers' intention and their mass abandonment would be a major contribution towards a better diet in a more rational world.

The despicable deep-freeze

Technologists and grocers do of course argue that without the deep-freeze, some people would have no "fresh" vegetables at all. After all, vegetables cannot be grown in extremes of latitude except in the all too brief summer; and must northerners again live on turnips through the winter, like the Saxon peasantry? What of people in big towns, cut off from the fields? It seems perverse to put up with tired green beans and pock-marked cabbages when the deep-freeze gives access to the best of all the world's crops, whatever the season, wherever people live. And what should be done about gluts? In the old days of course it was broccoli for breakfast, dinner and tea followed by brussels sprout fritters, sprouts *en casserole*, and sprouts *bourgignon*. Surely it is better to keep surpluses, perhaps in less than perfect form but nonetheless acceptable, until the appetite for them returns?

Such arguments are seductive (why else would there be a multimillion-dollar deep-freeze industry?) but they are 90 percent nonsense.

It is no longer true, and becomes less true almost by the week, that fresh vegetables cannot be supplied all year round. People outside the sixtieth parallels of latitude would be hard-pressed to produce a generous winter supply of vegetables, but very few people do live outside the sixtieth parallels, and those who do (such as Eskimoes and Lapps) are among the world's anomalous peoples who are well adapted to their own peculiar diets. Perhaps there are people in the extreme zones who actually want fresh vegetables, but it would be far cheaper to deliver them daily by airplane than to perpetuate the deep-freeze industry.

Anomalous Lapps and Eskimoes

Even people at the harsh edges of the temperate zones need not go short of fresh vegetables. The finest private vegetable gardens I have seen are in the notoriously harsh border country between England and Scotland. Even without the aid of plastic coverings the lowland Scots

Vegetables ad libitum

could have at least half a dozen kinds of fresh cabbage and cauliflower in winter, plus lettuce and some of the spinachlike leaves, as well as carrots and beets that have been stored, and rutabagas, salsify, radishes and leeks straight out of the ground, while exotics—such as tomatoes—could be delivered fresh from temperate greenhouses. Modern plant breeding and the modest technology of the protective plastic coverings are extending all plant seasons: already there are tomatoes that survive frost, and "long-day" onions from Japan via Israel that swell in the dying days of summer instead of in the lengthening days of spring.

Modern breeding and modest technology

As for the "unfortunate" town-dwellers, the truth is that major cities have become almost the only places in the West where you are guaranteed to find fresh vegetables; ironically, it is the small country towns that are deprived. It is merely a question of marketing.

But surely freezing increases variety? Even if there is a choice of about 20 fresh vegetables in January, is it not reasonable to add a few more? The answer is both yes and no. If the product is to be acceptable, then vegetables have to be frozen within minutes, or certainly hours, of leaving the ground. Commercial deep-freezing is a high-capital enterprise; it should be done on a large scale, or not at all. In practice, commercial deep-freezing is tightly integrated (farmer–processor–retailer) and highly mechanized.

Only a few vegetables—those that can be grown under field conditions, mechanically harvested and reduced easily to pieces of a suitable size for freezing—are suited to the commercial process. The pea, specially bred with prominent stalks that reach out to the combine harvester, just happens to be the most suitable candidate. Some vegetables such as carrots do not need to be frozen and some of the "variety" that the processors offer is a simple numbers game: peas with carrots, peas with corn, peas with corn and carrots, and so on.

Only a few species are suitable for freezing, and only a few varieties within those species; and it saddens me that seedsmen so assiduously develop new varieties not necessarily for flavor or for protein content, but for suitability for freezing.

The home freezing of surplus garden produce should not be necessary. Short-row planting, short-term cropping, and an appropriate blend of varieties should reduce gluts and—more to the point—ensure that fresh vegetables are never lacking. Why eat last month's green beans when you could be eating this month's brussels sprouts? If you do have a glut, then give the surplus away or put it on the compost heap. To use a freezer "economically" (although this seems to be a self-contradictory exercise) you have to grow vegetables specifically to keep it filled; and that really is boneheaded.

Gluts are for giving away

But the fundamental objection to freezing springs from the fundamental question, what are vegetables for? The first answer is that they provide fiber, which they will do equally well whether they are fresh, frozen, or canned. The second is that they provide vitamins and minerals and it is just possible that a frozen pea might contain marginally more vitamin C than a fresh pea that has been left lying around; but since peas are not a significant source of vitamin C in the Western diet this sort of point (which food technologists are fond of making) is hardly compelling. The chief purpose of vegetables is to provide flavor, and here the fresh vegetable wins hands down. The frozen pea is not a bad product, but it does not compare with an in-season brussels sprout or savoy cabbage, and it is no more than a weak pastiche of the fresh green pea, which is a thing divine. If you destroy or even detract from the flavor of vegetables then you have lost most of the point of growing them, and to eat them processed when they could so easily be made available fresh seems vaguely masochistic. Seasonality is not a hardship, but is one of the virtues of vegetables; the first fresh peas of summer, like the first fresh strawberries, are worth looking forward to, and there is nostalgia in the autumnal meals of green beans and in the wintry sweetness of turnips.

Peas divine

Most foods inevitably will be, and perhaps should be, produced by professionals, and it would be no bad thing if Western cities were surrounded and infiltrated by market gardens, as in China. Yet even the British, an urban people not renowned for their industry, are said to grow at least a third of their vegetables themselves. They do this without particular encouragement (from town planners, for example) and often with the old-fashioned technology that was largely cobbled together during World War II as part of the "Dig for Victory" campaign. If vegetable growing ever became fashionable and was not regarded merely as an eccentricity, then it could in a few years be transformed into the subtlest of the technological arts.

Methods of cultivation and the varieties to match are increasing in sophistication almost by the week. The well-spaced rows of exhibition-sized plants, double dug, weed free, chemically fertilized and metronomically rotated, are giving way to highly intensive short-row ecosystems of big, slow-growing plants—parsnips or brussels sprouts, for example—intercropped with dwarf, compact varieties of lettuce, cabbage, or even tomato, sprawling capsicums or ground cover of lamb's lettuce or dwarf strawberries, with the whole phantasmagoria planted in raised beds and nourished, warmed and moistened by still-rotting compost beds beneath. The margins are again breaking down between the productive kitchen garden and the merely decorative border: the natural beauty of artichokes or cardoons and the contrived elegance of red cabbage or purple kohlrabi or red-stemmed chard should not be allowed to pass unadmired. Some of the peasant gardens of France or Italy are almost wild in their profusion and intricacy, yet every square inch is productive and under control.

Decorative border vegetables

At the other extreme, techniques are being developed that obviate the need for gardens altogether. Tomatoes, peppers and scarlet runners (once grown exclusively for their beauty) are now raised in peat bags on balconies and patios. The nutrient film technique, in which plants are fed by a continuous flow of dilute nutrient solution in soilless channels, could enable anyone with a window or a flat roof to experience the delights of vegetables that were still growing only minutes before they were put in the pot. Such technology could turn an apartment building into a Babylonian garden, dripping with produce.

Who needs gardens?

The variety of vegetables—edible plants—is vast, and increasing by the month as the breeders develop new combinations of color and form.

Vegetables ad libitum

But it is useful, for gastronomic and nutritional purposes, to classify them partly on an anatomical basis and partly by their family relationships.

Leafy vegetables

Leafy vegetables have been sadly downgraded in the Western diet. The extraordinary variety that nature offers is reduced in many people's minds to a sad little catalog of less than half a dozen. Cabbage seems to have a bad name, associated with sulfurous exudates from subterranean kitchens; spinach, beloved by Popeye, seems to have fallen from grace since its generous iron and calcium content was found to be largely in indigestible form; and lettuce, one of the least interesting and nourishing of leaves, masquerades ubiquitously as "green salad," serving partly to clear the palate but mainly for decoration.

Fallen spinach

To restore leafy vegetables to a central position in our diet would be a major nutritional and gastronomic advance. Their nutritional qualities include their vitamin and mineral content, of course, but also—another of those stunning nutritional insights of the past few years that comes as such a shock to the meat-oriented Western dietitians—in some cases their protein content. Green leaf crops produce far more protein per acre than any other kind of crop (and, of course, far more than livestock produce) for the obvious reason that the protein that eventually winds up in, for example, a wheat berry or a bean was made first in the leaves. Leafy vegetables have a high fiber and water content, so unless the protein-rich pulp was first extracted (a process advocated by Mr N. W. Pirie in England, and now adopted in feeding programs in India), they probably could not act as the sole source of protein for human beings for they would be too bulky. But no single food should act as the sole source of protein or of anything else, and several kinds of leaf could act at least as significant sources of protein. So they should be eaten not simply for their micro-nutrients or for their many varied flavors, but almost as a staple; as nourishing, non-fattening bulk food. Indeed, if you set out each day to eat half a pound of green leaves—without a fatty dressing—you could be doing yourself a large nutritional favor.

Leafy vegetables for protein?

There are hundreds of thousands of different kinds of plants and few have leaves that are actually poisonous; but many are too fibrous, resinous, spiny, furry, sticky, small or bitter to make pleasant eating. The outstanding contributors of leaves that are both pleasant and nourishing belong to three families: the spinach group, Chenopodiaceae; the dock family, Polygonaceae; and the wallflower family, Cruciferae, which includes the extraordinary miscellany in the genus *Brassica*. In addition, the cow-parsley family, Umbelliferae, includes many plants (such as celery) with leaves of outstanding flavor, although only a few (such as parsley, with its remarkable vitamin C content) have particular nutritional merit. The daisy family, Compositae, offers the pleasant but arcane cardoon (ancestor of the globe artichoke), the endive, the dandelion and the overrated lettuce.

Nutritionally, the kings of the leaves are the Chenopodiaceae. The best-known example, rightly, is spinach, *Spinacia oleracea*, the leaves of which contain no less than five grams of protein per 100 grams (a quarter

King Chenopod

of a pound). If it is true, as the United Nations suggests, that the average adult needs only 37 grams of protein per day, then 800 grams of spinach—less than two pounds—could provide your daily protein needs. Nobody wants to eat two pounds of spinach, and its high oxalic acid content, not to mention its very high vitamin A content, might make such a feat nutritionally undesirable (vitamin A is one of the vital substances of which you can have too much). Nonetheless, spinach is worth including in the diet in bulk, especially if officiously combined with auxiliary protein sources. Luckily spinach does have an outstanding gastronomic affinity with potato (as in the Indian *sag alu*), pulses (*sag dhal*), liver, fish, eggs and yogurt. It is sometimes hard to credit that nature can be so beneficent.

The second outstanding chenopod is *Beta vulgaris*, which, like the egregious *Brassica oleracea*, manifests in several forms. One subspecies of *Beta vulgaris* has big sweet roots, and is called sugar beet. In others, the root is usually colored, juicy and not quite so sweet: these are the beetroots. But one subspecies of *Beta vulgaris* has relatively unswollen roots and spinachlike leaves that can be cropped continuously until the plant gives up the ghost. These are beet greens, or perpetual spinach. Yet another kind of *Beta vulgaris* has leaves like spinach beet and large, thick leaf stalks that can be eaten as a separate vegetable. This is sea kale beet, or chard. Some varieties have red leaf stalks and have already crossed the divide between the productive and the decorative.

Two chenopods whose sharp peppery flavor endeared them to Iron Age farmers (to those farmers' undoubted benefit) are Good King Henry, *Chenopodium bonum-henricus*, and Fat Hen, *Chenopodium album*, both of which deserve recognition. You will not find them in the food stores, but you will find them on wasteland throughout the temperate world. Eat the leaves raw or cook like spinach.

Good living in the Iron Age

The Polygonaceae have become esoteric, at least in Britain. They include the docks (nutritionally inferior only to spinach) which gardeners curse, poison, and root out to make way for lettuce; and sorrel, which is sometimes cultivated as a spinach substitute or salad but is available free of charge on grassland or wasteland.

But the family that has made the greatest culinary contribution to human happiness is the Cruciferae; and in particular the cruciferan genus known as *Brassica*. One single species of *Brassica*, *B. oleracea*, is one of the most varied (and perhaps the most varied) of all living things.

Unbeatable Brassicas

Brassica oleracea began its botanical career inauspiciously enough, as a sprawling and not outstandingly leafy plant of coastlands around Britain and the Mediterranean, which sent up a spike of four-petalled yellow flowers in its second year. (It is these cross-shaped flowers that gave rise to the family name, Cruciferae.) But primitive farmers obviously recognized some special talent in this hardy weed, for they began to cultivate it. They bred varieties that were still primitive, but were more leafy and were hardy and hot flavored. These are now known as kale. They developed some with a swollen but aborted terminal bud; we call them cabbages. In others the stem was lengthened, and the axillary rather than the terminal buds were encouraged to develop; these are brussels sprouts. Some kinds were bred with grotesquely swollen

Vegetables ad libitum

flower buds; we know them as cauliflowers and broccoli. Finally, varieties were bred with swollen stem bases; we call them kohlrabi.

The cabbage, like the potato, has suffered from its institutional image, and from bad cooking. In truth it is the prince of vegetables, with a generous range of minerals and vitamins and a by no means negligible quota of protein (a quarter pound of the heavy, wrinkled savoy cabbage contains more than three grams of protein; a half pound would theoretically provide almost a fifth of an adult's daily needs). Cabbage can and should be eaten raw, its pepperiness perhaps lightened, as in many a Greek salad, with shreds of lettuce. It can of course be cooked or pickled just for its flavor and color (from white through dark green to livid red), but it also deserves to be used almost as a staple, for its mildly fibrous but low-calorie bulk and for its ability to hold gravy and sauces like a sponge. The brussels sprout is slightly less versatile but even higher in protein; its four percent vies with spinach. Cauliflower is only a modest protein source (less than two percent), but its low-calorie, flavorsome bulk is a useful dilutant in diets which—as in Western countries—tend to be too concentrated in energy and fat.

Prince cabbage

The various Chinese cabbages are also *Brassicas*, although they are not *B. oleracea*. Bok Choy is *Brassica chinensis*, and Pe Tsai (which I have found one of the easiest crops to grow) is *B. pekinensis*. Both feature heavily in Chinese cooking, often fried rapidly in peanut oil with garlic and a touch of soy sauce. They are excellent raw (far superior to lettuce) and can be used as an edible "spoon." They are used thus in one of my favorite Chinese restaurants to wrap an odd but unforgettable granular mixture of spiced duck and wind-dried sausage; a kind of instant but superior *dolmades*.

Bok Choy and Pe Tsai

But when you have finished with *Brassica* you have not finished with the leafy Cruciferae. Sea kale, mustard and the various cresses are Cruciferae; and watercress in particular deserves recognition as the almost universal garnish. Because it grows naturally in streams that sometimes harbor the snails that carry liver fluke, a parasitic flatworm, it has at times been rightly regarded with suspicion. But it is now cultivated in clean, filtered water-beds; and varieties can be grown in gardens, in polyethylene-lined ponds. Rocket, *Eruca sativa*, is sometimes still grown as a salad plant but, as with sorrel, dock, or Good King Henry, is just as easy to gather wild.

Sea kale, mustard and cress

The Umbelliferae is one of those biochemically involved plant families providing a whole range of oils, unguents and alkaloids, some poisonous and some merely delicious. The umbelliferan herbs and spicy seeds include dill, chervil, sweet cicely, lovage, angelica, fennel, coriander, caraway and cumin. The types used for the flavor of their leaves or stems include parsley, celery and Florence fennel. Parsley is as rich in protein as spinach. It is an outstanding source of carotene (vitamin A) and is in the same league as black currants as a source of vitamin C. It certainly deserves its reputation as a garnish.

Ever so Umbel

The merits of celery are those that are particularly appropriate in a Western diet, which tends to be too rich rather than too poor. Celery is 93 percent water, is hardly outstanding in any nutrient, and possibly provides fewer calories than are required to chew it. I do not like it

Vegetables—in endless variety—are the key to good eating: high in bulk, low in calories, high in flavor. The Chinese simply mix them, cook them rapidly in a little stock, soy and sugar, and serve them hot but crisp.

Pickle sextet. **Back row, left to right,** *pickled cucumber; the great mustard pickle, piccalilli; and an almost instant "pickle," red cabbage with sesame seeds.*
Front row, left to right, *baby turnips tinted with beets, from the Middle East; mixed spicy pickles from India; and carrots, hot with mustard and peppers—highly esteemed in South-East Asia.*

*Vegetables at the extreme of their range—
heavily flavored and all but de-textured.*
Left, *stuffed tomatoes;* **top right,** *ratatouille;*
and **bottom right,** *carrot soup with zucchini
croutons, garnished with melted cheese.*

cooked, but as a crudité it is almost without peer.

Fennel provides superb aniseed-flavored seeds; and one of its cultivated varieties, the Florence fennel, also provides a bulblike mass of leaf bases, which develop just below ground. An *al fresco* meal I once had in Naples, with Mozzarella cheese, radishes, bread, fennel and Frascati wine, remains among my outstanding gastronomic memories.

The leafy, daisylike plants of the Compositae family include dandelion (which is another "weed" that perhaps deserves more than its usual dressing of paraquat), endive, chicory, the cardoon, which is ancestor to the globe artichoke and might merit wider recognition as a border plant that is also esculent, and the ubiquitous lettuce. Some of the new dwarf lettuces, such as the crisp, pointed Tom Thumb, are worth an airing as space fillers, intercropped between slower growing vegetables such as cabbages or beans. *Dandelion, lettuce and cardoon*

Finally, a whole range of families contribute just one or a few edible species each. Some speak highly of the nettle (Urticaceae) as a green vegetable, while New Zealand spinach, which some favor as a spinach substitute in hot, dry areas, is an ice plant, Aizoaceae. Asparagus is one of the lilies (Liliaceae) and bamboo shoots are, of course, grass (Gramineae). The nasturtium (Tropaeolaceae) deserves wider recognition as a salad plant; it should ease its way from the ornamental vine to the table just as the scarlet runner has done. Amaranthus spinach (Amaranthaceae) is a docklike weed which some American gardeners encourage when it turns up. One of the Amaranthus—*A. leucocarpus*—was a major grain crop of the Aztecs. *Lilies and nasturtium*

Roots and Stems

Roots are workhorse organs whose function is to conduct nutrients and water into the plant and in some cases to store food, but they provide some of nature's most pungent flavors. Ginger, turmeric, licorice and horseradish are so powerful that they are used only as spices or condiments, while the roasted roots of dandelion and chicory have both passed muster as ersatz coffee. Few roots are outstandingly nutritious, although some tribes in New Guinea have recently upset nutritional rubric yet again by living healthily on an almost exclusive diet of sweet potatoes, which are hardly superior, in protein or anything else, to turnips. The merits of food roots lie primarily in their astonishing range of flavors, from sweet to bitter, through infinite shades of indescribable subtlety; in their low-calorie bulk, which makes them, like cabbage and spinach, a fine vehicle for more nutritionally assertive foods; and in their availability, for they are designed by nature to act as store houses and can be kept for months either in clamps or, as with salsify, scorzonera, or parsnip, just left in the ground to be picked at will all winter long (provided you put some sacks or litter over the top, to prevent the ground freezing).

Root vegetables, like so many good things, have often been despised. Many people have written turnips off as cattle food, although in the hands of the Chinese and especially of the fastidious monks of Nepal, they become things of startling beauty; and I was mildly shocked to learn from a Canadian friend recently that she had never heard of the *Fastidious monks of Nepal*

Vegetables ad libitum

incomparable parsnip. Root vegetables, taken all in all, are wonderful. So long as plants continue to have roots, people can sleep easy in their beds at night.

The same families that supply the bulk of the edible leaves also provide most of the temperate roots. Only the incorrigibly leafy Polygonaceae are badly represented.

Thus the Cruciferae provides *Raphanus*, the radishes, whose name—from *radix*, as in radical—means root. Radishes have been in cultivation for so long that their wild ancestors have been altogether lost. Western countries tend to favor the extraordinarily quick-growing summer types, as fiery ingredients in salads. They are also fine as crudités, and far more appropriate as a predinner nibble than the peanut or salted almond, since they do nothing except clear the palate. But the West should also look harder at the slower-growing big radishes favored in the East. The big *daikon*, for example, is a large, mild white radish and is one of Japan's standard vegetables.

The disprized radish

The Cruciferan genus *Brassica* inevitably is represented. The turnip, *Brassica campestris*, has been cultivated for thousands of years and can be pureed, roasted, used as bulk in stews, or as a garnish. The larger rutabaga may have arisen in Bohemia (Czechoslovakia) in the seventeenth century, as a hybrid of *B. campestris* and *B. oleracea*. The turnip is not truly a swollen root, but a swollen hypocotyl; the bit of the plant between the root proper and the first embryonic leaves. The rutabaga includes a swollen hypocotyl fused to the swollen stem base. The way to distinguish rutabagas from turnips is not by color—the flesh of both rutabagas and turnips may be either yellow or white, and the skin color is highly variable—but by the presence of leaf scars around the "neck" of the rutabaga. In kohlrabi (*Brassica oleracea*) the swelling is confined to the stem. It is as if *Brassicas* just have a tendency to lay down big round food stores, which move up and down the stem and root from species to species like a can of beans in the neck of a pantomime ostrich.

Maculate rutabagas

The Compositae contributes several fine roots, which tend, as a group, to be largely neglected. The Jerusalem artichoke is a native of North America. Not only does it have oddly sweet roots that make excellent soup but it also throws up tall, leafy stems that form a useful garden screen. The Jerusalem artichoke is, after all, a *Helianthus*; a close relative of the sunflower. Pigs are fond of the aromatic Jerusalem artichoke, and John Seymour records in *The Fat of the Land* (Faber and Faber, 1961) that he plowed and weeded a field by planting it with these tubers and then setting pigs to grub them up.

The neglect of *Tragopogon porrifolius*, the salsify, astonishes me. Although it is native to southern Europe, it will grow elsewhere and its roots, which are extremely hardy, can be "stored" in the ground all through winter. Salsify's flowers are dandelion like (only bluey-purple). Its roots, too, are long and narrow like a dandelion's, but their flavor is wonderful, with an oddly maritime tang that has earned them the nickname of "vegetable oysters." In the old days, when oysters were common and cheap ("poverty and oysters always seem to go together," as Sam Weller put it), people used them to eke out their meat pies and puddings. Now that oysters are dear, salsify could and should emerge as

Poverty and salsify

a comparable pie filler. I once made a pigeon and salsify pie, just to prove the point. Salsify is also good when pureed, baked, or roasted; indeed, it is the Compositae's answer to the parsnip.

Scorzonera, another southern European "dandelion," also deserves mention; but its black-skinned roots are inferior to salsify's and I would rather grow the latter.

The Umbelliferae's contribution to the roots includes the carrot, parsnip, celeriac, and "turnip-rooted" forms of parsley and chervil. The carrot is rightly renowned as a source of vitamin A (the night-vision vitamin; hence the saw that carrots help you to see in the dark) and also contains a particularly potent form of dietary fiber. I like carrots because they taste nice: they are among the outstanding crudités and they can be so sweet that they have featured in many a dessert. The potent carrot

The parsnip hardly deserves less fulsome praise than the salsify, and being bigger is much easier to handle in the kitchen. Parsnips dug from the frosted earth and roasted alongside the meat are one of winter's delights. Chenopodiaceae has a stake in roots, again through *Beta vulgaris*. I have a friend who grows sugar beet as a vegetable although this seems to me mildly eccentric, but the common beet, in its blood-red and golden forms, deserves exploration. In its common English setting, boiled, sliced and pickled in vinegar, the beet belongs in the landlady tradition of sulfurous cabbage and moldering seedcake, but it can be roasted or baked or frittered in *pakoras*, and it sweetness and color make a fine contrast to yogurt. Explore the beet

Finally, a range of tropical or subtropical roots deserve mention, partly because they serve some people as staples and partly because they are finding their way into Western shops, and into the United States as crops. They include *Manihot*, alias cassava, which is a staple in parts of Africa and provides Westerners with tapioca; *Moranta*, or arrowroot, which Westerners use for its starch; *Colocasia*, or faro, which is one of the plants known as sweet potato in the Pacific islands; *Ipomoea*, which is what most people mean by sweet potato, and which originated in South America and has spread throughout the tropics, and northward to Spain and New Jersey; and *Dioscorea*, from the briony family, also known as the yam. As long as such sweet roots are available they are perhaps worth a try (and they have given rise to a pleasant, eclectic West Indian cuisine of curries and pasties), but they seem to me to have no obvious advantage for temperate countries over, for example, the parsnip or potato. All kinds of sweet potato

The Onion Group

The genus *Allium* is one of those natural oddities which, like yeast, has had an outstanding influence on world cuisine. The group includes the onion, shallot, Welsh onion, chive, garlic and leek. *Alliums* have at times been classified as lilies, and placed in the Liliaceae, and at times have been put in the Amaryllidaceae alongside snowdrops and narcissi. But botanists now recognize their unique status, as cooks have always done. *Alliums* now have their own family, the Alliaceae.

The onion is a bulb of the species *Allium cepa*, manifesting in hundreds of varieties, in an astonishing range of shapes, colors and

Vegetables ad libitum

sizes: from the pencil-thin, white scallions to vast livid or golden orbs. Onions are used as a bulk vegetable, roasted, baked, or even stuffed. They are allowed to melt into the background in curries, sauces, and soups of every idiom, and they can be sprinkled raw or pickled to make a piquant garnish.

Shallots, too, are *Allium cepa*, although they were once classified as a separate species. They are planted in winter to produce clusters of bulbs by midsummer, in time to leave the beds clear for other summer crops. The tree onions are an odd group producing little bulbs—bulbils—on flower heads; but these are more of a curiosity than a worthwhile crop.

King Arthur's onions

Welsh onions, *Allium fistolosum*, also grow in shallotlike bunches. They have nothing to do with Wales, and are grown, if at all, in kitchen rather than market gardens to be used as scallions and herbs.

The chive, *Allium schoenoprasum*, is an elegant little plant that grows wild from arctic Russia to Japan, from the Mediterranean to the Himalayas, and in North America. Its narrow leaves are a delightful garnish, and will improve the flavor of potatoes when boiled with them. Every garden should have a patch of chives.

Every garden should also have a patch of garlic, *Allium sativum*, which is expensive in the shops but one of the easiest crops to grow, if you have the right soil; just plant the cloves in autumn and harvest complete bulbs the following summer. Garlic is at home in most non-sweet dishes, and seems to enhance the flavor of other foods. Eaten in large quantities, it evidently lowers blood cholesterol levels; although it is theoretically preferable to avoid high levels through a low-fat diet than to use garlic as a drug to treat established excess.

Easy garlic

If onions have a fault (and how churlish it seems to suggest that they might) it is their lack of substance, or "bite," when cooked. Yet the *Allium* group has catered for that, too, with *Allium porrum*, the leek. Leeks probably originated in the Near East—the Israelites ate them before they left Egypt—but they rapidly spread north. They are a great standby, giving texture and flavor to austere meals as in the wondrous leek pudding of the north of England; and no plant better deserves to be a national emblem, as it is for Wales.

Substantial leeks

Fruits

Convention has established that fruits should be considered as sweet things, while vegetables are not. Yet a fruit in the botanical sense is merely that organ of the plant that bears the seeds, and at least as many fruits (in the botanical sense) are used as vegetables as serve as dessert. A few, such as the apple and banana, belong in both camps. Here I will discuss fruits that cooks regard as vegetables.

Fruits, whether sweet or not (and with a few exceptions such as the avocado, banana and olive), are nutritionally unexceptional. They are positively deficient in protein and low in energy: the apple, for instance, contains only half as many calories as the potato, which is itself a modest energy source. A few are outstanding in some mineral or vitamin—sweet peppers, black currants and oranges are a rich source of vitamin C for example. But fruits should be eaten in large amounts precisely because they are bulky; they have a useful fiber content and are low in calories. The old adage of plump ladies, that everything that tastes good makes you fat, is a poor generalization and obviously is not applicable to fruit.

The leaves and roots come mostly from the same five families; but the edible fruits come from a quite different set.

Corn on the cob is the immature fruiting head of *Zea mays* from the grass family, Gramineae. Corn contains sugar, which begins to change into starch within minutes of picking, so theoretically it should be taken at the run from field to cooking pot; but it is perfectly good when bought at the store. Cooking, in boiling water, is mainly for heating purposes; five minutes is enough. Some people freeze corn, but the result is a sad pastiche of the real thing. The real thing is worth waiting for, and is one of the pleasures of late summer. *Sweet cobs*

The Leguminosae is known mainly for its dried seeds—pulses—but also includes a clutch of edible fruits, or pods. The mangetouts, or snow peas, are varieties of *Pisum sativum*, the ordinary garden pea, which Americans sometimes, rather flatteringly, call the English pea. The asparagus pea, noted as a foil for omelets, is *Lotus tetragonolobus* (which means its pods have four-angled lobes). The edible-podded beans include *Phaseolus vulgaris*, the green bean; *Phaseolus coccineus*, the scarlet runner; and *Psophocarpus tetragonolobus* (more four-angled lobes), alias the winged bean or Goa bean. *Edible pods*

The Cucurbitaceae is an opulent and primitive family from America, Asia and Africa; it includes the cucumbers and gherkins, marrows and squashes, pumpkins and melons, watermelons and gourds. The fruits are mostly non-sweet, although some are sweet, and some have uses other than culinary. The gourds serve many societies as vessels and ornaments, and the fibrous skeleton of one of them manifests as the loofah. *Opulent and primitive*

The genus *Cucumis* spans the world, with three major continents contributing intriguingly different variants. *Cucumis sativus*, which probably originated in southern Asia, is the cucumber. It has long been cultivated in India, and the Ancient Greeks and Romans knew it too. Cucumber has little nutritional value (it is almost as deficient in energy as celery, and is hardly outstanding in other departments) but it is a superb garnish for spicy meats and strong cheeses; it does after all provide a metaphor for coolness. *Cucumis anguria* comes from America. This is the gherkin, renowned worldwide as a pickle, sweet, sour, or hot, and particularly favored by the Jews of Eastern Europe to enliven their kosher austerity. *Cucumis melo*, which probably came first from Africa, is the melon. Its culinary status is peculiarly hybrid, between vegetable and fruit; it can be served as dessert, or, quite legitimately, as a palate-clearing starter. *Peculiarly hybrid*

Africa also contributed the watermelon, *Citrullus vulgaris*; a fine, thirst-quenching fruit, but it also provides oily and nutritious seeds which some societies at least have the prudence to eat.

Cucurbita pepo probably arose in America; it is one of those species, like *Brassica oleracea*, that manifests in vastly different forms. The archetype is perhaps the vegetable marrow, which can be fried, baked or stuffed and is a load of wet nothing when boiled. The smaller zucchini are marrows bred to be picked when only a few inches long, and are

Vegetables ad libitum

usually considered more exciting; they are pleasant when half disintegrated in *ratatouille* and can be fried and floated in thick soups like croutons. The flat and intriguing custard marrow has been grown in English gardens for 400 years but has rightly remained in a minor culinary league; but the fibrous spaghetti squash, which opens into long thin fronds, is an amusing substitute for noodles, although it lacks the latter's food value. Americans make much of summer squashes, and also of the pumpkin. Pumpkin seeds are rich in oil and protein, and are commonly eaten deep fried.

Finally, Americans are favored by *Cucurbita maxima*, the winter squash, which has a more floury texture than marrow and is generally more versatile.

The Solanaceae is full of surprises. It makes few contributions to the human condition but those it does make are striking. It gives us the potato on the one hand and deadly nightshade on the other, and a whole catalog of plants, including belladonna, which are used as drugs. It also gives us the tomato, the eggplant, the many varieties of sweet pepper and chili pepper.

The tomato, *Lycopersicon esculentum*, is from the misty, temperate regions of the lower Andes. Ancient, exotic, at one time allegedly aphrodisiac, it now manifests itself in a vast range of forms from the size of a marble to the size of a melon. It may be round, ellipsoidal, or pear shaped; golden-yellow or red. The big, fleshy, sweet Mediterranean kinds are best for cooking; the aromatic English kinds belong with raw cucumber and onion among the world's great garnishes. English tomatoes should be grown at home. The finest are thin skinned with a bouquet as delicate as Rhine wine. Only the tough ones travel; they are bred for that purpose.

Temperate tomatoes

The eggplant, *Solanum melongena*, is not only related to the potato but is in the same genus. It comes from tropical Asia, and, as *brinjal*, is greatly favored in India. The people of the Middle East regard eggplants as poor man's meat and like to stuff them with rice, herbs and nuts. But they no longer need be considered in such exotic context; even the British can grow them under glass in the spring.

Brinjals and pimientos

The sweet peppers, alias paprika or pimiento (the name depends on variety and region), are *Capsicum annuum*. Originally from tropical America, the sweet peppers are spreading farther and farther into temperate regions. Their pungency is provided by the compound capsicin; but it varies in amount from variety to variety and, erratically, from fruit to fruit. So some sweet peppers are sweet, and some are hot, Sweet peppers are bright red, bright green, or yellow, and are fine either cooked or raw.

Chilies, *Capsicum frutescens*, are also variable and unpredictable. They are often served pickled and you can eat one, casually, as if it were a carrot, and then be paralyzed by the next. But the risk is worth taking.

Nature is often cruel and has no particular interest in the human race; but if she cared for us like a mother she could hardly provide a finer selection of edible plants. People complain about the time it takes to wash vegetables and sometimes to peel them. But the only appropriate emotion is gratitude.

Vegetable recipes

Theme I
The road to pickledom

The question "why?" echoes loud and clear over all vegetable cookery: why cook them at all when so many are so good when eaten raw? Raw vegetables, not necessarily turned into salads but simply cut bite sized as crudités—carrot, cauliflower, celery, fennel, radish, turnip—could stand in as a course in almost any meal, and linger on as a perpetual side dish as bread should do. Raw vegetables more finely cut—tomato, cucumber, pepper, onion and celery—could almost be a ubiquitous garnish. Fresh vegetables and good bread are half of sound nutrition and good gastronomy.

Vegetables eagerly accept dressing; with oil, to counter their fatlessness; with herbs and spices, including sugar and salt; with acid vinegar or lemon, lime or tamarind to sharpen them; and with all manner of fermented materials—vinegar, of course, and soy sauce and *miso*, and alcohol such as the Chinese sweet white wine *mirin*, and yogurt as in the Indian *raitas*. Such dressings can be used as dips, or applied at the last minute, but if the vegetables are dressed heavily in such agents they grade quickly and imperceptibly into pickle.

The gratuitous use of salt and sugar—as of fat—should be avoided; both are lavished into Western (and sometimes into Eastern) cooking in absurd amounts, and possibly with evil nutritional consequences. If they are overused, the palate merely adjusts to a higher level, until unsalted or unsweetened food seems literally tasteless. But sugar and salt can both be used as spices in dishes that would be nonsensical without them but which are eaten only in small amounts and therefore do not make major nutritional inroads. Salt and sugar both come into their own in pickles.

VINAIGRETTE
Here is perhaps the simplest dressing of all, the classic French dressing.

**3 tablespoons olive oil
1 tablespoon wine or cider vinegar
Ground pepper (optional)
A pinch of salt**

Beat the oil and vinegar together, perhaps with pepper and a little salt. Olive oil and vinegar can simply be presented on the table as separate condiments.

Vinegar, sometimes with oil and often with salt and sometimes with sugar, is the basis of a whole spectrum of pickles from all over the world, some designed to be eaten almost instantly and some that can be stored for up to a year. Here is a simple pickle from Japan.

SWEET AND SOUR CABBAGE WITH SESAME
Except for the sesame seeds this pickle has a universal feel, and although it comes from Japan it could as well be Lancastrian.

**2 tablespoons white sesame seeds
$\frac{1}{2}$ cup wine vinegar
1 tablespoon sugar
$\frac{1}{2}$ teaspoon salt
1 lb ($\frac{1}{2}$ kg) red cabbage**

Toast the sesame seeds in a dry iron pan until they begin to change color and leap about. Bring the vinegar, sugar and salt to a boil and add the sesame seeds. Then allow to cool.

Cut the cabbage into thin strips—this, I think, is the ideal form for raw cabbage—and put it into a bowl. Pour in the spiced vinegar, making sure the cabbage is well coated. Stand a plate on the cabbage and weight down with a pile of saucers or a large jar of jam. Serve after 2 hours.

RED CABBAGE AND TURNIP
Here is a fairly hot version, again universal, that takes a little longer. Red cabbage is the basis, but many other vegetables can be added, such as cauliflower and kohlrabi.

**1 lb ($\frac{1}{2}$ kg) red cabbage
1 small turnip
2 small dried chili peppers
2 cups cider vinegar
1 tablespoon salt
1 teaspoon sugar**

Cut the cabbage into chunks. Cut the turnip into $\frac{1}{2}$-inch (1 cm) slices and cut across to make half moons. Arrange the vegetables in a glass jar, alternately, with the chilies in the middle. Mix 2 cups of water with the vinegar, salt and sugar and pour over the top. Close tightly.

The pickle will be ready in 10 days.

Vegetables ad libitum

PICKLED CUCUMBERS

1 lb ($\frac{1}{2}$ kg) small pickling cucumbers
2 garlic cloves
A few sprigs Chinese parsley
6 black peppercorns
1 tablespoon salt
2$\frac{1}{2}$ cups white wine vinegar
1 teaspoon sugar

Pack the cucumbers in a jar with the garlic, Chinese parsley and peppercorns dotted at intervals. Mix the salt, vinegar and sugar and pour over the top.
  Close tightly and leave in a warm place, for 10 to 14 days.

PICKLED TURNIPS WITH BEET AND FENNEL

In this variant, beet is used to color turnips, which in some countries are regarded as cattle food but east of Suez and north of the Scottish border are treated with appropriate reverence.

1 lb ($\frac{1}{2}$ kg) baby white turnips
1 small beet, peeled and sliced
A few sprigs Chinese parsley
1 garlic clove
1 tablespoon salt
1 teaspoon fennel seeds
2$\frac{1}{2}$ cups white wine vinegar

Peel and cut the turnips into halves or quarters and the beet into small half moons. Pack into a jar, with the Chinese parsley and garlic suitably spaced. Add the salt and fennel seeds to the vinegar, bring to a boil and pour over the top. Cover tightly; ready in 10 days.

PICCALILLI

Piccalilli is a great pickle, ideally suited to the suburban gardener who grows small amounts of all sorts of vegetables.

6 lb (3 kg) mixed vegetables: cauliflower, cucumber, squash, green beans, snow peas, green tomatoes and baby onions are all suitable
1$\frac{1}{4}$ cups salt
8 cups white vinegar
4 green chili peppers
6 whole cloves
1$\frac{1}{2}$-inch (3 cm) piece fresh ginger root
1 cup sugar
6 tablespoons dry mustard
3 tablespoons turmeric

Begin by cutting the vegetables into small pieces. Put them on a dish and cover with the salt. Leave for 24 hours, then rinse and drain.
  Pour 5 cups of the vinegar into a large saucepan, and add the chilies, cloves and ginger tied in cheesecloth.
  Add the sugar and stir until it dissolves. Add the vegetables and simmer for 20 minutes.
  While the vegetables are simmering, mix the mustard and turmeric with the remaining vinegar. Stir the mixture into the vegetables and simmer for another 10 minutes.
  Pour into jars and seal.

INDIAN VEGETABLE PICKLE

Here is a more complex variant on the sweet-sour theme from India.

2 lb (1 kg) turnips
1 lb ($\frac{1}{2}$ kg) young carrots
1 lb ($\frac{1}{2}$ kg) cauliflower
4 garlic cloves
2-inch (5 cm) piece fresh ginger root
1 large onion
$\frac{1}{2}$ cup corn oil
1 to 2 teaspoons chili powder
1 teaspoon ground cumin
1 teaspoon turmeric
1 tablespoon salt
1 cup brown sugar
1$\frac{1}{4}$ cups wine vinegar

Peel and slice the turnips and cut into half moons. Slice the carrots. Break the cauliflower into florets.
  Slice the garlic, ginger and onion finely and fry in the oil, until they are strongly aromatic. Then add the rest of the spices and fry for a few more minutes. When cool, stir in the salt and the vegetable pieces. Put the spicy vegetable mixture into jars.
  Stir the sugar into the vinegar and when it has dissolved bring to a boil. When it is cool, pour over the vegetables. Cover tightly. The pickle will be ready after 2 days.

HOT CARROT PICKLE

Mustard grows obligingly the world over and is the key to a fine range of pickles. It may, of course, be included in a vinaigrette. Here is a mustard-hot version of the normally sweet carrot pickle, from the Middle East.

1 lb ($\frac{1}{2}$ kg) carrots
1 teaspoon salt
1 tablespoon mustard seeds
$\frac{1}{2}$ teaspoon fennel seeds
6 green chili peppers
1-inch (2.5 cm) piece fresh ginger root, sliced thinly
2 garlic cloves, sliced
$\frac{1}{2}$ teaspoon sugar
1$\frac{1}{4}$ cups wine vinegar

Slice the carrots along their length and then halve. Put them in a dish, and sprinkle with salt. Leave in a warm place for a day. Add the mustard seeds, fennel seeds, whole chilies, sliced ginger, garlic and sugar to the vinegar and mix well in with the carrot. Transfer to jars, cover, shake well, and leave in a warm place for a few days.

JAPANESE PICKLED CUCUMBER
In the East, soy may stand in for vinegar. Here is a simple Japanese example, with cucumber.

1 lb ($\frac{1}{2}$ kg) cucumber
2 dried red chili peppers
4 tablespoons soy sauce
A generous pinch of sea salt

Cut the unpeeled cucumbers along their length. Remove the seeds and cut the cucumbers into 1-inch (2.5 cm) pieces. Slice the chilies thinly. Add the soy sauce and salt and mix in well. Put a weighted plate on top and leave for 12 to 24 hours.

CHINESE PICKLED CABBAGE
A more complex version with vinegar and lemon from China.

1 lb ($\frac{1}{2}$ kg) Chinese cabbage
1 shallot or small onion
1 sweet red pepper
$\frac{1}{2}$ lemon
3 tablespoons light soy sauce
3 tablespoons wine vinegar
A generous pinch of salt

The insubstantial leaves of Chinese cabbage are not shredded, like the robust European cabbage; the inner leaves are left intact and the outer ones

are cut into strips, about 2 inches by 1 inch (5 by 2.5 cm). Parboil the strips by pouring boiling water over them in a colander, and then drain thoroughly.

Chop the shallot or onion finely—as finely as you can; cut the pepper into thin rings and cut the lemon first in thin rounds, and then cut each round in half. Put all the ingredients in a bowl, and toss to mix. Put a weighted plate on top and leave for 1 to 2 hours.

PERSIAN CUCUMBER RAITA
Raitas are not normally classified as pickles, but I see no reason why they should not be.
Serves 4

1$\frac{1}{4}$ cups yogurt
1 cup chopped cucumber
1 scallion, chopped finely
1 tablespoon golden raisins
1 teaspoon chopped fresh mint

All is simply beaten in with the fresh, cool yogurt.

Theme II
Cooking vegetables

People do dire things to vegetables, elaborate and fiddly things, but it is hard to improve upon the intact softened entity; the roasted baby turnip, white and bronzed, the patiently steamed leek. Root vegetables wrapped in foil and baked, or parboiled and then given half an hour around the roasting meat, or cauliflowers and half cabbages in sealed casserole dishes with a little water are things of delight.

BAKED ONIONS
Here is the ultimately simple but almost unimprovable side dish.

6 large onions

Trim the onions but do not peel. Put them upright in a fireproof dish or roasting pan, and bake in a 400°F (200°C) oven for about 1 hour.

The antithesis—which should appeal particularly to the gardener, who finds himself with one of this and two of that and a small handful of something else—is to chop and mix the

Vegetables ad libitum

vegetables and provide just enough liaison for coherence but not enough to blur the colors. Chinese Mixed Vegetables deserve to be used in many contexts—not simply Chinese.

CHINESE MIXED VEGETABLES
Use almost any vegetable for this dish.
Serves 2

2 large or 6 small mushrooms (perhaps include a small Chinese dried mushroom, but they are powerful)
1 small onion (optional)
1 large carrot
5-inch (13 cm) piece unpeeled cucumber
1 sweet green pepper
½ lb (240 g) bean sprouts or cabbage or Chinese cabbage
Corn oil
⅔ cup light stock or water
A good pinch of salt
A good pinch of sugar
½ teaspoon soy sauce
1 teaspoon cornstarch

Trim and slice the vegetables delicately and appropriately. Leave mushrooms whole if small, or slice them if large. Slice the onion thinly. Cut the carrot in thin diagonal slices; cut the cucumber in a similar manner and the pepper in strips; shred the cabbage or, if it is Chinese cabbage, cut into small pieces.

Heat a little oil in a large saucepan and cook the onion until it just begins to soften. Add the green pepper and stir for another 30 seconds and then add the carrot and cook for 2 to 3 minutes. Add all the other vegetables. Toss them until they are well coated with the oil.

Then add the stock or water, salt, sugar and soy sauce, and allow to simmer for 2 minutes or until the vegetables are cooked to your taste.

While the vegetables are simmering, blend the cornstarch with 2 teaspoons of cold water to make a smooth, thin paste. Stir the cornstarch into the vegetables when they are almost done. Continue cooking for 1¼ minutes. Serve at once.

STUFFED TOMATOES
Serves 4

4 large beefsteak tomatoes
Olive oil
8 tablespoons dry breadcrumbs
1 garlic clove, crushed
2 tablespoons chopped fresh parsley
1 tablespoon chopped fresh basil
Salt and pepper
A large pinch of sugar
4 tablespoons grated cheese

Slice the tops off the tomatoes, and scoop out the pulp. Turn the hollow cases upside down to drain.

Chop the pulp finely and mix with 1 tablespoon of olive oil and all the other ingredients. Spoon the mixture into the tomatoes, balance their caps on top, and brush with oil.

Bake in the oven at 375°F (190°C) for about 20 minutes or until the tomatoes are soft and thoroughly hot.

RATATOUILLE
The formerly subtropical fruits such as zucchini, eggplant and green pepper are reduced almost to mush, to make a substantial dish that can be eaten either hot or cold as a main course, a starter or an accompaniment. Ratatouille is a classic.
Serves 4 to 6

1 lb (½ kg) zucchini
1 lb (½ kg) eggplant
1 lb (½ kg) green peppers
1 lb (½ kg) onions
1 lb (½ kg) tomatoes (preferably the big beefsteak kind)
2 garlic cloves
4 to 6 tablespoons olive oil
A large pinch of oregano
A large pinch of basil
Salt and pepper

Slice the unpeeled zucchini, eggplant and green peppers thinly. Slice the onions. Cut the tomatoes into wedges and crush the garlic.

Soften the onions and garlic in the oil in a large saucepan. Add the green peppers, eggplant, zucchini, tomatoes, herbs, salt and pepper. Cover tightly and cook, stirring occasionally, until the vegetables are soft. Uncover the pan halfway through to allow the excess liquid to evaporate.

A valuable motif in vegetable cooking is the creation of substance—body or bite—which vegetables tend to lack. Leaves, if close packed, are perhaps most substantial. The leek, made up of concentric rings of thickened leaf, has often stood in for meat; and spinach, the most proteinaceous of the commonly eaten leaves, even has some of meat's nutritional properties.

SAG ALU
Spinach cooked with potatoes and spices in Indian style. Serve piping hot with *chapatis* and yogurt.
Serves 4

2 lb (1 kg) boiled potatoes
1 lb (½ kg) spinach
1 onion
1 garlic clove
1-inch (2.5 cm) piece fresh ginger root
2 tablespoons oil
1 teaspoon mustard seeds
1 teaspoon ground cumin
1 teaspoon turmeric
½ teaspoon chili powder
¼ teaspoon ground fenugreek
A large pinch of salt

Cube the potatoes and chop the spinach.
 Fry the chopped onion, garlic and ginger in the oil in a large saucepan, together with the mustard, cumin, turmeric, chili powder, fenugreek and salt until the onion is soft. Add the potatoes and stir into the frying spices. When the potatoes are hot and thoroughly coated with the spicy oil, add the spinach. Stir, then put on the lid, turn the heat low, and allow the spinach to disintegrate into the mixture.

Spinach should be cooked without water: just warmed in a saucepan until it begins to sweat and then, the heat turned up, cooked in its own remarkable quantities of juice. If the spinach is chopped before cooking the resulting puree is solid enough to be fried like a cake, perhaps coated first with oatmeal.
 In India, where people are into spinach in a big way, they make balls—*koftas*—of spinach, stiffened with *besan* (chickpea) flour.

SPINACH KOFTAS
These traditionally would be served with a curry sauce; but they are at home in almost any company.
Serves 4

1 lb (½ kg) spinach
2 garlic cloves
½-inch (1 cm) piece fresh ginger root
1 green chili pepper

A large pinch of cinnamon
A large pinch of fenugreek
A large pinch of salt
½ teaspoon ground cumin
Besan (chickpea) flour
Oil for deep frying

Chop the spinach finely and cook it without water until it has disintegrated. Then mix in the chopped garlic, ginger and chili and the spices and stir in the *besan* flour, a little at a time, until the mixture is stiff. Make little balls of the mixture and deep fry.

Theme III
Fat and flour

The fatlessness and low calorie content of vegetables leaves room to exploit their obvious affinity for fat and flour. The modern custom of daubing all vegetables with butter (perhaps designed to compensate for the frozen vegetable's lack of flavor) is to be abhorred. Legitimate forms range from the thick soup, where the fat and flour provide liaison between the separate points of flavor and bite; through the various fat-and-flour sauces, flavored at will, which are applied separately to the clean, pristine vegetables; and from the *fritter*, *tempura* or *pakora*, where the pieces of vegetable are first dipped in batter and then fried—usually deep fried; to the stuffed pancake, *samosa*, pie, pudding, or stuffed dumpling (as in some of the Chinese *dim sum*), in which the vegetables are usually cooked separately and then encased in substantial pastry.

BASIC WHITE SAUCE
This is a basic white sauce in which the starch of the flour is dispersed through water to produce a matrix that holds the droplets of fat.
 The sauce is richer if you use milk, or a milk and water mixture, and can, of course, be made with stock. Nutmeg is an appropriate spice (or mace in the interest of delicacy) and herbs can be added at will.
 The same sauce with ½ cup of grated cheese stirred in will transform poached cauliflower, leeks or broccoli into a fine dish, especially if you cast off with a sprinkling of nutmeg and brown under the broiler or in the oven.

Vegetables ad libitum

2 tablespoons fat (I would use corn oil)
2 tablespoons flour
1¼ cups water
Seasoning

Heat the oil, stir in the flour and cook, stirring, for 2 to 3 minutes. Add the water a little at a time—stirring all the while to eliminate lumps—and cook for another 5 minutes or so. Season to taste.

THICK VEGETABLE SOUP
Grated cheese sprinkled on top of the soup and browned under the grill adds flavor and substance to the soup and is a good way of using up old Cheddar.
Serves 4

½ lb (240 g) carrots
½ lb (240 g) turnips
½ lb (240 g) leeks
1 onion
1 sweet red pepper
½ lb (240 g) potatoes
3 tablespoons oil
1⅓ cups split peas, soaked
5 to 6 cups stock or water
1 teaspoon yeast extract or a small
    piece *miso* (either of which stand
    in for salt)
2 tablespoons flour
Freshly ground black pepper

Slice the carrots obliquely, cut the turnips into little wedges and slice the leeks, onion, red pepper and potatoes.
  Heat half the oil in a large saucepan, add the vegetables and cook them, stirring for 5 minutes—there is hardly enough oil to "fry" them; but there should be enough to coat and seal them. Add the stock or water, stir in the yeast extract or sprinkle in the *miso*, and simmer for 30 minutes.
  Heat the remaining oil in a frying pan, stir in the flour and cook for 2 to 3 minutes. Add a cup of the vegetable liquid a little at a time, stirring all the while, to make a cream. Then stir this white sauce into the soup, pepper liberally, and simmer for another 5 minutes until the vegetables are tender.

CARROT SOUP WITH ZUCCHINI CROUTONS
This is a substantial soup; which is not undistinguished.

Serves 4

1½ lb (¾ kg) carrots
A sprinkling of thyme
A pinch of salt
2½ cups stock or water
2 tablespoons oil
1 tablespoon flour
2 zucchini
¾ cup grated hard cheese

Slice the carrots into disks. Put them in a flameproof casserole with the thyme, salt and the stock or water, and boil for about 12 to 15 minutes or until the carrots are soft.
  Heat the oil in a saucepan, stir in the flour and gradually add some of the carrot water to make a cream; cook for 5 minutes. Add the cream to the carrots and cook for another 5 minutes.
  Meanwhile slice the zucchini and fry them in a pan that has been only lightly brushed with oil, until they are soft and slightly browned.
  Arrange the zucchini on the surface of the soup, then sprinkle on the grated cheese. Put the dish under the broiler until the top is lightly browned.

INDIAN PAKORAS IN WESTERN STYLE
One of my favorite inventions is the mixed vegetable *pakora*. The beet lends color; a soft pinkness that suffuses through the gold.
Serves 4

1 white turnip
1 rutabaga
1 potato
1 parsnip
1 beet
1 cup flour
1 teaspoon ground coriander
½ teaspoon ground cumin
½ teaspoon turmeric
½ teaspoon chili powder
A pinch of salt
A touch of lemon juice
Oil for deep frying
1 small onion
2-inch (5 cm) piece cucumber
1¼ cups yogurt

Peel the turnip, rutabaga, potato and parsnip, cut them into cubes a little under 1 inch (2.5 cm) across and boil for about 12 minutes or until they begin to soften. Boil the beet separately, and whole, for about 30 minutes, then peel and cut into similar cubes. This precooking can be done in advance; it doesn't matter if the vegetables become cold.

Mix the flour, spices, salt and lemon juice and add enough water to make a batter. When you are ready to serve, heat the oil (you want it really hot); coat the vegetable cubes in the batter and deep fry.

Pile the fritters, or *pakoras*, on a plate and garnish with raw chopped onion and cucumber, and serve the yogurt separately as a sauce; or stir the onion and cucumber with a little seasoning into the yogurt to make a *raita*.

Theme IV
The vegetable as sauce

In the above recipes the vegetables provide the substance and white sauce or yogurt provides the liaison; but the vegetable, pureed, may itself serve as a sauce. The technique is ancient—the bashed neep (mashed rutabaga) is the traditional and unbeatable accompaniment to haggis—but Michel Guérard has recently elevated the puree to *haute cuisine* in his *Cuisine Minceur*, which he designed as an antidote to what has become the traditional heavy sauces of butter and cream. The puree can provide flavor without heavy infusions of fat and calories, and deserves wider acknowledgement.

BASHED NEEP
This mashed rutabaga dish is an excellent accompaniment to all manner of sausage and roast meats.
Serves 4

2 lb (1 kg) rutabagas
2 tablespoons butter
A pinch of nutmeg
A heavy sprinkling of black pepper
A pinch of salt

Peel the rutabagas and cut into 1-inch (2.5 cm) cubes. Simmer in water for at least 30 minutes or until they are very soft. Drain the rutabagas and mash them with the butter, nutmeg, pepper and salt.

NEEP PURRY (TURNIP PUREE)
This recipe comes from the pseudonymous Meg Dods, who cooked for the Cleikum Club, an early nineteenth-century cabal of Scottish gourmets.

2 lb (1 kg) turnips
2 tablespoons butter
White pepper
$\frac{1}{2}$ teaspoon ground ginger
A pinch of salt

Meg Dods suggests that the turnips should be boiled for up to 2 hours; but it perhaps was customary to pull turnips when they were bigger and tougher than is the custom now. Then she mashed them with the ginger, which the Cleikum members rightly thought a splendid touch, and the other ingredients.

Cauliflower and broccoli are eminently amenable to the puree treatment; just simmer the florets in water for 15 minutes or until they are soft, and then puree them in the blender with nutmeg, pepper and salt and perhaps a touch of milk. M. Guérard suggests four parts spinach and one part pears (quartered and boiled for 15 minutes) pureed together.

And here is a more robust Middle Eastern version, using eggplant.

EGGPLANT PUREE
Such smooth, all but fatless, purees are an excellent foil for the fattier vegetable *pakoras* or fritters.

2 eggplants
2 tablespoons olive oil
Juice of 1 lemon
2 tablespoons chopped parsley
(ordinary or Chinese)
2 garlic cloves
Black pepper
Salt

Cook the eggplants whole over a naked flame or under the broiler, until the skins are black and blistered and the flesh is soft. Then peel them by rubbing off the skins under the cold tap. Mash the eggplant flesh with a fork or in a blender, working in the oil and lemon juice as you go. Finally, mix in the parsley, crushed garlic and seasoning.

Serve cold.

The alternative lifestyle-the fungi

There is something about fungi that brings out the extremes in people. The mushroom has always been a creature of fantasy—the home of the little people that springs from the onanistic semen of the tupping ram—and the misconceptions and calumnies persist: that it can be grown only on horse dung, preferably from well-fed racehorses, and that, once grown, it has no food value.

On the other hand the phenomenal growth rate and versatility of yeasts and molds has led many a respectable scientist to declare that they are world savers: and to point out that a half-mile-square yeast factory could provide the protein needs of the world, and even to imply that such a calculation is relevant to the real predicaments of real people.

The truth, as ever, lies between these extremes of euphoria and calumny. Fungi will never be such a valuable food source worldwide as, for example, potatoes. Yet they have enormous and exciting potential, as fermenting agents to preserve food and provide new and exquisite flavor, and as modest but at times critical providers of protein, energy and micronutrients. During 4,000 years of wine and cheese and bread and *miso*, we have explored only the margins of this potential.

Critical providers of protein and energy

Fungi represent, in the modern phrase, an alternative life-style. Green plants are autotrophs, which means that they feed themselves, using the sun's energy to cobble together assorted, scattered atoms into protein, fat, nucleic acids, sugars, starch and cellulose, and the thousand other props of living tissue. Animals are heterotrophs, consuming the living tissue that the plants have put together, and pressing it into their own service. But all flesh dies, and then fungi (and bacteria) feed upon it, which is an animallike thing to do except that they can digest materials (notably cellulose) that animals, unassisted, cannot digest. Yet they also utilize inorganic materials, such as nitrates and phosphates, which is a pathognomonically plantlike thing to do. Fungi are called saprophytes, from the Greek word *sapros*, meaning putrid. In essence they are middlemen, duckers, weavers and opportunists. They are important as a food source partly because they are themselves flesh, and can be consumed by human heterotrophs, and partly because the world produces an awful lot of dead organic material, from dung and straw to oil and wood pulp, for them to feed upon.

Indeed, it is easy to see why so many scientists in recent years have suggested that fungi, and in particular yeasts, are the food of the future, and to see why an impressive list of companies, including most of the major food and oil firms in the United States, Europe, the Soviet Union, Japan and the Third World, have begun investing in the single-cell proteins, or scps, that yeasts produce. The case is seductive; yet this apparently outstanding function of fungi will not help significantly to solve the world's food problem, and may even detract from its solution.

The seductive but erroneous case for single-cell proteins

In essence, the case is simple. Microorganisms, properly prepared, are high-protein foods, comparable, for practical nutritional purposes, to meat. But whereas a calf takes four weeks to double its weight, and a chicken takes four days, a microbe such as a yeast can double its weight in four hours. If you began with a pound of yeast at midnight, and fed it well, then by midnight the following day you could have 64 pounds. In another 24 hours you would have two tons. And by midnight of the third day you would have 100 tons of high-protein material: the protein equivalent of several hundred head of cattle.

Yeast at midnight

Every country can provide suitable substrates. The industrial countries have agricultural and forestry wastes, of course—the leaves and stalks of the potato plant, for example—but also the thousands of tons of organic by-products from the oil-based petrochemical industry. Even methane gas, from coal, can be processed to feed microbes. Third World countries have millions of tons of plantation waste, from cacao and coffee plants, sugarcane, palms and pineapples, that are commonly left not only to rot but to pollute.

In the early 1960s, when the thin stream of capital that had for many years been flowing into SCP production swelled to a flood, the world's food problems were ascribed, primarily, to lack of protein. Livestock production on the Western scale clearly was not appropriate for the majority of the world, which included most of the hungry and allegedly protein-deficient people. Microbial protein was the obvious answer.

The unarguable value of single-cell proteins . . .

The only major objection to this apparently unassailable argument seemed to be that SCPs might not be as good as had been claimed. They are rich in nucleic acids, including the purines, which are thought to be involved in producing gout. Some of the materials on which yeasts could be grown—notably oil by-products—theoretically could contain carcinogens; and it is difficult to eliminate these from the SCPs themselves. But difficult does not mean impossible, and, besides, the immediate problems of hunger were far more serious than the distant and only theoretical prospect of cancer. These caveats seemed small compared with microbes' obvious advantages.

But there proved to be other difficulties. The phenomenal predicted growth rate of yeast is only theoretical; at least, it may be achieved on the scale of the laboratory flask, when we are talking about a doubling of weight from one gram to two grams, say, but the physical problems posed by scale-up are of the kind that give engineers sleepless nights. How do you ensure that each of the tiny cells in a huge mass of yeast has reasonable and constant access to substrate? How do you provide each cell with sufficient oxygen, and keep it free from its own waste products, which would inhibit growth? And how do you stop any one of a thousand wild microorganisms invading the culture, and perhaps producing toxins? How do you monitor the final product, to ensure that it really is safe—nontoxic, noncarcinogenic?

. . . except, that is, for the snags

The answer is that to produce SCPs safely and in bulk you must build a factory complete with bulk tanks, germ-free laboratories and temperature-controlled growing rooms that is at least as sophisticated as a modern brewery. That, and the fact that the waste on which the yeasts are supposed to be grown always has a market price—oil by-

The alternative lifestyle-the fungi

products have alternative uses, and even pineapple tops at least must be transported to the factory—has meant that SCPs are not cheap, and never can be. Indeed, the countries that can afford to buy them are those that could afford to buy conventional foods. SCPs are not directly going to help poor people.

If you can afford single-cell proteins, you do not need them

Yet the rich people who can afford SCPs have no need to run even the small theoretical health risk of eating them: they have no immediate starvation problems to set against that risk. So in practice, and in the foreseeable future, SCPs are destined to be used as animal feed. Yet meat production is not vital to human survival, and the intensive livestock factories for which SCP feeds are most appropriate are liable to detract, if anything, from the world's ability to feed its people. And what do we gain from the alleged efficiency of yeasts if we are obliged, in the end, to push them through inefficient, old-fashioned livestock?

But the final blow to the SCPs-will-save-the-world thesis came from the nutritionists. They pointed out, as we have seen, that human protein needs have been exaggerated; that world food shortages were, after all, literal food shortages, and not specifically shortages of protein; that if you produced enough grain then you would thereby produce enough protein; and that if you did not produce enough grain then there was no obvious point in peddling high-protein supplements.

So where does that leave SCPs? As a profitable industry, is one answer, for the reality is that European and American intensive livestock units will be with us for some time. But, to be less cynical, they could yet bring some less equivocal benefits.

Yeast and algae as cleaners-up

SCPs become useful when they are themselves produced as a by-product of other essential processes. For instance, it is ridiculous to pretend, as has sometimes been claimed, that the problems of plantation-based economies can be solved by growing SCPs on plantation wastes. Modern political precedents suggest that a country that specializes in sugarcane, for example, and which cannot feed its people, would do better to grow less sugar and more wheat, and hence become self-reliant in food—in which case it would have no need for SCPs. On the other hand a country such as Malaysia could feed its people reasonably comfortably and yet leave vast areas to spare for the profitable production of exportable pineapples or palm oil. (It is a pity Malaysia does specialize in palm oil, which is a highly saturated fat; but this is just an example.) Already, in practice, the pineapple and palm plantations are causing awesome pollution problems: palm effluent is particularly offensive. These effluents could be—and are being—used as substrates for microbes, just to get rid of them, or at least to render them more innocuous. SCPs could be, and are being, produced as a result; but only in passing, as a bonus. Used as animal feed they possibly will not make a great contribution to the Malaysians' nutrition. But their sale will help to finance the inescapable chore of cleaning up the environment.

The SCP manufacturers complain (although less so now, as the case for using them as human food grows more threadbare, and the profits from animal-feed sales mount up) that they have been dogged by prejudice. People, they say, will not eat microbes, because microbes are

*Mushrooms enjoy a unique position in cookery.
Their texture and flavor are reminiscent of
meat, while their nutritional qualities are akin
to those, say, of green peas; and they and their
relatives could be grown in abundance all over
the world.* **Top,** *mushroom soup;* **left,** *stuffed
mushrooms, and* **bottom right,** *mushrooms en
croûtes—that is, in a baked bread case, which
should be thick.*

Mushrooms almost at their simplest: **above,** *with olive oil; and,* **below,** *extending and flavoring baked fish.*

germs. That is only half true: yogurt, beer and Roquefort, which is as shamelessly moldy as damp bread, have enjoyed a pretty sound reputation these past few centuries. What is true is that microbes and molds have usually served only as relishes: food very definitely of the third kind. To eat them in bulk as significant sources of protein and energy is the conceptual leap, not just the mere eating of them. The main failure of SCPs is that their production requires high technology, and is therefore expensive: and that the end product may serve as a nutrient in certain contexts but would never pass muster as food. The fungus that does seem to be working its passage from a mere relish to a major food source is one that is already acknowledged as a thing to be eaten: to whit, the mushroom, and some of its relatives.

Mushrooms have presumably been popping up in fields, quickly and without warning, for as long as there have been fields. They have no palpable seed to plant, but only minute spores; that they should have been cultivated at all—not, traditionally, by introducing spores but by planting bits of the threadlike underground "roots," or hyphae—was one of those major technological leaps, like the invention of the windmill or of crop rotation, that has been absorbed as if (in retrospect) the discovery was merely inevitable. But cultivation of the European mushroom, *Agaricus* (formerly *Psalliota*), was begun in France in the seventeenth century by the market gardeners around Paris, who inoculated the spent hotbeds in which they had grown their melons. Until recently, when mushroom cultivation began to emerge as a precise technology, the empirical methods of the original gardeners had hardly been changed.

The technological leap into mushroom cultivation

Like most of the big edible fungi, the mushroom is a basidiomycete (exceptions are the truffle and morel, which are ascomycetes). The bulk of the fungus is a mass—mycelium—of hyphae, probing a little bit like roots and a little bit like worms, through organic material. When conditions are right—and there is a very large prize for anyone who can work out exactly what "right" means in this context—a mass of hyphae, bunched together, pushes through the surface of the substrate to form a fruiting body. Slung beneath the cap of the fruiting body are either gills, as in the mushroom, or tubes, which are sometimes fused to produce a muffinlike series of pores. On the gills and within the tubes are formed the spores, destined to be scattered by wind and water and (given an extraordinary amount of luck) to give rise to a new mycelium.

The conditions that produce vigorous mycelia, able to throw up plenty of fruiting bodies, are not the same as those that will induce the fruiting bodies to form: putting it crudely, you need to give the mycelium a good time to get it to grow, and then give parts of it a hard time so that it will fruit. In short, as the technologists like to put it, mushroom cultivation involves solid fermentation on a two-substrate system.

The SCP manufacturers, in a sense, cheat: they work under sterile conditions, like brewers or manufacturers of antibiotics, to make absolutely certain that the only fungus growing on the medium, oil or malt or whatever, is the one they want to grow. The mushroom grower cannot afford such effete maneuverings and it is not even clear that they would help him if he could, for mushrooms, at least in a state of nature,

Nothing effete about mushrooms

The alternative lifestyle-the fungi

seem to require the presence of other microbes. In lieu of an aseptic compost, the mushroom growers must simply create conditions that favor mushrooms rather than the thousand other organisms that would be happy to put in an appearance in their place.

The main part of the two-substrate system, the part that favors mycelial growth, is compost: traditionally a mixture of dung and straw. Compost, ecologically, is extremely complex stuff. It is first attacked by thermophilic bacteria that may heat it almost to the boiling temperature of water. As it cools, fungi of the actinomycete group take over and, after them, an inoculum of mushroom will flourish. In practice, then, the mushroom grower commonly creates vast compost heaps of manure, arranging them in long parallel windrows for ventilation and for easy handling, and then packs what remains after the flush of heat into trays, into which the mushroom spawn is inoculated. These trays traditionally are kept in natural caves (such as those along the Loire), in quarry tunnels or, nowadays, in concrete sheds that will similarly preserve the autumnal temperatures that mushrooms need.

The ecology of the mushroom heap

The second component of the two-substrate system, which induces the growing mycelium to fruit, is a cap of earth, or peat and chalk, or (in one experimental process) fiberglass, laid over the top of the compost. In this superficial layer water and nutrients may be deficient and it is in these harsh conditions (as is so often the case in nature) that reproduction takes place. Yet fructification evidently requires more than starvation. It will not take place in pure culture. Certain bacteria that have not yet been completely identified are required to provide the final spur.

An enormous number of things can go wrong in mushroom cultivation. If conditions are too hot or too cold, too acid or too alkaline, too airy or too dank, provide too much nitrogen or not enough, then growth does not happen or takes place too slowly to be of use; and a dozen other importunate fungi will put in an appearance. When it has grown, the mushroom may be victim of an impressive catalog of pests and infections. In short, it requires delicate husbandry; and when a formula was found that worked it was hardened into ritual. Mushrooms have always been elusive, otherworldly things; and even after cultivation they preserved some of their mysterious, quasi-supernatural aura.

Delicate husbandry

What has changed the entire scene is science. Mushrooms have traditionally been grown on horse manure; its open texture and rapid rotting seemed exclusively to provide the right conditions. Dr W. A. Hayes from Aston University in England, and his colleagues, have shown that the mushroom's prime requirement is simply for cellulose, the brittle material of which plant cell walls are made. Mushrooms will grow on straw, paper or pieces of sugarcane; and they can be fertilized with any kind of manure, including the chicken manure that should be available worldwide, provided it is presented in the right form. It is even possible to use artificial fertilizer. Dr Hayes has also emphasized that mushrooms are far from negligible as a source of protein and energy. They contain more than 90 percent water, when fresh, but the dry matter is 18 percent protein and six percent fat. The protein is rich in lysine, which is the amino acid most required by people on a high-cereal diet; and the fat is largely polyunsaturated.

Mushrooms on paper, mushrooms on straw, mushrooms in every back yard

Every country in the world has straw to spare. Every country has sources of manure. Mushroom cultivation tends to be labor intensive, because the fruits appear sporadically and must be picked by hand; and the poor countries, that have most need of extra food, have plenty of labor. Suddenly all the world is interested in mushrooms. Consumption is increasing by ten percent per year.

Every country has room for mushrooms

Nutritionally the mushroom should be considered as a superior vegetable: comparable, say, to the fresh pea. But because of its muscular texture and its savor, it is, gastronomically, closer to meat. Indeed, as the recipes show, it can be used in any context; as garnish, relish, bulk or accompaniment. The only certainty is that it deserves to take a central role in all the world's cuisine.

Despite its complexity, the mushroom seems to be the easiest edible macrofungus to cultivate; at least it is the one that has caught people's imagination. Yet the mushroom is only one representative of a whole class, as potentially significant as the classes of animal or vegetable.

The genus *Agaricus* itself contains three common, edible types. The one that has taken most readily to cultivation is *A. bisporus*, but *A. campestris*, the wild field mushroom that was first cultivated, has a superior flavor; and so too does the yellow-tinted horse mushroom, *A. arvensis*, with its whiff of aniseed.

Another candidate for the compost-heap style of cultivation—indeed, already cultivated for many centuries by the Chinese—is *Volvariella volvacea*, the paddy-straw mushroom. Rice straw is the usual substrate, although tapioca and other residues have been used. Conventionally, the straw is arranged in long windrows on an earth base, and piled up about 30 inches, with the fungus inoculated at intervals. The compost first heats and then cools and produces a crop after about 12 days, without the aid of a casing layer. Yield is unpredictable by these traditional methods; but plastic houses are on the way in and China is moving rapidly from its postrevolution, peasant-wisdom agriculture into the pleasures of high science, It will be surprising if *Volvariella* does not rival the ascendancy of *Agaricus*, at least in wet, subtropical, rice-growing countries.

Most of the large edible fungi are, however, associated with trees: sometimes, like some bracket fungi, growing unashamedly as parasites, but often taking part in subtle fusions of hyphae and tree roots, known as mycorrhizae; symbiotic fusions whose origins are so deeply embedded in arboreal history that the forest trees need the fungi almost as much as the fungi need them. Successful cultivation of most fungi, then, will depend partly on the extent to which foresters are prepared to extend the uses of their forests, and partly on the technologists' ability to prize the fungi from their origins.

Fungi in the forests

Thus, the only other mushroom that has so far challenged *Agaricus* in cultivation is *Lentinus edodes*, the *shiitake*, which is grown in eastern Asia—primarily Japan—by inoculating into holes drilled in hardwood logs: oak, chestnut, alder, maple and hornbeam. During the first seven or eight months, when the mycelium spreads through the logs, the *shiitake* prefers Mediterranean temperatures, 75° to 82° Fahrenheit, but during fruiting, when the logs are stacked, neatly crisscrossed, in the

How to grow the perfect shiitake

The alternative lifestyle-the fungi

raising yards, they prefer a modest 55° to 68° Fahrenheit. The seven months required for preliminary growth is a long time, but cropping can be continued for three to six years. The Japanese have shown what a delightful thing the *shiitake* is; it is a little like garlic and a little like mushroom and is astonishingly aromatic. It can be bought, dried, in Europe and the United States. But surely it could be cultivated in those rolling hardwood forests of New England, or in southern Europe?

Boletus edulis, the cèpe (or in Italy, *porcini*, meaning piglets) and its relatives, form another delightful woodland group that could theoretically be encouraged; they belong with morels and girolles in the finest cooking. *Tricholoma*, too, including the marvelous *T. matsutake*, which grows under pine trees in Japan and is available, dried, in the West, as well as the European blewits, are also fit subjects for cultivation and for world cuisine. The example of the oyster mushroom, *Pleurotus ostreatus*, which is traditionally grown like the *shiitake* on logs (primarily beech) but is now being grown on crushed corn cobs, shows that it should be possible to sever fungi's cumbersome association with trees: and even that prince of fungi the morel, *Morchella*, has now been raised on beds made from apple residue and paper waste. If the truffles, *Tuber melanosporum* and *T. marginatum*, could be induced to forget that they evolved on the roots of hardwood trees, then world cooking would never be the same again.

Cèpes, truffles and matsutake

The grower of mushrooms and of SCP microbes is interested in harvesting the fungi themselves; the substrate—oil, compost or whatever else is used—is emphatically left behind. The more common way to use fungi and other microbes in food production is to set them to work upon a substrate, and then eat the substrate, pleasantly rotted, with or without the microbes. Thus yeast is set upon flour to produce leavened dough, and upon grains and fruit to produce beer, wine and cider; and milk products are abandoned to lactobacilli to produce cheese. It is odd that the three components of the traditional plowman's lunch— bread, cheese and beer, wine or hard cider—which in different forms are at the core of a dozen cultures, should all be products of fermentation (controlled microbe attack). Or perhaps it is not so odd, because microbial attack produces acids and alcohols from the original carbohydrates or fats of the substrate; and these acids and alcohols combine to form a vast array of aromatic esters. The three new-formed groups of chemicals act as preservatives, and add flavor and color. Bread, wine, beer and cheese are discussed elsewhere in this book: microbes inevitably permeate a cookbook as they do all life. But here it seems appropriate to discuss the major, future role of fungi in producing sauces and foods from grains and beans; in the production, that is, of *shoyu* (soy sauce) and *miso* (soybean paste) and their actual or potential relatives.

Fermented plowman's lunch

The husbandry of fungi in *shoyu* or *miso* production is conceptually different from SCP or mushroom cultivation. In SCP production sterile conditions prevail; the required organism is the only one allowed near the substrate. A whole pharmacopoeia of microbes is allowed a crack at mushroom composts, but conditions are arranged so that the planted mushroom, alone, eventually predominates. In *shoyu* or *miso* produc-

Miso, soy sauce and a hundred variants

tion (or in several hundred comparable fermentations in Asia and Africa) the exact nature of the functional microbes is of little consequence; and in practice, although a few species of aspergilli, yeasts and lactobacilli tend to dominate, the catalog of microbes that could be involved in any one fermentation can run into several pages—assuming, that is, that all the participants could be identified. Fermentation is never far removed from putrescence, and it is one of nature's most pleasant miracles that the only half-controlled rotting of a vast range of materials should so often yield products that are not only nontoxic and tolerable, but nutritious and pleasant.

Shoyu and *miso* have been produced in China and Japan for perhaps 3,000 years. *Shoyu* production is now the world's third largest food fermentation industry, second only to bread and booze, and the sauce is now known worldwide. *Miso* is as deeply ingrained in Japanese culture as beer is in Britain's. It is finding its way into Britain through the health food shops and oriental stores, and has already reached supermarket status in the United States. It epitomizes the theme of this book; an ancient, established food that is very much a food of the future.

Both *shoyu* and *miso* production involve the creation—and creation is the proper word for this ancient craft—of a *koji*. A soy sauce *koji* is made (commonly, although not necessarily) by mixing soybeans that have been washed, soaked and cooked, with whole wheat that has been toasted and crushed, or with wheat flour that has been steamed or subjected to dry heat (parched). Then an inoculum of mold is mixed in—either from a specially prepared seed *koji*; or, traditionally, as a portion of *koji* from a previous fermentation; or, often, in the big-business, brewery-type production that now prevails, as a laboratory-prepared suspension of prescribed fungal spores. These molds are aspergilli; more specifically they are strains of *Aspergillus oryzae*, one of the few aspergilli that is not actually poisonous.

The Zen art of cultivating koji

The inoculated bean-grain-mold mixture is then spread in shallow trays, traditionally made of woven bamboo, through which the air can circulate freely. It is kept in a humid room at the subtropical temperature of 86° Fahrenheit, and is turned regularly. After 72 hours, the *koji* is ready. If it is left longer than this, the aspergilli sporulate, and the *koji* becomes moldy, "off" and ammoniacal.

That is phase one. But in *shoyu* production the 72-hour *koji* is then mixed with 18 percent brine to produce a *moromi*; and this saline mixture is attacked first by lactobacilli and then by yeasts, to produce, after months or years, the mature, intriguing sauce. The lactobacillus-yeast combination is common in such "natural" fermentations; presumably before the biology of yeast was worked out in the nineteenth century, and pure yeast cultures were prepared, the fermentation of bread and beer would have been similarly mixed, and the product would have been pleasantly sour.

Shoyu, traditionally, is as varied as wine: different proportions of soybean and different kinds of grain may be used in the *koji*, and the use of one *koji* to inoculate the next would ensure that each producer, shop, household or monastery would produce individual sauces whose character was determined by the particular mold strains that became established. The modern mass-produced soy sauce is more uniform. Japan alone produces more than 100,000 million quarts annually; and such high-volume production inevitably implies a certain amount of standardization.

Shoyu is a relish; it has a respectable protein content but is a mere fluid, and its salt content is too high to allow it to play a major part in twenty-first-century nutrition. But the related *miso* is a vast family of pastes, sometimes smooth, sometimes crunchy as peanut butter, and is a food; intrinsically variable, and amenable to endless further variation, it is at home in all gastronomic contexts. *Miso*, like *shoyu*, is traditionally too salty for nutritional comfort; but there are low-salt forms, and potassium salts, which can taste pleasant enough, could perhaps be substituted for the customary sodium chloride.

Variations on a theme of miso

The lineage of *miso* may be even older than that of *shoyu* and is so variable that all generalizations about it must be largely wrong. But its production differs from *shoyu* in that only the grain component—rice in *kome miso*, and barley in *mugi miso*—is inoculated with aspergilli in the initial culture; whole soybeans are added later and subjected only to the lactobacillus–yeast fermentation. Except, of course, in the case of *mame* (*hatcho*) *miso*, in which no grain is used, and a portion of the beans is fermented with aspergilli.

When the first *koji*—or barley, rice, or portion of beans—is mature, it is mixed with more cooked rice, barley, and/or beans; salt is added, and a lactobacillus–yeast fermentation, that may last two years or more, begins.

This, roughly, is the route to traditional *miso*; but the process can be quickened by various industrial devices and elaborated with pickles or nuts, for example, to produce a range of *misos* that may be salty or sweet, red, brown, yellow, or light buff, and flavored almost at will. And although *miso* is the daddy, South-East Asia also boasts *tempeh*, which as yet seems to have escaped exhaustive study but is basically soybean fermented mainly by the mold *Rhizopus*. One United States authority recently listed more than 100 established Asian fermentations; and Africa can boast a comparable if less formal list (including *ogi*, *pinto*, rice wine and *ogorogoro*) in which cassava, maize, millet, banana and other foods are subjected to the ritualized ravages of fungi and bacteria.

The general point—the lesson for the future—is that any living thing can theoretically be subjected to the gentle attentions of a whole host of microbes; and the results, if controlled, can be both delicious and nutritious. *Miso*, in all its variety, has shown the way and is based on the temperate, subtropical soybean, which should probably be left to grow in the warm countries. But scientists at the Kansas State University have already produced *miso* and *tempeh* from chickpeas and horse beans, and Dr Brian Wood at the University of Strathclyde in Britain is hoping to produce them from field beans (*Vicia faba*). At the meeting place of staples and microbes is a near infinity of foods with precisely that texture and savory tang that future generations, obliged to be sparing with meat, will seek out. This, in the borrowed jargon of the agribusinessmen, is the most exciting growth area of all.

Fungi are odd, hybrid creatures, a bit like plants and a bit like animals, and their cuisine is equally hybrid. Because they are chewy and contain at least some protein, mushrooms, like pulses, are useful meat extenders. As with pulses, too, their protein is rich in lysine, which cereals tend to lack; and the mushroom-cereal theme runs through world cookery like the tandem of pulse and cereal. But mushrooms have their own clear, middle-toned flavor; and—another aspect of mushroom contrariness—although they appear dry, they are more than 90 percent water. Because of these two characteristics they are—unlike pulses—an excellent garnish; the many elaborate recipes for mushroom sauces and stuffings seem largely superfluous because mushrooms become sauce (or stuffing) if they are merely cooked gently alongside (or inside) the meat. The mushrooms' spongy texture—formed from a mass of hyphal threads—makes them avid recipients of fat. They are commonly cooked in butter or olive oil, and are egregious moppers-up of meat juices. In short, mushrooms are at home in almost every context; and since they can also be eaten raw it really is difficult to go wrong with them. The chief danger (other than burning) is to make them greasy by exposure to too much fat.

The simplest way to eat mushrooms is as they come; and Dorothy Hartley recalls in *Food in England* that country people used to slice them thinly, sprinkle them with lemon juice, and eat them between brown bread and butter; or they can be sliced fairly thickly, sprinkled with pepper and laid on top of beef in sandwiches. Thus they act as garnish, keep the sandwich moist, complement the bread cereal and extend the meat.

The following few recipes from the vast mushroom cuisine show them in all their principal contexts: fried, baked, stuffed, *en croûtes*, in soups, stuffings and duxelles and as a meat extender in pies.

MUSHROOMS IN OLIVE OIL
The simplest way to cook mushrooms is to fry them in a small amount of fat—bacon, butter or oil—until they have exuded enough moisture to cook in their own juice. Here is a minor extension of that basic idea from Greece, exploiting the affinity of mushrooms with sharp clean flavors. Such a dish served with pita (or any unleavened wheat bread) is a gastronomic delight.

Serves 4

3 tablespoons olive oil
$\frac{1}{2}$ lb (240 g) small button mushrooms
Black pepper
A pinch of salt
Juice of $\frac{1}{2}$ or 1 lemon
$\frac{1}{2}$ teaspoon dried thyme
1 to 2 garlic cloves, crushed
4 tablespoons finely chopped parsley

Pour the oil and 1 tablespoon water into a deep frying pan, add all the remaining ingredients except the mushrooms, and bring to a boil.

Wipe the mushrooms clean, halve them if they are too massive and add them to the pan. Simmer for 10 minutes, turning the mushrooms now and again. Serve cool or cold.

BAKED FISH WITH MUSHROOMS
In many traditional dishes mushrooms simply nuzzle alongside the cooking meat or fish, swapping juices and ending up as a garnish. In a future world such a role may prove too luxurious; the mushroom must stand in for flesh as well as flavoring. Hence equal proportions in this recipe. I suggest turbot not only because it works—the oily fish with the fatless mushroom—but also because it is eminently farmable and may be readily available in a future world. However, where fresh turbot is not available, flounder or sole is an acceptable substitute.

Serves 2

1 lb ($\frac{1}{2}$ kg) turbot fillets
Pepper
1 onion or 4 shallots
Oil
1 lb ($\frac{1}{2}$ kg) mushrooms
1 tablespoon chopped mixed herbs
A pinch of salt
Flour

Pepper the fish and let it stand for a few minutes. Fry the chopped onion or shallots in a very little oil until soft and beginning to change color. Pile in the sliced or whole mushrooms—turn up the heat slightly if they produce too much juice—and add the herbs and salt, stirring. When it is all just beginning to cook, take the pan off the heat.

Take a piece of foil large enough to

The alternative lifestyle-the fungi

enclose the fish completely and spread a third of the mushroom mixture in the middle of it. Coat the fish with flour and put half of it on top of the mushrooms. Add more mushrooms, then the rest of the fish and top with the remaining mushrooms. Fold the foil to make a neat, airtight package. Bake in a 325°F (170°C) oven for about 25 to 30 minutes.

CHICKEN STUFFED WITH MUSHROOMS

With poultry there is no need to provide the additional skin of foil. In one classic French dish truffles are simply inserted beneath the skin of a roasting chicken; mushrooms can be similarly tucked in, albeit with less spectacular results.

The body cavity of chicken or duck also provides a suitable oven for mushrooms. I have tried making a proper stuffing by chopping mushrooms with breadcrumbs and herbs but find that cultivated mushrooms do not have the flavor to counteract breadcrumbs and wild fungi are best left unadulterated. Chestnuts, however, are a fine autumnal complement to fungi and this Chinese dish uses them not with field mushrooms but with the delightful *shiitake* (the dried mushrooms with crinkly tops that are sold in Oriental food stores.

Serves 4

1 chicken, about 3 lb (1½ kg)
4 to 5 *shiitake* mushrooms
½ lb (240 g) chestnuts
1 onion
3 tablespoons soy sauce
A pinch of salt
Pepper
1 tablespoon sherry
1 tablespoon oil

Soak the mushrooms in hot water for 30 minutes. Drain the mushrooms, discard the stems and slice the caps. Slit the flat side of the chestnuts. Put them in a pan of cold water and bring to a boil. Simmer for 20 to 30 minutes then shell and peel while the nuts are still hot.

Chop the chestnuts and onion and mix with the mushrooms, two-thirds of the soy sauce, the salt and a good sprinkling of pepper. Stuff the mixture into the chicken and truss securely.

Rub the bird with a mixture of the sherry, the remaining soy sauce and the oil. Put the chicken on a rack and cook in the oven at 375°F (190°C) for 1 hour or until the bird is cooked.

MUSHROOM AND BARLEY SOUP

In this soup I use *miso* instead of the usual chicken stock. *Miso* is available at Japanese food stores.
Serves 4

1 small onion
1 small carrot
½ celery stalk
¼ cup butter
3 tablespoons *miso*
⅔ cup pearl barley
½ lb (240 g) mushrooms, chopped
A pinch of salt
A sprinkling of pepper
1 rounded tablespoon flour
Fresh dill or parsley, chopped

Chop the onion, carrot and celery and cook them gently in half the butter for about 10 minutes in a large saucepan. Melt the *miso* in 7½ cups of boiling water to make a stock. Pour the stock onto the frying vegetables. Add the pearl barley, the chopped mushrooms, salt and pepper and simmer for about 1 hour or until the barley is cooked.

Meanwhile, melt the remaining butter in another saucepan. Stir in the flour and after a few seconds add some of the stock from the other pan. When the mixture is smooth pour it into the simmering soup and stir well to blend. Simmer for a further 20 minutes, stirring frequently and adding more water if the soup is too thick. Sprinkle with dill or parsley before serving.

MUSHROOM SOUP
Serves 4

1 lb (½ kg) mushrooms
2 tablespoons olive oil
1 garlic clove
2 tablespoons chopped parsley
Nutmeg
Salt
Pepper
1 thick slice bread
5 cups chicken stock
2 tablespoons yogurt

Wash the mushrooms and pat them dry, then chop them into small pieces.

In a large saucepan, heat the oil and add the mushrooms, cooking them gently until they are soft. Add the chopped garlic, half the parsley, a grating of nutmeg and the seasoning, and continue cooking for a few minutes.

Discard the crusts from the bread, and soak it in a little of the chicken stock. Squeeze out the liquid and add the bread to the pan, stirring it well. Pour in the stock, and simmer for 25 minutes.

Blend the soup until smooth, then return to the pan and gently stir in the yogurt. Sprinkle over the remaining parsley and serve.

PIGEON AND MUSHROOM PIE

In this recipe the mushroom fulfills all its roles: provider and extender of flavor; provider of moisture, extender of meat and complement to cereal. Because of their moisture content and relative blandness, mushrooms are natural and traditional accompaniments of all manner of game.
Serves 2

1 large onion
Oil
½ lb (240 g) mushrooms
6 pigeon breasts
Flour
A pinch of salt
Pepper
1 large carrot
Pie crust made with 2 cups flour
  (equal quantities of whole wheat
  and all-purpose flour)

Chop the onion and fry gently in a very little oil until soft. Add the mushrooms, either leaving the tops and stems whole and separate or cutting them in half. Cook, stirring, until the mushrooms begin to give off moisture.

Cut the pigeon breasts into strips, about ½ inch (1 cm) wide, dust lightly with flour, salt and pepper and put in a fireproof casserole. Place the onion and mushrooms on top, then the sliced carrot and a good sprinkling of pepper. Pour in enough water to barely cover and bring to a boil on top of the stove. Cover and simmer in a 375°F (190°C) oven for about 1 hour.

Roll out the pastry, lay it over the pie and bake for a further 30 minutes.

MUSHROOMS EN CROÛTES
Serves 4

1 large loaf day-old bread (unsliced)
Oil
¼ cup butter
2 tablespoons flour
2 cups chicken stock
2 tablespoons milk
Salt
Pepper
Lemon juice
½ lb (240 g) button mushrooms
1 cup chopped cooked ham
⅔ cup grated Gruyère cheese

First, make the bread cases. Cut 4 slices of bread about 3 inches (8 cm) thick. Using a cookie cutter, cut out 4 large circles. Then, using a smaller cutter or a sharp knife make a circular incision in the middle of each circle, but do not cut quite to the bottom. Scoop out the bread from the center using a knife or your fingers. Brush the croûtes with oil, and bake at 450°F (230°C) for about 5 minutes or until the croûtes are lightly browned.

Meanwhile, make the sauce. Melt half the butter in a pan, add the flour and mix well to make a roux. Cook gently until the roux becomes straw colored, then add the stock a little at a time. Bring to a boil, then lower the heat and simmer for 5 minutes or until the sauce has reduced a little. Add the milk, a pinch of salt, a generous sprinkling of pepper and a squeeze of lemon juice. Simmer for a few minutes more, then remove from the heat.

Cook the sliced mushrooms in the remaining butter for a few minutes, then stir in the sauce, the chopped ham, the grated cheese, a pinch of salt and a little pepper.

Divide the mixture between the bread cases, then cook them in a 375°F (190°C) oven for about 10 to 15 minutes. Serve immediately.

STUFFED MUSHROOMS
Serve as a first course, or for a light lunch with plenty of mashed potato.

The alternative lifestyle-the fungi

Serves 2 to 4

1 lb ($\frac{1}{2}$ kg) large mushrooms
4 tablespoons fresh breadcrumbs
3 garlic cloves, crushed
1 tablespoon chopped parsley
1 tablespoon chopped chives
Salt
Pepper
Butter

Wipe the mushrooms clean and remove the stems. Chop the stems and mix them with the breadcrumbs, garlic, herbs and seasonings. Fill each mushroom with this mixture.

Put 1 or 2 flakes of butter on each stuffed mushroom and place under a medium to hot broiler until the breadcrumbs turn golden brown.

DUXELLES

Duxelles is a concentrated paste made from mushrooms which can be used for flavoring stews, soups and stuffings. It will keep for weeks, if it is tightly covered, in the refrigerator. Butter is used; but in this context of a highly concentrated flavoring it is justified.

1 lb ($\frac{1}{2}$ kg) mushrooms
2 shallots
$\frac{1}{2}$ cup butter
Salt
Black pepper

Chop the mushrooms very finely. Enclose them in a cloth and twist to extract any moisture. Chop the shallots finely and fry them in the butter for about 5 minutes. Add the mushrooms and seasoning and cook, stirring frequently, for about 45 minutes or until all the liquid has evaporated and you have a rich, thick mixture. Let the duxelles cool before putting in a jar.

MUSHROOMS AND SHRIMP ON SKEWERS

This splendidly easy dish should be served with stir-fried vegetables and rice. The rice may be plain boiled or "fried" as in the mock fried rice recipe that I give here. The mushrooms and shrimp must be of equal size—about one inch (2.5 cm) round. If shrimp of this size are not available, alternate the mushrooms with pieces of sweet green pepper or pineapple chunks and stir small shrimps into the rice.

Serves 4

32 button mushrooms
24 cooked shrimp
3 large garlic cloves
Juice of 1 lemon
A pinch of salt
Black pepper
2 tablespoons finely chopped basil
Olive oil

Mock fried rice
$\frac{3}{4}$ lb (360 g) long-grain rice
A pinch of salt
Olive oil
Soy sauce
1 bunch scallions

Clean the mushrooms and remove their stems. Put the mushroom caps and the shrimp in a bowl. Crush the garlic and mix it with the lemon juice, salt, a generous sprinkling of pepper, the basil and a little olive oil—there should be just enough marinade to coat the ingredients. Pour the marinade over the mushroom caps and shrimp, toss well and set aside while you prepare the rice.

Wash the rice thoroughly and soak in water for 30 minutes. Drain the rice and put in a saucepan with a pinch of salt. Cover with water, which should lie no more than $\frac{1}{4}$ inch (0.5 cm) above the rice, and bring to a boil. When the rice is bubbling furiously, cover the pan tightly and reduce the heat to very low (or if you are cooking on an electric hob, turn the heat off). After 15 minutes uncover the pan and sprinkle a little olive oil and soy sauce over the rice. Toss the rice with a fork, adding more soy sauce, if necessary, to get the right color. Chop the scallions, white and green parts, and stir them in.

Thread the mushroom caps and shrimp alternately onto 8 small skewers. Cook under a hot broiler for $1\frac{1}{2}$ to 2 minutes on each side and serve immediately with the rice.

MUSHROOMS WITH CHICKEN IN CHINESE STYLE

Serve this adaptation of a Chinese dish with steamed rice and mixed fried vegetables, particularly cabbage.

Serves 4

3 dried Chinese mushrooms
½ lb (240 g) fresh mushrooms
½ lb (240 g) boned chicken breast
1 tablespoon cornstarch
A pinch of salt
1 small onion
1 small piece fresh ginger root
3 tablespoons oil
4 tablespoons chicken stock
1 tablespoon dry sherry
1 tablespoon soy sauce

Soak the dried mushrooms in boiling water for 30 minutes. Drain the mushrooms (reserve the water), discard the stems and slice the caps. Slice the fresh mushrooms.

Cut the chicken breast into thin, small pieces. Mix half the cornstarch with the salt and rub this mixture into the chicken pieces. Set aside for 15 minutes.

Chop the onion. Cut the ginger into thin slices and then into small julienne strips. Fry the onion and ginger in 2 tablespoons of the oil, stirring, for 20 seconds. Add the chicken pieces and stir-fry for 2 minutes. Lift out the chicken, onion and ginger from the pan and set aside.

Add the remaining oil to the pan and stir-fry the mushrooms for 1½ minutes. Add the chicken, onion and ginger and fry for 30 seconds.

Mix the remaining cornstarch with the stock and add it to the pan with 2 tablespoons of the reserved mushroom water, the sherry and the soy sauce. Increase the heat to very high and cook, stirring, for a further 30 seconds. Serve immediately.

MUSHROOM SAUCE TO GO WITH SPAGHETTI

For this sauce you need those large, open, dark-gilled mushrooms which let out an inky juice when cooked. You can make the sauce well in advance as this gives the flavors a chance to mingle.
Serves 4

1 onion
2 garlic cloves
2 tablespoons olive oil
1 lb (½ kg) mushrooms
2 lb (1 kg) ripe beefsteak tomatoes
1 teaspoon basil
1 teaspoon oregano
A pinch of salt
Black pepper

Chop the onion, crush the garlic and fry them gently in the olive oil. When they are soft and just beginning to color, add the sliced mushrooms. Increase the heat and fry, stirring, for a few seconds until the mushrooms begin to cook and let out juice.

Skin and chop the tomatoes and add them to the mushrooms along with the herbs, salt and pepper. Stir to mix. When the sauce is bubbling, cover the pan, reduce the heat to very low and simmer for 35 to 40 minutes. Uncover the pan and if the sauce is too liquid, cook uncovered until it is the right consistency.

KOREAN MISO SAUCE

Miso does not contribute mass, it is a flavoring with a few nutritional advantages and is perhaps at its best when made into a sauce and used as a dip or a topping for such vegetables as tomato, celery or cucumber; it is also used to enliven bowls of rice or noodles. *Miso* is available at Japanese food stores.
Makes about ½ cup

1 garlic clove
1-inch (2.5 cm) piece fresh ginger root
2 green chili peppers
1 small onion
1 tablespoon sesame oil
Tabasco sauce
3 tablespoons red, barley or *Hatcho* *miso*
2 tablespoons soy sauce
2 tablespoons *sake* or white wine (optional)

Chop the garlic, ginger root, chilies and onion. Heat the sesame oil in an iron skillet or heavy frying pan. Add the garlic, ginger, chilies, onion and a dash of Tabasco. Cook for 2 minutes and stir in the *miso*, soy sauce and *sake* or wine, if you are using it, and bring just to a boil, stirring. Serve cool.

One of our small eggs

One of my abiding memories of postwar British food rationing is of long, long queues at far-flung farmhouses for illicit boiled-egg teas. There is nothing like a shortage to help people to appreciate food, and there is no food more worthy of appreciation than the egg. Neither has any food caused so much controversy, indeed so much rancor, as the egg has done in the 1960s and 1970s.

The first area of controversy has been agricultural. Mass egg production, which has made so many fortunes and lost a few, is based on the battery cage. Peasants have been tying cows by the neck for thousands of years, dormice have been fattened in little jars, monkeys have been chained from the waist to barrel organs and parrots shackled to perches, but never in all history has the biology of a fellow creature been so disregarded, and on such a scale, as in the modern poultry battery system. The birds are kept three to twelve to a cage, several tiers deep, tens of thousands or even hundreds of thousands to a unit. Debeaking is one of the mutilations already employed to reduce "vice," and the removal of wings (perhaps by breeding from deformed birds) is one that has been proposed to save space. Automation is the key to the battery's commercial success, but one of the inescapable tasks of the few remaining workers is to fish out all the corpses each morning. In some countries there are "codes of practice" to stem the worst excesses, but there is little in the way of legislation and no effective way of enforcing what there is.

The obvious excesses of the battery farm

Like all such intensive farming, the battery system has been under fire because of its inherent wastefulness. Feeding is automated, and with so many birds so expensively housed it is vital to ensure maximum and uniform biological performance. So the birds are fed not on scraps but on custom-milled feed.

It is impossible to "prove" that battery hens suffer, although some animal behaviorists point out that the perpetual racketing they make is not the sound of contentment, but the primitive call of alarm. Besides, to demand "proof" of suffering seems merely perverse. Domesticity in animals is never more than a veneer, as any dog or cat owner knows. All animals are wild, and a system that confines wild animals to such a degree defies common sense.

The proper niche of chickens is the traditional one: on farms, and in small units near where people live. I have found that a family of five produces enough food trash to maintain a flock of eight birds with only a small supplement of proprietary feed. Chickens eat everything, from potato peelings to old bones, and if you do not like killing snails and slugs, the hens will make short work of them too. In return, such a flock provides the family with all the eggs they need.

Chickens as scavengers and pest controllers

While agribusinessmen and animal welfarists have battled over the hen, nutritionists have gone to war over the egg itself. Throughout all the clashes of nutritional theory, it has been the favored missile.

In the early 1960s, when protein and vitamins were in vogue, the egg was life's elixir. Eggs are three-quarters water, but they contain 12 percent protein; which means that protein accounts for 48 percent of all the solid content. This protein is of such high quality that it is used as a reference, against which all other natural food proteins are judged. Eggs also, as befits the sole food store of an unborn animal, contain an impressive selection of minerals and vitamins, including vitamins A and D, and some of the B series.

The egg is impressive nutritionally . . .

Then scientists of various persuasions became worried by cholesterol and saturated fat. As explained earlier, the body manufactures most of its own cholesterol and the dietary contribution is probably minor. Nonetheless, when the link between heart disease and high blood cholesterol first became apparent, it seemed reasonable to advise people to cut down on cholesterol-rich foods. Eggs are not the richest source of cholesterol—their 450 milligrams per quarter pound is modest compared with the 2,000 milligrams per quarter pound in brains, for example—but because people eat a lot of them, they are in practice by far the greatest single source of dietary cholesterol. In addition, eggs contain ten percent fat, of which about one-third is saturated. The word went round: cut down on eggs. American egg producers finally started suing for defamation and at least one professor suddenly found that his office was full of heavies and that his research papers were under subpoena. It was all very bizarre.

. . . but is its cholesterol dangerous?

Some authorities have said that since eggs can cause trouble, then they must be modified. The simplest method is to acknowledge that the white and the yolk are quite separate entities, and to treat each on its merits. The white is innocent: it contains nine percent high-grade protein, barely a trace of fat, and no cholesterol. The yolk is the villain of the piece, with 30 percent fat and all the cholesterol that the egg contains. Some American doctors accordingly suggest that you should eat only egg whites, and give the yolks back to the chickens.

One trouble with this proposal, besides its innate wastefulness, is that the innocent white is also innocuous: it is 90 percent water, and has a poor vitamin content. The maligned yolk contains only 50 percent water but has 16 percent protein and contains the bulk of the vitamins.

Other academics, of more technical bent, have suggested that the egg's biochemistry should be modified at source. Why not breed a hen that lays low-cholesterol eggs? Or, if this should prove impractical (as it almost certainly would), why not at least try to reduce the egg's saturated fat content, by feeding hens on a diet rich in polyunsaturates? This has been tried, but one of several difficulties is that polyunsaturated fats are far too expensive to feed to chickens. Another is the understandable lack of enthusiasm for such an effete project.

High science bent on impractical ends

I feel that the answer—as is usual in nutritional matters—is to apply common sense. If eggs are eaten as part of a high-meat, high-fat diet then they might indeed provide the nutritional straw that breaks the arterial camel's back. The egg tossed on top of the hamburger as casually as if it were no more significant than a slice of pickle is a symbol

One of our small eggs

of the modern Western diet and of the role of eggs within it. If eggs are treated as if they were meat, served with reverence and used to garnish vegetables and staples, it is hard to see how they could do much harm.

Indeed, some of the peoples who do not suffer from coronary heart disease, such as the rural Spanish and Chinese, eat quite a few eggs; but their diet is mainly made up of cereals, potatoes and beans. The Romans doted on eggs, yet made no mention of heart attacks among their many references to disease. We hear much of the Romans' indulgences, but they had no intensive beeves or dairy cattle, no battery chickens and no factory pigs and they simply could not have eaten much meat. There is less flesh on a peacock than on a modern broiler and it takes a lot of larks' tongues to make up for one pork chop. By our standards their diet was austere, and they used to thank their gods for eggs.

The Romans loved eggs, but did they suffer heart attacks?

The biological significance of eggs—as the lacto-ovo-vegetarians recognize—is that they are one of the few forms of high-quality, high-flavor animal protein which can be taken (theoretically) without harming the animal. (Milk can too, and blood; but we may leave the latter to the Masai.) Furthermore, wild birds may lay more eggs than they can hatch, or lay them out of season; so judicious culling may even be helpful to them.

The plover is a well-established object of the cull; the earliest clutches of its fine speckled eggs fare badly but the bird will lay again if these are taken. Gulls, too, have long been plundered without significant harm— and that new phenomenon, the urban herring gull, could usefully be regarded as a resource, rather than a menace. Three thousand pairs now nest in more than 100 places in British towns, although very few ever did so before 1940. They are noisy and messy, and government councils have squandered small fortunes on their removal; but the hassle of nesting on a block of offices, even when harassed by the city council, is nothing compared to that of the birds' natural, congested sea-cliff, and they are here to stay. So are their eggs, if anyone cares to risk the birds' ice-pick beaks to collect them.

In Africa, ostriches lay eggs in communal nests, up to seven birds laying up to 13 eggs each in one shallow scrape. The boss hen and her mate do all the incubating; but since they can cover only 20 they kick out the surplus (although they make sure that they hang on to their own). An ostrich egg is a fine thing; and many may be taken with impunity.

Among more conventional livestock, the eggs both of the turkey and goose are at least as good as the chicken's, and a taste for those of the highly prolific duck is well worth the acquisition. Quails belong in that small select category of creatures—along with trout, bees, and Roman snails—that are worth keeping not for their nutritional merits but for the delicacy of their products. Their tiny eggs are supreme, in flavor, shape and color.

So eggs are powerful agents, but whether for good or evil depends on context. Mr Woodhouse, father of Jane Austen's Emma, had grasped the point, although he was perhaps a little too diffident: ". . . let me propose your venturing on one of those eggs. An egg boiled very soft is not unwholesome . . . you need not be afraid . . . one of our small eggs will not hurt you."

The fault of eggs, if such a divine conception can be faulted, is that they are too accommodating. It is easy just to drop them into things, for a touch of color, flavor or texture, as if they were mushrooms or spices. It is easy to forget that they carry enormous nutritional weight—they are an excellent source of protein and vitamins but possibly too high in cholesterol for complete comfort. I do not think you should be afraid of eggs, but treat them reverentially, like meat or fish. Use them only to make much of them; and match them with vegetables and staples, perhaps with slivers of fish or ham or some strong-flavored meat. A hamburger "topped with a fried egg," as the menus have it, epitomizes the egg's misuse.

Because eggs are so accommodating and so ubiquitous (the hen is now one of the commonest land vertebrates, matched only by rats and human beings) they find expression in every cuisine, in every idiom. But recipes fall conveniently enough into four main categories: variations on a theme of boiled, poached or baked eggs; the use of hard-boiled eggs; the fried egg; and the intricate and endlessly interesting passage from scrambled egg, through omelets (which deserve their own book) to soufflés and meringue; although the meringue uses only the white of the egg and I feel the twenty-first-century cook should come to terms with the yolk, rather than throwing it away as some doctors have recommended.

Theme I
Eggs boiled, poached and baked

Many cookbooks make much of the art of boiling eggs, but I am not sure I believe that it is that subtle; or rather, the way the egg contents behave when heated depends partly on the egg's age and partly on its size, and to fiddle about with 15-second timings one way or the other when faced with such variables seems to me perverse. Eggs on the whole are pleasantly soft-boiled if you lower them into boiling water, allow the water to come back to a boil and then let them simmer for three to three and a half minutes. But a new-laid egg (and you cannot know what a fresh egg is unless you keep chickens) has a white that is more clearly differentiated into stiff protein and fluid, and takes about four to four and a half minutes to cook convincingly.

New-laid eggs come into their own when poached because they do not disintegrate as the older egg may do. To poach an egg, break it into a cup and slide it into water that has just come to a boil. When the water comes back to a boil, take the pan off the heat, cover with a lid and leave for three and a half to four minutes. Lift out the poached egg with a perforated spoon. Those so-called egg "poachers" in fact produce steamed eggs, which are nothing like so succulent.

Poached, boiled and baked eggs integrate effortlessly with vegetables and staples, which is the egg's proper role; poached eggs go on toast and soft-boiled eggs, or *oeufs mollets*, are used as garnish. But I like eggs baked in the oven in a hundred variations; poached in any kind of sauce; or stirred into soups, not gratuitously but to provide the "meat."

EGGS WITH SPINACH
Serves 4

2 lb (1 kg) spinach
A large pinch of salt
Freshly ground black pepper
½ teaspoon ground cumin
A large pinch of ground fenugreek
4 eggs

First cook the spinach: chop it and ram it into a saucepan. Mix in the salt and spices and allow the spinach to cook over a low heat until the juices begin to exude, then turn the heat up.

When the spinach is pleasantly mushy, tip it into a heated ovenproof dish, make 4 shallow depressions in the top, and break an egg into each depression. Bake in a moderate oven, 350°F (180°C), for 15 minutes.

EGGS WITH POTATO AND TURNIP
There are endless variations on the potatoes-mashed-with-other-things theme; and all are natural foils for eggs.
Serves 4

2 lb (1 kg) potatoes
1 lb (½ kg) rutabagas or white turnips
½ cup milk
A large pinch of salt
A large pinch of nutmeg
A small pinch of ground ginger
A generous sprinkling of black pepper
4 eggs

Peel the potatoes and the rutabagas or

turnips and cut them into egg-sized pieces. Cover with water, bring to a boil and boil for 15 to 20 minutes. Then drain and mash with the milk, salt and spices.

Turn the mixture into a casserole dish, make 4 depressions in the top, break an egg into each, and bake in a moderate oven, 350°F (180°C), for 15 minutes or until the eggs are set.

POACHED EGG CURRY

And here in similar vein is a modest but pleasant egg curry. Serve with plain boiled rice or with a vegetable risotto.
Serves 4

1 large onion
1-inch (2.5 cm) piece fresh ginger root
3 to 4 tablespoons oil
2-inch (5 cm) piece cinnamon stick, broken up
1 teaspoon turmeric
2 fat garlic cloves
2 tomatoes
1 teaspoon ground cumin
1 teaspoon ground coriander
A large pinch of ground cloves
Seeds of 2 cardamom pods, crushed
1¼ cups yogurt
A large pinch of salt
4 eggs

The Garnish
Raw onion slices
Parsley (ordinary or Chinese)

Slice the onion and ginger finely, and fry gently in the oil for 2 to 3 minutes or until the onion is soft. Add the cinnamon, the turmeric and the finely sliced garlic, and fry for another 2 minutes. Then add the sliced tomatoes, the cumin, coriander, ground cloves and the cardamom and fry until the tomatoes are soft.

Mix the yogurt with an equal amount of water, pour into the frying spice mixture, bring to a boil, cover the pan and allow to simmer for about 10 minutes to produce a rich, well-cooked, spicy-yogurty sauce.

Sprinkle on the salt, then break the eggs gently into the curry mixture—they must remain intact—and poach, covered, for 20 to 25 minutes.

Serve garnished with the onion slices and chopped parsley.

CLEAR CHICKEN SOUP WITH POACHED EGG

Eggs also poach pleasantly in consommé, to turn a light soup into a light meal.
Serves 4

5 cups clear chicken stock
1 red chili pepper
4 scallions
1 garlic clove
1 tablespoon soy sauce
1 teaspoon ginger sherry (see page 47)
Salt
4 eggs

Bring the chicken stock to a boil. Add the finely sliced chili pepper, the coarsely chopped scallions and the whole garlic clove. Stir in the soy sauce, the ginger sherry and a pinch of salt.

Bring the soup back to a boil and simmer for 5 minutes. Then take off the heat, remove the garlic and break the eggs gently into the soup. Put the pan back on to a low heat and seethe gently until the eggs are poached.

CONSOMMÉ WITH EGG
Serves 4

4 slices of bread
4 eggs
Salt
5 cups strong beef consommé
Grated Parmesan cheese

Toast the bread on both sides. Put the toast in four heated soup bowls. Break the eggs carefully (the yolks must remain whole) one on each piece of toast. Sprinkle a little salt over each egg. Bring the consommé to a boil and pour it gently into the soup bowls (not directly onto the yolks, or you will break them). Serve immediately with the cheese.

FISHY EGG-DROP SOUP WITH MUSHROOMS
Serves 4

1 dried Chinese *shiitake* mushroom
2 cups chopped mushrooms
4 scallions
5 cups clear fish stock
1 tablespoon soy sauce
4 eggs

Eggs can be at their finest in soups, to which
they add the final touch of nutritional quality,
texture and color. Here is an Italian version:
consommé poured over raw egg.

Variations on a theme of omelet:
Chinese, **top** *; and a Japanese stuffed version, used as*
a garnish, **left.** *Fried eggs deserve liberation: here is*
minty fried egg, with mushrooms and lemon
juice, **right.**

Soak the Chinese mushroom in hot water for 30 minutes. Drain, discard the stem and chop the cap. Chop the fresh mushrooms and the scallions. Put the stock and soy sauce into a large pan, add the scallions and mushrooms and bring to a boil, then immediately take the pan off the heat.

Break the eggs into a bowl and stir until mixed, but do not beat. Pour the eggs in a thin trickle into the hot soup, stirring as you go. The idea is to produce long thin threads of cooked egg: if you pour the eggs in too quickly you may get ugly lumps, and if the soup is actually boiling when you pour in the egg it may simply disintegrate and curdle, and float to the top.

When the egg is all in, bring the soup back to a boil and serve.

BAKED POTATOES WITH EGGS AND YOGURT

Baked potatoes always make good eating, but when they are stuffed with eggs and yogurt, they make a meal.
Serves 4

4 large potatoes
2 tablespoons butter
4 scallions
Salt
A generous sprinkling of pepper
A large pinch of nutmeg
4 tablespoons yogurt
4 eggs
$\frac{2}{3}$ cup grated Cheddar cheese
A bunch of watercress, for garnish

Scrub the potatoes, prick them with a fork and bake them for $1\frac{1}{2}$ hours in a moderate oven, 375°F (190°C).

When the potatoes are cooked, take them out of the oven (but do not turn the oven off) and lay them on their sides. Cut off a small piece from the top of each potato and scoop out the insides.

Mix the scooped-out potato with the melted butter, the finely chopped scallions, a little salt, the pepper and the nutmeg, then stir in the yogurt and the beaten eggs.

Stuff the mixture into the 4 potato skins, and top each potato with a little grated cheese. Return the potatoes to the oven for about 10 minutes. Serve garnished with the watercress.

Theme II
The hard-boiled egg

The egg, once hardened by boiling for ten minutes, becomes a discrete, solid and special thing which taken alone is as versatile as, for example, the mushroom (although it is far more nutritionally significant). Hard-boiled eggs are, of course, delicious by themselves or they may be dipped into cumin and finely chopped mint or flavored with tarragon.

TARRAGON EGGS

If you like tarragon and eggs this is a fine way of bringing them together; the eggs literally absorb the herb flavor.
Serves 4

4 eggs
Fresh tarragon leaves

Wrap each egg in tarragon leaves and then in foil or plastic wrap. Wrap well to seal. Put the eggs in the refrigerator for 24 hours.

Remove the wraps and hard boil or soft boil the eggs in the usual way.

EGG PILAU

Where the Americans would use potatoes, the Eastern peoples would use rice. The nearest thing to an egg and potato pie, using rice, is Egg Pilau.

This is a grand little *pilau*, which is gently spiced and goes well with the lightest of cool white wines.
Serves 6

3 cups long-grain rice
2 onions
2 tablespoons corn oil
2 garlic cloves
1 teaspoon ground coriander
1 teaspoon ground cumin
$\frac{1}{2}$ teaspoon ground mace
A large pinch of cinnamon
$1\frac{1}{4}$ cups yogurt
A large pinch of salt
1 tablespoon almonds
1 tablespoon pistachio nuts
2 tablespoons raisins
6 hard-boiled eggs

The Garnish
2 tomatoes
Chinese parsley

One of our small eggs

Wash the rice, and soak in $4\frac{1}{2}$ cups of water for 1 hour. Then bring to a boil and simmer gently for 5 to 10 minutes or until the water is absorbed.

Meanwhile, chop 1 onion and fry gently in the oil for 5 minutes or until soft. Then stir in the finely sliced garlic and the coriander, cumin, mace and cinnamon. After 2 to 3 minutes, when the spices are strongly aromatic, pour in the yogurt, add the salt and continue cooking until hot and pleasantly mixed.

Halve the almonds, and toast them and the pistachios and raisins in a dry pan until the raisins swell up and the almonds are beginning to color. Shake the pan constantly.

Take a large casserole dish and line the bottom with thin slices of the second onion. Cover with a layer of rice, followed by slices of hard-boiled egg, then by the yogurty-spicy mixture, and by a sprinkling of the toasted nuts and raisins. Then repeat, finishing with a layer of rice.

Cover the dish tightly and bake in a moderate oven, 350°F (180°C), for about 30 minutes.

Turn the *pilau* out onto a hot serving dish (so the onions that were on the bottom are now on top) and decorate with thin slices of raw tomato and sprigs of fresh Chinese parsley.

Serve immediately.

Theme III
Fried eggs

Fried eggs might seem out of place in a nutrition-oriented cookbook; the once forbidden fruit cooked by the forbidden method. But the Western mistake is to associate frying in general, and fried eggs in particular, with meat: eggs and bacon, eggs with bacon and sausage and eggs on steak. In the Far East, people fry everything, vegetables at least as much as meat (of which they have little), but usually they use minimal amounts of oil. Rethink the fried egg into the context of vegetables and aromatized oils and it becomes eminently respectable.

Natural and willing confederates of the fried egg are the mushroom and tomato, the bean-sprout and the asparagus pea; and although garlic is a little coarse with fried eggs, cumin, coriander, mint, lemon and chili peppers are

quite at home. So here are two variations on a theme of fried eggs, just as simple as eggs and bacon, and better for you.

SPICY FRIED EGG AND TOMATO
Serves 4

1 green chili pepper
4 tablespoons corn oil
$\frac{1}{2}$ teaspoon cumin
8 tomatoes
A large pinch of salt
Pepper
4 eggs

Chop the chili pepper finely and fry lightly in the oil for 1 minute. Stir in the cumin and fry for another minute.

Cut the tomatoes in half, and add them to the pan with the salt and pepper. Fry lightly on both sides. Do not let them burn, as they so easily do, or they will taste nasty and spoil everything.

When the tomatoes are soft, lift them out onto a heated plate and keep warm while you fry the eggs in the remaining spicy oil. Add a little more oil if necessary.

Serve immediately with the tomatoes.

MINTY FRIED EGG WITH MUSHROOM
The mint in this recipe may be left out and any other herb included instead.
Serves 4

1 small red chili pepper
2 tablespoons oil
$\frac{1}{2}$ lb (240 g) mushrooms
1 teaspoon chopped fresh mint
A squeeze of lemon juice
A pinch of salt
Pepper
4 eggs

Chop the chili finely and fry gently in the oil for 1 minute. Add the mushrooms (halved, sliced or left whole, depending on size), scatter on the mint and add a few drops of lemon juice and the salt and pepper. Cook the mushrooms gently and remove them when they are soft to a heated serving dish and keep warm. Add a little more oil to the pan, if necessary, and fry the eggs briskly. Put the eggs on top of the mushrooms and serve immediately.

Theme IV

Scrambled eggs, omelets and soufflés

When an egg is beaten it becomes a thing apart; a new form of "meat," like the hard-boiled egg. Mix with a fork, heat, and go on mixing over the heat, and you have scrambled eggs. Less stirring during cooking nudges the scrambled egg into the realm of the omelet, perhaps the most variable and versatile as well as one of the simplest and most satisfying and nutritious of all cooking's forms.

Separate yolk and white and you have two distinct entities; the latter in particular may be beaten to a froth that can be far lighter than snow and can then be mixed back with the beaten yolks to be fried into a fluffy omelet, or baked to produce one of cookery's most astonishing caprices, the soufflé.

But let us begin at the beginning.

SCRAMBLED EGG

Broiled tomatoes, fried zucchini or mixed vegetables are fine additions and toast is not unknown.

Serves 2

3 eggs
Pepper
A pinch of salt
1 tablespoon milk

Break the eggs into a bowl, add the pepper, salt and milk and stir with a fork but do not beat; the idea is merely to mix yolk and white but not to froth, and odd flecks of pure white or yolk in the finished dish are no bad thing.

Cook slowly in a cast-iron or non-stick pan, stirring all the while, until the eggs are pleasantly set but still moist.

SCRAMBLED EGGS WITH SCALLIONS AND CHILI

Anything light and discrete can be stirred in with scrambled eggs: fresh peas, asparagus peas, slivers of endive or fennel, the odd shrimp, pieces of leftover fish; and a touch of cumin or finely chopped mint or thyme can hardly come amiss. Scallion and chili is a fine combination, with a faint echo of the Middle East.

Serves 2

2 scallions
1 small red chili pepper
2 teaspoons corn oil
Lemon juice
3 eggs
1 tablespoon milk
A pinch of salt
Pepper

Chop the scallions—including the green tops—and slice the chili finely. Fry for a minute in the oil and add a few drops of lemon juice.

Break the eggs into a bowl, add the milk, the salt, pepper and the chili and scallion mixture and stir until mixed. Cook the egg mixture slowly in a cast-iron or nonstick saucepan, stirring all the while, until the eggs are set but still soft and moist.

Serve immediately.

Scrambled eggs grade into omelets (anyone who says they do not is a pedant), and omelets are of four main kinds. There is the French omelet, made with lightly beaten eggs in a very hot pan; the moment the bottom is set the omelet is folded over and served immediately with the center still liquid. Fresh herbs, grated cheese, lightly fried sliced mushrooms, stewed tomatoes, chopped ham and many other ingredients may be used as fillings. There are those omelets made just by beating eggs and frying flat, which can be eaten as they are or in sandwiches, or used to wrap things in, or as garnish (for vegetables or rice, not for meat). There are those in which the beaten egg is impregnated in greater and greater proportion through the range of Spanish omelets, to the point achieved in some Arab omelets where the egg is mere binding and the omelet is a cake: nutritionally acceptable if the things that are bound are relatively innocuous, such as potato and other vegetables.

Finally, there are the light fluffy omelets, made by beating white and yolk separately and then folding together; and these fluffy omelets can also be impregnated with herbs and light adornments, from scallions, bean sprouts and watercress to chopped ham and shrimp, or they can be used to wrap things in.

I feel that the omelets made by beating the eggs together, which have a texture, should be used to wrap heavy stuffings, such as meat; the fluffier kind should have lighter fillings, such as fish or mushrooms.

One of our small eggs

SIMPLE OMELET
All the books will tell you to cook omelets in butter, but this is gratuitous use of fat, a cardinal sin.
Serves 2

3 eggs
1 tablespoon milk
Freshly ground black pepper
A pinch of salt

Break the eggs into a bowl, add the milk, pepper and salt, and beat with a whisk until the mixture is frothy.
  Heat a large, well-seasoned iron or nonstick pan, and when it is decidedly hot, pour in the beaten eggs. Stir lightly so that the liquid on the top can run through to make contact with the hot metal beneath. Stop stirring when the surface is still moist, but there is little spare liquid, or you will not finish up with a properly integrated omelet.
  Serve flat or flipped over.

OMELET SANDWICH
An omelet sandwich comes as close to nutritional perfection as anything simple can be, although it is a little short on vitamin B_{12}. For each person just prepare a one-egg flat omelet, and a small loaf made by any of the methods described in the chapter on bread (pita or barley bread would be fine). Slit open the bread, fold in the omelet with a little chopped raw onion, tomato, cucumber, fennel, shredded lettuce or cabbage. Sprinkle with pepper, olive oil and a little salt, and serve.

The omelet is also used as garnish for vegetables or staples. Its color is enticing but its nutritional power should not be forgotten.

VEGETABLE RISOTTO WITH OMELET
Serves 4

1 cup long-grain rice
1 carrot
$\frac{1}{4}$ lb (120 g) Belgian endive
2 scallions
1 small dried red chili pepper
$\frac{1}{2}$-inch (1 cm) piece fresh ginger root
2 garlic cloves
1 cup white cabbage
4 tablespoons corn oil

A handful of fresh peas
$\frac{1}{2}$ teaspoon salt
3 eggs
Soy sauce

First wash the rice, and soak it in $1\frac{1}{2}$ cups of water for 30 minutes.
  Slice the carrot thinly on the diagonal. Slice the endive. Chop the scallions coarsely, then chop the chili, ginger and garlic finely. Shred the cabbage.
  Fry the chili, ginger, garlic and scallions lightly in the oil for a minute, then add the carrot and stir-fry for a good 5 minutes, until it is beginning to soften. Then add the peas, cabbage and endive and fry for a few more minutes, until all is hot and the cabbage is beginning to soften.
  Drain the rice, reserving the water. Add the rice to the cooking vegetables and stir-fry for another 5 minutes. Then add the reserved water and the salt, bring to a boil, cover, and allow to simmer for 10 minutes.
  While the rice and vegetables are simmering, cook a flat omelet.
  Turn out the rice-vegetable mixture onto a hot oval dish. Slice the omelet into strips and lay along the top and sprinkle with soy sauce.
  Serve immediately.

JAPANESE STUFFED OMELET
The Japanese are fond of using stuffed omelets as garnish; stuffed, for example, with spinach.

1 teaspoon sesame seeds
$\frac{1}{2}$ lb (240 g) spinach (if it does not all go in the omelet it can easily be used for something else)
A pinch of salt
2 eggs

Toast the sesame seeds in a dry saucepan until they begin to jump about. Then put the finely shredded spinach and the salt on top and toss around to mix the seeds well in. Turn the heat down, put the lid on and allow the spinach to sink and puree.
  Meanwhile, make a thin, flat omelet.
  Finally, put the spinach in a line down the omelet, about $1\frac{1}{2}$ inches (3.5 cm) from one edge. Fold the shorter edge over the spinach, then roll up the omelet neatly like a jelly roll.

Cut the roll into 1-inch (2 cm) lengths,
which, in an ideal world, should emerge
as neat, tight targets of green encased in
soft yellow. Very heraldic.

Serve immediately.

OMELET STUFFED WITH MUSHROOM AND KIDNEY

Note that the mushrooms in this recipe
provide the bulk; the minute amount of
kidney is merely garnish, which is the
kidney's main role—in cooking at least.

Serves 2

1 small lamb's kidney
1 small red chili pepper
3 tablespoons corn oil
2 cups sliced mushrooms
A generous sprinkling of black pepper
A pinch of salt
1 tablespoon chopped chives
1 tablespoon cornstarch
3 eggs

Make the filling first. Chop the kidney
and slice the chili finely, and fry
lightly—the oil hardly hot—so that the
kidney exudes its juices and becomes
succulent. After about 5 minutes'
patient stirring, add the chopped or
sliced mushrooms, and stir-fry for
another minute or so: they should be hot
and oiled, rather than cooked, at this
stage. Now sprinkle on the pepper and
salt, scatter on the chives, add $\frac{2}{3}$ cup of
water, bring to a boil, and allow to
simmer gently for 5 minutes.

Put the cornstarch into a cup, and stir
in about a tablespoonful of the cooking
liquor and mix to a thick paste. Add a
little more liquor and mix to a thinner
paste. Continue adding a little more
liquor until you have a smooth floury
fluid. Pour this back into the pan with
the kidney and mushroom mixture, and
cook for 3 minutes or until the sauce is
pleasantly thick.

Sauces of this kind lose nothing by
being allowed to stand in the warm for a
short time; indeed, they benefit, as the
ingredients get to know one another. So
put to one side and take time off to
make the omelet.

Lay the ingredients along the middle of
the omelet and fold in first one side and
then the other.

Serve immediately.

CHINESE OMELET

Serves 4

1 onion
$\frac{1}{2}$-inch (1 cm) piece fresh ginger root
1 garlic clove
4 tablespoons oil
1 cup cooked small shrimp
1 cup bean sprouts
Salt and black pepper
6 eggs
$\frac{1}{2}$ sweet green or red pepper
2 tablespoons dry sherry

Slice the onion thinly. Cut the ginger
into thin slices and then into julienne
strips. Finely chop or crush the garlic.

Heat half the oil in a small frying pan
and stir-fry the onion, ginger and garlic
for 1 minute. Add the shrimp, bean
sprouts, a pinch of salt, a generous
sprinkling of black pepper and stir-fry
for 1 minute.

Beat the eggs with a pinch of salt and a
little pepper until frothy.

Heat the remaining oil in another
frying pan. Add the finely sliced pepper,
stir for a few seconds and then pour in
the eggs. Shake the pan to allow the egg
to coat the bottom evenly.

When the egg begins to coagulate, stir
the top with a fork and pour in the
onion-shrimp-bean sprout mixture.
Scramble lightly without disturbing the
bottom. Pour in the sherry and mix
lightly. Serve when lightly set.

Spanish omelets easily become great piles of
tedious leftovers precariously linked by egg.
But with a modicum of cool and a sense of
adventure the heavily impregnated omelet is no
mean thing. Spanish omelets should be thick
enough to cut in wedges for serving.

SPANISH OMELET IN NORTH MEDITERRANEAN STYLE

Serves 4

1 large onion
5 tablespoons oil
2 zucchini
1 large tomato
$1\frac{1}{2}$ cups cooked diced potatoes
A handful of fresh cooked peas
Black pepper
A pinch of salt
A pinch of mixed herbs
6 eggs

One of our small eggs

Chop the onion and fry in the oil until soft, then add the sliced zucchini and stir-fry until they are soft. Add the coarsely chopped tomato and potatoes and the peas. Pepper generously, add the salt and stir-fry until the potatoes are thoroughly heated and covered in oil. Sprinkle on the herbs, then pour in the well-beaten eggs and stir until everything is thoroughly mixed and the egg is well on the way to setting. Then stop stirring, to allow the bottom to set. Put the pan under a hot broiler for a few minutes to allow the top to brown.

SPANISH OMELET IN EASTERN STYLE
Serves 2 to 4

1 teaspoon sesame seeds
1 teaspoon fennel seeds
3 tablespoons oil
1 large onion
1 small red chili pepper
2⅓ cups cooked diced potatoes
2 large garlic cloves
A pinch of salt
1 teaspoon ground cumin
4 eggs
A handful of Chinese parsley

Toast the sesame and fennel seeds in a dry pan until the sesame seeds jump about. Add the oil, and when it is hot, fry the thinly sliced onion and chili until soft. Then add the coarsely diced potato, the chopped garlic, salt and cumin. Stir-fry until the potatoes are hot and beginning to cook again.

Beat the eggs and mix in the chopped Chinese parsley, then pour onto the frying potato-onion mixture. Stir until the egg is well on the way to setting, then cook on until the bottom is set. Put the pan under a hot broiler for the top to brown. Serve immediately.

GREEN FLUFFY OMELET
And so to the opposite extreme: the fluffy omelet, which, I feel, is suited to the light filling. This, I think, is one of my finest creations.

There is a nice nutritional touch in using parsley with egg, for parsley is extremely rich in vitamin C, which is one vitamin that eggs lack.

Serves 2

6 oz (180 g) white fish fillets (carp, pickerel, yellow perch or yellow pike)
1 head Belgian endive
1 garlic clove
½-inch (1 cm) piece fresh ginger root
3 tablespoons corn oil
A generous sprinkling of black pepper
A pinch of salt
1 tablespoon cornstarch
3 eggs
A large bunch of parsley

First make the filling. Slice the fish into slivers, about 1¼ inches (3 cm) long and ⅛ inch (0.25 cm) thick. Slice the endive leaves to about the same length. Slice the garlic and ginger finely.

Fry the garlic and ginger lightly in the oil for 1 to 2 minutes. With the heat still low, add the fish and endive pieces. Just toss the fish around lightly; the idea is to heat and to bring out the moisture rather than to cook. If you smell frying fish you are overdoing things.

After a minute, pepper generously and add the salt, then pour in 1 cup of water. Bring to a boil and allow to simmer for about 5 minutes. Put the cornstarch into a cup, add a spoonful of the fishy liquor to make a thick paste, then add a little more to make a thinner paste, and so on until you have a smooth, thin white fluid, then pour this back into the simmering fish. Stir gently until the sauce thickens.

Next make the omelet. Separate the eggs. Beat the whites until frothy but not stiff. Beat the yolks until they are as frothy as yolks can get. Chop the parsley and fold it and the yolks into the whites. Then pour the mixture into a hot, dry, nonstick or heavy iron pan, and stir until the top begins to set.

Spoon the fish-endive filling in a band across the middle of the omelet, and fold one side over and then the other.

Serve immediately from the pan.

FLUFFY OMELET WITH VEGETABLES
Asparagus peas and salsify both belong in that intriguing and marginal category of foods that taste like themselves, but with a hint of something else. Asparagus peas of asparagus; salsify of oyster.

Egg recipes

Serves 2

½ cup sliced salsify (oyster plant)
1 garlic clove
2 tablespoons oil
1 cup asparagus peas
1 cup bean sprouts
1 teaspoon chopped chives
1 teaspoon cornstarch
Black pepper
A large pinch of salt
3 eggs

To make the filling, peel and slice the salsify thinly and the garlic very thinly, and fry them gently together in the oil until the salsify is soft. Then add the asparagus peas, bean sprouts and chives and toss about until these are hot.

Meanwhile, mix the cornstarch with a little water to make a thick paste. Then add more water and continue to mix well to a smooth floury fluid. Pour this onto the vegetables and toss about until they are hot and steamy.

Make a fluffy omelet as described in the previous recipe, but without the parsley. Spoon the vegetables in a band across the middle of the omelet and fold over both sides.

Serve immediately.

CHEESE SOUFFLÉ

Soufflés must be eaten immediately they are cooked otherwise they will collapse and the whole point will be lost. To make it easier for the cook, the first part of the preparation—up to the addition of the egg yolks and grated cheese—can be done in advance.

Serves 4

3 tablespoons butter
3 tablespoons flour
1¼ cups milk
Salt
Pepper
A pinch of cayenne pepper
1 teaspoon prepared Dijon mustard
4 egg yolks
½ cup grated Gruyère cheese
¼ cup grated Parmesan cheese
5 egg whites

Melt the butter in a saucepan. Stir in the flour and cook over low heat for 1 minute. Remove the pan from the heat and add the milk, a little at a time,

stirring constantly to avoid lumps. When all the milk has been added return the pan to the heat and bring the sauce to a boil, stirring constantly. Remove the pan from the heat and mix in a pinch of salt, pepper, cayenne and the mustard.

When the sauce has cooled a little, beat in the egg yolks, one at a time, and then the grated cheese.

Beat the egg whites until stiff. Mix 1 tablespoon of the egg whites into the sauce then fold in the rest.

Pour the mixture into a well-buttered soufflé dish and bake in a 375°F (190°C) oven for 25 to 30 minutes or until the soufflé is well risen and is golden brown on top.

Serve immediately.

SPINACH SOUFFLÉ

Serves 4

3 tablespoons butter
3 tablespoons flour
¾ cup milk
4 tablespoons pureed spinach
Salt
Pepper
⅓ cup grated Gruyère cheese
¼ cup grated Parmesan cheese
4 egg yolks
5 egg whites

Melt the butter in a saucepan. Stir in the flour and cook over low heat for 1 minute. Remove the pan from the heat and add the milk a little at a time, stirring constantly. When all the milk has been added stir in the spinach. Return the pan to the heat and bring the sauce to a boil, stirring all the time. Reduce the heat and cook for 2 to 3 minutes until the sauce is thick and smooth. Stir in a little salt, plenty of pepper and the cheese and cook for a further 2 minutes. Remove the pan from the heat and when the sauce has cooled a little beat in the egg yolks.

Beat the egg whites until stiff. Mix 1 tablespoon of the egg whites into the sauce then fold in the rest.

Pour the mixture into a well-buttered soufflé dish and bake in a 375°F (190 C) oven for 25 to 30 minutes or until the soufflé has risen and is nicely browned.

Serve immediately.

Shepherds of fish

The Neolithic revolution might at last be concluded in the twenty-first century as the last of the prey animals that we now pursue are brought into honest domesticity. I speak of course of fish; the marine kinds that may be managed to the point of ranching and ranched to the point of farming: and more particularly the freshwater kinds, notably trout and carp, that may be for the twenty-first century what broiler chickens and the now precious cod have been for the twentieth century.

Fifteen years ago it seemed, at least to some commentators, that the sea would solve all humankind's food problems. The land covered a mere two-fifths of the world, and was two-dimensional. The sea covered most of the world and was a mile deep. Protein was thought to be the chief requirement and fish contained about 20 percent high-grade protein. It was just a question of pulling them out. The bigger the boats, the more they caught, and the boats accordingly grew bigger and faster. With their Sonar and landing gear they could locate and scoop out entire shoals as neatly as Little Jack Horner pulled out his plum.

Scooping out fish by the shoal

There were of course logistic problems. Big boats are expensive and their owners could not afford merely to catch fish when the going was good; they had to catch all the time and to go on catching. The great loads they brought home had to be dealt with immediately for nothing spoils quicker than fish, and the smart new fleets were supported by smart new packing factories, which in turn had to be paid for by bigger and bigger catches.

There were also irritations. The Organization of Petroleum Exporting Countries (OPEC) was one, because fast, heavily laden boats on cruises of a thousand miles must burn egregious quantities of oil. Legal difficulties were another, because the old sea laws, initially conceived for the offshore boats of local industries, proved inadequate.

But the biggest irritation was the sea itself. It is just not that opulent. Fish live where there is plankton, the tons of small animals and plants that float near the surface. Plankton has to be nourished constantly by minerals stirred up from the bottom; and minerals are not stirred up from the bottom except by odd currents, rough weather, or the sea glancing off a continental shelf or a ridge on the ocean bed. Fish do not fill the oceans like pickles in a jar. They live in tightly circumscribed regions that can be clearly defined; cod and herring in the North Sea and anchovies in the South Pacific. Industrial-scale fishing overwhelmed the resource. Cod, herring and anchovy have all been under severe pressure and are unlikely to be given much of a chance to recover.

Where are the sea's riches?

Industrial fishing will continue. The sea will never be fished out (for fishing would become absurdly uneconomical long before this happened) and species that hitherto have been minor, such as sand-eel, will fill at least part of the ecological vacuum caused by the herring's depletion. But the euphoria at least is over. Fish provide remarkably little human food—less than four percent of the world's dietary protein—and this alone should suggest that they should be regarded not as a major protein source but as a delicacy. The expense of pulling them out, and the depleted stocks, support this view. As long as people regard any food as a delicacy they are prepared to pay for it; and if they are prepared to spend at least as much for fish as they would for meat, then fish farming will be worthwhile.

Many people, such as the old Scottish crofters, have combined fishing and farming; but there is plenty of evidence that the two require different temperaments, and one reason for the law's failure to contain overfishing is, perhaps, that fishermen are not conservative by nature. They are adventurers; tomorrow they may be rich or they may be drowned. When oyster beds in Holland were modernized, the fishermen who had hitherto plundered them were invited, even beseeched, to stay on as farmers; but of course they did not. Real farmers, erstwhile of cows and corn, eventually took over the oyster farms.

There have been many attempts at sea farming. So far they have been most successful with static creatures such as mussels and oysters which are not fish at all. Lobsters too are remarkably static, despite their formidable muscle and armament, and are content to sit in holes hardly bigger than themselves for decades at a time. Lobsters are not so much farmed as encouraged; and one method, practiced in France, is to sink old cars in the shallows, which with the aid of a few barnacles and fronds of seaweed develop quickly into a crustacean paradise. Rubbish, dumped into the sea, can be depressing, and the deepest trawls sometimes come up with cargoes of suntan lotion bottles. But the creative use of rubbish, including old cars, should be taken seriously.

Cultivating lobsters: the creative use of rubbish

The difficulty is that the oceans are far too big to farm collectively—yet the beneficence of the sea depends on its constancy of temperature, and its intricacy of chemistry and life, which cannot easily be imitated in a confined space. To farm fish as opposed to mollusks or crustaceans, the marine farmer must enclose a piece of sea in such a way that the natural waters flush in and out while the fish are trapped. In practice he is obliged to use odd coves or inlets, or perhaps estuaries, where the natural topography provides most of the essential architecture. There are not all that many suitable places.

Yet the most valuable North Sea fish, Dover and lemon sole, turbot, halibut, mullet and plaice, are eminently farmable; and some, like turbot, seem positively to enjoy the cramped conditions of intensive farming. There are some strange problems of biology, but these can perhaps be solved by selective breeding or crossing. Flatfish, for example, have a strong sense of social hierarchy, and their growth rate reflects their position in the pecking order. The dominant ones grow very fast, and raise everybody's hopes about the fishes' astonishing potential, while the meek remain incorrigibly weedy.

Feudal flatfish

The second, less tractable problem is that the marine food-fish are all

Shepherds of fish

carnivores. If they themselves need to be fed on flesh, or at least on high-grade protein foods, then what advantage do they have over, say, intensive pigs, which eat their way through so much cereal? None, is the short answer; but it is at least possible to raise algae on sewage, and to feed shrimp on the algae, and use the shrimp to feed fish, so that the fish become a by-product of sewage disposal. There is something mythological, not to say aesthetically pleasing, in producing such delicacy from such stercoraceous origins.

The untapped potential of freshwater fish

Freshwater fish farming is in many ways more promising; anyone can build a pond, and some at least of the possible freshwater species are omnivorous and could be slotted into a farm or household economy as unobtrusively and beneficially as free-range chickens. Many freshwater or sometimes freshwater fish can be, and are, eaten: salmon and trout, pike, eels, minnow, bass, yellow perch, lake herring, carp, *Tilapia*. But by far the most promising of these, for husbandry purposes, are the salmonids (salmon and trout, and particularly trout) and the carp.

Salmon and trout are among the few fish which, after a brief period of adaptation, can live either in seawater or in fresh water; although many trout in practice spend their whole lives in fresh water. The archetypal *curriculum vitae* for a salmonid is to be born in a fast-flowing river; to migrate to sea, to grow and mature; and to return to the same river to breed a few years later.

Salmonid rivers are clean—that is, contain little organic material—cold and sometimes fast running. Organic detritus soaks up oxygen, warmth drives it off, and stagnancy reduces the chances of more dissolving; so the outstanding feature of good salmonid waters is that they are rich in oxygen. In addition, because water with a low organic content contains few living things (by definition), the river salmonids inevitably are largely surface feeders, eating mostly insects. Hence the noble sport of fly-fishing.

The carnivorous salmonids . . .

The salmonids' two outstanding biological demands—for oxygen and for a rich, carnivorous diet—are also the outstanding constraints on husbandry. Some trout farms make use of existing, fast-running streams; but further expansion will depend more and more on custom-built pools. These are becoming popular in the United States, but the lives of the thousands and sometimes tens of thousands of dollars' worth of fish that they contain depend upon the good order of the oxygen pump. Power failure is one obvious drawback, and although the farms may have their own generators, these too may give up the ghost. Perhaps it is my own clumsiness that causes me to fear such second-by-second reliance on machinery.

Secondly, the salmonids' carnivorousness makes them expensive to feed, and again suggests that however profitable salmonid farming may be it will not solve many human food problems, for livestock that needs high-protein feed is to some extent competing with us for food as well as supplying it.

. . . and the omnivorous carp

The fish that does have an exciting and eminently defensible farming future is the carp. Its only drawback, at least in Britain and the United States, is the lack of a ready market. But in Europe, and particularly in Eastern Europe, carp is regarded as a feast; among other things, a traditional Christmas-time dinner. There surely are enough Poles and Germans in Britain and the United States to push the market along, not to mention Jews, who are forbidden to eat the eggs of the sturgeon (because it is a fish without scales) and so eat the caviar of carp instead.

Carp have all the advantages that salmonids lack. They live in dirty water; not polluted, but rich in organic detritus. This means they do not need a great deal of oxygen, and can be kept in static pools—as they have been kept in monastery gardens for at least a thousand years. They are omnivorous, and indeed can be well-nigh vegetarian. Thus they are theoretically cheap to feed, and are able to live on materials that human beings reject; in Japan, they have been fed on mixtures of chopped grass and silkworm pupae.

Carp have all the advantages

Finally, again by virtue of their low oxygen demand, they do not object to warm (and hence de-oxygenated) water, and indeed grow faster if the water is warm. The fish farmer can raise the temperature of his carp pond with ample solar-traps—that is, with sheets of glass or polyethylene angled over the water—and by protecting the surface from the wind. But power plants are the most obviously exploitable heat source. One way to cash in on the endless warm water that flows from them, which otherwise is wasted and is regarded as thermal pollution, is to use it to force vegetables; and another is to fill warm lagoons with carp, and particularly the mirror carp, which responds well to such treatment. Britain's Central Electricity Generating Board is taking both vegetables and carp seriously. The usual complaint against such ideas is that they are not "realistic"—that is, that they do not make money in the short term. It is comforting that the ecologically desirable may sometimes coincide with the almost immediately profitable.

Fish in the power plants

Carp are adaptable. The Chinese traditionally keep them in their drainage ditches, in pleasant harmony with ducks, whose ordure increases the organic content of the water and hence the fish's food supply. In addition, the grass carp at least (like the manatee) is an admirable clearer of waterways and some have even been imported to Britain to do just that.

Some say that carp flesh is superior to trout, but whether it is or not I hope the carp catches on. Neither I, nor eight hundred million Chinese, can think of anything bad to say about it.

The *Tilapia* is the traditional lake fish of Africa; one that illustrates the point that although fish seem to contribute little statistically to the mass of mankind, for some communities they are vital. *Tilapias* could probably be raised in Britain's power plant water, and they are now being taken seriously in the United States—where, in the south, they may thrive without artificial heat. On the other hand, some African countries are keen to import carp, but never having tasted *Tilapia* I cannot comment on the relative merits of the two.

Fish farming is not new (the Chinese have been farming carp for thousands of years) but it is new to Westerners and to Western science. It has come to us at a time when the husbandry of all livestock is undergoing constant and even frenetic revolution, and when the cereal breeders have already shown that genetic engineering is a reality. The

Shepherds of fish

changes that scientists will make in fish farming in the next few decades and in the fish themselves will be spectacular, and although they will not necessarily benefit the human race (any more than the spectacular, germfree intensive piggeries do) they are worth a brief review.

Selective breeding and intensive husbandry are liable to transform present species. Twenty-pound trout, a yard or more long, are already well within the farmers' compass, although the market will probably continue to demand smaller beasts. Crossbreeding—hybridization—will produce extraordinary changes. The traditional zoological view that a species was a group of living things that could not produce fully viable or fertile offspring if crossed with other species is already defunct; and it never really did apply to fish which happily hybridize in the wild not only with members of different species, but even with members of different families to which, according to zoology textbooks, they are not even closely related. Fertilization of fish eggs often occurs externally, and there is little need for psychological commitment from either participant. The behavioral difficulties that proscribe copulation between opposing land animals do not usually apply.

Crossbreeding is intrinsically useful because the offspring of differing types tend to show "hybrid vigor" and outstrip both their parents. In Russia the giant sturgeon known as the beluga, which may weigh more than a ton, has been crossed with the modest one-pound sterlet, and the offspring grow faster than the beluga. In France, trout have been crossed with salmon. Halibut, which is of outstanding quality but is none too easy to farm, might usefully be crossed with flounder, which is less desirable but eminently tractable. Flatfish, which grow unevenly because of their strong sense of hierarchy, might perhaps be crossed with roundfish, whose politics are more democratic. We can envisage not simply new varieties comparable, say, to the Ayrshires and Anguses that have been developed among cattle, but whole new species; creatures quite different from anything ever seen before.

But what I find more exciting are the possibilities that fish offer for exploiting that difficult twilight zone between husbandry and conservation. Instead of simply filling ponds with carp, why not make ponds into stable ecosystems, stage managed to be both productive and of value to all wildlife—comparable with the sheep-grazed chalk grassland of an earlier age, and with the woods full of blewit and *shiitake* mushrooms that might be established in the future? The carp is outstanding, but other species have much to offer, at least as members of a mixed system; the minnow, for example, the small boy's archetypal little fish, is said to compare with herring sprats. Rivers that now are managed to accommodate salmon, and others that are not, might also be adapted to the elver, migrating larva of the eel, and to the grayling, said by some to be the most graceful of fish. The trend is already afoot; rivers and ponds are officiously stocked for fishermen, fishing is one of the world's most popular sports (the most popular of all in Britain), and many anglers have deep regard not simply for the trophy but for the integrity of nature. People are more likely to be sympathetic to the natural world if it gives them some small payoff. Fish do this with interest, and they could do far more.

Fish is at its best when it first falls onto the bank or into the ship's hold; so good is it fresh, and so irrevocably is the first flush of flavor lost, that deep into the nineteenth century, carp were cut up alive and cooked, and many restaurateurs still invite their customers to select their meal from the tank. Fish in its first phase of delicacy can be eaten raw; if cooked it requires only the most reticent embellishment or none at all. The less subtly fleshed species (and there are plenty of those), or the finer kinds past their fleeting prime, can take more robust treatment.

Theme I
Raw fish

Eating raw fish seems to be against the spirit of twenty-first-century conservatism because only the best parts of the finest fish will do. But there are plenty of things to be done with the lesser cuts, from pies to curries and fishcakes, and in truth the essence of conservatism is to make the best possible use of all parts of a beast: the bones no less than the finest flesh, and the finest flesh no less than the bones.

RAW FISH JAPANESE STYLE
The original recipe employs the specifically Japanese ingredients of *daikon* (Japanese radish), *wasabi* (Japanese horseradish) and light soy sauce. More readily available ingredients feature in this version, but the effect is similar.

This is a fine fresh starter and best eaten with chopsticks.
Serves 4

$\frac{1}{2}$ lb (240 g) raw delicate fish or other seafood—trout, tuna, sole, halibut, sea-bass, salmon or shrimp
$\frac{3}{4}$ cup carrot
$\frac{3}{4}$ cup parsnip
$\frac{1}{2}$ teaspoon cumin seeds
$\frac{1}{2}$ teaspoon white sesame seeds
Lemon juice, to moisten
Watercress
Grated horseradish

Each fish is filleted according to its shape and skeletal details; but the usual principle is to remove the skin from one side and then, using a sharp knife, ease the flesh away from ribs and backbone, and then repeat on the other side.

Slice the fillets into slivers about $1\frac{1}{2}$ inches by 1 inch (3.5 by 2.5 cm) and $\frac{1}{8}$ inch (0.25 cm) thick (or thicker if you prefer), and arrange these attractively on 4 plates. Grate the carrot and parsnip coarsely, toss in the cumin, sesame and lemon juice, and put a mound on each plate. Garnish with watercress and give each person a separate little bowl of horseradish.

SEVICHE
This is a Peruvian dish in which the fish is "cooked" in lime juice. After the fish has marinated for 90 minutes it turns opaque and, if it is freshly caught, should be ready to eat after another 3 hours. Store-bought fish will benefit from a longer soak. In Peru, the fish is garnished with corn on the cob and sweet potatoes.
Serves 4 to 6

$1\frac{1}{2}$ lb ($\frac{3}{4}$ kg) skinned fish fillets (any firm-fleshed white fish)
2 cups fresh lime juice or, if not available, use fresh lemon juice
$1\frac{1}{2}$ teaspoons salt
1 garlic clove
1 dried red chili pepper
2 onions
Black pepper
Lime slices
Sweet red pepper

Cut the fish into $\frac{1}{2}$-inch (1 cm) cubes and put into a bowl. Combine the lime juice with the salt, crushed garlic, the seeded and chopped chili, the finely sliced onions and a generous sprinkling of black pepper. Pour the mixture over the fish and toss well. Cover and refrigerate overnight. Serve garnished with lime slices and strips of sweet red pepper.

Theme II
The art of simplicity

Fish is never tough; the point of cooking it is to improve flavor, and perhaps to make it hot and to improve texture, but not, as is often the case with red meat, to make life easy for the jaws. One way to test if fish is cooked is to prod it with a fork, for the raw flesh offers some resistance whereas the cooked flesh offers none at all. The

Shepherds of fish

protracted boilings and simmerings that play such a part in meat cookery, play no part in fish cookery—except, that is, for simmering bones to make stocks and jellies.

The techniques that have evolved for cooking fish are those a fisherman might use; indeed, only fishermen know what fish can really taste like. Reasonably solid fish that is not too oily, such as haddock, cod or salmon, can simply be steamed or poached; and poaching means cooking in water at less than boiling point. You can cook haddock fillets simply by putting them in cold water, bringing them to a boil, then turning off the heat and allowing them to bathe in the cooling water for ten minutes. Kippers, too, are at their best when simply poached—put them into a pitcher or bowl, cover with boiling water and leave for ten minutes.

One Saturday I tried a range of mackerel recipes. I wrapped the fish in foil with various stuffings and sauces, but found that the best were the ones I did for the children, who do not like stuffings and sauces. These were simply placed on the rack in the middle of a preheated oven set at 375°F (190°C) with a baking pan underneath to catch the drips, for 35 minutes. The mackerel emerged with their edges pleasantly crisped and their unsullied flesh running with juice.

Foil does have its place, for fish can be pleasantly moist and oily enough to require no added fat (and I deplore the modern habit of smothering fish in butter, not simply on nutritional grounds but because of the insult to the fish). Cooking in close confinement can ensure that nothing is lost. People have been wrapping fish in leaves and cooking it between hot stones since the beginning of time. They have wrapped fish in paper wherever it crept into their culture, so foil can be seen as the modern version of an ancient technique. Some say that the best way to cook a salmon is by slow baking in foil at 300°F (160°C). An hour should suffice for a fish or piece of fish weighing between two and six pounds (1 and 3 kg). Allow ten minutes per pound for larger fish and be careful not to overcook it. But if aluminum became more expensive than gold and foil disappeared from the kitchen, the cook need lose no sleep over it.

Theme III
More flavors for the fish

That great English cook the late Philip Harben pointed out that you cannot aromatize fish,

tempting though the idea is, simply by flavoring the water in which it poaches. Other routes must be adopted. The first is marination, whereby powerful flavors are induced to seep into the flesh, over many hours; and the second is to flavor the surface of the flesh so that it either consolidates the absorbed marinade, or contrasts with the unsullied fish.

Here are three approaches to marination: a classic method from northern Europe; one from Japan; and one from India.

ROLLMOPS
Marination German style.
Serves 4

4 fresh herring
4 gherkins
6 shallots or 2 medium onions
12 peppercorns
2 small dried red chili peppers
A large pinch of mustard seed
5 cups white wine vinegar (or enough to cover)

Take 2 fillets from each herring. Lay each fillet on a board, skin side down. Slice the gherkins and the shallots wafer thin and put a row of each along each herring fillet; then roll up the fillets and secure them with little wooden skewers.

Put the rollmops into a wide-necked jar, toss in the peppercorns, chilies and mustard seed, cover with the vinegar and put on the lid. They will be ready for eating in 2 to 3 days.

TERIYAKI
Marination Japanese style.
The German marinade uses one product of fermentation: vinegar. The Japanese *teriyaki* uses three more: soy sauce, the sweet rice cooking wine known as *mirin*, and the drier rice wine *sake*. The marinated fish is then cooked. It is excellent served with rice and stir-fried mixed vegetables.
Serves 4

3 mackerel
1 garlic clove
4 tablespoons dark soy sauce
4 tablespoons *sake*
4 tablespoons *mirin*

Fillet the mackerel and cut each fillet in half so that you have 12 pieces in all.

Chop the garlic, add it to the mixture of soy sauce, *sake* and *mirin* and bring to a boil. Cover the fish with the soy-wine-garlic mixture and leave to marinate for 20 to 30 minutes.

Preheat the broiler to a moderate heat, and cook the fish pieces for 1 to 2 minutes on each side, basting intermittently with the marinade.

Serve immediately.

SPICED FISH
Marination Indian style.
In this version, the fish is cooked (fried this time) as in the Japanese recipe, but yogurt takes over as the inevitable fermented agent in the marinade. Spice to taste; fiery hot with chilies, or soothing with mace or cumin.
Serves 4

4 fish fillets: any firm white fish will do
½ teaspoon salt
Seeds of 6 cardamom pods, crushed
1 teaspoon ground cumin
1 teaspoon ground cinnamon, cloves and black pepper in equal amounts
A pinch of nutmeg
A pinch of mace
⅔ cup yogurt
Oil for frying

Skin the fish fillets. Mix the salt and spices with the yogurt and rub the mixture well into the fish. Pour whatever is left on top and allow the fish to marinate for 3 hours.

Remove the fish pieces, and fry gently in a small amount of oil for a few minutes on each side. Then add the rest of the marinade and cook until the flesh offers no resistance to a fork.

Serve at once.

Cereal is used with fish and meat as a means of holding flavor to the surface; it is sometimes cooked into the surface, as in dredging; and sometimes it is applied separately, as a sauce. Here are four approaches: from Scotland, Japan, England and China.

HERRING IN OATMEAL
Serve the herring with boiled potatoes and broiled tomatoes, or, just to pay lip service to the pulse and grain theme, with lentils or peas.

Serves 4

4 fresh herring
A large pinch of salt
A pinch of dry mustard
A generous sprinkling of black pepper
3 tablespoons fine oatmeal
1 tablespoon oil, or less if possible

Clean the herring, and dry the insides. Mix all the seasonings into the oatmeal, and press the herring into it, so that as much as possible adheres.

Heat the oil and fry the herring for 3 to 5 minutes on each side.

A WESTERN TEMPURA
The English, of course, are fond of frying fish in batter, which is an easier way to induce cereal to form a tasty coat. The Japanese, who have a lighter touch, also employ this method and they call the result *tempura*. Here is a highly simplified form, as appropriate with French fries as with oriental rice, and excellent with stir-fried vegetables.
Serves 4

1½ lb (¾ kg) firm but not too oily fish: flounder, cod, haddock or jumbo shrimp
Corn oil for deep frying

The Batter
1 egg
A pinch of salt
1 teaspoon soy sauce
1 teaspoon vinegar
2 drops sesame oil
½ cup all-purpose flour
2 tablespoons cornstarch

First make the batter. Beat the egg, beat in ½ cup of water then add all the seasonings and the sesame oil and stir in the flour and the cornstarch.

Cut the fish into fillets. Skin and cut the fillets into pieces about 3 inches (8 cm) long and 1½ inches (3.5 cm) wide.

The oil should be moderately hot, about 350°F (175°C) if you have a thermometer, but if not drop a teaspoon of batter into the oil—it should sink a little, then rise quickly and sizzle, and be browned in less than a minute.

When the oil is hot enough, coat the fish pieces in the batter and submerge just a few pieces at a time; do not put them in all at once or they will cool the oil and come out greasy. They should be nicely golden in less than a minute. Lift out and dab quickly with absorbent paper before serving.

The third way to use cereal to hold flavor on the surface is to make a sauce. In purist terms this is preferable, as a sauce need contain no fat (except what is in the stock), although a modern chef would normally incorporate butter. Flavored white sauces of one kind or another are suitable with virtually any fish, and a mustard sauce, for example, goes supremely well with herring or mackerel. But the most aesthetically satisfying way to make a sauce for fish or meat is to incorporate the stock in which the flesh was first boiled or poached; and you would not normally poach such an oily fish as mackerel or herring. So the white sauces are best suited to the poachable fish; and the classic dish is smoked haddock with parsley sauce. There is in this a marvelous clash both of flavor and color, for parsley sauce should be green (not white with green flecks) and the heraldic juxtaposition of green and gold would have brought joy to the medieval cook.

POACHED SMOKED HADDOCK WITH PARSLEY SAUCE

Haddock with milk, cereal and such a fine sauce of vitamin C (parsley) is good food, although tending, if anything, to err on the side of protein richness and perhaps of fattiness. Lots of boiled potatoes and big floury white beans, notably butter beans, are an admirable nutritional and gastronomic foil.

Serves 2

$\frac{3}{4}$ lb (360 g) smoked haddock fillets
$1\frac{1}{4}$ cups milk
White pepper
1 tablespoon flour
A good handful of parsley

Trim the ugly dried edges off the haddock fillets. Put the fillets in a pan, cover with the milk and sprinkle with white pepper (black will do, of course, but it speckles the sauce). Bring almost to a boil, simmer for a minute or two over low heat, then turn off the heat and allow the fish to poach in the cooling fluid for 10 minutes. Prod the fillets with a fork; if the flesh flakes easily the fish is cooked.

To make the sauce, put the flour into a

cup, and add no more than 2 teaspoons of the poaching liquid. Stir to a thick paste. When all the fluid is absorbed, add another 2 teaspoons of the stock and stir again. Repeat this gradual thinning until the paste thins and becomes positively fluid.

Now remove the haddock from the pan and keep it hot. Put the pan back on the heat and stir in the thin flour-stock mixture. Keep stirring until the fluid comes to a boil, whereupon the sauce should immediately thicken. Turn off the heat but keep stirring for a few more seconds to ensure all is smooth.

Add a good handful of finely chopped parsley to make a rich green sauce. Pour the sauce over the haddock.

Serve immediately.

Haddock complemented by large quantities of staple is essentially being used as a garnish, although six ounces (180 grams) per person is a lot for such a role; and, of course, the carnivorous Westerners like to emphasize that their fish is flesh, and to leave it intact. The Chinese are happy to emphasize that the fish is a mere garnish and to put it in the orchestra with other assertive flavors such as peppers and onions. Nutritionally—in its balance of water, fat, cereal and fish—the following Chinese fried fish is almost identical to the poached haddock dish, with water and oil taking over from the milk, and the vitamin C-rich peppers standing in for parsley. Logistically the dish is the same, too, with the cereal holding the flavor to the fish's surface. But the idiom is quite different.

CHINESE FRIED FISH

The fish is used sparingly and adventurously but with proper respect for its delicacy. This is good cooking. Of all the staples, only rice or new potatoes have the delicacy to match it.

Serves 4

1 lb ($\frac{1}{2}$ kg) white fish fillets: sole, flounder or halibut
1 tablespoon cornstarch
1 teaspoon ginger sherry (see page 47)
2 drops sesame oil
$\frac{1}{2}$ teaspoon sugar
A pinch of salt
Oil for deep frying

The Vegetables
1 sweet red pepper

It is sound nutritional advice to eat more fish: but there is not enough to go around and fish, like meat, must be treated as a delicacy. **Top**, *rollmops, marinated in German style;* **left**, *raw fish in Japanese style; and* **right**, *a classic from Peru, seviche, in which fresh fish is marinated in lime juice.*

*Scenes from a British high tea: baked bass, **top**; mackerel pâté and baked mackerel, **center**; herrings in oatmeal, **bottom left**; and potted shrimp, **bottom right**.*

A little fish going a long way: in fish cakes,
top*; lightly fried in Chinese style, with*
vegetables, **left** *; and a Western version of*
Japanese tempura, **right.**

1 sweet green pepper
1 onion
1 tomato
2 garlic cloves
½-inch (1 cm) piece fresh ginger root
2 tablespoons corn oil
1 teaspoon soy sauce
A pinch of sugar
A pinch of salt

The Garnish
4 scallions, made into "flowers" (see page 45)

Cut the fish fillets diagonally into neat, bite-sized pieces, about 1 by 1½ inches (2.5 by 3.5 cm).

Add 4 tablespoons of water gradually to the cornstarch. Add the sherry, sesame oil, sugar and salt. Coat each piece of fish with this mixture and set aside to marinate while you attend to the accompaniments.

Seed the peppers and cut them, the onion and the tomato into pieces only a little bit smaller than the fish pieces. (The onion should remain more or less intact and should still be decorative at the end of the cooking time; it is not intended to disappear as in so many Indian dishes.) Slice the garlic and ginger thinly.

Heat the corn oil, and fry the garlic and ginger for 1 minute; then throw them out, for their job is done.

Add the onion to the oil and keep it moving in the pan for a minute, then add the pepper pieces and stir-fry for another minute. Finally, add the tomato pieces and all the remaining ingredients. In another minute all the vegetables should be sufficiently hot and cooked. Take the pan off the heat.

Deep fry the fish pieces in a frying basket in clean hot oil until they are slightly colored; 2 minutes or less should suffice. Drain on paper towels.

Now add the fish pieces to the vegetables and cook again, stirring gently, so as not to break up the fish, for another 30 seconds.

Serve immediately, decorated with the scallion flowers.

MACKEREL BAKED IN FOIL
A simple way to bring extra flavors to fish is to wrap it up—in foil, for example—with whatever you want to flavor it with. The flesh itself is not flavored by such treatment; that is an illusion. But the accompaniments blend with the exudant juices, to make a simple, pleasing sauce.

I see no point in using butter to cook mackerel, as is so often recommended; it is oily enough already, and its oil is unsaturated. Butter in such a context is merely a nutritional pollutant. I use a little corn oil in this recipe, simply to bind the seasonings.

Whole baked tomatoes and boiled potatoes are fine accompaniments.
Serves 2

2 mackerel
2 shallots
2 garlic cloves
1 tablespoon corn oil
Juice of 1 lemon
A large pinch of dried tarragon
A large pinch of cayenne pepper
A large pinch of sugar
A pinch of salt
A generous sprinkling of black pepper
4 tablespoons chopped parsley

Clean the mackerel, but you can leave the heads on. Chop the shallots and garlic finely, and then grind these together in a mortar with the oil, lemon juice, tarragon, cayenne, sugar and the seasonings, to produce a gooey paste. Then stir in three-quarters of the finely chopped parsley.

Wash and dry the mackerel. Lay each fish on a piece of foil big enough to wrap it in. Spoon the onion mixture into their insides and wrap in the foil.

Bake the mackerel in a 400°F (200°C) oven for 30 minutes, or 40 minutes if the fish are large.

When you unwrap the fish, make sure you retain all the liquid. Sprinkle the fish with the remaining parsley, and pour the liquid over.

Serve immediately.

STUFFED CARP
Carp, too, is a fine candidate for stuffing, as in this version from Eastern Europe.

Serve hot with red cabbage and carrots or turnips, and boiled potatoes. Or serve cold with brown bread.

Shepherds of fish

Serves 4 to 6

2 to 3 lb (1 to 1½ kg) carp
1 tablespoon fresh breadcrumbs
¼ lb (120 g) black olives
1 tablespoon chives
2 garlic cloves
1 tablespoon olive oil
Juice of 1 lemon
A generous sprinkling of
  cayenne pepper

Gut the carp. Lightly toast the breadcrumbs on a dry griddle. Mix in the pitted and halved olives, the chopped chives and garlic, and the olive oil, lemon juice and cayenne. Stuff the carp with the mixture, wrap in foil, and bake in a 350°F (180°C) oven for 1 hour or until cooked through.
  Serve immediately.

BAKED BASS
There are endless variations on this theme, including the ginger sherry, garlic and soy combination of China (excellent with carp) and the more acquired taste of the soy, *sake* and *miso* triad of Japan. But here is a version from India that would do fine things to many a middle-sized fish that was not too oily.
  Pleasantly spiced rice, a vegetable dish incorporating spinach (such as *sag alu*), and pickles, raw onion and tomatoes, would be fine accompaniments.
Serves 4

2 lb (1 kg) bass
2 garlic cloves
1 teaspoon cumin seeds
1 teaspoon ground fennel
½ teaspoon ground mace
½ teaspoon ground fenugreek
Freshly ground black pepper
A large pinch of salt
2 teaspoons corn oil

The Garnish
Sliced raw onion
Chinese parsley

Clean the fish but leave the head on. Chop the garlic finely and mix with the spices, salt and oil. Make cuts in the fish surface, and rub the spicy mixture well in. Wrap the fish in foil and bake in a 400°F (200°C) oven for 40 minutes or until cooked through.

Serve on a hot dish. Retain whatever liquid escapes into the foil and pour over. Garnish with the raw onion and Chinese parsley.

Theme IV _____
Fish comminuted

Little bits of leftover cooked fish are among the most useful ingredients in the kitchen.

MACKEREL PÂTÉ
Serves 2

1½ cups cold cooked mackerel
Juice of ½ lemon
Salt
Black pepper
Cayenne pepper

The Garnish
1 slice lemon or parsley (fresh or
  Chinese)

Carefully pick the bones out of the fish, then add the lemon juice, a little salt and a generous sprinkling of black pepper. Mash with a fork until smooth but not entirely devoid of texture, put into a pleasant dish, sprinkle lightly with cayenne and garnish with a lemon slice or sprigs of parsley.

POTTED SHRIMP
Shrimp can border on the tedious, and can be expensive. To pot them is the answer. Butter appears here in its proper guise, as a rare delicacy; but a little goes a long way.
Serves 4

1 cup cooked small shrimp
1 cup white fish fillet
½ teaspoon ground mace
A large pinch of cayenne pepper
1 drop anchovy paste
¾ stick butter
1 to 2 tablespoons melted butter, to seal

Peel and remove the heads of the shrimp. Put the fleshy tails to one side. Simmer the heads and shells in 1¼ cups of water until it becomes pink. Strain, and reserve the water.
  Cook the fish in the shrimp water until it is tender. Drain and when the fish is

cool, pound it to a smooth paste with the mace, cayenne, anchovy paste and the butter. When all is smooth, stir in the whole shrimp.

Press the mixture into a small earthenware dish. Stand the dish in a pan of boiling water for 10 to 15 minutes until it is heated through. Pour the melted butter on top to seal. Serve cold.

FISH CAKES

Fish cakes are among the most variable and malleable of all dishes. They can express almost every idiom from homely Scottish to Indian Raj and it is difficult to make them unpleasant. Here is a simple recipe with finely chopped parsley adding color (and vitamin C). Serve these fish cakes with broiled tomatoes or ratatouille.

Makes 12 small fish cakes

$2\frac{1}{2}$ **cups cooked potato**
Milk
$\frac{1}{2}$ **lb (240 g) cooked white fish**
Salt
Black pepper
2 heaping tablespoons chopped parsley
2 to 3 tablespoons oatmeal
Oil for frying

Mash the potato with a dash of milk until it is smooth. Carefully bone the fish, and mash it roughly in with the potato. Add a little salt, pepper generously and stir in the parsley.

Break off pieces a little smaller than a golf ball, flatten to about $\frac{3}{4}$ inch (2 cm) thick, coat with oatmeal as thickly as possible on all sides, and fry in a little oil until the fish cakes are pleasantly browned on both sides.

SPICY FISH KOFTAS

To convert fish cakes into something mildly exotic is simplicity itself. Serve these *koftas* with *dhal*, rice and a yogurty vegetable curry.

Makes 12 to 15 koftas

1 cup cooked white fish
1 small onion
2 to 3 tablespoons oil
2 garlic cloves
1 small red chili pepper
1 small green chili pepper
1 teaspoon turmeric

1 teaspoon ground coriander
1 teaspoon ground cumin
$\frac{1}{2}$ **teaspoon mustard seed**
$2\frac{1}{2}$ **cups cold mashed potatoes**
2 to 3 tablespoons oatmeal
Oil for deep frying

Bone the fish, and break into small flakes. Chop the onion and fry in a small amount of oil until soft, then add the garlic and chilies, both finely chopped, and fry for another 2 minutes. Stir in the spices until they are well mixed and beginning to aromatize, then add the fish and stir for 3 to 5 minutes; add a little more oil, if necessary.

Mix the spicy fried fish with the potatoes. Break off balls about $1\frac{1}{2}$ inches (3.5 cm) across, coat them in oatmeal (an easy way is to coat your hands thickly with oatmeal and toss the balls about a bit) and deep fry in hot oil until they are pleasantly golden.

Variations on a theme of milk

If cows had been left where they belong, where nothing much except grass will grow, and their milk and its derivatives where they belong, as Food of the Second Kind, guarantors of quality and sources of exciting flavor, then the present doubts about the usefulness of milk and the desirability of butter and cream need never have arisen.

Of course milk is excellent stuff; of course butter is an outstanding fat. But both are rich, and if milk producers and dietitians cajole people to drink the stuff by the pint, and if cookbook authors decorate every dish with knobs of gleaming butter and dollops of cream, then the inevitable excess is liable to do harm.

All mammals produce milk (which is how mammaldom is defined) and its nutritional quality varies with the particular baby's needs. Human milk is weak stuff, less than two percent protein, but then human babies take four months to double their birth weight. Reindeer milk sometimes contains more than ten percent protein and more than 20 percent fat, but baby reindeer must double their birth weight within a few brief autumn weeks, or they will not survive their first Arctic winter. Ewe's milk is also rich—more than five percent protein and six percent fat—but goats and cattle both produce a more modest fluid, less than four percent protein and about four percent fat. Mare's milk, about two percent protein and one percent fat, is closer to human's. Goats and sheep are admirable milch animals; they are virtually the only source of milk in some Mediterranean countries, except for the odd water buffalo, and the self-sufficient Westerner might be better off with a big milky ewe than with a small cow. Horse milk seems an odd kind of food to Westerners, but the Russians keep nearly a quarter of a million milch mares, and horses, sheep and goats are admirably suited to many areas—where it is hilly and rough, or impossibly dry—in which cattle languish. Cattle will and should dominate the Western dairy scene, but it is at least a pity that we neglect other admirable species.

Russian milch mares

Cow's milk is 88 percent water, but many solid foods, including green leaves and carrots, are even more watery, and even beefsteak contains 70 percent water. It is not the high water content that makes milk fluid but the molecular arrangement; the fat is held in separate droplets to form an emulsion, and the proteins held both in suspension and in solution. A small rearrangement of molecules—as in curdling—quickly turns milk solid. The protein in milk is mostly casein, which is unique to milk. The fat consists mostly of short-chain fatty acids, which are easily digested, and is about 60 percent saturated and 40 percent unsaturated (although very little of it is polyunsaturated). The 4.7 percent of sugar is also in a form unique to milk, namely lactose, which is about one-sixth as sweet as sucrose (table sugar).

Milk contains a reasonable spectrum of vitamins, including carotene—vitamin A—which puts the yellow tinge into cream. But it is a poor source of vitamins E and C. Minerals are its strong point, particularly phosphorous and calcium; indeed, dairy products supply Americans with 75 percent of their daily calcium. Some nutritionists claim that human beings could not meet their calcium requirements without dairy products, and this idea has been used in Britain as an advertising pitch. If you match people's alleged calcium requirement against the modest calcium content of most foods, this claim seems to be true, but on commonsense grounds it seems ludicrous, since nature could hardly have designed human beings so badly that they actually need the arcane secretions of an alien creature.

Overall, milk emerges as a fine emergency food—a quick and easy ration for people whose diets are obviously deficient but not in specific ways that can easily be identified or put right. But for most people on a reasonably rich and balanced diet, milk should be no more than one modest dietary component among many. To superimpose the potentially massive nutritional contribution of large volumes of milk on a diet that is not conspicuously lacking is to run a rather obvious risk of excess.

Fine emergency food

Milk can be processed in three main ways. First, its components can be separated in various permutations, and the water may then be squeezed out of each extraction. Second, each of the separated components may be salted, to preserve them and add flavor.

Third, the whole milk, or one component or permutation of components, may be fermented by bacteria or fungi or both; briefly, or over many months or years. Since milk is so complex and varies so much from species to species, breed to breed, place to place and season to season, and since the number of feasible processes is so great, the number of possible milk products could theoretically approach infinity and in practice runs into many hundreds. But those many hundreds of products can be grouped in remarkably few categories.

Infinite variety

Fat is lighter than water, and floats to the surface to form the thick emulsion known as cream; or, as is usual in commercial circles, the cream can be separated by applying artificial gravity in a centrifuge. If the cream is then stirred—churned—the fat globules combine, and instead of a matrix of water holding fat droplets, it becomes a matrix of fat holding water droplets. Squeeze out the water, or most of it, and you have butter, which is mostly fat but contains 15 percent water, a miniscule (0.4 percent) amount of protein, a little calcium and an impressive quota of vitamin A. What is left after extracting cream is skimmed milk, and what is left after making butter is buttermilk, which in effect are the same thing. Skimmed milk contains most of the protein in the original milk (all but a trace), and virtually all the lactose. American supermarkets sell it for drinking and low-fat yogurt and some cheeses are made from it.

The second main way to split milk into its components is to coagulate, solidify, or "curdle" the principal protein (casein). This is done in two ways: by applying acid—such as lemon juice; by introducing "lactic acid bacteria"; or by the enzyme rennin, found in the stomach wall of young milk-fed animals, and generally used in its extracted form,

Lemon juice, rennin and nomads' pouches

Variations on a theme of milk

rennet. No one knows how people first discovered the use of rennet: but nomads were often shepherds and were forever carrying things in pouches made of sheeps' stomachs, and perhaps found that such transport solidified their lunch beautifully.

The casein, once curdled, forms a three-dimensional latticework which holds the milk fats, and the whole coagulum is called curd. Squeeze out surplus moisture from this curd and you have a primitive cheese. Pickle the primordial cheese in saline, or with bacteria and/or fungi, and you have unequivocal cheese. The liquid remaining after the curd is removed from milk is the whey. It contains very little fat but it does contain the milk sugar (lactose) and some of the non-casein soluble proteins. These can in turn be coagulated to form whey cheese, of which perhaps the best known is the Norwegian Mysost.

There are plenty of ways to produce curd; many ways of extracting the whey afterward, from cutting and straining to hanging in wicker baskets or perforated jars; many kinds of organism, both bacteria and fungi, that are happy to ferment the finished curd, living either on the surface, as in Camembert, or sunk deep into the fabric as in the blue-veined cheeses; and many ways of modifying each kind of fermentation, through temperature, length of time of maturation, and so on. Each modification affects the flavor of the finished cheese. You cannot make every kind of cheese from every kind of milk, but each principal class of milk has given rise to its own prodigious catalog of cheeses.

Curds and whey

But it is possible, and worth while, to classify the world's otherwise bewildering list of cheeses into six main groups.

Group I are the soft cheeses, unripened and ripened. Low-fat varieties such as cottage cheese, and high-fat varieties including the cream cheeses, and the version of Neufchatel made in the United States, are among the unripened types. The ripened soft cheeses include Bel Paese, Brie, Camembert and the French version of Neufchatel (which one might be forgiven for thinking is the authentic one).

Group II are the semi-soft cheeses. Some of these are ripened principally by bacteria; these include Brick and Munster. Some are ripened both by bacteria and by surface bacteria and fungi; examples are Limburger and Port Salut. Some are ripened mainly by *Penicillium* molds injected deep into their fabric; they include Roquefort, Gorgonzola, Blue Stilton and Wensleydale.

Group III are the hard cheeses. Those ripened by bacteria, but without "eyes"—big trapped bubbles—include Cheddar, Cheshire and Cacciocavallo. Those ripened by bacteria but finishing up with intriguing cavities (the archetypal cartoonists' mouseholes) are the Swiss Emmenthal and Gruyère.

Group IV are the very hard cheeses; so hard they are used mainly for grating. Romano, Sapsago and Spalen are examples, but the most famous is the one coveted by the marooned Ben Gunn in *Treasure Island*, Parmesan.

Group V are the processed cheeses, usually made into passable products by adding citrates and phosphates and perhaps dried skim-milk powder to ripened hard or semi-hard cheese of poor quality.

Group VI are the whey cheeses: Primost and Mysost are examples.

Cheeses are highly variable nutritionally, but as a group they are potent. Cheddar is the most common type in the West and on the whole is fairly middle order. For example, it contains about 37 percent water. The range of water content runs from 23 percent in Parmesan and—surprisingly—in Stilton, up to nearly 80 percent in cottage cheese.

Potent cheeses

Cheddar, with 406 Calories per quarter pound, is pretty calorific: but the drier Parmesan (408) and Stilton (462) outstrip it, as does the fatty cream cheese (439). Cheddar is 26 percent protein: only Parmesan, with 35 percent, is significantly more proteinaceous, while the watery cottage cheese with 13.6 percent, and cream cheese with just over three percent protein, are significantly less so. But Cheddar is fatty: 33.5 percent, which is slightly more than most of the hard cheeses (Edam, for example, is less than one-quarter fat). Cream cheese is nearly 50 percent fat, but cottage cheese contains only four percent.

Cottage cheese emerges with the most favorable ratio of protein to fat, but it is watery and boring—which is a severe drawback in a Food of the Second Kind, the prime role of which is to add interest to staples. The one to be avoided is cream cheese, about which it is hard to find anything favorable to say; it even lacks flavor, unless it is shot through with chives. I would opt, as usual, for the strong-flavored cheeses. A little goes a long way, and it is hard to eat too much Stilton, for example, or the mature Cheddar, precisely because they are so pungent.

The world's range of fermented milks—either whole milk, or with some of the fat removed—is briefer than its catalog of cheeses, for two main reasons. First, the processing is less complex and there are fewer opportunities for variation, and second, fermented milks do not store as well as many cheeses so there has not been such incentive to develop new types. But the list is impressive nonetheless, with cow, goat, sheep, horse, buffalo, yak and reindeer well represented. A few examples are *lait caillé* of France, *dickmilch* of Germany, *prostkvasha* of the Soviet Union, yogurt of the Balkan countries and now of the West, *laban* of Egypt, *jub-jub* from the Lebanon, *kurut* from Afghanistan, *dahi* from India, and the alcoholic *kefir* and *koumiss* from the Soviet Union—the former made from ewe's milk and the latter from mare's milk.

Fermented milks

All these products—some staples and some delicacies, some liquids and some near solids—depend on the action of lactic acid bacteria: small round kinds, called *Streptococci*, or rod-shaped kinds known as *Lactobacilli*, or (as in yogurt) both. The lactic acid bacteria are like yeasts, in that their outstanding influence on human diet and history depends upon one rather simple and superficially unimpressive biochemical trick. They feed upon carbohydrate but they do not attack proteins or fats; so if they find their way into milk they break down the lactose, but leave the other components more or less intact.

The outstanding influence of lactic acids

Furthermore, the approach of lactic acid bacteria to lactose is profligate. If they were good, efficient, thrifty organisms they would break the lactose down to carbon dioxide and water (as a human being would do) and thus extract the last available calorie. But they do not. They merely effect a partial breakdown, comparable with the burning of wood to form charcoal, or of coal to form coke; in fact, they break down the lactose only as far as lactic acid.

Variations on a theme of milk

This restrained breakdown, however, has three advantages. First, although it is theoretically profligate it releases a great deal of energy vary rapidly. So once lactic acid bacteria are established, they grow extremely quickly.

Second, this partial breakdown rapidly uses up all available oxygen, which suits lactic acid bacteria very well because they are anaerobes, but discourages many other microbes that might otherwise compete.

Third, as lactic acid accumulates, the acidity of the milk obviously increases. Lactic acid bacteria thrive in acid conditions, but almost all other types perish.

So invasion by lactic acid bacteria has two characteristics. It is an all-or-nothing affair; if the lactic acid bacteria once become established, they quickly take over the whole culture, but if they do not, then a host of molds and other microbes will quickly change conditions irrevocably. So an established culture of lactic acid bacteria is a pure culture, for it will be too acid for other microbes. This has two implications: first, that a lactic acid bacteria fermentation is preservative, and makes excellent food, provided you like the flavor; second, that you can theoretically start a new culture just by using a sample from the previous one.

Yogurt is produced by *Streptococci* and *Lactobacilli* working in concert and to some extent in sequence. In practice the yogurt manufacturer infects milk with a fifty-fifty mixture of *Streptococci* and *Lactobacilli*; but the *Streptococci* tend to become established first, and as the acidity increases the *Lactobacilli* take over and may make the final yogurt too acid even for the *Streptococci*. It is easy to make yogurt at home, but it is difficult to produce a reliable product indefinitely because of the shift in the bacterial flora as the fermentation proceeds.

Milk into yogurt

In nature, where you find *Lactobacillus* you tend to find yeast. Fermentations that are predominantly based on yeast often take an acid turn because of *Lactobacillus*, which accounts for the sour-dough breads and sour beers that are not only common but usual among pre-technological people who have not yet learned to culture yeast in pure form. Conversely, predominantly *Lactobacillus* fermentation can take a yeasty turn. I have made some distinctly yeasty yogurts in my time (not at all unpleasant) and the fermentation of mare's milk to *Koumiss* and of ewe's milk to *kefir* involve yeast. Both have a modest alcohol content.

There is a widespread belief that yogurt is life's elixir. Some people living in the Urals are said to be at least 100 years old and are said to owe their longevity to yogurt. There are too many "saids" in this statement for intellectual comfort, but there can be little doubt that on nutritional and culinary grounds alone, low-fat yogurt is fine stuff. Low-fat yogurt in the United States (and it varies from country to country) contains six percent high-grade protein, with less than one percent fat and an impressive spectrum of minerals. I use yogurt in cooking all the time, with abandon, in recipes in which it is specified and as a substitute for sour cream. It is not the same as sour cream either in flavor or texture, but it is excellent in its own right and, if modern nutritional theory is even half correct, is far more desirable.

A hundred years old in the Urals

In short, there is plenty of room for dairy farming and its products in the twenty-first century. But restraint is the watchword, as always.

Low-fat yogurt can appear in almost any recipe: here it manifests in a whip, with sherry, raisins and nuts, **top left***; in a drink, with honey,* **top right***; and in watercress soup,* **bottom.**

Cheese in various roles: as a sauce for fish on a bed of spinach, **top***; as a sauce for leeks, in leek mornay,* **left***; in Greek cheese salad,* **center bottom***; and with yogurt and pears,* **right.**

The classic Welsh rarebit, melted cheese on toast, is infinitely variable. This version, **in the foreground,** *includes apple and walnut.* **Top,** *yogurt again, with fresh fruit.*

Like eggs, milk and its derivatives can appear in all kinds of cooking and in all contexts; in sweet and non-sweet dishes, as unobtrusive creators of texture or as principal agents of flavor. As with eggs, it is easy to overlook dairy products' nutritional potency. Milk has an almost unparalleled ability to turn a marginal diet into an adequate one, but also, particularly in the form of cream and butter, an unparalleled facility for converting nourishing and harmless meals into powerhouses of calories and saturated fat. Three-quarters of a stick of butter used to cook the meat before making a stew adds 500 Calories; one and a quarter cups of light cream used to enrich it adds another 400. I try to use butter minimally, as an excellent fat worthy of reverential and hence of sparing treatment, and avoid cream altogether. But I make much of low-fat yogurt, which contains less than 200 Calories per pint. Four principal themes emerge.

Theme I
Drinks, dips and cocktails

Low-fat yogurt is low on calories and, of course, on fat, and can reasonably be diluted both with milk and with honey.

YOGURT

To make your own yogurt the only ingredients you need are milk and a little yogurt. The milk is best if it is skimmed of all cream and any commercially made yogurt will do. The problem in a temperate climate is to provide a constant warm environment in which the yogurt will set in firm curds. The ideal temperature is between 90° and 100°F (32° and 38°C). An electric oven set at its lowest setting or the back of an old-fashioned cooking range is ideal. Or use a yogurt maker.

If you make yogurt regularly, remember to reserve a little yogurt to make the next batch. After two to three weeks the culture will become too acid and you will have to begin again with a fresh culture.

Makes 2 cups

2 cups milk
2 teaspoons yogurt

Bring the milk to boiling point and as it rises in the pan, lift the pan off the heat

and put it immediately in cold water.

While the milk is cooling, smear the yogurt on the inside of a bowl. When the milk has cooled—you should be able to put your finger in without discomfort—pour it onto the yogurt and stir well. Put the bowl in a warm place and leave undisturbed for at least 5 hours.

Serve cold.

YOGURT WITH SAFFRON

A pleasant sour-sweet concoction to serve after a spicy meal.
Serves 4

3½ cups yogurt
2 tablespoons honey
½ teaspoon saffron
2 tablespoons chopped pistachio nuts

Line a strainer with cheesecloth and put it over a bowl. Pour in the yogurt and leave it to drain for 3 hours or until no more whey drips out.

Turn the curds into a bowl. Dissolve the saffron in a tablespoon of hot water and beat it into the curd along with the honey. Serve chilled in very small bowls garnished with the pistachio nuts.

YOGURT AND HONEY DRINK
Serves 4

1 tablespoon honey
⅔ cup low-fat yogurt
Juice of 1 lemon
2½ cups milk

If the honey is hard, melt it gently in a saucepan. Then stir it in with the yogurt and lemon juice, add the milk, stir well and refrigerate.

YOGURT WHIP WITH SHERRY, RAISINS AND NUTS
Serves 4

⅓ cup raisins
3 tablespoons medium sherry or Madeira
1¼ cups low-fat yogurt
Juice of 1 lemon
1 tablespoon pistachio nuts
2 egg whites

Soak the raisins in the sherry or Madeira for an hour or two before using. Mix the yogurt, lemon juice, chopped nuts, raisins and sherry. Beat the egg whites until stiff, and fold in.

Divide the mixture between 4 dishes and keep cool in the refrigerator before serving; but serve within the hour.

FRESH FRUIT YOGURT

An even more dashing dessert. It has some of the texture of the traditional English strawberries and cream and the astringency of the French strawberries with lemon juice.
Serves 4

1 cup low-fat yogurt
Juice of 1 lemon
2 tablespoons brandy, kirsch, or fruit schnapps
2 egg whites
1 to 2 lb ($\frac{1}{2}$ to 1 kg) seasonal fruit: a mixture of raspberries and strawberries, or whatever is available

Mix the yogurt with the lemon juice and brandy, kirsch or schnapps. Beat the egg whites until stiff and fold them in. Spoon over the fruit and serve.

Theme II
Spreads, canapés and fancies

The strong flavor and high nutritional value of cheese and yogurt make them admirable abettors of such worthy but bland staples as bread, toast, oatcake, rye bread and potato.

CHEESE PÂTÉ

Serve the pâté with toast for lunch or as part of a buffet.
Serves 4

1 small onion
1 garlic clove
$1\frac{1}{2}$ cups grated crumbly medium-hard cheese
$\frac{1}{2}$ cup cottage cheese
1 tablespoon yogurt
1 teaspoon prepared mustard
1 teaspoon capers
2 small pickles
2 tablespoons chopped walnuts

Chop the onion and garlic very finely, and mix them in with the two kinds of

cheese, the yogurt and the mustard. Stir in the chopped capers, pickles and walnuts. Spoon into a pleasant dish.

Chill lightly before serving.

SMOKED MACKEREL AND COTTAGE CHEESE PÂTÉ

And here is a more elaborate version with smoked mackerel.
Serves 4

$\frac{1}{4}$ lb (120 g) smoked mackerel fillets
$\frac{1}{2}$ cup cottage cheese
2 tablespoons yogurt
Juice of 1 lemon
A pinch of salt
Black pepper
Paprika
1 tablespoon chopped chives

Pound all the ingredients except the chives together until the mixture is homogeneous, then stir in the chopped chives. Spoon into a serving dish.

WELSH RAREBIT
Serves 4

$2\frac{1}{2}$ cups grated old cheese (I used ancient Roquefort and Cheddar)
2 teaspoons oil
$\frac{1}{2}$ teaspoon nutmeg
$\frac{1}{2}$ teaspoon cayenne pepper
$\frac{1}{2}$ teaspoon paprika
1 teaspoon dry mustard
4 tablespoons dark beer
4 thick slices toast

Stir the grated cheese into the oil in a frying pan. Keep the heat low and sprinkle on the spices and add the beer. Stir as the cheese melts so that the whole forms a firm paste, with a kind of alcoholy-cheesy aroma reminiscent of fondue. Ladle the mixture onto hot toast, and then serve directly or brown briefly under the broiler.

WELSH RAREBIT WITH NUTS AND APPLE

Fruit and nuts are a superb foil for cheese and both are incorporated in this pleasant variant of Welsh rarebit.
Serves 4

$1\frac{1}{4}$ cups grated Cheddar cheese
1 medium-sized eating apple

1 tablespoon coarsely chopped walnuts
Worcestershire sauce
4 slices toast

Peel and grate the apple. Mix the cheese
and apple with the nuts and a dash of
Worcestershire sauce. Spread the
mixture on the toast and put under a
hot broiler. Keep your eye on it because
the apple tends to blacken before the
cheese is properly cooked. This can be
overcome by smoothing the surface now
and again with a knife.

CHEESE AND PEARS
Cheese and apple go well together; so do
cheese and pear.
Serves 6 to 8

3 large ripe pears
1 sweet red pepper
$\frac{1}{2}$ lb (240 g) crumbly cheese
Juice of 1 lemon
$1\frac{1}{4}$ cups low-fat yogurt

Peel the pears, remove their cores, and
cut them into thin strips. Halve the
pepper, discard the seeds and slice
thinly. Cut the cheese into cubes, as far
as is possible with a crumbly cheese.
Mix the lemon juice with the yogurt,
and pour over the cheese, peppers and
pears. Toss lightly to mix.

CHEESE FONDUE
The ultimate cheese dip, and one of the
finest variations on a theme of bread
and cheese, is the Swiss cheese fondue.
Recipes vary, but a mixture of cheeses
and dry white wine is mandatory, while
kirsch, the cherry liqueur, is usual.
  Theoretically, of course, virtually any
hard cheeses could be used for fondue,
and herbs, spices and alcohol, from
stout to aquavit, could be added at will.
But Swiss fondue has evolved from two
native cheeses, Gruyère and
Emmenthal, and Kirsch, one of the
many fruit liqueurs that the Swiss make
so well. Take away these native
connotations and the dish loses much
of its point.
Serves 6

$1\frac{1}{2}$ lb ($\frac{3}{4}$ kg) Gruyère cheese
$1\frac{1}{2}$ lb ($\frac{3}{4}$ kg) Emmenthal cheese
1 garlic clove

1 bottle dry white wine
Black pepper or nutmeg, optional
6 tablespoons kirsch
2 large French breads, cut into cubes

It is best to begin the fondue on the
stove and then transfer it to the fondue
burner, which is, of course, essential.
  Begin by grating all the cheese and
rubbing the fondue pan with the garlic
clove. Pour the wine into the pan, add
the cheese, and cook over moderate heat
until the cheese is melted. Then sprinkle
with black pepper or nutmeg—if you
think this is necessary—and stir in the
kirsch. Transfer to the fondue burner in
the middle of the table.
  The diners dip cubes of bread into the
cheese mixture, on long thin forks. A
fine way to spend an hour.

Theme III
Soups, casseroles and sauces

Milk and yogurt serve not only to enrich the
texture of soups but also to add that extra touch
of nutritional quality to a predominantly vegetable soup, as a garnishing of meat may do. Here,
first, is a basic "country" soup.

THICK LEEK AND MUSHROOM SOUP
Serves 4

1 onion
$\frac{1}{2}$ lb (240 g) potatoes
1 lb ($\frac{1}{2}$ kg) leeks
1 tablespoon oil
$2\frac{1}{2}$ cups milk
$\frac{1}{4}$ lb (120 g) mushrooms
$\frac{1}{2}$ teaspoon salt
1 teaspoon black pepper
1 tablespoon flour
Grated cheese

Chop the onion finely, dice the potatoes
and slice the leeks finely and fry gently
in the oil for 5 minutes. Then add $2\frac{1}{2}$
cups of water and half the milk. Tip in
the halved mushrooms and add the salt
and pepper. Bring to a boil, then
simmer gently for 25 minutes.
  Mix the flour to a thick paste with 1
tablespoon of the remaining milk. Add
more milk, then more and more until
all the remaining milk is used up, with

Variations on a theme of milk

the flour evenly dispersed. Add the mixture to the soup, bring back to a boil, and simmer until it thickens. Sprinkle with cheese and serve at once.

CUCUMBER SOUP WITH YOGURT
The fresh summery trio of yogurt, cucumber and milk will do grand things to a light chicken stock.
Serves 4

1 medium cucumber
1 small onion
5 cups chicken stock
Salt
3 tablespoons finely chopped mint
$\frac{2}{3}$ cup yogurt

Peel and chop the cucumber coarsely. Chop the onion finely. Simmer them in the stock until the onion is tender. Blend the soup until smooth and return to the heat. Add a pinch of salt and simmer for 5 minutes. Add the chopped mint, bring to a boil, and simmer for a further 3 minutes. Take the soup off the heat, stir in the yogurt and serve.

WATERCRESS SOUP WITH YOGURT
Serves 4

1 large onion
2 garlic cloves
4 tablespoons olive oil
$\frac{1}{2}$ lb (240 g) potatoes
Salt
Black pepper
$1\frac{1}{4}$ cups chicken stock or water
A large bunch of watercress
$2\frac{1}{2}$ cups milk
$\frac{2}{3}$ cup yogurt

Chop the onion and garlic finely and sauté gently in the oil until the onion is soft but not colored.
 Slice the potatoes finely and add them to the pan. Sauté for a minute or two until the potatoes are pleasantly oiled, then sprinkle with a little salt and black pepper. Add the stock or water, bring to a boil, lower the heat and simmer gently for 5 minutes or until the potatoes are beginning to soften.
 Reserve a few sprigs of watercress for garnish. Remove the leaves from the remaining sprigs and chop some of the stems. Add the leaves and chopped stems to the potatoes. Then add the milk, bring to a boil and simmer gently for 15 to 20 minutes.
 Take the pan off the heat and stir in the yogurt. Blend or purée the soup and return it to the pan. Heat again, but do not boil. Garnish the soup with the reserved watercress sprigs.
 Serve immediately.

THICK LIMA BEAN SOUP WITH YOGURT
This theme of pulse with dairy is repeated throughout world cooking. Here is a more robust autumn or winter version of pea soup. Chinese mushrooms provide the edge of flavor.
Serves 4

$1\frac{1}{2}$ lb ($\frac{3}{4}$ kg) fresh lima beans, or dried lima or butter beans
6 Chinese dried mushrooms *(shiitake)*
$2\frac{1}{2}$ cups water
$2\frac{1}{2}$ cups milk
Bouquet garni
$\frac{1}{2}$ teaspoon mace
$\frac{1}{2}$ teaspoon salt
Black pepper
$\frac{2}{3}$ cup yogurt

If the beans are dried, soak them overnight. Soak the mushrooms in hot water for 30 minutes; drain, discard the stems and chop the caps.
 Simmer the beans in enough of the water to cover, until tender. Puree them in a blender and return to the pan with the rest of the water, the milk, bouquet garni, all the seasonings and the mushrooms. Simmer gently for 15 minutes. Take the pan off the heat, remove the bouquet garni, stir in the yogurt, and gently heat up again without bringing to a boil.

MEXICAN BEANS WITH CHEESE
A Mexican version of the pulse-dairy theme, this time with cheese.
Serves 6 to 8

5 cups red kidney beans
4 large onions
4 garlic cloves
2 chili peppers
3 tablespoons oil
2 lb (1 kg) beefsteak tomatoes
1 teaspoon oregano

1 teaspoon salt
1 cup diced Cheddar, or similar cheese

Soak the beans overnight. Drain, cover with fresh water, simmer for 30 minutes and drain again.

Chop the onions and garlic, slice the chilies finely, and fry in the oil in a flameproof casserole until the onion is tender and transparent. Add the beans and continue to fry until they are heated through. Add the finely chopped tomatoes, the oregano and salt. Cover the pan and continue to cook over low heat until the tomatoes are mushy.

Cut the cheese into small pieces and stir it in. When the mixture simmers, cover the casserole and put it into a 300°F (160°C) oven for 3 hours.

THICK LENTIL SOUP
Serves 4

1 lb ($\frac{1}{2}$ kg) lentils
1 slice bacon
1 large onion
1 garlic clove
2 tablespoons oil
1 sweet red pepper
A large pinch of salt
$1\frac{1}{4}$ cups milk
1 tablespoon mild paprika
$\frac{1}{2}$ cup grated hard cheese

Small yellow lentils need no soaking, but bigger ones should be soaked for 1 hour before using.

Chop the bacon, onion and garlic finely and fry in the oil. After 5 minutes add the finely sliced pepper. Continue to fry for 1 to 2 minutes. Stir in the lentils and salt then pour in the milk and $2\frac{1}{2}$ cups of water, bring to a boil, and simmer until the lentils are soft (the small ones take only 10 minutes).

Sprinkle the paprika and cheese on top and cook for another minute.

BORTSCH
Bortsch is a classic soup in which cultured cream is used not as a thickening but as a topping. Low-fat yogurt must stand in for soured cream.
Serves 6

$1\frac{1}{2}$ lb ($\frac{3}{4}$ kg) beets
1 lb ($\frac{1}{2}$ kg) onions

$7\frac{1}{2}$ cups meat stock
$1\frac{1}{2}$ tablespoons sugar
2 tablespoons wine vinegar
3 cups shredded white cabbage
1 teaspoon salt
1 teaspoon black pepper
$1\frac{1}{4}$ cups yogurt

Peel the beets and onions, and slice them thinly. Put them in a large saucepan and simmer in the stock with the sugar and vinegar for about 30 minutes. Add the cabbage to the pan. Simmer for another 10 minutes. Add the salt and pepper, and simmer for a further 20 minutes.

Serve in hot bowls and put a large swirl of yogurt in the middle of each.

FISH WITH SPINACH AND CHEESE SAUCE
Milk and cheese enhance many a fish dish. The following recipe is suitable for heavy fish, swordfish, for example. Serve with plenty of potatoes, boiled in their skins, sliced and well peppered.
Serves 4

$1\frac{1}{2}$ lb ($\frac{3}{4}$ kg) spinach
4 fish fillets or boned steaks, about $\frac{1}{4}$ lb (120 g) each: use swordfish, halibut or pike
2 cups milk
1 bay leaf
6 peppercorns
1 tablespoon flour
$\frac{1}{2}$ teaspoon salt
A large pinch of mace
$\frac{1}{2}$ cup grated cheese
2 hard-boiled eggs

Chop the spinach and cook it in a dry saucepan until mushy.

Simmer the fish in the milk with the bay leaf and peppercorns for about 15 minutes: the idea is to cook the fish and to flavor the milk at the same time. If this is done in an open pan on top of the stove, the milk will reduce slightly, which is all to the good as you will need about $1\frac{1}{4}$ cups for the sauce. Remove the fish from the pan and set aside.

Add a tablespoon of the fishy milk to the flour in a bowl to make a thick paste, then add a little more of the milk until the mixture is liquid. Stir in the salt, mace and half the grated cheese. Add this mixture to the rest of the

Variations on a theme of milk

milky stock in the pan and cook,
stirring, until the sauce thickens.

Put the spinach into a shallow flameproof dish; lay the fish pieces on top,
interspersed with slices of hard-boiled
egg. Cover with the sauce, sprinkle with
the remaining cheese and brown under
the broiler or in a hot oven.

FISH AND MUSHROOM PIE
Serves 4

2 lb (1 kg) potatoes
2½ cups milk
A pinch of salt
Pepper
¾ lb (360 g) smoked haddock fillets
¾ lb (360 g) mushrooms
Butter
1½ tablespoons flour

Boil the potatoes, and mash them with a
little milk, salt and plenty of pepper.

Poach the fish in the rest of the milk
for 10 minutes. Drain and flake the fish,
discarding any skin and bones. Reserve
the milk. Put the flaked fish into an
ovenproof dish.

Slice the mushrooms if large, or keep
whole if small, and fry them in a small
amount of butter for a few seconds. Add
the mushrooms to the fish and season.

Mix the flour with a little of the
reserved milk to make a paste.
Gradually mix in the rest of the milk.
Return the sauce to the pan and
simmer, stirring, until thick. Season and
pour over the fish and mushrooms.
Cover with a thick crust of mashed
potato and bake in a 350°F (180°C) oven
for 30 minutes or until nicely browned.

FISH BAKED IN YOGURT
Fish bakes pleasantly in yogurt, too.
Serve with potatoes and lima beans.
Serves 4

1 cup yogurt
1 lb (½ kg) white fish, in 4 fillets
Juice of 1 lemon
1 tablespoon dry white wine
½ teaspoon salt
¼ teaspoon cayenne pepper
Chopped chives

Two hours before you begin cooking, put
the yogurt in a cheesecloth-lined sieve to
allow the whey to drain off.

Put the fish fillets in an ovenproof dish.
Mix the yogurt, lemon juice, wine, salt
and pepper. Pour over the fish and bake
at 350°F (180°C) for 25 to 30 minutes.
Garnish with the chives and serve.

Cheese sauce poured over fish is extravagant by
twenty-first-century standards, nutritionally
and economically. A fine strong-flavored vegetable is more to the point. Cauliflower is an
obvious candidate but leek is more subtle.

LEEK MORNAY
Serves 2 to 4

**4 large leeks (about 1½ inches/3.5 cm
  thick)**
Bouquet garni
2½ cups milk
¼ teaspoon salt
2 tablespoons flour
½ cup finely grated cheese
Paprika

Wash and trim the leeks. Lay them side
by side in a pan just big enough to hold
them in a single layer. Shred finely any
of the green part that you need to cut
off to fit them in, and put it alongside
the leeks. Put in the bouquet garni,
cover with the milk, add the salt and
bring to a boil. Simmer until tender.

Lift the leeks out carefully and put
them into a hot dish. Throw out the
bouquet garni. Mix a little of the
cooking liquor with the flour in a bowl,
then add a little more and a little more
until the mixture is quite liquid. Stir the
flour mixture into the rest of the stock
with the grated cheese, and cook and
stir until the sauce thickens and the
cheese melts. Pour the sauce over the
leeks and sprinkle on a little paprika.

YOGURT POTATOES
Serves 2 to 4

2 lb (1 kg) potatoes
A large handful of parsley
1 cup grated cheese
A pinch of salt
Black pepper
1¼ cups yogurt

Slice the potatoes very thinly. Chop the
parsley finely and mix it with three-

quarters of the cheese, the salt, plenty of pepper and the yogurt. Layer the potato slices in a casserole or soufflé dish. Spread some of the yogurt mixture on each layer. Sprinkle the remaining cheese on the top. Cover the dish and bake in a 400°F (200°C) oven for 30 minutes. Remove the cover and bake for a further 30 minutes or until the potatoes are cooked and brown on top.

NOODLES BAKED WITH CHEESE
Serves 4

4 tablespoons corn oil
½ lb (240 g) button mushrooms
3 tablespoons flour
2½ cups milk
1 cup grated cheese
A pinch of salt
Pepper
1 lb (½ kg) noodles

Heat the oil and fry the mushrooms for 2 minutes. Stir in the flour and cook, stirring, for a few seconds. Add the milk gradually, stirring vigorously to avoid lumps. Bring the sauce to a boil and simmer until thick. Stir in three-quarters of the cheese, the salt and plenty of pepper. When the cheese has melted and the sauce is smooth, remove the pan from the heat.

Boil the noodles and drain them. Mix them into the sauce. Tip the mixture into a greased baking dish, sprinkle the remaining cheese on top and bake at 400°F (200°C) for 25 minutes or until heated through and golden brown.

Theme IV
Cheese as meat

Cheese has all the flavor and nutritional quality, and some of the texture, that is needed in a substitute for meat. Endless variations on a theme of cheese pie and tart are possible, but the following, a kind of vegetarian Scotch egg, is simple and ingenious.

VEGETARIAN SCOTCH EGGS
Serves 6

1½ lb (¾ kg) potatoes
Milk

1 teaspoon mixed herbs
½ teaspoon salt
½ teaspoon black pepper
1½ cups finely grated cheese
6 eggs
½ cup oatmeal
Oil for deep frying

Boil the potatoes and mash with a dash of milk, mixing in the herbs, salt, pepper and the cheese as you go. Hard boil the eggs.

Coat the eggs in the potato mixture, coat the surface with oatmeal, and deep fry until golden and beginning to brown.

GREEK CHEESE SALAD
Serves 6

½ lb (240 g) Feta cheese
1 cucumber
1½ lb (¾ kg) tomatoes
12 black olives
1 tablespoon wine vinegar
4 tablespoons olive oil
A pinch of oregano or mint
A sprinkling of black pepper

Dice the Feta and cucumber, peel and chop the tomatoes, pit the olives and put them all in a bowl. Make the dressing with the vinegar, oil, pepper and oregano or mint, and pour it over the cheese and vegetables.

Toss well and serve.

Cumin, cockles and chrysanthemums

Food of the Third Kind should be eaten precisely because it is unnecessary; for when nutrition has been taken care of, gastronomy comes into its own.

There are three justifications for eating foods in this category. First, they, more than any other ingredients, give each dish its character. The finest meat, fish or vegetable may need no embellishment, but much worthy and doubtless necessary food can be seen, gastronomically, merely as a vehicle for pungent leaves or aromatic seeds. You can switch the idiom and mood of a dish, from Indian to Mexican, from English to Greek or from winter to summer, just by manipulating a few spices; although I am most intrigued by the hybrids—the dishes which incorporate both the rich sweet spicing of medieval England and of India, the fusion of Spanish technique and Aztec ingredients that gave rise to Mexican cooking, and the marvelous hodgepodge of Indian, Chinese, Dutch and French cooking that you find in much of South-East Asia. I hope twenty-first-century cooks preserve their sense of time and place, for the associations of classic dishes are part of their charm; but I hope too that everyday cooking will be eclectic, with *dosa* and *falafel* and fresh English fruit turning up in the same lunch.

Eclectic cooking

Second, these merely indulgent third-kind foods provide a point of contact between human beings and their environment; contact that is so easy to lose. All but a few of the most recalcitrantly tropical spices, such as ginger and turmeric, will grow in the most temperate garden and anyone with even a modest patch has room for at least 100 different culinary plants, each offering a different gastronomic experience. In addition, many herbs and spices of the garden also grow wild in Europe and North America, as horseradish does, or else have wild relatives that perhaps have something different to offer—as marjoram has oregano.

Widespread interest in wild foods could of course be disastrous. If everyone started picking berries or scooping up cockles whenever they went for a walk, we might in the end revert to the excesses of nineteenth-century natural history, when gentlemanly and maidenly interest in the surroundings reduced entire natural populations to museum curios.

Again, it would be a bad thing if people planted trees, shrubs or herbs without regard for the local ecology; but the boundaries between wilderness and park and park and farm not only will but probably should become more blurred. It might be a sin to fill Britain's woodlands with fancy rhododendrons, as is happening here and there, but why not encourage the native hazel, partly for its value to local wildlife but also, as a bonus, for the odd nut?

Rhododendrons a sin, hazels a bonus

Finally, interest in the arcane reaches of gastronomy can be a lifetime's adventure, which is another name for cultural experience. The adventure is of course gastronomic, for the familiar foods even of the delicatessens contain only a fraction of life's flavors: as Richard Mabey says in his admirable *Food for Free* (1972), speaking only of northern Europe: "there is a whole galaxy of powerful and surprising flavors preserved intact in the wild stock, that are quite untapped in

Almost everything that grows can theoretically be eaten, and sometimes improves with pickling. **Back row, left to right,** *fruit vinegar and pickled pears.* **Front row,** *herb vinegar and sweet and sour rose petals.*

Twenty-first-century cookery will again blur the margins of sweet and non-sweet. Here are cherry soup, **top,** *pear soup,* **right,** *and,* **in the foreground,** *sloe jelly.*

cultivated foods: tart and smoky berries, strangely aromatic fungi, crisp and succulent shoreline plants." It would be a pity not to see the Taj Mahal before you die, and it would be a pity not to taste *shiitake* mushrooms or sea lettuce; but you can buy *shiitake* at a Chinese supermarket, and find sea lettuce on the beach.

The adventure is intellectual, too, for the modest cultivation of a row of herbs can develop into an obsession with all that grows. Every wayside weed has a hundred million years of botany behind it and has probably been intricately involved, for good or evil, with the human history of food, magic and medicine. Then again, the search for new foods can be a physical adventure, whether you go to dubious country shacks in search of bootleg liquor or to sea cliffs for the nests of swifts.

Obsession with all that grows

A brief look at trees will make the point. Trees, more than any living thing, are the makers of landscape. They determine what it looks like; they largely determine the nature of the soil or whether there is soil at all; they determine the climate on the small scale and influence it on the grand scale, and so they determine what else will grow. A country with a hundred million trees has a great deal to its credit.

A tree is not an inanimate object, it is an ecosystem. It usually brings pleasure to the eye, but whether it does good or evil or nothing at all for the indigenous flora and fauna depends on what kind of tree it is and whether it is put in the right place. Few countries have enough trees, but many are frenetically planting thousands upon thousands of them that are of little use to man or beast; and I refer now not to the softwood timber trees that are sown as a cash crop, but to trees that people plant specifically for the good of humanity and their fellow creatures.

For instance, the oak, or at least *Quercus robur*, is native to Britain and supports more than 100 kinds of invertebrate, which in turn support birds. Plant an oak, and you have planted a wildlife sanctuary. On the other hand, the sycamore is extremely common in Britain and can be a fine tree, but it is an exotic. Most British insects do not get on with it and, in comparison to the oak, the average sycamore is an arboreal wilderness. The world is full of beautiful trees that will grow as well in Europe or North America as in their native Asia or Africa; but if, as is often the case, they are planted just because they are exotic and different then good looks is all they may contribute. It seems a pity to get only one advantage from a tree when you could get half a dozen.

Generous oak and barren sycamore

I would like to see trees planted in large numbers wherever there is a space for them; but usually with a motive that goes beyond mere appearance. The linden or lime, *Tilia*, is marvelous to look at and provides excellent timber, and both in America and Europe it supports wildlife. Its young leaves are an excellent, peppery-sharp salad herb, that can be put in sandwiches alone or with cheese and egg or chopped up in pancakes and *dosa*. Its flowers make marvelous tea when dried and they are there for the taking by the fistful in June and July. Why not plant a linden, then, not for yourself but for the next century?

Or why not plant a beech, which gives fine furniture timber, creates its own ecosystem and provides sweet salad leaves? Every few years it also produces vast amounts of seed—beech mast—which is good to eat roasted if you can spare the time, and can yield prodigious quantities of

Versatile beech

Cumin, cockles and chrysanthemums

oil from which a vegetarian butter is made. Beech does of course illustrate the leading disadvantage of trees, which is their time scale; for plant breeders could undoubtedly turn beech mast into a highly desirable crop, just as they once produced apples from crab apples and potatoes from gnomish little mountain tubers. But you would need Faustian powers to embark on a beech improvement program.

Oak is not just for the birds, for its acorns are edible even if they are not particularly nice. But the walnut, *Juglans*, the pecan, *Carya*, and the sweet chestnut, *Castanea*, all deserve to be planted more widely in all the temperate countries. Here we have some conflict, for the North American pecan would obviously be exotic in Britain and perhaps would not favor wildlife—yet that could be an advantage in a tree grown partly for food. The point is not to be purist, but merely to ensure that plants as big and significant as trees should do more than occupy space. With walnuts and pecans we are within the purlieus of Food of the Second Kind, for every quarter pound of walnuts provides 525 Calories, 10.6 grams of protein and more than 50 grams of fat; and although ripe walnuts contain barely a trace of vitamin C, green (and subsequently pickled) walnuts contain up to three percent of the vitamin and so are one of nature's richest sources. Although some populations have sometimes relied heavily on nuts for food, there just are not enough walnut trees around for their seeds to be more than a delicacy. There could be, however, if we start planting now. The chestnut is nutritionally disappointing—a mere two percent protein and two percent fat—but the flavor is half of European autumn; magnificent with brussels sprouts, Goethe thought.

Make way for walnuts

Less physically impressive but definitely to be taken seriously are *Corylus*, *Sambucus*, *Crataegus* and *Sorbus*. *Corylus avellana* is the hazelnut or cob, often truncated in the hedgerows but capable of growing 20 feet tall, and a fine sight in late winter with its bright yellow catkins; *Corylus maxima* is the filbert, which is even bigger and produces nuts (seven percent protein and 36 percent fat) that go well with pancakes, in yogurt, in mueslis, or indeed with almost anything.

Sambucus is the elder. Its flowers make one of the best of all the flower wines and a classic preserve with gooseberries, and may also be used to make oddly English fritters. Its purple-black berries lend an edge to apple pie and feature in ancient English sauces.

Crataegus can serve, albeit modestly, to usher in the Rosaceae, which are to fruit what the Cruciferae are to green vegetables. If you want to classify something large and juicy, guess Rosaceae and more than half the time you will be right. *Crataegus* includes the hawthorn, *C. monogyna*, whose leaves are worth trying both as a salad and as a sharp spinach, and whose haws at least are worth a nibble. The grander *Crataegus azarolus* provides the yellow azaroles, bigger and generally more worthwhile than haws, prized in France (of course) and used there and elsewhere in southern Europe to make liqueurs. The English grow azaroles but only to look at. There, in their different approach to this humble fruit, is the symbol of those two countries' mutual disdain.

The rose's succulent relatives

Sorbus includes *S. aucuporia*, the rowan, or mountain ash, which even in insouciant Britain is used for jellies to serve with game.

First of the major fruit trees among the Rosaceae is *Malus*, the apple. Mother of them all is *Malus pumila*, the crab apple, which grows wild in Europe, Asia and North America, and is worth encouraging for the jelly that can be made from its fruits. But even more worth while—although in the garden rather than the wild, for they are a little too hospitable to local fauna—are the many hundreds of cultivated derivatives that people have developed these 3,000 years past. The modern growers produce fruit of uniform size and color, middle-of-the-road flavor (but sometimes with no flavor at all), and with tough skins for traveling. But there are apples with a whiff of pineapple, or of orange, or of banana, or of nothing except themselves, marvelously aromatic but often delicate. Only private gardeners can afford to keep these fragile and erratic varieties in existence—unless we all become connoisseurs and are prepared to buy fruit as fastidiously as some people buy wine.

The world cannot have too many apples. They are incomparable raw, produce some of the finest liquor and can be used in cooking almost as freely as onions.

Pyrus, the pear, is the apple's more southerly relative; it has the same peculiar fruit, a "pome," formed from the swollen receptacle of the flower. In theory, pears can do all that apples can do, but their flavor is more elusive and their texture more uncertain.

Pyrus and Prunus . . .

Prunus includes the cherries, an astonishing variety of plums, sloe and bullaces (wild plums); the damsons and gages; the apricots, peaches and nectarines; and, just for luck, the almond.

Just to complete the list of edible Rosacean trees, we should mention the once-favored quince, *Cydonia*, and the hardier medlar, *Mespilus*.

. . . quince and medlar

All the trees cataloged above can be grown specifically for food and most have been; but they will yield something even if planted simply in the spirit of landscape gardening. And since most landscapes and townscapes benefit from the odd evergreen, we might make more of *Laurus nobilis*, which grows to 60 feet and produces the marvelously aromatic leaves known as bay; or of a little cypress tree called *Juniperus communis*, whose berries provide the flavor in gin, and feature in many a medieval soup; and a whole group of pines, mostly from Mediterranean or warmer climates, but capable of growing at least as far north as Britain, which have seeds that can be eaten with almost any sweet or non-sweet dish. The seeds of *Pinus pinea*, the stone-pine, are the highly flavored pine nuts or pignoli of Italy; the Mexicans have their nut pine, *Pinus cembroides*; and other types are gathered in Switzerland, Russia and the Himalayas. People stick little evergreens in their gardens, just to hide the shed. Why not plant one you can eat?

Pine trees for supper

Trees take so long to grow, of course. "He who plants pears, plants for his heirs" is an old saw. But then if our ancestors had not been so generous we would not have our few remaining specimen forest trees; and if they had not been so careless we would have a lot more.

The National Academy of Sciences, Washington DC, are now encouraging research on some extraordinary and underexploited tropical fruits that may be grown in Third World countries to supplement the local diet, or as export crops for cash. These include the naranjilla, *Solanum quitoense*, a marvelously juicy dessert fruit from

Cumin, cockles and chrysanthemums

Peru, Colombia, Ecuador and Guatemala—another relative of the potato and tomato. Pejibaye, *Guilielma gasipaes*, is one of several palms that remain remarkably underexploited; its chestnutlike fruits have a balanced quota of carbohydrate, protein, oil, minerals and vitamins.

For immediate returns go for herbaceous plants and shrubs, and the hundreds of flavors they have to offer, from their roots, tubers, stems, stalks, leaves, flowers, seeds, and—in the case of saffron—their stigmas.

The buttercup family, Ranunculaceae, is considered primitive, for its floral parts are simple and all too emphatically separate. The buttercup itself is poisonous. But the peony, *Paeonia*, is also Ranunculaceae and its flowers make a fine wine, or can be stewed with onions or made into syrup. Cooking with flowers has gone out of fashion, but the Romans made much of them and so did the Tudor English; and so, still, do the Japanese. Flowers for eating should usually be grown in the garden, for all but a few of the commonest wild flowers would be too easily ravaged if everyone went after them, and florists' flowers are liable to be heavy with insecticide. A flower garden that you can eat is a wonderful thing.

So is a water garden that you can eat; and *Nymphaea alba*, of the Nymphaeaceae, the white water lily, has edible rhizomes in its pond bed. The lotus, *Nelumbo nucifera* of the Nelumbonaceae, has seeds and rhizomes that are highly esteemed in China. The water chestnut, *Trapa natans*, however, is related to the willow herb (Onagraceae), while the Chinese water chestnut, *Eleocharis*, is a sedge.

Cruciferae dominated the chapter on greens and inevitably turn up among the herbs. If you ever establish *Armoracia rusticana* in your garden you may regret it, for its roots are ineradicable; but since, when grated, they are horseradish, you may think this is no bad thing. The mustards are *Brassica*: black, *nigra*, and white, *alba*, rightly esteemed both for their seeds and leaves. But do not ignore the humble Jack-by-the-Hedge, *Alliaria petiolata*, for its hot garlicky leaves are excellent and may be picked from such a common weed with a clear conscience.

Jack-by-the-Hedge and sweet violet

Viola, of the Violaceae, belongs in the garden; violets may be common enough locally but in general are far too rare to be picked from the wild. *Viola odorata*, sweet violet, is the outstanding type, without which no Roman garden was complete. It goes, as flowers inevitably do, into soups, salads and summer drinks.

And what garden could not accommodate cowslip, *Primula officinalis*, of the primrose-primula family, Primulaceae? It is said to have a delicate aniseed flavor, and is used in pancakes and pickles as well as in salads.

Two common members of the Caryophyllaceae illustrate the gardener's cavalier disregard for the niceties of family. He would cultivate *Dianthus*, the pinks and carnations, but root out *Stellaria media*, the chickweed. The former are fine culinary flowers, in pickles, pancakes and jam; the latter is in the category of herbs that border on the substantial, like sorrel, and are cooked like spinach. Perhaps the best way to get rid of weeds is to acquire a taste for them.

Carnations, chickweed and mallows

Malvaceae, the mallows, have much to offer. The glutinous leaves of some varieties feature in an Egyptian soup, *melokhia*, and the flowers of that most spectacular mallow, the hollyhock, without which no Englysshe cottage garden is compleat, are fine in salads.

The Leguminosae family, which gives us the pulses, is also the source of intriguing flavors. *Glycyrrhiza glabra* is a perennial leguminous herb whose roots, pulped and boiled, yield licorice. It is associated with southern Europe and the warm parts of Russia and was once grown widely even in England, and especially in Yorkshire, where it gave rise to the Pontefract cake. There is a hint of licorice too in the leaves and seeds of *Trigonella foenum-graecum*, alias fenugreek. This plant is at home in Mediterranean countries (and the Israelis are stepping up cultivation), but there are temperate equivalents including the European *Trigonella ornithopodioides*. Those ubiquitous legumes the clovers, *Trifolium*, should not be left to the cattle. Their flowers make pickle and wine and do interesting things to sandwiches.

Pontefract cake, fenugreek and clovers . . .

Then of course there is the Rosaceae family, again. The type genus, *Rosa*, includes the wild dog-rose, *Rosa canina*, ancestor of many domestic roses; its hips make syrup that is an outstanding source of vitamin C, and its flowers have flavored dishes as diverse as apple pie and omelet. The Romans doted upon the rose, for its scent and its appearance, but perhaps most of all for its culinary possibilities. The strawberries are Rosaceae, of the genus *Fragaria*; and their soft leaves are edible as well as their fruits. *Poterium sanguisorba*, the salad burnet, is a miniature rose relative whose leaves, its only culinary asset, may be used as garnish. Then there is the extraordinary genus that vies with *Prunus* in variety, namely *Rubus*, which includes raspberries, blackberries, dewberries and the little yellow cloudberries favored in Scandinavia—and all their hybrids, such as loganberries, boysenberries and youngberries. The fruit of the raspberry plant is of course incomparable; but do not overlook its leaves, which make one of the most convincing of the non-camellian teas. Barberry, too, is a rose, *Berberis vulgaris*; its sharp berries are fine with fatty meat.

. . . and back to roses

Not to be confused with *Rubus* are the *Ribes*, the currants of the Grossulariaceae. *R. rubrum* and *sativum* pass muster as red currants, and white currants are merely a colorless and somewhat less acid variant. *R. nigrum* is the black currant. *R. grossularia*, just in the interests of confusion, is the gooseberry. All these fruits make excellent jams, jellies and sauces; traditionally, red-currant jelly is served with meat, and gooseberry jelly or sauce goes well with fish.

Then there is the Umbelliferae family, whose contribution of carrots, parsnips, parsley, celery and Florence fennel has already been noted, and which provides the herbs and spices used in almost all the great cuisines. Many grow wild in temperate countries, although care is necessary because the Umbelliferae often have deeply notched or feathery leaves that are easily confused, and they include such poisonous plants as hemlock. But many "weeds" are worth gathering. Cowparsley, *Anthriscus sylvestris*, is said to be good in salads and for flavoring bland dishes, and the despised ground elder, *Aegopodium podagraria*, which has ruined many an English garden, was obligingly brought to Britain by the Romans as a sharp form of spinach. Perhaps, as with chickweed, the best way to get rid of it is to eat it.

Other umbelliferous plants grown for their leaves, leaf stalks or stems include the towering herb angelica, *Angelica*, whose stems make a

Cumin, cockles and chrysanthemums

famous decorative candy; coriander, *Coriandrum*, whose chopped leaves, commonly known as Chinese parsley, give a sharp edge to Greek, Middle Eastern and Indian cooking but which can be grown perfectly well in temperate climates; chervil, *Anthriscus cerefolium*, a diminutive relative of cowparsley with its delicate hint of aniseed; lovage (*Levisticum*), used both as a vegetable and as a herbal tea; and sweet cicely (*Myrrhis*), offering a hint of aniseed.

The seeds of umbelliferous plants have perhaps contributed even more to world cuisine. The seeds of coriander and cumin, *Cuminum*, are almost definitive of India, along with turmeric of the ginger family. The seeds of celery and fennel have found their way all around the world. Dill, *Anethum*—both seeds and leaves—help turn cucumbers into one of the world's great pickles. Caraway, *Carum*, is the aroma of English and European tea shops, and aniseed, *Pimpinella*, lends its definitive flavor to concoctions as diverse as French liqueurs and Chinese boiled tripe.

If you don't like Indian umbellifers . . .

The daisy family, Compositae, has already appeared in this book; with the sunflower, Jerusalem artichoke, lettuce, globe artichoke, dandelion and salsify. But the composites, like the Solanaceae, are full of surprises. The small white petals of *Bellis perennis*, the "daisy" of the suburban lawn, make a pleasant wine and may lend interest to salad. The orange petals of marigold, *Calendula*, have been used as a cheap substitute for saffron, and also became one of the outstanding culinary treats of eighteenth-century England and could appear in every course—in soups, in soufflés, in entrées and in desserts. The coltsfoot, *Tussilago farfara*, is a fine plant in a garden, with culinary and medicinal associations going back at least to the Romans. Its leaves can be eaten like spinach and its flowers aromatize wine or *dosas*. The Japanese in particular make much of the petals of the chrysanthemum, *Chrysanthemum indicum*, in soups and salads; and the leaves of the humbler *Tanacetum vulgare*, alias tansy, were piled with abandon into medieval English dishes of all kinds. The artemisias include tarragon, *Artemisia dracunculus*, beloved of Greek cooks and often used to flavor vinegar; and also the intriguing wormwood, *Artemisia absinthium*, which flavors absinthe and in excess is hallucinogenic; and southernwood, cudweed and the mugworts, which between them have a long, sometimes honorable and sometimes distinctly shady history in magic and medicine. The plants known as camomile, favored in teas for their aroma or their medicinal effects, come from several composite genera; but the one featured in the works of Beatrix Potter is *Chamaemelum nobile*, alias *Anthemis nobilis*, the sweet or English camomile.

. . . or edible daisies . . .

The Labiatae, now there's a subject, as Sam Weller said about pork. If you want a subject, take the Labiatae. Their name implies lips, which their flowers have; and their stems tend to be square in cross section.

. . . take the Labiatae

The dead nettles, *Lamium*, are labiates, and may be cooked like spinach. Far more interesting is that other lover of cool moist places, *Mentha*, the mint. There are many kinds, some tasting of apple, some of eau-de-cologne, some striped in pink or yellow or white. The one chopped in vinegar for English mint sauce and widely used with lemon in all kinds of contexts in the Middle East is spearmint, *Mentha spicata*.

198

Mentha aquatica, the water mint, features in old English cookery but has risen to fame mainly through its marriage with *M. spicata*: their hybrid offspring is *M. piperita*, the peppermint, whose oil turns up in toothpaste, cordials, medicines and candy.

Basil, a prince among herbs, is a labiate. *Ocimum basilicum* is sweet basil and *O. minimum* is the diminutive bush basil. They often feature with tomatoes, but go well with many other vegetables.

The savories, too, are labiates: *Satureja hortensis*, from the Mediterranean, is the summer savory and was one of the Romans' favorite herbs, used in meat stuffings and in vinegar. Winter savory, with similar uses, is *Satureja montana*, also from southern Europe.

The thyme group are labiates. *Thymus vulgaris* is the one everyone knows. *T. herba-barona* has a hint of caraway, and lemon thyme, *T. citriodorus*, with its variegated variety *variegatus*, is reminiscent of lemons. Other thymes, with small, profuse flowers and soft leaves, are excellent for rockeries. There is a strong hint of lemon in many of the labiates: notably in balm, *Melissa officinalis*.

Marjoram, in all its varieties, is a labiate; including sweet marjoram and *Origanum vulgare*, the oregano. Rosemary, *Rosmarinus officinalis*, is a labiate: a fine shrub that can grow more than six feet high, widely used in perfumery, and excellent with poultry and lamb. Sage, *Salvia officinalis*, is a labiate; and in England is *the* herb to flavor poultry.

The lavenders, *Lavendula*, are labiates. Their flowers are made into jelly with mint and are used to flavor honey; and, as seems the inevitable fate of the entire family, are used to aromatize vinegar.

I like the botanical approach to food plants because of its innate tidiness; but it is full of pleasant surprises, too. The genus *Vaccinium* includes *V. myrtillus*, the blueberry, *V. oxycoccos*, the cranberry, and *V. vitis-idaea*, the huckleberry, which can be made into tarts and sauces for strong meats. They are of the heather family, Ericaceae. The flowers of heather itself, *Calluna*, are used to make tea. *Arbutus*, the strawberry tree, is also Ericaceae, although its oddly exotic fruits are disappointing.

Hundreds of kinds of animals can be eaten too, but gratuitous pillaging of our fellow creatures is even less justified than it is with plants. When the world's food crisis was at its height in the early 1970s there was much heady talk of eating snakes and worms; but in this, as in most food matters, common sense should prevail.

Shellfish can be worth the gathering, however, if they are not gathered to extinction. The lowlier kinds have nothing much to offer. Some people eat limpets, but they can be as tough as boots. Winkles are nature's gift to all who would waste time pleasantly, a kind of Zen mollusk. Oysters were once a protein standby, and mussels may be again: India is among the countries interested in their cultivation, probably on rafts out at sea, as a significant protein source rather than as a delicacy. Some shellfish, notably the scallop and the Japanese *awabi*, are among nature's supreme delights. Boiled or baked, they can be superb. Perhaps, above all, they should be used as in the old days in England, as spices and as supplements to meat: cockles with lamb, and oysters in all manner of meat pies. It will take only a lifetime to work out all the possibilities.

Cumin, cockles and chrysanthemums

The whole point of Food of the Third Kind is that anything goes. Attempts to discern themes would be fatuous, and I make none. Here instead is a small selection of exotica.

SWEET APPLE SAUCE

This sauce is for cold pork. Store it in jars, and apply it thickly to a piece of baking pork belly ten minutes before it has finished cooking. When the meat is cold, slice it thinly for sandwiches.
Makes about 5 lb (2½ kg)

4 lb (2 kg) windfall apples
2 cloves
2 lb (1 kg) sugar

Peel and core the apples, chop them up, and simmer in 5 cups of water with the cloves until they are disintegrated. Mash to make a puree; there is no need to bother with the blender. Add the sugar, stir well, and simmer for about 1 hour or until you have a thick, smooth, golden fluid. Seal in sterilized jars.

PICKLED PEARS

Any hard pears will do for pickling.

5 cups cider vinegar
¼ cup pickling spices: whole cloves, bruised ginger root, cinnamon sticks, allspice berries
2 teaspoons salt
2 lb (1 kg) sugar
4 lb (2 kg) hard pears

Begin by spicing the vinegar: tie the pickling spices in a piece of cheesecloth or in a muslin bag and add to the vinegar. Add the salt. Bring to a boil and simmer for 5 minutes.

Remove from the heat, and scoop out the bag of spices. Add the sugar to the vinegar and stir to dissolve.

Peel, halve and core the pears—or leave whole if they are small. Add them to the sugared spiced vinegar and simmer in a covered pan until they are tender. Then lift them out gently and pack them in sterilized jars.

Finally, bring the vinegar mixture to a boil and let it boil rapidly down until it forms a thin syrup. Pour this over the pears and seal, preferably with a vacuum-sealed lid. Eat after 4 weeks, or preferably 6 weeks.

SWEET AND SOUR ROSES

Flower petals can be used like any other herb: dried or fresh; piled into pastries or pancakes, soups, stews or summer drinks; or infused in hot water to make tea, or in vinegar or oil for dressings. And they may be pickled.

1 cup rose petals
1 cup sugar
1¼ cups wine vinegar
½ teaspoon each nutmeg, cinnamon and ground ginger

Put the petals (not whole flowers) into a heat-resistant pickle jar. Dissolve the sugar in the vinegar, add the spices and bring to a boil. Simmer for a few minutes, then pour over the petals. Seal, and store in a cool place.

SLOE JELLY

The sloe is the fruit of the blackthorn bush and its blue-black berries are found in hedgerows during the autumn. Sloe jelly tastes good with roast meat.
Makes about 4 pounds (2 kg)

1 lb (½ kg) sloes
1½ lb (¾ kg) apples or windfalls
Juice of 1 lemon
Sugar

Prick the sloes with a needle. Cut the apples into halves or quarters, depending on their size. Put the fruit in a large saucepan with the lemon juice and just enough water to cover. Simmer for about 1 hour or until the fruit is soft. Break up the berries as they cook.

Pour the fruit and liquid into a scalded jelly bag and let drip all night. If you do not mind a cloudy jelly, squeeze the bag. But if you want a clear jelly, leave the dripping mixture alone.

Measure the liquid and put it into a saucepan. To every 2½ cups add 2 cups of sugar. Stir over low heat until the sugar has dissolved completely. Then raise the heat and boil fast for about 10 minutes until the jelly has reached setting point. Pour into jam jars and seal while hot.

CHERRY SOUP

A soup to serve either at the beginning of the meal or as a dessert. When yogurt is used in this way it is best to get rid of

the excess water. Put the yogurt in a sieve lined with cheesecloth, and allow the whey to drip out. A gentle squeeze will help to quicken the process.
Serves 4

1½ lb (¾ kg) cherries
1¼ cups red wine
Peel and juice of 1 orange
Sugar
1 teaspoon arrowroot
⅔ cups yogurt

Pit the cherries and put them in a saucepan with the wine, 1¼ cups of water, and the orange juice and peel, and simmer for about 10 minutes or until the fruit is soft.

Discard the orange peel and blend or sieve the fruit. Stir in sugar to taste. Dissolve the arrowroot in a spoonful of water and stir it into the soup. Put the soup back on the heat and simmer for 2 minutes. Serve either hot or chilled with a spoonful of yogurt.

PEAR SOUP
Serves 4

2 lb (1 kg) ripe but firm pears
2½ cups white wine
1 vanilla pod
Sugar
4 tablespoons medium sherry
4 tablespoons toasted slivered almonds

Peel, core and slice the pears. Put them in a saucepan with the wine and vanilla pod. Poach gently for 30 minutes.

Remove the vanilla pod and sieve or blend the soup. Add sugar to taste and chill in the refrigerator.

When ready to serve stir a spoonful of sherry into each bowl of soup and sprinkle the top with the almonds.

ROSE-HIP SYRUP
Rose hips, the red fruit of the wild rose, were used in medieval times as a filling for tarts. During World War II they were highly valued for their vitamin C content (four times as much as black currants and twenty times as much as oranges).

1 lb (½ kg) rose hips
1 cup sugar

Wash the hips and put them through the meat grinder. Bring 5 cups of water to a boil in a saucepan. Put in the hips and bring back to a boil. Immediately remove the pan from the heat and set aside for 20 minutes.

Pour the contents of the pan through a scalded jelly bag. When it stops dripping, return the pulp to the pan. Pour in 2 cups of water and bring to a boil. As soon as it boils remove the pan from the heat and set aside for 10 minutes. Pour through the jelly bag.

When the dripping has stopped, pour all the juice into a clean pan and bring to a boil. Boil briskly until the liquid measures about 2 cups. Reduce the heat and stir in the sugar. When the sugar has dissolved, boil for 5 minutes.

Pour the syrup into clean bottles. If you make large quantities then you will have to seal and sterilize the bottles. A small quantity can be safely kept in the refrigerator for a week or two.

ELDER FLOWER PANCAKES
Exquisitely perfumed elder flowers lift pancakes into the realms of the exotic.
Makes about 8 pancakes

1 cup flour
A small pinch of salt
1 egg
1¼ cups milk
12 elder flower clusters
Melted butter
Sugar

Sift the flour and salt into a bowl. Make a well in the middle, drop in the egg and half the milk. Beat well until frothy then stir in the rest of the milk. Set aside for 20 minutes.

Wash the elder flowers thoroughly in salted water. Pick off the heads and fold them into the batter.

Put just enough melted butter into a cast-iron or nonstick frying pan to coat the bottom, and make the pancakes in the usual way.

Serve with a dusting of sugar.

GOOSEBERRY SAUCE
A sharp sauce to serve with mackerel or any other oily fish. It is also good with roast goose or pork.

Cumin, cockles and chrysanthemums

Serves 6

1 lb ($\frac{1}{2}$ kg) green gooseberries
Butter
Sugar

Top and tail the gooseberries. Put a small knob of butter in a saucepan, pile in the gooseberries and cook over low heat until they are soft.

Sieve or blend the gooseberries if you like a smooth sauce, or crush them with a fork or the back of a spoon if you prefer a lumpy one. Stir in sugar to taste, but do not make the sauce too sweet; it is meant to be sharp to cut through the oiliness or fattiness of the fish or meat.

PESTO
A sauce of Genoese origin which is tossed into freshly cooked spaghetti or noodles just before serving.
Serves 4

1 tablespoon pine nuts
A large bunch of fresh basil
2 garlic cloves
$\frac{1}{2}$ to $\frac{3}{4}$ cup grated Parmesan cheese
$1\frac{1}{4}$ cups olive oil

Toast the pine nuts in a dry iron pan, gently shaking the pan all the while. Using a blender, or a pestle and mortar, blend the nuts, the chopped basil and the garlic into a paste. Gradually incorporate the cheese. Dilute with olive oil to make a thick sauce.

PICKLED NASTURTIUM SEEDS
These make an excellent substitute for capers. The nasturtium seeds must be pickled as soon as the flowers fade and before they become hard.

$2\frac{1}{2}$ cups wine or cider vinegar
$\frac{1}{4}$ cup salt
10 peppercorns
Mace
Horseradish
1 small onion
1 bay leaf
Nasturtium seeds

Put the vinegar into a saucepan. Add the salt, peppercorns, a few shreds of mace, a few gratings of horseradish, the chopped onion and the bay leaf. Bring

to a boil and simmer for 5 minutes.

Pour the vinegar into a bowl, cover and allow to cool. When the vinegar is quite cold, strain it into a glass or earthenware jar.

Pick the nasturtium seeds as the flowers fall and drop them into the spiced vinegar. Keep the jar tightly covered in a cool place.

Leave for at least 30 days before eating the "capers."

FLAVORED VINEGARS
The most common flavoring for vinegar is tarragon, but all sorts of other ingredients can be used, from rose petals to raspberries.

HERB VINEGAR
Whatever the herb—sage, marjoram, rosemary, or even a mixed bunch—you will obtain the best results if you pick the sprigs before the plant flowers. Put them into a bottle and pour over the best vinegar. A pinch of salt may be added, and, if you are using a particularly strong herb such as thyme or rosemary, a peppercorn.

The vinegar will be ready to use after 2 to 3 weeks.

FRUIT VINEGARS
Vinegars flavored with fruit, such as raspberries, were once taken to ease sore throats; today they may accompany plain steamed puddings.

$2\frac{1}{2}$ cups good wine vinegar
1 lb ($\frac{1}{2}$ kg) raspberries, blackberries or other soft fruit

Put the vinegar and fruit into a large jar or bowl, cover, and leave for 1 week.

Strain off the juice into a pan, boil for 5 to 6 minutes, then pour into a warmed bottle. Sugar may be added to this recipe, but it is more practical to sweeten the vinegar as you use it.

ROSE PETAL VINEGAR
For a romantic addition to summer salads, pour 5 cups of vinegar onto 2 cups of rose petals. Leave for 10 days before using in a vinaigrette.

Bibliography

An exhaustive list of all my sources would be tedious rather than helpful.
The following are particularly relevant.

Michael Allaby, *World Food Resources*, Applied Science Publishers Ltd.,
  Barking, Essex. 1977
Michael Allaby, Colin Blythe and Colin Hines, *Losing Ground*, Earth
  Resources Research Ltd., London. 1974
Michael Allaby and Colin Tudge, *Home Farm*, Macmillan London Ltd.
  1977
Kenneth Blaxter FRS, "Can Britain Feed Itself?," *New Scientist*, 20 March
  1975, p.697
Kenneth Blaxter FRS, "Deer Farming," *Scottish Agriculture*, Winter
  1971/72, pp.225–30
George Borgstrom, *The Hungry Planet*, Collier Macmillan Ltd., London.
  1967
Georg Borgstrom, *World Food Resources*, International Textbook Co. Ltd.,
  Aylesbury, Bucks. 1973
Jean-Anthelme Brillat-Savarin, *The Philosopher in the Kitchen*, Penguin
  Books Ltd., Harmondsworth. 1970
Edward Espe Brown, *The Tassajara Bread Book*, Shambhala Publications
  Inc., Berkeley. 1970
Helen Burke, *Chinese Cooking for Pleasure*, The Hamlyn Publishing Group
  Ltd., Feltham, 1965
D. P. Burkitt and H.C. Trowell (eds), *Refined Carbohydrates and Disease*,
  Academic Press, London. 1975
John Burnett, *Plenty and Want*, Thomas Nelson, London. 1966
T. L. Cleave, G. D. Campbell and N. S. Painter, *Diabetes, Coronary
  Thrombosis and the Saccharine Disease*, John Wright & Sons Ltd., Bristol.
  1969
T. L. Cleave, *The Saccharine Disease*, John Wright & Sons Ltd., Bristol.
  1974
D. J. A. Cole and R. A. Laurie (eds), *Meat*, Butterworths, London. 1975
Michael and Sheilagh Crawford, *What We Eat Today*, Neville Spearman
  Ltd., London. 1972
Elizabeth David, *English Bread and Yeast Cookery*, Allen Lane at Penguin
  Books Ltd., London. 1977
Department of Health and Social Security/Medical Research Council,
  Research on Obesity; compiled by Dr W. P. T. James. Her Majesty's
  Stationery Office, London. 1977
Jane Grigson, *The Mushroom Feast*, Penguin Books Ltd. 1978
Jane Grigson, *Charcuterie and French Pork Cookery*, Penguin Books Ltd.,
  Harmondsworth. 1970
Michel Guérard, *Cuisine Minceur*, Pan Books Ltd., London. 1978
Ross Hume Hall, *Food for Nought*, Harper and Row, New York. 1974
Philip Harben, *The Grammar of Cookery*, Penguin Books Ltd.,
  Harmondsworth. Revised 1965
Dorothy Hartley, *Food in England*, Macdonald, London. 1954
K. W. Heaton, *Bile Salts in Health and Disease*, Churchill Livingstone,
  Edinburgh and London. 1972
C. R. Hensman, *Rich against Poor*, Penguin Books Ltd., Harmondsworth.
  1971
Russell Kyle, *Meat Production in Africa. The case for new domestic species*,
  University of Bristol. 1972

Bibliography

Frances Moore Lappé, *Diet for a Small Planet*, A Friends of the Earth/Ballantine Book, New York. 1971

Gerald Leach, *Energy and Food Production*, IPC Science and Technology Press Ltd., Guildford. 1976

Richard Mabey, *Food for Free*, William Collins & Co. Ltd., Glasgow. 1972

Donald D. McLaren, "The Great Protein Fiasco," *The Lancet*, 1974, vol. 2, p.93

F. Marian McNeill, *The Scots Kitchen*, Blackie & Son Ltd., London. 2nd ed. 1963

Peter and Joan Martin, *Japanese Cooking*, Penguin Books Ltd., Harmondsworth. 1972

G. B. Masefield, M. Wallis, S. G. Harrison and B. E. Nicholson, *The Oxford Book of Food Plants*, Oxford University Press, Oxford. 1969

Kenneth Melanby, *Can Britain Feed Itself?*, Merlin Press, London. 1975

National Academy of Sciences, Washington DC, *Underexploited Tropical Plants with Promising Economic Value*, 1975

R. Palme Dutt, *India Today*, Victor Gollancz Ltd., London. 1940

A. A. Paul and D. A. T. Southgate, *McCance and Widowson's The Composition of Foods*, Her Majesty's Stationery Office, London. 1978

Philip Payne, "Protein Deficiency or Starvation?," *New Scientist*, 7 November 1974, p.393

H. C. Pereira, "Research and Development for Britain's future food supplies." Lecture at the Twelfth British Weed Control Conference, Brighton, 19 November 1972

N. W. Pirie, *Food Resources, Conventional and Novel*, Penguin Books Ltd., Harmondsworth. 1969

J. W. G. Porter and B. A. Rolls (eds), *Proteins in Human Nutrition*, Academic Press, London. 1973

R. W. Reilly and J. B. Kirsner (eds), *Fiber Deficiency and Colonic Disorders*, Plenum Press, New York. 1975

Claudia Roden, *A Book of Middle Eastern Food*, Penguin Books Ltd., Harmondsworth. 1970

Redcliffe Salaman, *The History and Social Influence of the Potato*, Cambridge University Press, Cambridge. 1949

Jack Santa Maria, *Indian Vegetarian Cookery*, Rider and Company, London. 1973

George Seddon and Helena Radecka, *Your Kitchen Garden*, Mitchell Beazley Publishers Ltd., London. 1975

John Seymour, *The Fat of the Land*, Faber and Faber, London. 1961

J. E. Smith and D. R. Berry, *The Filamentous Fungi*, Edward Arnold, London. 1975

John S. Steinhart and Carol E. Steinhart, "Energy Use in the US Food System," *Science*, 1974, vol. 184, pp.307–16

F. Steele and A. Bourne (eds), *The Man/Food Equation*, Academic Press, London. 1975

Gunnar Thorson, *Life in the Sea*, Weidenfeld and Nicolson, London. 1971

The Transnational Institute, *World Hunger: Causes and Remedies*, Amsterdam. 1974

Hugh Trowell, "Obesity in the Western World," *Plant Foods for Man*, 1974, vol. 1, pp.157–68

Colin Tudge, *The Famine Business*, Faber and Faber, London. 1977

Colin Tudge, "Preventive Medicine, California Style," *World Medicine*, July 1977, pp.17–21

John Yudkin, *Pure, White and Deadly*, David-Poynter Ltd., London. 1972

General index

Recipe index

Recipe index